W9-AVW-283

The
Building
Professional's
Guide to
Contract
Documents

Third Edition

Waller S. Poage, AIA, CSI, CVS

*The
Building
Professional's*

Guide to
Contract
Documents

Third Edition

Waller S. Poage, AIA, CSI, CVS

RSMeans

Copyright 2000
Construction Publishers & Consultants
63 Smiths Lane
Kingston, MA 02364-0800
(781) 422-5000

The editor for this book was Danielle Georges. The managing editor was Mary Greene. The production manager was Michael Kokernak. The production coordinator was Marion Schofield. The electronic publishing specialist wasJennifer Harvey. The proofreader was Joseph Augusta. The book and cover were designed by Norman R. Forgit.

Printed in the United States of America

10 9 8 7 6 5 4 3 2

Library of Congress Catalog Number Pending

ISBN 0-87629-577-4

 Reed Construction Data

To Elizabeth for a quarter century of unconditional friendship, wise counsel and sacrifice, but most of all for sharing those things without price which make life a worthwhile adventure.

In Memory of Rob for what is and not what could have been, the gifts of Tammy, Wynn, Angela, Nicholas, Alexia and Ian Michael who have so enriched our lives.

To Ann for your example of excellence in all that you do, but most of all for always being there when it counted.

To Cathy for your freedom of spirit and mastery of challenge, not to ask why, but why not!

To Betsy for the gifts of Scott and Natalia Elizabeth, the ninth generation of Robert Poage of Virginia.

To Meg for your example of faith, courage, persistence and fortitude and the sure belief that the best is yet to come.

Table of Contents

Preface

Construction in the 20th century became a major industry on which a great part of society came to depend for its livelihood as well as its shelter. Mankind expanded the collective knowledge of construction more in the 20th century than in the previous 40 centuries of recorded history. The "built" environment more than doubled in the last half of the past century.

Looking ahead to the 21st century, we can reasonably expect to see the work of the construction industry more than double again. The buildings we create will not only be larger and more complex in the new century, but "smarter" as expanding technology produces buildings that can practically "think" for themselves. We will produce more, waste less, and design and construct buildings with useful life that is measured in centuries rather than decades.

The effort required to construct the modern "built" environment incorporates many elements. Among them are the ambition of the owner, the art of the designer, and the ingenuity of the engineer, together with the leadership of the contractor, the skill of the tradesman, and the product of the manufacturer. The welfare and economy of the community are also major considerations. There are few human endeavors that require more coordination and communication skills than the work of today's construction professional who directs the profusion of trades and skills needed to erect a modern building. The common "touchstone" relating owner, professional, manager, tradesman, and producer is that series of documents known in the industry as the *Contract Documents*.

Construction documents consist of drawings, technical specifications and other related material which include agreements, conditions of agreements, instructions, and modifications. Such instruments are all necessary to the construction of modern building projects. They serve as the product, or the tool, of the modern construction professional. Design professionals will spend a great part of their professional lives preparing contract documents. Building professionals will spend a like amount of time interpreting and following such documents. Owners will spend large sums of money to have construction documents created and used.

Now is the time to establish an improved formula for understanding, using, and controlling construction documentation. After thirty-five years of professional practice, and eight years dedicated to teaching the construction sciences, the author continues to recognize the need for an improved text that examines the complex subject of construction documents.

This book, his response to that need, now in its third edition, covers the preparation and use of documentation and communication between owners, architects, engineers, contractors, subcontractors, material producers, and the many others that comprise the construction industry.

Legal issues, as well as legal documents and their use, are discussed in this text. Much of the material included has important legal consequences and implications. It is the explicit recommendation of the author, editors, and publisher that an attorney should be consulted on all legal matters and that all construction documents receive a thorough and competent legal review.

Acknowledgments

We appreciate and wish to acknowledge the following organizations whose documents and efforts have provided direction and content to this volume: The American Institute of Architects, the Engineer's Joint Contract Documents Committee, the Construction Specifications Institute, the American Society for the Testing of Materials, the Society of American Value Engineers, the Design/Build Institute, and the editors and staff of the R. S. Means Company.

The author also wishes to acknowledge the support and influence of the principals and staff of Henningson, Durham and Richardson, Inc.; Hayes, Seay, Mattern and Mattern, Inc.; Morse Diesel International; James W. Hudson and Associates, and the Gilbane Building Company, all of whom aided in inspiring and shaping this third edition.

There are a number of references made throughout this book to the Construction Specifications Institute (CSI) and documents produced by CSI. *MasterFormat*™ is published by CSI and Construction Specifications Canada (CSC), and is used with permission from CSI, 2000. The Construction Documents Fundamentals and Formats Module (1996 edition) and the Construction Specifications Practice Module (1996 edition) are from CSI's *Manual of Practice* and are used with permission from CSI, 2000. For those interested in a more in-depth explanation of *MasterFormat*™, Construction Documents Fundamentals and Formats Module, and Construction Specifications Practice Module and their use in the construction industry, contact: The Construction Specifications Institute, 99 Canal Center Plaza, Suite 300, Alexandria, VA 22314, Tel: 800-689-2900, Fax: 703-684-0300, URL: http://www.csinet.org

Introduction

From the beginning, human beings have been organizers, inventors, constructors, and artist/designers. As with other creatures, the primary motivation was survival, but humanity's competitive and challenging spirit set it apart from other creatures. Not satisfied for long with the simple elements of survival, humans designed shelters, that have reflected their personality and ego. Throughout history, humans have built an ever-expanding, complex, and colorful environment.

Construction has, over time, reached mammoth proportions, and growing along with it has been the requirement for documentation. As we investigate construction documentation today, it is appropriate to look back to the origins of this far-reaching venture.

Early Construction

The simple need for food and shelter required early man to become organized and to use teamwork. Clans were formed and then tribes, each with established territories. The common need for food and shelter also led to specialization by trade. Members of the tribe were trained for different tasks and arts to become part of the community effort. Father taught son, mother taught daughter, and master taught student. Available space in caves and other forms of natural shelter were outgrown as new generations increased the populations of the tribes. This population growth and the necessity to maintain communities led to the construction of shelter.

History does not contain a record of the first structure built, nor does it recognize the first architect or contractor. The first structure was probably a residence, made from the rough elements and materials available in the surrounding area. Archaeological evidence suggests that the familiar coolness and safety of the cave prompted the first builders to excavate below the surface. Consequently, retaining and supporting walls had to be built, using stones of a size which could be hand carried, sometimes from great distances. The earliest roof structures were made from tree limbs lashed together with thatched reeds, bonded with a covering of mud.

Anthropologist/archaeologists pose an interesting theory as to how we may have emerged from nomadic hunter/gatherer to builder and dweller of permanent structured communities—the first towns and cities. The theory suggests that the discovery of wheat was an important factor. Unlike its ancestor grasses, kernels of wheat are heavy and not easily blown by the wind from their stalks or place of growth. As a result, wheat grew near the place where it fell, creating natural fields of edible grain. About 10,000 years ago, as nomadic humans came upon these "windfalls" of wheat, they remained nearby, without the need to continue roaming in search of food. From the wheat grains they made bread, and they baled and stored the stalks and leaves for their livestock. For this reason, it is thought that the first permanent villages were constructed near wheat fields, and that these early structures of stone and brick were the beginning of civilized community life. The town of Bethlehem, Israel, lies a few miles from the historical city of Jerusalem and is known to be one of the oldest places of continued inhabitance in the world. The name "Bethlehem," translated from the original Hebrew means, "place of bread."

Early Documents

The first known documents were sketches drawn on cave walls, depicting the excitement of the hunt. These sketches can be seen in the caves of Lascaux located in the Vezere Valley in France. The first known record-keeping documents were clay tablets inscribed with symbols that communicated stories and made records of transactions. The excavation of the ancient city of Ebla, now in modern Syria, has uncovered thousands of these clay tablets. Their existence is evidence of humanity's having lived in permanent communities with documentary skills for more than 10,000 years.

About 4,000 years ago, in Egypt, artisans found that they could transform the pith of certain reeds that grew along the rivers into a crude form of paper that has come to be known as "papyrus." Using a brush made from animal hair, they could write on this medium with ink made from the carbon of burned organic matter. The first known "books" were actually scrolls written on long sheets of papyrus glued together.

Papyrus was used to record some of the first known construction documents in the Septiguent Bible, written in the Greek language and first transcribed around 300 BC. One of the first specifications appears in the book of Genesis, describing the Ark, built to save a remnant of humankind and selected animal species from the Great Flood. Here we find divine instructions given to Noah as to how and of what material he and his sons were to construct the Ark.

Twenty-first-century humans live in a veritable sea of paper; its benefits to their knowledge and survival are many. The invention of the printing process in the 16th century gave us the ability to document our discoveries and knowledge, and stimulated achievement and understanding through writing, education, science, and invention.

The Master Builders

The traditional master builder has been architect/engineer, artist, and contractor. He or she not only designed the building, but also directed or managed the construction. Although the master builder's job is now often divided into two professions, that of the design professional, and that of the contractor or project manager, this design/build approach still goes on in many parts of the world today, as it has for many centuries.

Master builders directed the construction of the pyramids of Egypt. These structures are among the world's oldest reminders of civilization's early zeal to design and build on a grand scale. Although there is much speculation as to the methods by which the pyramids were constructed, it is evident by the structures themselves that their master builders were able to achieve a high degree of engineering accuracy, measurement, and control of form. By the Fourth Dynasty of Egypt (2575 BC) humankind's talent in master building was reaching classic proportions. The first true pyramids were built by the Egyptian ruler Snofru, who reigned from 2575 to 2551 BC.

By far the most famous of the pyramids is the Great Pyramid of Khufu. The exactness of measurement, the relationship of the perimeter of the base (which is divisible by 2 pi), the obvious skill in scheduling the time of construction to match the lifetime of the monarch, and the management of the tremendous amount of material and manpower all indicate a highly developed architectural design, and some form of architectural documentation. The Great Pyramid contains an estimated 2,300,000 blocks of stone with an average weight of two and one half tons each. The volume of this structure could easily contain five or more of the great cathedrals of Europe, including St. Peter's in Rome, the largest church in Christendom. The pyramid has a nearly perfect square base with sides 756 feet long. It covers 13 acres of ground, equal to approximately ten New York City blocks. The four sides vary in length less than eight inches in overall dimension, an error of less than one in 1100. (Today we specify an acceptable error in masonry of one in 500.) The Pyramid's original height has been computed at 481 feet, about two thirds of the height of America's first high rise building, the Woolworth Tower in New York.

Throughout history, the master builder has considered it a duty and a privilege to train understudies in the art and science of building design and construction. Until the early 18th century, and before the creation of the modern day school of architecture, much of the master builder's education consisted of actual practice in building skills such as masonry, stone cutting, concrete manufacture and placement, and carpentry. Training behind a drawing board was incidental to the main exposure, which thrust the student physically into learning the theory and science of building construction by doing. As we shall see, the professionalism of the master builder/architect, and the master builder's training participation in the building process (for reasons of ethics and other considerations) took a much different turn with the creation of the American Institute of Architects in the 19th century.

Unlike the traditional master builder, the American design professional (architect/engineer) has kept apart from any financial or functional interest in the actual construction process. The intent was to keep his or her service and advice to the client free of any conflict of interest. Such conflicts could be potential profit from the production and marketing of materials, or from the construction process. Today, the American design professional concerns himself or herself with the building design, its form, envelope, structure, site improvements, and mechanical and electrical service and function. He or she defines the work by creating certain professional documents. During construction, the architect or the engineer becomes an interested observer in the employ of the owner, administering and interpreting the intent of the Contract for Construction, and documenting the flow of information throughout the process. From time to time, he or she is called on to express judgment in the case of questions or disputes. Design professionals have recently become more entwined in the construction process in the roles of owner, developer, and construction manager. The same basic ethic prevails, but it has become more complicated, as we shall see in subsequent discussion.

The Age of Discovery
The development of the wheel gave us a revolutionary new tool with which to construct buildings. The wheel provided the means to transport materials of great bulk and weight, and the pulley allowed

the use of hoists, the block and tackle, and other labor-saving devices such as the wheelbarrow. All of these are basic tools today. No-one is certain just when the wheel was invented, but it is clear that construction was not the primary motivation behind its development.

It is interesting to note that the inspiration behind most of these inventions and discoveries was not a desire to construct spectacular buildings. The structural use of the arch, for example, was the result of the experiments and discoveries of the Greek mathematician and scientist, Archimedes. Archimedes lived in the third century BC when Greek civilization was in its prime. It was this civilization that had a great influence on the development of architecture as an art form. In addition to the arch, Archimedes gave us the mathematical relationship of the surface area of a sphere to its circumference, diameter, and volume. Despite the fact that Archimedes was not a builder, his discoveries led to major advancements in construction. The arch was used extensively by the Romans during the next five centuries. An understanding of the arch led to the development of the vault, the dome, and the flying buttress, all common elements in the great cathedrals of Europe from the 4th century AD well into the 19th century.

It was the invention of the steam engine by James Watt and the discovery of electricity around 1746 which would lead humans, master builders, to the achievement of the dream to build higher structures. Electricity produced safer and cheaper artificial lighting as well as the electric motor, without which we would not have mechanical ventilation, elevators, power tools, or communications. Modern blast furnaces produced steel, thereby allowing buildings to be constructed more quickly and cheaply, and to greater heights. The development of refrigeration provided air-conditioning for buildings. The Fourcault process allowed for the economical production of glass, and the Bayer process produced pure aluminum. The availability of electricity has enhanced almost every industry related to building construction—from the lumber sawmill to the modern brick and concrete kilns. It was the growth of technology that allowed the American builder to participate in the largest building boom in the history of mankind. In a brief period of 200 years, the North American continent would see as much building construction as had taken place in the whole of Europe and Asia in 4000 years.

Production of Materials

With the Industrial Revolution came the development of industries related to the extraction and refinement, or manufacture of building materials and systems of all kinds. In 1824, in England, Joseph Aspidin patented a hydraulic cement he called "Portland Cement," because it resembled the gray limestone mined on the isle of Portland. The development of energy resources such as coal and natural gas allowed for the production of great quantities of Portland Cement in furnaces or kilns. This material, one of the major ingredients of modern building, was introduced to the marketplace in Pennsylvania in 1872. The blast furnace was developed by Henry Bessemer in 1847, the open-hearth furnace by the Siemens brothers of England in 1868, and the electric furnace in the United States in 1906—all for the production of steel. The Fourcault and Cobern processes were developed for producing sheet glass, and the Bayer process for aluminum.

All of these advances brought the building material industry into full focus in the early 20th century. With such industries came the need for expanded engineering and technical drawing. The processes themselves brought about the need for technical specifications and new forms of labor specialization. The corresponding explosion of new building created the need for management and design techniques that would blend skill, labor, materials, and assemblies to create the complex buildings that so totally dominate the skyline of modern cities in the world today.

The Shaping of Technology

Throughout history, technological advancements have been reflected in achievements in building construction. From the time of the Great Pyramids until just over 200 years ago, building structures, tools, and techniques were evidence of the limitations of technology. However, from that time until today, humans has been striving for larger and higher structures. That goal and dream has certainly been achieved in the present age, but the technology required to construct large, habitable buildings was slow to evolve. The pyramid builders produced spectacular structures, yet over the following 40 centuries, the most significant developments in building technology were the invention of the wheel, the arch, and the development of concrete. Consequently, architectural documents remained relatively uncomplicated for many centuries, and construction management was largely achieved by using simple drawings, verbal instructions issued on the job, and the most basic of technical specifications.

In Khufu's time, it took a quarter of a century to construct the Great Pyramid. Today, we are able to construct in less than three years a structure such as the World Trade Center in New York City, a remarkable 110-story building complex capable of housing more people than the total population of the average U.S. city. The world's largest office building, the Pentagon in Arlington, Virginia, has 3,705,397 square feet (344,243 square meters) of office and other space. The Petronas Towers, in Kuala Lumpur, Malaysia, the world's tallest buildings, are 1,483 feet (452 meters) high.

In the early 1980s, a group of computer scientists finished compiling a data bank that listed biographical data on everyone in recorded history who had been known to have invented anything or made a major discovery. The evidence showed that almost 80% of all the people who had made such a contribution were still living. Indeed, the technical advancements related to science in general, and building construction in particular, have been rapid and far-reaching in the latter half of the 20th century.

In the mid-seventeenth century, the English mathematician and scientist, Issac Newton, developed the first major advances in mathematics and physics since Archimedes almost 2000 years before him. Newton gave us the theory of gravity, the mathematical principal of the lever arm, calculus, and differential equations. From Newton's work, we have derived the mathematical ability to analyze the structural behavior of buildings. One of the by-products of this technology is the need to create more detailed documents that would include structural calculations and requirements for the various sections and connections. A diagram of the building's structural assembly has also become a requisite.

From the time of the pyramids, it was about 4500 years before any portion of a man-made structure surpassed the record height of 482 feet achieved in the Great Pyramid of Giza. The Washington Monument, completed in 1884, is 555 feet high, and the Eiffel Tower of Paris, completed in 1889, is 984 feet high. While these monumental buildings will always hold a significant place in the history of architecture, it must be remembered that none of them was built for human habitation. It was the American "skyscraper," designed to house large numbers of people, which would finally surpass the height record set by the ancients. The first true high-rise building to be constructed in the United States was Cass Gilbert's 58-story Woolworth Building completed in New York City in 1913.

From the beginning, we have been builders and shapers of our environment. In solving the need for shelter over a period of some ten thousand years, we have become inventors, artists, architects, engineers and constructors. In today's complex society, specializations have evolved to support the ambitions and creature comforts that characterize modern humankind. The construction industry recognizes and depends upon the coordination of talents, skills, trades, professions and products in order to continue constructing the built environment. The cord that binds the package is that collection of information we call "Professional Documents." Every individual who becomes part of the construction industry, no matter what his or her role, will spend more than half of his or her available time dealing with or preparing that package of information called the Contract Documents to which this book is dedicated.

Chapter One

The Construction Industry

The construction industry owes its existence to the needs of the entity identified in construction documents as the *owner*. The owner's needs translate into the *project*, which leads to the employment of the *design professional*, whose product, the *contract documents*, describes the work of the *constructor*. Once employed by the owner, the constructor becomes the *contractor*. The contractor may delegate portions of the work to the *subcontractor*, who in turn may delegate portions of his work to the *sub-subcontractor*. The contractor, the subcontractor and the sub-subcontractor all rely on the *producer* for the manufacture, production, distribution, and sales of all the materials, components, equipment, and assemblies that go into the construction of a modern building. The producer's representative, often called the *product representative,* brings products for the consideration of the design professional and the constructor.

The entities mentioned above are together what is known as the construction industry. A description of their work and relationships is set forth in a listing of information the construction industry calls the *contract documents*.

The business or work of the construction industry is the creation of the *built environment*, and the government has the responsibility of ensuring that this business is conducted in a manner that protects the rights and safety of the general public. *Building codes* have been established to provide for public safety. They are enforced by *building officials* who represent government on behalf of the public.

The "OPC" Relationship

Building construction, by its nature and complexity, requires contractual relationships between owners who wish to build, design professionals who conceive the design, and constructors who accomplish the actual work of building. Understanding the relationships that develop between these parties is important in understanding the contract documents.

For a project to be constructed, someone must first establish the need for the project, identify an appropriate site, and establish the means by which the project cost will be satisfied. The owner usually takes the initial step. The owner generally will require the technical and artistic skills to establish a statement or program describing the functional requirements of the building, or the ability to design the project. For this work, the owner will generally employ the services of a licensed architect or engineer who will document decisions concerning the aesthetic effect, shape, size, and arrangement of space and function, as well as the organization of the materials and methods of construction. The Design Professional's services also involve ensuring the project's conformity to local and state building codes, other ordinances, and applicable federal law and regulation. To carry this process out, the owner employs the services of an architect or an engineer, or both. This text will refer to the entity responsible for design, licensed for practice by the state, regardless of discipline, as the *design professional.*

The process of construction requires the services of the entity this text identifies as the *constructor,* who is employed by the owner to provide the skill, labor resources, and tools needed to construct the building. Building construction takes place through agreements between the owner, design professional, and constructor. This text will frequently refer to the contractual relationships between these parties as the *Owner/Professional/Constructor,* or *OPC,* relationship. Figure 1.1 illustrates the traditional OPC relationship.

In the traditional OPC relationship shown in Figure 1.1, the design professional provides a service directly to and for the owner. That service is described in the *Agreement between Owner and Architect or Engineer.* To complete the OPC relationship, the owner employs the constructor to conduct the work that is described in the *Agreement*

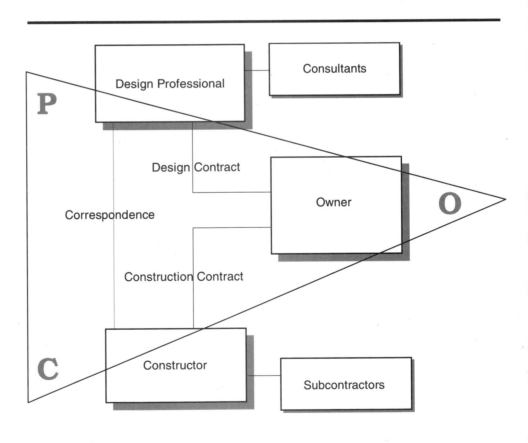

Figure 1.1 The OPC Relationship

between Owner and Contractor. This triad relationship is the "design/bid/build" or "traditional" method of project delivery. It has been used successfully in the United States for almost three centuries.

The design professional may employ by subcontract other design professionals ("consultants" or "subconsultants") to accomplish certain defined services that may be highly specialized. The constructor, in similar fashion, may employ by subcontract other constructors to provide specialty work.

Inherent in the OPC relationship is the *prime responsibility* of both the design professional and the constructor. Each is a prime participant in the service to the owner, with no direct contractual relationship to one another. The word "prime" identifies a primary and independent entity in contract with the owner and totally responsible for any services or work that he may subcontract to others. The term *prime contractor* becomes a significant definition, as we will see in the discussion of alternative project procurement methods later in this text (see Chapter 7, "Project Delivery").

While the traditional OPC relationship continues to be employed by many owners in the United States, other methods of project delivery may be used, depending on the owner's particular needs. For example, circumstances may suggest, and even dictate, that the owner employ more than one prime constructor, with each called on to perform highly specialized work. In such cases, the owner may need to employ a *construction manager* to manage the work of multiple-prime constructors. If a project, for example, requires a number of design delivery and construction specialties, the owner may have need of a *program manager.* In still another situation, the owner may wish to have his or her project delivered under a single *prime contract,* in which case he or she employs a *design/build contractor* for his or her purposes. These alternative project procurement methodologies are discussed in more detail in Chapter 7, "Project Delivery."

The Owner

Legally, the owner must be able to meet the minimum standards of competency defined by state law in order to execute a valid and binding contract. As a practical matter, he or she should also be able to fulfill all his obligations under the agreement. These responsibilities may include paying for the project; providing title to real property; providing for insurance; arranging for and paying interest, if required; and supplying basic and relevant information to those whom he or she employs. The owner must also have the ability to make legally binding decisions and approvals. These are most often the owner's primary contractual responsibilities in both the "Agreement between Owner and Design Professional," and the "Agreement between Owner and Contractor." Chapter 2 discusses various classifications of ownership, along with relevant economic influences and methodologies of doing business.

The Owner's Other Consultants

In addition to the design professional, the owner may need to employ the services of an attorney, an accountant, an insurance specialist, and a financial adviser. These professionals may be necessary to ensure that a proposed project will not only be successful, but lawful, and profitable as well.

The Design Professional

As stated previously, the term *design professional* as used in this text may refer to either an architect or an engineer. Although this text deals chiefly with the architect as the prime design professional, under the laws of most states, an architectural or engineering license can only be held by an individual, since the state examines and certifies for practice only those individuals who meet the standards and requirements established by that state for professional practice. A partnership, corporation, joint venture, or other entity, however, may practice professionally by virtue of the direction and control of the practice of partners, shareholders, directors, officers, employees, or others who are authorized to act on behalf of the entity and who are licensed by the state registration board. State laws vary widely with respect to how individuals within the entity must be licensed. Some states require, for instance, that all the stockholders of a corporation be licensed, while others simply require that the employee who performs or directs the professional services be licensed. Some states require that the employee who performs or directs the professional services be licensed. Some states require that the entity itself obtain a certificate of authorization from the registration board, others do not. Chapter 3 examines the various classifications of design professionals.

Depending on the nature of the project, the owner will employ either an architect or an engineer as the prime design professional. This individual or firm may then hire by subcontract professionals from other disciplines to act as consultants. For the majority of buildings constructed in the United States, the owner hires an architect as the design professional, and the architect hires—with the approval of the owner—engineers and others of various disciplines for assistance. An engineer is usually hired as the design professional in a construction project involving utilities, streets, highways, drainage structures, bridges, municipal subdivisions, and similar projects.

By virtue of his license to practice, the architect provides the artistic and technical skills necessary to confirm the owner's program. He also prepares the building design, which determines or recommends the materials and methods of construction. In the traditional OPC relationship, the architect prepares the documents necessary for construction, assists the owner in the selection of a constructor, and acts as the owner's representative in the construction process.

The Relationship of Architect to Engineer

In recent years, public sector owners, particularly agencies of the federal government, have increasingly made reference to the "Architect/Engineer" or "A/E" in contract language. While these two disciplines are usually complementary, they are not interchangeable, nor is the existence of one necessarily dependent upon the other. Many professional firms present themselves as A&E firms, employing representatives of both disciplines. However, the majority of practitioners in the United States prefer to practice separately, each with the option to employ the other as a consultant when the need arises.

Unless the architect is part of an A&E firm, he will likely procure the services of an engineering consultant for much of the technical design work, particularly the elements of structure; plumbing; heating, ventilating, and air conditioning; electrical; and site work.

In projects where engineering is the prime discipline involved, the engineer will be hired as the prime design professional and employ an architect to design any buildings that may be part of the project. An example of this type of project is a utility treatment plant requiring a building to house administrative and control functions.

The Constructor

This text uses the term *constructor* to represent that entity most commonly known in the industry as the Contractor, or the Prime or General Contractor. Technically, the constructor is not a contractor until he is a party to a contract; therefore, we will refer to him as "constructor" in the general sense and as "contractor" in the context of his contractual relationship to the owner.

The constructor can be an individual, a partnership, a corporation, a limited liability company, or a joint venture. Many states require that constructors who act as general contractors for building projects be licensed for that purpose. The constructor demonstrates by his experience, education, and financial ability that he is equipped to provide the skills, labor, materials, equipment, and other resources necessary to construct the project required by the owner.

The large sums of money that flow through the constructor's hands as he fulfills his contractual duties require that he be financially sound, well capitalized, and adequately managed. Chapter 4 details how the constructor does business.

The Subcontractor

The 20th century may be remembered as the "Age of Specialization." In our highly specialized economy, the construction industry has recognized its own series of experts. Commonly referred to as *subcontractors*, these professionals have developed a particular specialty within the scope of the "total project." Their work usually requires individual licensing as well as special skills, tools, and techniques. The term *sub*, used as a prefix to the term *contractor*, connotes the usual subordinate role of the subcontractor.

Like the constructor, the subcontractor can be an individual, a partnership, a corporation, a limited liability company, or a joint venture. The subcontractor is usually employed directly by and at the discretion of the constructor in his role as prime or general contractor. Depending upon project needs and the approach to construction chosen by the owner, however, the subcontractor may also be employed by the owner or construction manager, or by another subcontractor to the project.

In most cases, the subcontractor is not in a direct agreement with the owner since he is not a party to the Contract for Construction or Agreement between Owner and Contractor. This is an important point to consider when preparing contract documents. We will see in subsequent chapters that typically, where a single Contract for Construction is awarded, the language should enforce the contractor's total responsibility for the work to be done. In such instances, the subcontractor, while a recognized entity in the performance of the work, is not a part of the special relationship that exists between owner, professional and constructor. The subcontractor is instead responsible primarily to the contractor with whom he has an agreement. Nevertheless, the contract between owner and contractor applies to the subcontractor as well, as he is obliged to perform his work in accordance with its provisions.

When an individual or company that normally performs work as a subcontractor is employed directly by the owner, construction manager, or program manager, it is identified as a "separate contractor." (The term is used even though the actual work to be performed may be the same as that which would be performed as a "subcontractor.") This agreement provides a direct relationship with the owner, construction manager or program manager and requires cooperation with other contractors under similar contracts.

Primary Subcontractors

Primary subcontractors perform work that may require licensing by the state or subdivision responsible for issuing building or construction permit certificates. They generally provide and install equipment and accessories related to the following:

- Plumbing
- Heating, Ventilating, and Air Conditioning
- Electrical
- Specialized Equipment, Design, and Installation

Secondary Subcontractors

The list of secondary subcontractors is long and not as well defined as that of primary subcontractors. Secondary subcontractors perform work requiring special skills, applications, tools, and equipment, but are not generally required to possess special licensing. Their areas of work include but are not limited to the following:

- Earthwork and / or Paving
- Concrete Placement and Finishing
- Masonry
- Steel Erection
- Carpentry
- Moisture and Thermal Protection
- Insulation
- Sheet Metal
- Glass and Glazing
- Painting and / or Decorating
- Tilework
- Flooring
- Ceiling
- Security Systems
- Communication Systems

The Sub-Subcontractor

The *sub-subcontractor* is an entity in a contractual relationship with a subcontractor who is, in turn, in a contractual relationship with a contractor or other third party. Sub-subcontractors may work in the following areas:

- Concrete Placement and Finishing
- Welding
- Gypsum Board Installation

- Finishing or Finish Material Installation
- Special Carpentry
- Special Equipment Installation

The Producer

In this text, the *producer* is defined as a resource that serves the construction industry by providing products for installation by the constructor. A producer may provide basic materials such as masonry units, combinations of basic materials such as "ready-made" concrete, or sophisticated assemblies of basic materials such as pre-cast concrete structural members.

Producers are the primary source for new and useful technology in the construction industry. They are critical to the successful constructor, who constantly seeks to employ improved means and methods of building to balance the primary "drivers" of the construction process: *cost, quality,* and *time.* (These drivers will be discussed in more detail in Chapter 7). For instance, the innovation of the adjustable height, self supporting, long span overhead crane—the Linden crane—has allowed constructors to move large amounts of materials and assemblies quickly and more efficiently. Because of this innovation, the contractor may minimize labor, save time, and improve quality.

The Product Representative

Product representatives are both salespeople and experts in assisting design professionals and constructors with the proper application of particular products. They are frequently construction professionals themselves, or have at the very least developed a deep knowledge of the product or products they represent. They furnish catalogs and samples and are constantly on the alert for marketing opportunities.

The Building Official

Municipal regulations for building construction are called *building codes* and have become "the law" within the jurisdiction in which construction takes place. Codes, commonly administered by local government representatives called *building officials*, define buildings by type of construction, function, and occupancy. They regulate design and direct the use of construction materials and methods to provide optimum protection to the building's occupants, the property itself, the surrounding property, and the public. Similar regulations and codes have been enacted to protect construction workers.

Building Codes

Over the years, municipalities around the country have adopted certain model codes and standards as law. Model codes are written by panels of experts and are frequently revised. The following are among the most commonly accepted codes, listed with the organizations responsible for their content:

The Uniform Building Code (UBC)
The International Conference of Building Officials (ICBO)
5360 South Workman Mill Road
Whittier, CA 90601
www.icbo.org

The Standard Building Code
Southern Building Code Congress, International (SBCCI)
900 Montclair Road
Birmingham, AL 35213
www.sbcci.org

The Basic Building Code
Building Officials and Code Administrators, International (BOCAI)
4051 West Flossmoor Road
Country Club Hills, IL 60477
www.bocai.org

Some model codes concentrate on specific disciplines. BOCAI, for instance, writes the National Plumbing Code and the National Mechanical Code. The National Fire Protection Association (Batterymarch Park, Quincy, Massachusetts 12269; www.nfpa.org) writes the National Electrical Code and the National Fire Code.

Several organizations are involved in keeping code administrators and other officials informed and advised. These organizations have an influence on code enforcement and have helped bring uniformity to the content and format of the codes. Advisory organizations include:

International Code Council (ICC)
5203 Leesburg Pike, Suite 708
Falls Church, VA 22041
www.intlcode.org
Note: The ICC has produced the International Building Code, intended to unify the model codes.

**National Conference of States on
Building Codes and Standards (NCSBCS)**
481 Carlisle Drive
Herndon, VA 22070
www.ncsbcs.org

Uniform Standards
Some organizations are dedicated to determining *uniform standards* of composition, quality, testing, and installation of materials, assemblies and methods of construction. These published model standards have come into general use and are accepted by architects, engineers, contractors, building officials, and other industry professionals.
The following are among the most prominent of these agencies.

The American Society for Testing Materials (ASTM)
100 Barr Harbor Drive
West Conshohocken, PA 19428-2959
www.astm.org

American National Standards Institute (ANSI)
11 West 42nd Street
New York, NY 10036
www.ansi.org

Underwriter's Laboratory (UL)
333 Pfingsten Road
Northbrook, IL 60062-2096
www.ul.com

Federal Specifications
Superintendent of Documents
U. S. Government Printing Office
Washington, DC 20402
www.access.gpo.gov

Industry Services

Since 1950, the construction industry has spawned many service organizations that have improved communication and made significant contributions to the industry as a whole. The *plan rooms* that service organizations sponsor in practically every major city and many smaller communities have been particularly helpful. These rooms advertise, display, and provide facilities for the study of current bidding documents (provided by owners and design professionals) for local projects.

Several service companies and trade organizations also publish journals, newsletters, and special reports. These publications keep subscribers informed of projects available for bidding, and post results (when publicly available) of competitive and negotiated bid awards. They also address technical innovations, new products, labor relations, and legislative and code changes. Most prominent among these organizations are the Associated General Contractors of America (AGC) and the FW Dodge Corporation.

Industry Influences

Chapter 7, "Project Delivery," shows that cost, quality and time are the defining factors in the owner's choice of project delivery method. "Quality" would be difficult, if not impossible, to define without the existence of generally accepted *standards* that may be taken as a basis of comparison or degree of excellence.

Standards

The last 25 years have produced a series of standards that benefit the owner and his interests. These standards are commonly accepted by the construction industry and have become woven into the fabric of contract documents. Standards that relate to design and construction can be grouped into several categories:

- Life Safety Standards
- General Building Design Standards
- Building Protection Standards
- Structural Design Standards
- Environmental Design Standards
- Producer's Quality Standards
- Institutional Standards
- Government Standards

The Appendix contains a listing of the major standards organizations in each of these categories.

Patents, Trademarks, and Copyright Law

A *patent* is a document issued by a national government that grants an entity exclusive rights to an invention for a limited time. It gives its owner the right to prevent others from making, selling, importing, or using the invention in the country that granted the patent—creating, in essence, a legal monopoly. In the United States, utility patents and plant patents provide this protection for 20 years, while design patents are issued for 14 years. A patent can be renewed only by a special act of the United States Congress.

A *trademark* is a word or words, a name, a design, a picture, a sound—or any combination of these elements—that distinguishes the products of one company from those of another. A *service mark* identifies the source of a service rather than a product. For example, an electric company may use a light bulb as a symbol of the service it offers to its customers.

A *strong trademark* consists of a word that has no recognizable meaning as a word, such as Sheetrock®, a trademark of the United States Gypsum Corporation. A *weak trademark* may consist of a common word, such as "Premier," or a word that suggests some characteristic of the product, such as "Quick-Set." Weak trademarks receive less protection, unless the public identifies them with a certain manufacturer as a result of wide advertising and long, continuous use.

Most countries have laws that protect the rights of trademark owners. A firm must establish its rights in each country in which it seeks protection.

Registration of a trademark serves as notice of a company's claim of ownership. Registration is not needed to sue for trademark infringement, but it gives the owner much stronger legal protection.

The term *copyright* refers to a body of exclusive rights that protect original works from unauthorized use. Copyright generally extends to original works of literary, dramatic, musical, artistic, or intellectual expression.

Copyright law covers the overall form of an architectural work and the unique arrangement of elements and spaces in its design.

It also covers the expression of the design in the form of drawings and/or specification as well as the specific expression of the design in the form of drawings and/or specification. The United States has participated in many international conventions and bilateral agreements to provide its citizens with copyright protection abroad.

Proprietary technology is technology that is owned by one individual or group, protected by patent or copyright, and made available to others under a *license agreement* for a price. Examples of proprietary technology in the construction industry include:

- The use of forming systems used to place and shape concrete into structural components.

- The application of special coatings that protect certain materials and systems from the elements.

- The use of electronic hardware and software for the automatic control of mechanical and electrical systems in buildings.

The development and licensing of proprietary technology has become a major industry, and will continue to have enormous impact on the built environment and the OPC relationship.

Summary   This chapter has identified the construction industry's major players, discussed the importance of the OPC relationship, and reviewed many of the principles and influences that shape that relationship. Subsequent chapters will examine each of these topics in greater detail and describe the documentation used to define the OPC relationship. The primary focus of this work is to outline the composition of construction documents as well as the issues and concerns that commonly affect their use. Our hope is that construction professionals will see that excellence in communication and record keeping is a key ingredient for continuing prosperity.

Chapter Two

The Owner

We saw in Chapter 1 that building construction takes place through agreements between the owner, design professional, and constructor. This text refers to the contractual association between these parties as the *Owner/Professional/Constructor*, or *OPC*, relationship.

This chapter will discuss the owner's requirements in order to build, and will examine how projects are funded. It will also look at other influences the owner must consider, such as the economy, and restraints imposed by government in the form of building regulations and codes as he interacts with design professionals, constructors, and producers.

The owner in the OPC relationship might be an individual, a partnership, a corporation, a limited liability company, a political subdivision, or any one of a number of agencies of municipal, county, state or federal government. No matter what form he takes, the owner and his objectives are continually influenced by the economy.

The Economy of the United States

There are two basic forms of economy: capitalism and socialism. Capitalism is based on rights of the individual to contribute to the greater economy of all citizens. Socialism is based on control of the economy by government for the greater benefit of the society. Neither has ever existed in pure form, as the economic systems of all nations involve some degree of government control and some degree of private choice. However, economies that rely for the most part on private decisions are usually described as capitalist. Those that rely on action by the government are considered to be socialist.

In the landmark book *The Wealth of Nations* (1776), Scottish economist Adam Smith laid out the basic argument for capitalism as the United States of America was being formed. Smith maintained that a government should not interfere with a nation's economy but instead let individuals act as "free agents" who pursue their own self-interests. Such free agents, he argued, would naturally act in ways that would bring about the greatest good for society.

Adam Smith's ideas first became influential during the early 1800s. Capitalism soon spread to other major trading nations, and the newly formed United States adopted Smith's economic model.

In a capitalist economy such as ours, the prices of labor, capital, and goods and services are determined by the market forces of *supply and demand.* Generally, the market will force prices to fall when supply exceeds demand, and to rise when demand exceeds supply. *Competition* exists when many suppliers try to sell the same kinds of things to the same buyers. A supplier who charges lower prices or improves the quality of his or her products may attract potential purchasers away from competitors.

Competition among employers for workers and among workers for jobs helps establish *wage rates*. Businesses need to pay wages high enough to attract workers with skills that are needed. When jobs are scarce, however, workers may accept lower wages. Similar competition helps determine *interest rates,* which are essentially the cost of borrowing money.

In *The Wealth of Nations,* Smith spoke of *perfect competition* whereby privately owned businesses, driven by a desire for profit, would decide what goods or services to produce, how much to produce, and what methods to use in production. In theory, perfect competition would produce exactly the right combination of goods and services to match the tastes and buying power of the consumers. In addition, it would lead firms to adopt the most economical production methods, and prices would drop to the lowest levels permitted by manufacturing costs. Inefficient firms would lose money and be driven out of business by firms with sound management.

Capitalism as it exists today differs in significant ways from the ideal of perfect competition, as government is far more involved than Smith envisioned. It works to ensure competition, stabilize the economy, protect the public interest, and equalize wealth distribution among the citizenry. Government also taxes households and businesses, and uses those taxes to purchase goods and services, and to provide for the needy.

The Private Sector Owner

Owners exist in two fundamentally different sectors, the *private sector* and the *public sector.* The private sector owner in the United States is a beneficiary of capitalism. In capitalist economies, private decision-makers determine how resources will be used, what mix of goods and services will be produced, and how goods and services will be distributed among the members of society. Moreover, most land, factories, and other capital is privately owned in capitalist systems, while government owns most of the capital used in production in socialist economies. Figure 2.1 shows the relationships and resources available to the private sector owner as his project gets underway.

The private sector owner can be an individual proprietorship, a partnership, a limited partnership, a joint venture, or a corporation.

Individual Proprietorship
Individual proprietorship means individual ownership of a property, a business, or a means of production or distribution of goods. The owner makes all decisions, receives all profits, and is legally responsible for any business debts. Single proprietorships are the most common form of business ownership in farming, construction, and many other industries, as proprietors can start a business with a small amount of capital and few legal formalities.

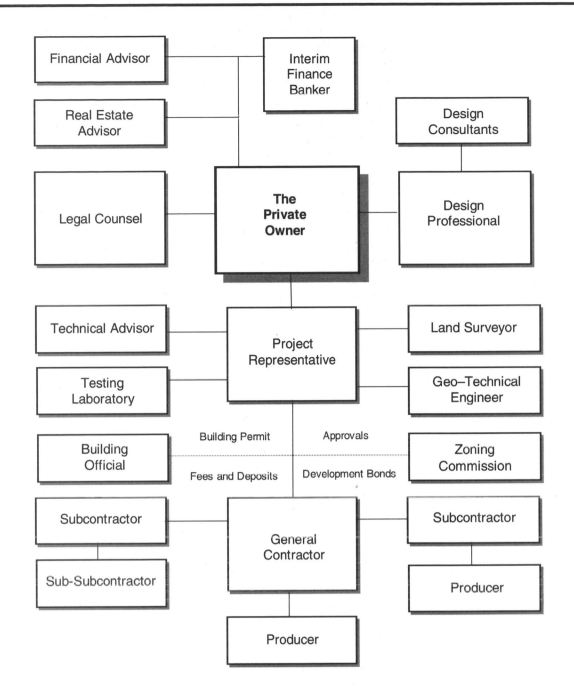

Figure 2.1 *The Private Owner's Resources*

Partnership

A partnership is an association of two or more individuals for the purpose of jointly creating or owning a business. Partners share in profit and loss, and are jointly and severally responsible for all business debts. They may sign a legal agreement that specifies the amount of work and capital each person contributes and the percentage of profit each receives.

Nearly all partnerships are small businesses. They are typically formed to provide professional services such as architecture or engineering, law, medicine, and real estate. A partnership can be dissolved by mutual agreement or by the withdrawal of any of the partners.

Limited Partnership

A limited partnership is similar to a partnership except that the participation in management, the distribution of profit, and the liability for loss is not shared equally. In a limited partnership, one or more of the partners are identified as the *general partner* and the others become *limited partners*. All of the partners contribute capital and share potential profits established by formula in the partnership agreement. However, the general partner assumes the entire risk for the business, though he may have some recourse to the limited partners based on the partnership agreement.

Joint Venture

A joint venture is a business organization created by two or more individual proprietors, partnerships, or corporations—or any combination of the same. They are usually formed for purposes of a single business venture, but may also organize for multiple purposes. A joint venture may be formed, for example, to develop a commercial office building or a shopping center. A design professional and a general contractor may enact a joint venture to provide design/build services for an owner.

Corporations

A corporation is a business created by an individual or group of individuals who charter a company with certain legal rights and privileges. A corporation can own property, buy and sell, manufacture products, and generally operate as if it were an individual. The business corporation is the most common. Other types include municipal or government-owned corporations, nonprofit corporations, and professional corporations. A corporation is formed under the general laws of the state in which it incorporates, but can do business in other states if it files certain forms and pays required fees in those states.

Corporations may be either privately owned or publicly traded. The public corporation obtains funds by selling ownership shares, called capital stock, to large numbers of investors. A public corporation is governed by a board of directors elected by stockholders at regular meetings. The directors establish the policies of the corporation.

Private corporations, unlike public corporations, have a limited number of owners. In such corporations, stockholders often manage the company, rather than appoint others to do so. There is no open market for the sale of stock of private corporations.

Municipalities may form corporations to operate certain enterprises, such as the distribution of water. Likewise, federal, state, or local governments may establish corporations to provide certain public welfare functions. Federal corporations include national banks and certain federal businesses such as the United States Postal Service.

Quasi-public corporations join private and government investors in high-risk investment situations, such as the development of space satellites. In these ventures, the government usually subsidizes or insures the private investor.

Nonprofit corporations provide community services. They consist of members instead of stockholders and provide no dividends.

Limited Liability Company

A Limited Liability Company (LLC) is a business organization that mixes features of a partnership and a corporation. A relatively new and increasingly popular business entity, the LLC provides participants with the limited personal liability found within the corporate structure, as well as the taxation advantages of the partnership. LLCs exist for a limited amount of time, and transfer of ownership does not happen as easily as does the ownership of stock.

Limited Liability Partnership

A Limited Liability Partnership is a form of Gerneral Partnership whereby a partner is not personally liable for the debts, liabilities, or obligations of the partnership or other partners, or the acts or omissions of any other partner, simply by virtue of being a partner. LLPs can operate more informally than corporations and are generally accorded full partnership tax treatment.

Private Sector Finance

The owner can seldom finance a major project without the services of a *lender.* Commercial banks most commonly fill this need. Other lenders include commercial insurance companies, savings and loan associations, and, on occasion, individuals.

Because the lender has an obligation to its investors, stockholders, or depositors, a commercial loan to the owner must be secured by value in the form of pledged assets called *collateral.* Collateral can take many forms. To safeguard against *default,* or the failure of the borrower to repay the loan, the lender will often require that collateral be in the form of real estate, stocks and bonds, money, and other assets that could be readily liquidated if necessary to repay the loan. Assets used as collateral are encumbered by a *lien,* which prevents the transfer of those assets throughout the term of the loan.

Interim Finance

In construction finance, the primary element of the required collateral is often the project itself. Of course, the project is far from finished when its financing is being arranged, so it is often necessary for the owner to seek a financial institution that is willing to provide short-time financing with alternative collateral arrangements.

Permanent Finance

Once the project is completed, the owner transfers his loan from the interim lender to a permanent lender in a procedure called *closing.*

At closing, the interim lender's loan plus any earned interest is paid off and the period of permanent financing begins. The permanent loan is paid off in regular installments that are calculated to include both principal and interest for the agreed period of the loan.

The collateral for the permanent loan is often, in part or in whole, the title to the project and all of its improvements. Such collateral is usually in the form of a mortgage, a legal instrument in which the permanent lender obtains a lien on the property or, in some jurisdictions, requires a *deed of trust*, a legal instrument in which actual title to the property is entrusted to both the owner and the permanent lender with the provision that neither party can liquidate the asset without the express permission of the other. If the owner fails to make regular payments to the permanent lender, the lender may, upon notice to the owner, cause a *foreclosure* in which the lender takes sole legal title to the property and may liquidate it to satisfy the debt.

The Public Sector Owner

The concept of government as owner is usually referred to as *public sector ownership*. Projects developed by the public sector can be thought of as property actually owned by the citizens of the political subdivision leading the development. Figure 2.2 shows the relationships and resources available to a public sector owner.

Public sector owners include municipalities, counties, states and a variety of federal government institutions.

Municipal Government
A municipality is an organized city, town, or other community. Municipal governments provide a variety of services for residents, including police and fire protection, street maintenance, and health and welfare services. An incorporated municipality is a corporation under the law with a charter from the state defining its powers, responsibilities, and organization. The United States has about 19,000 incorporated municipalities.

Forms of City Government
There are two major forms of city government in the United States: the *mayor-council* form and the *council-manager* form. A small and steadily decreasing number of cities use a third type of government called the *commission* form.

The mayor-council form is the oldest type of city government in the United States. Patterned after city government in England, it initially had a council, which was the chief organ of government, and a mayor, who was a member of the council and presided over it. Under most mayor-council systems today, the mayor operates from a separate office and is not a member of the council. The people elect both the mayor and the council. More than one-third of the cities in the United States with populations of 25,000 or more have the mayor-council system.

A chief feature of the council-manager form of government—also called the *city manager plan*—is the centralization of administrative responsibility. An elected city council hires a professional administrator called a city manager to supervise all municipal affairs. The city manager appoints the heads of all departments and is responsible for

18

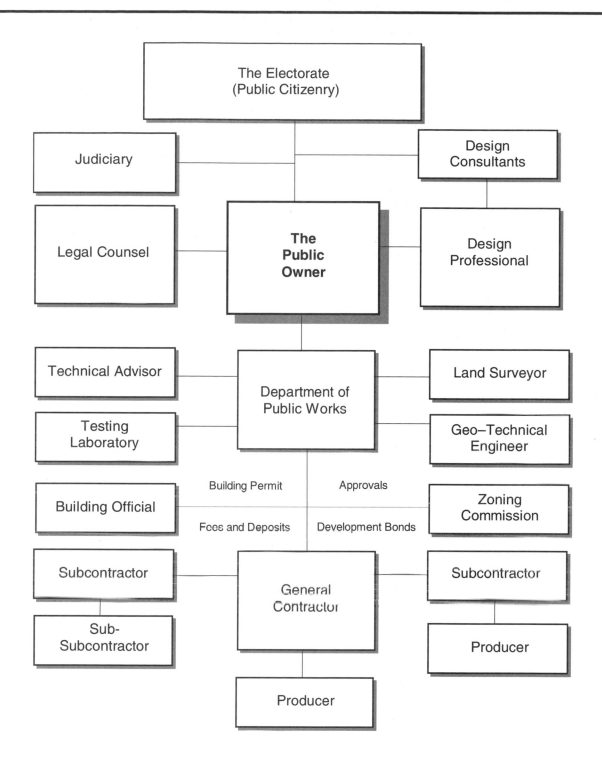

Figure 2.2 *The Public Owner's Resources*

managing all of the city services. This plan is the most common form of city government in the United States for cities with populations of 25,000 or more. Figure 2.3 illustrates the council-manager form.

The commission form of government combines legislative and executive authority in an elected group of commissioners. The commission as a body has the power to pass ordinances, impose taxes, distribute funds for city needs, and appoint officials. One of the members may be designated as mayor for ceremonial functions and for presiding over commission meetings.

County Government

Most county governments have a decentralized administration, with no executive head. The main county institution is an elective board that, in most cases, is called a board of commissioners or supervisors. The members of some boards are elected at large, while others are elected from districts, wards, or townships. Some counties, especially urban ones, have an executive office that controls all other county offices. The executive office is headed by an elected county executive or by an administrator or manager appointed by the elective board.

In counties where large cities occupy the entire county area, city and county governments may form a single unit. Denver, Honolulu, and San Francisco, for example, have combined city and county governments. In counties that are only partly covered by a city, the city and county may share responsibility for providing services to county residents. Cities like Baltimore and Roanoke, Virginia, are not part of any county and do not form a part of county government. In these cities, municipal officials perform many of the duties that are ordinarily handled by county officials.

State Government

In the United States, state government maintains law and order and enforces criminal law. It protects property rights and regulates business. It supervises public education, including schools and state universities. It provides public welfare programs, builds and maintains highways, operates state parks and forests, and regulates the use of state-owned land. The state has direct authority over local governments, counties, cities, towns, townships, villages, and school districts.

Public Sector Finance

The necessity for governments to borrow in order to finance initiatives has led to the development of various forms of public debt that have become a central feature of all capital markets in the United States. Government bonds, notes, bills, and certificates of obligation all represent public debt, and all require specified payments to the debt holders at designated times. For the most part, public debt differs from private debt only in that it is an obligation of government rather than of private individuals or corporations.

Maturity

Maturity of public debt ranges downward from very long periods to as little as a month or even a few days. A large portion of government debt consists of bonds with specific maturities of 5 to 99 years or longer. Twenty- and thirty-year bonds—often known as long-term or *funded* debts—are common.

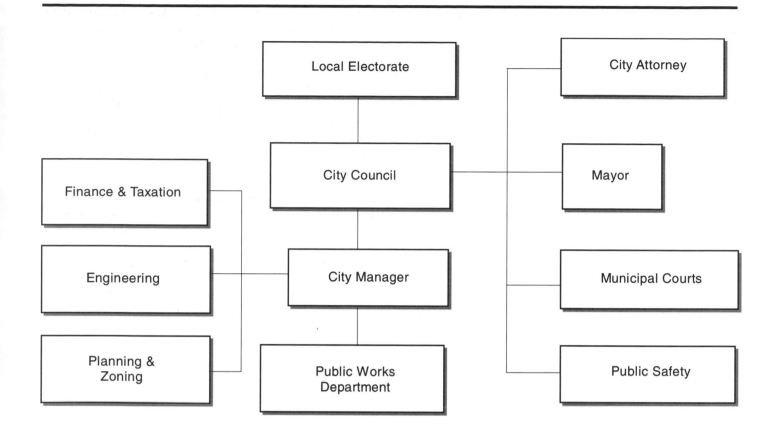

Figure 2.3 *Council-Manager Form of Municipal Government*

Debt with maturity of less than five years is often called short-term or *floating* debt and may take several forms:

- Notes, with maturities from one to five years.
- Treasury bills, with maturities from one month to a year.
- Certificates of obligation, with similar maturity periods but available at a fixed interest rate.

The length of the maturity period affects what is known as the *liquidity* of the debt—that is, how quickly it can be converted into money. Securities with very short maturity periods are constantly repayable in money and thus have maximum liquidity. As the period of maturity increases, the liquidity falls, unless a capital loss is to be incurred and the pure debt characteristic increases.

Types of Issue

Government debt may be issued directly by a government or by semiautonomous governmental organizations such as provincial power authorities. Government debt issues may be guaranteed by a governmental entity through *general obligation bonds*, or the debt obligation may rest solely upon the enterprise in debt and paid out of revenues. The latter are known as *revenue bonds*.

The great bulk of all government debt consists of marketable securities known as *government or municipal bonds*, which are negotiable and are sold freely on the market. They are usually issued in relatively large denominations and interest is paid by check or coupon on a periodic basis. Since they are salable, their price fluctuates from time to time, going above maturity value when the current market interest rate falls below the interest rate that they bear. When the market interest rate rises, or when fear develops about the government's ability to pay interest, the price may fall below the maturity value.

Other types of bonds bought by the public are not marketable but can be redeemed, at least after a specified period, for their principle plus accrued interest. An example of this type is the U.S. savings bond.

City and County Finance

City and county governments have traditionally relied on property taxes to finance government services. The city collects these taxes from property owners, businesses, and other taxable property. However, city and county governments also receive financial aid from state and federal governments. Much of this assistance comes in the form of *grants-in-aid*, which are funds made available under certain conditions or for a specific program. Most grants from state governments may be used for general purposes, but the city must meet certain standards established by the state. Most federal aid consists of grants for such specific purposes as airport construction or improvements in city sewerage systems. The federal government also offers *block grants*, which cities may use for various projects within a broad category, such as housing or education.

State Finance

Grants-in-aid from the federal government rank as the largest single source of state income. In the early 1990s, such grants totaled about $120 billion a year. Other major sources of income include state lotteries and taxes on general sales, individual and corporate incomes, and goods such as motor fuel, liquor, tobacco, and motor vehicles. Most of the money in a state's budget goes into payments for education, transportation, public welfare, health and hospitals, insurance trusts for the retirement of employees, and unemployment insurance.

Federal Government Acquisition
The federal government is the largest single purchaser of goods and services in the United States. Government construction contracts, like all federal procurement activities, are carefully regulated by legislation. The following acts are among the most significant.

Federal Acquisition Regulations
Perhaps the most important regulations directly related to federal procurement are the Federal Acquisition Regulations (FARs). The FARs were established to codify uniform policies for acquisition of supplies and services by executive agencies and are periodically supplemented by departmental and agency regulations.

Competition in Contracting Act
The Competition in Contracting Act (CICA) revised the FARs to encourage competition for all types of government contracts. The goal of the CICA is to create savings for the government by generating lower bids. The CICA requires that all proposed contracts expected to exceed $25,000 be published in the federal publication known as *Commerce Business Daily*.

Prompt Payment Act
Under the Prompt Payment Act, the government must make contract payment within 15 days of the payment date required by contract. If the government is late in its payment, it must also pay a penalty charge.

Davis-Bacon Act
The Davis-Bacon Act established minimum wages for various job classifications on all federal construction projects. Wage rates are determined annually by the Secretary of Labor.

Miller Act
The Miller Act provides protection of government interests by requiring contractors to furnish performance and payment bonds on contracts exceeding $25,000.

Civil Rights Legislation
In 1964, Congress passed comprehensive civil rights legislation to end discrimination based on race, color, religion, or national origin. It banned discrimination by trade unions, schools, or employers involved in interstate commerce or doing business with the federal government. It also assured nondiscrimination in the distribution of funds under federally assisted programs.

In the years that followed, the policy of affirmative action was embraced by federal agencies enforcing the Civil Rights Act. Special efforts were taken to allocate jobs and resources to those who had been discriminated against, such as minorities and women. By the late 1970s, however, affirmative action policies had led to court challenges and charges of "reverse discrimination" usually against white males. The most noteworthy case was *Regents of the University of California* v. *Bakke* (1978), in which the Supreme Court ruled that fixed quotas may not be set for places for minority applicants for medical school if white applicants are denied a chance to compete for those places. It was an inconclusive victory for opponents of affirmative action, and in *Fullilove* v. *Klutznick* (1980), the court upheld the federal law requiring that 10 percent of funds for public works be allotted to qualified minority contractors.

The Supreme Court began to seriously restrict affirmative action in 1989. In several decisions that year the Court gave greater weight to claims of reverse discrimination, outlawed the use of minority set-asides in cases where prior racial discrimination could not be proved, and placed stricter limits on states' use of racial preferences than it did on the federal government. In *Adarand Constructors* v. *Peña* (1995), the Court placed stricter limits on federal affirmative action programs, stating they were unconstitutional unless they fulfilled a "compelling governmental interest."

Chapter Three

The Design Professional

From the earliest times, humanity's involvement with religion and politics, and the desire for immortality, have given the *design professional* opportunity to ply his or her art. Archaeologists continue to unearth remnants of ancient civilizations that evidence not only the milestones of our evolution, but also our fascination with the designed environment. We cannot say with certainty that design is the world's oldest profession, but it surely was among the first special services demanded by the community.

Professional Practice

Two major developments led to the emergence of professional practice in the construction industry. First, public officials enacted licensing laws to govern those who design the built environment in order to safeguard the public interest. Next, licensed practitioners organized to promote a system of acceptable ethics and excellence in their work.

All 50 of the United States have enacted licensing laws for architects and engineers in the last half-century. Over the past 25 years, interior design has also been recognized as a design profession in some states. These licensing laws and registration procedures require those who wish to become professional practitioners of these disciplines to show qualifications related to education, workplace experience, and knowledge of building materials and methods. To these basic requirements are added comprehension of civil, structural, mechanical, and electrical design as well as an understanding of building codes and safety regulations. A candidate for licensing must exhibit, by written examination, a thorough knowledge of the community, the physical environment, and the relevant areas of the law. An architect, interior designer or professional engineer must also be well versed in the many facets of labor, material cost, and the amount of time required for project construction.

A design professional must be an astute businessperson as well as a technical expert. Good judgment based on knowledge and experience is his stock in trade, and his success is generally measured by how well his judgment serves the needs, desires, and economic goals of his client. Survival often depends on his ability to manage a staff of multi-disciplined personnel while producing a profit under conditions that limit the fees he can charge for his services.

The Architect

Thomas Jefferson, a man renowned for his prowess as a statesman, lawmaker, and businessman, was also an architect. He was one of the first Americans to design buildings that were more than copies of the work of 17th-century Europeans. His design innovations in his beloved Monticello suggested that the form of a building should be a product of its function. A century later, Louis Sullivan, the mentor of Frank Lloyd Wright, would coin the phrase "form follows function."

The drawings that survive from Jefferson's work on the University of Virginia seem rather simple when compared with the documents that today's design professional produces. The difference illustrates the enormous changes that have taken place in the profession over the past 200 years. In Jefferson's day, it was not unusual for an architect to visit the job site frequently to direct the work of the constructor. Christopher Wren, the architect who designed St. Paul's Cathedral in London just a generation before Jefferson, was on site daily to sketch details of current work.

Over the years, however, it became necessary for the design professional to include more and more documentation in what grew to be known as the "working drawings." Competition among constructors intensified and the owner's need for competitive bids became commonplace. As a result, the design professional was called on to provide more detailed drawings and specifications. The contract documents for a building comparable to St. Paul's Cathedral would likely contain hundreds of drawings today. The *project manual*, which collects all drawings, specifications, and other documents, would probably be published in several volumes. (Chapter 11 examines the project manual in detail.)

The design professional known as the *architect-of-record* no longer practices in the capacity of "master," as Christopher Wren and Thomas Jefferson did. As a result, his role in the OPC relationship has fundamentally changed. He continues to visit job sites and issue directives during the process of the work. However, his visits are described as *observations* for reasons we shall discuss in Chapter 6, "Legal Concerns and Insurance."

The Interior Designer

A number of buildings, especially office buildings for multiple tenants, are designed and completed in two separate phases that involve different design professionals and contractors. The first phase usually focuses on the building *shell* or *envelope*, which includes the basic structural, mechanical, and electrical systems and public spaces such as lobbies and corridors. It also addresses the building's *core*—its elevators, stairs, maintenance closets, mechanical and electrical service rooms, and toilets. The second group of contracts focuses on the design and *build-out* of the tenant spaces. As the number of buildings designed in this manner has increased, more and more design professionals have come to specialize in the design of interiors.

In the early 1980s, several states and the District of Columbia enacted licensing laws that recognized interior design as an independent professional discipline. Others have since followed suit. The National Council for Interior Design Qualifications (NCIDQ) has created national standards for the examination and licensing of interior design professionals.

The Engineer

Engineering might be described as the practice of using science to convert the resources of nature to the uses of humankind. According to the Engineers Council for Professional Development (ECPD), it is the creative application of scientific principles to design, where design is the development of structures, machines, apparatus, or manufacturing processes, or works utilizing them singly or in combination. The term is sometimes more loosely defined, especially in Great Britain, as the manufacture or assembly of engines, machine tools, and machine parts.

The words *engine* and *ingenious* are derived from the same Latin root, *ingenerare,* which means "to create." The early English verb "engine" meant "to contrive." Thus the engines of war were devices such as catapults, floating bridges, and assault towers; their designer was the "engine-er," or military engineer. The counterpart of the military engineer was the civil engineer, who applied essentially the same knowledge and skills to designing buildings, streets, water supplies, sewage systems, and other projects.

A great body of special knowledge is associated with engineering, and preparation for professional practice involves extensive training in the application of that knowledge. Standards of engineering practice are maintained through the efforts of professional societies, with each member acknowledging a responsibility to the public over and above responsibilities to his employer.

Unlike the scientist, the engineer is not free to select the problem that interests him. Instead, he must solve problems as they arise. More often than not, his solution must satisfy conflicting requirements—he must balance efficiency with cost, for instance, and safety with complexity of design. The engineering solution is the optimum solution, the end result that, taking many factors into account, is most desirable. It will be the most efficient for a given cost, or the simplest that will satisfy certain safety requirements.

Branches of Engineering

Although engineering problems may vary in scope and complexity, the same general approach to them is always applicable. First comes an analysis of the situation and a preliminary decision on a plan of attack. In line with this plan, the problem is reduced to a clearly stated categorical question. This question is then answered by deductive reasoning from known principles or by *creative synthesis,* the process of putting ideas together in new ways. The answer is always checked for accuracy and adequacy. Finally, the results for the simplified problem are interpreted in terms of the original problem and reported in an appropriate form.

The major engineering branches and their primary functions are listed below in order of decreasing emphasis on science.

- **Research** uses mathematical and scientific concepts, experimental techniques, and inductive reasoning to seek new engineering principles and processes.
- **Development** applies results of research to useful purposes, such as the creation of a new electrical circuit, chemical process, or industrial machine.
- **Design** selects methods, specifies materials, and determines shapes that will satisfy technical requirements and meet performance specifications.

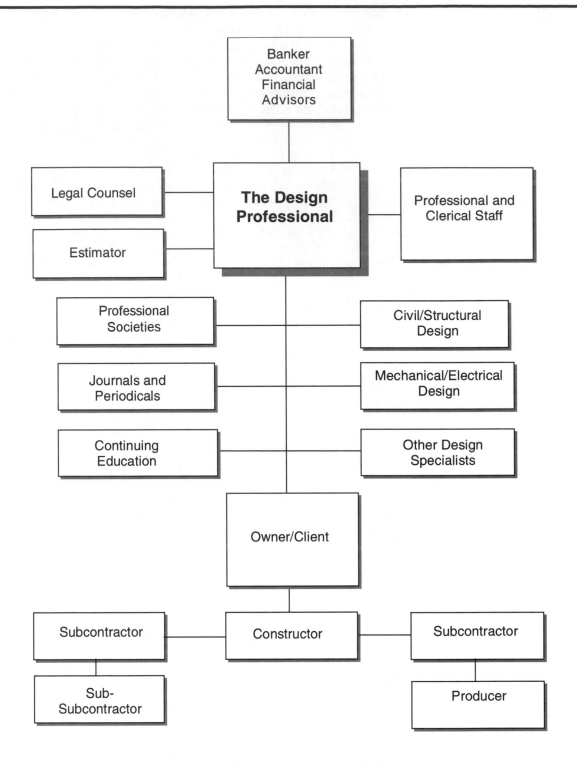

Figure 3.1 The Design Professional's Resources

- **Construction** prepares the job site by directing the placement of materials, organizing personnel and equipment, and determining procedures that will economically and safely yield desired results.
- **Production** designs plant layout, selects equipment and processes, integrates the flow of materials and components, and provides for testing and inspection.
- **Operation** controls machines, plants, and organizations that provide power, transportation, and communication; determines procedures and supervises personnel to obtain reliable and economic operation of complex equipment.
- **Management** analyzes customers' requirements, recommends units to satisfy needs, and resolves related problems.

Professional Institutions

Professional societies have been formed in each design discipline to establish and maintain the highest of moral and professional ethics. (A listing of professional societies and related organizations appears in the Appendix.) Although full membership is usually limited to licensed individuals in the mainstream of professional practice, associate memberships are often made available to those in the early stages of career development. Professional societies have published standards of practice, codes of ethics, suggested formats for the documentation of technical material, recommendations for business practice, and disclosures of advancements in technology. Most also publish magazines and other literature wherein practitioners share experience and judgment with their peers on technical solutions and other matters of mutual interest.

American Institute of Architects

The American Institute of Architects (AIA) has provided its members with support and a variety of services since 1857. Membership is often three-tiered, as a member of the AIA belongs to the national organization, a statewide affiliate, and in some cases a local chapter. The association provides programs for professional development, member and component services, and liaison with government at all levels. It also forms committees to work on issues like historic resources and preservation, regional and urban development, and areas of special focus such as architecture for health, education, and aging.

The AIA has been an industry leader in providing model contracts and associated documents for the construction industry. The use of these documents, and similar ones like those in this text, has important legal consequences and implications. To assure their proper use, consultation with an attorney is recommended.

Engineering Societies

Unlike architecture, engineering encompasses many varied and sometimes dissimilar disciplines. As a result, there are a number of different, often overlapping engineering societies. Among the most prominent are the National Society of Professional Engineers (NSPE), the American Consulting Engineer's Council (ACEC), and the American Society of Civil Engineers (ASCE). (More are included in the list of associations in the Appendix.)

In recent years, organizations have begun to work together on professional engineering documents. Most notably, the ACEC, ASCE, and NSPE have joined forces to create the Engineers Joint Contract

Documents Committee (EJCDC), which develops and periodically updates fair and objective standard documents.

Construction Specifications Institute

The Construction Specifications Institute (CSI) is made up of members from all areas of the construction industry. It is a nonprofit technical organization that provides a forum for architects, engineers, contractors, subcontractors, material manufacturers, suppliers and others. CSI is dedicated to the improvement of professional documentation, and more specifically, to the improvement of specifications and building practices through service, education, and research.

Before the days of organizations like CSI, there was no universally accepted format for the preparation of professional documents in the United States. The language of construction varied from state to state and city to city, with terminology for even the most common construction items varying greatly. For example, a suspended ceiling in one locale might be a furred ceiling in another, and a modular ceiling in yet another. The nomenclature, character, and organization of the specifications were left to the discretion of the individual specifier. As buildings, systems, and constructor practices grew more complex, the bidding process became increasingly difficult, and disputes and misunderstandings became more common and acute.

The CSI has provided a universal language and a common format for the writing of construction specifications. Its contributions to the industry are many, but the improvements it brought to the contract documents are especially significant.

Methods of Practice

In the early 20th century, it was common for architects to practice individually and hire engineers as subcontracted consultants (*subconsultants*) for certain aspects of the design. Since engineers tend to specialize by individual disciplines, the architect often employed a civil engineer for design of the site and a structural engineer for design of the foundation and superstructure. He may also have employed a mechanical engineer for the plumbing and HVAC systems and an electrical engineer for lighting and circuitry.

By mid-century, however, things were changing. As projects became larger and more complicated, architects and engineers began to offer their services jointly under a single firm. Because projects were now more expensive, more and more owners wanted to have their projects detailed and quantified before they began to pay for design or construction services. This gave rise to the *professional planner* who performed studies of an owner's needs. The planner's duties include basic functional programming, justifying costs for budget purposes, and identifying alternatives in site location and design and construction methodology.

Today, it is most common to find a design professional—often referred to as the Architect/Engineer or A/E—practicing with a firm that offers architecture, engineering, and planning services under a single umbrella. Planning services are usually performed by an architect regardless of the structure of the firm.

Professional Compensation

At one time, professional organizations like the AIA and the NSPE regularly established and published schedules that set standard minimum fees for specified professional services. These standards had been agreed on by a majority of professionals within a common discipline and were generally accepted among owners in the private and public sectors. The result was that professionals were rarely forced to compete with each other solely on the basis of fee. Competition was instead based on depth of experience, skills of staff, the ability to respond to an owner's needs quickly and efficiently, and the quality of references provided by other clients.

In the late 1960s and early 1970s however, the nature of competition for work began to change. Several professionals offered their services at prices lower than those in minimum fee schedules. The associations objected on the grounds that the lowered fees were a violation of their basic code of ethics. Several cases were litigated, and the results favored the maverick professionals. The Supreme Court eventually ruled that minimum fee schedules were unlawful violations of the "price fixing" provisions of the Sherman Anti-Trust Act.

Since that ruling, professionals have come under increasing pressure to compete on the basis of cost as well as qualification. They are forced to "streamline" services to adequately serve the needs of clients while remaining competitive in their fee structures.

Design Fees

The professional fees that are acceptable to most design professionals vary from a low of 6% of the cost of construction to a high of 12% or more. The design fee is affected by a number of factors.

The most direct way to determine the adequacy of a design professional's fee is to consider it in relation to the project cost. For example, the time required to design and produce contract documents for a six-classroom elementary school costing $450,000 will approximate 50% of the time needed to perform the same services for a school of 24 classrooms costing $1,600,000. If the larger project garners a fee of, say, 6% of the construction cost, or $96,000, then the corresponding fee for the smaller project ought to be $48,000, or 10.7% of the cost of construction.

Complexity of project design is the second most direct variable in determining the adequacy of a fee. The design of a hospital costing $16,000,000 is considerably more complex, for example, than the design of a high school of similar cost. The time spent designing and producing contract documents for the high school might be 70% of the time required for the hospital. If a 6% fee, or $96,000, is considered a competitive fee for the high school, then the fee for the hospital should be $137,000.

Selecting the Design Professional

Sometimes, the owner selects an A/E without going through a formal evaluation process. Perhaps the owner and the A/E have worked together in the past, or the A/E's reputation is such that the owner does not feel compelled to consider others. On the other hand, as is the case with some public owners, law or political decorum may demand that a competitive selection process be employed. Such processes usually involve an advertisement of the owner's needs, a review of the respondent's credentials, and a series of interviews with a "short-list" of qualified candidates.

Either way, an A/E should be selected because of design abilities, experience, communication skills, and proven leadership in the project delivery process. The A/E must also be able to recognize and insist on a quality of materials and construction methods that will meet or exceed the needs of the owner.

Comparative Selection of the Design Professional

While it is not always necessary to do so, there may be valid reasons for an owner to select the design professional by a comparative selection process. By formally comparing the credentials of candidate firms, the owner is often able to find the "best" fit for his needs. The several approaches to comparative selection are discussed below. No matter what approach is taken, it is helpful to all involved parties if the owner clearly states his selection criteria in advance.

The One-Step Comparative Selection Process

The one-step comparative process is conducted by advertising a detailed *Request for Proposal* (RFP). The RFP describes the project in detail, establishes detailed criteria for A/E firms or teams, and requests a written response from interested parties that includes the following:

- A description of the respondent's design and technical ability and experience, and that of any proposed subcontractors or consultants.
- An indication that the respondent fully understands the owner's needs and the nature of the project.
- An explanation of the respondent's unique qualifications and relevant background for such a project.
- A summary of the A/E services that the respondent proposes to provide to the owner, and the methodology that will be used to deliver those services.
- A description of the respondent's current workload and availability of personnel for the project.
- The qualifications and experience of the personnel that the respondent is willing to pledge to the project.
- A list of references, or clients for whom similar services have been performed, with addresses and telephone numbers.

Responses to the RFP are usually due by a specific date and time. At that time, the owner reviews the responses and makes a conditional selection. Pending a successful negotiation of fee for the work, the A/E is contracted for the services.

The Two-Step Comparative Process

The two-step comparative process is similar to the one-step process. The difference is that the owner prepares a *Request for Qualifications* (RFQ) asking that candidates submit a statement of qualification, experience, and availability for the project. Through the RFQ, the owner may determine the size and financial strength of a firm, the history of its practice, its experience with certain building types, and the availability of its key staff persons.

After responses to the RFQ are reviewed, the owner develops a list of two or more of the most qualified firms. These "short-listed" firms are then invited by RFP to prepare *technical proposals,* including a proposed *work plan* and detailed description of similar projects that the candidate has served. They may also be asked to participate in an interview before the final selection is made.

The Three-Step Comparative Process
This process is similar to the two-step process in that it begins with an RFQ issued by the owner. As with the last approach, the responses to the RFQ help the owner develop a short list of the most qualified firms, who are then invited to provide a detailed proposal. The third step in the process is the development of a second short-list of candidates, based on the strength of proposals, who will be interviewed by the owner. After the interviews are complete, the owner selects the firm he believes to be the best qualified for the job.

As an optional fourth step in the process, the owner may request in the RFP that each short-listed firm also submit a sealed fee proposal with its response. These fees are opened only after all interviews have been conducted and the leading candidate has been identified. If the fee proposal of the leading candidate is unacceptable to the owner, he may review the fee proposal of his second or third choice before he makes a final selection.

The Design Competition Method
On occasion, an owner will decide to stage a design competition to evaluate design professionals for a project. This is seldom an advantageous approach, as many qualified firms will not participate because of the high costs that are often associated with such competitions. In the United States, design competitions have been successful only where the project has been highly visible and where the owner's budget has few constraints.

Professional organizations such as the AIA have developed guidelines in an attempt to keep design competitions equitable. Their recommendations include the following:

- The owner should plainly document the criteria of the competition to ensure "apples to apples" comparisons of designs.
- A jury of peers, rather than the owner or a representative, should be retained to judge the entries.
- A series of cash awards should be offered as incentive to the participants. In the past, winning the commission alone has seldom been enough to attract the best or most able participants.

Most associations consider it acceptable, and even advisable, for the owner to reserve the right to award the commission to any participant, regardless of the outcome of the jury's ranking of the submissions.

The Problem with "Bidding" Professional Services
Many voices in the industry, including this one, strongly caution owners against competitive bidding for proposed design fees. There are a number of reasons why the practice may not be in the best interest of the owner. When design professionals are asked to compete on the basis of fee as opposed to qualifications, they are often obliged to cut corners on the project. They may use less experienced personnel, or evaluate fewer design alternatives.

Perhaps the greatest danger is that the quality of contract documents may suffer. The owner hires the design professional to prepare thorough documents that expertly describe the work required to construct the owner's project. If the documents are prepared with minimal detail, the whole construction process will suffer—and probably be more expensive. There is also likely to be more decision-making in the field by the constructor. Finally, long-term costs may also be higher, as designers may select systems that require minimum time to design rather than those that are most cost-effective over time.

The best firm to do the job may not be the cheapest, as the professional with the best skills and most experience will likely cost more than those less qualified. Better technical and human resources will also make a firm's *overhead*, or "cost of doing business," higher. Selecting a design professional based on cost without first weighing other factors is unlikely to yield positive results.

Primary Responsibilities of the Design Professional

Once the selection process is completed, the owner can expect the design professional to provide certain *basic services*. These services are usually uniform and common to any project, regardless of the method of project delivery that has been chosen, and form the core of the design professional's responsibilities.

Often, there are issues that must be addressed by the design professional before the basic services can begin. These elements are often called *pre-design services,* and can include:

- Identification of special project requirements.
- Architectural program development or confirmation of the owner's program of design.
- Development of design concepts and alternatives.
- Analysis of building code requirements and other applicable jurisdictional restrictions.
- Site selection.
- Budget analysis.

Likewise, special circumstances may require the design professional to perform additional services while delivering the basic services. Examples include:

- Demolition documents.
- Environmental studies.
- Design of off-site utilities.
- Design for fast-track construction methods.
- Life-cycle cost analysis.
- Value engineering.
- Study of funding alternatives.

Finally, the design professional may be called upon to provide additional assistance after the basic services are complete. These *post-construction services* usually include follow-up inspections of the completed building.

Schematic Design
The first basic services come during the *schematic design (SD),* or *preliminary design,* phase. During the SD phase, the design professional provides a basic project definition and illustrates the scale and relationship of project components. Drawings are usually limited to the following:

- The site plan.
- Building plan.
- Exterior design (elevation) sketches.

Drawings usually consist of diagrammatic, "one-line" floor plans of buildings and the site. The design professional may wish to create studies of building cross-sections and prepare conceptual sketches or simple models of building form and massing. Security requirements should also be identified. At the completion of the SD phase, the design professional should review probable project costs.

Design Development

The *design development (DD)* phase expands on the work done during the SD phase. It provides definition to the following:

- Exterior design.
- Interior design.
- Landscape design.
- Security systems design.
- Mechanical and electrical systems design.
- Special systems and processes.

Drawings produced during this phase may consist of floor and roof plans, building and wall sections, and exterior elevations. Security perimeters should be identified for both the site and the building. The DD phase should identify all local, state, and federal building code requirements and the special requirements of other agencies, then factor them into the design.

Basic engineering services provided during this phase include defining site improvements; evaluating structural design; developing plumbing, heating, and air-conditioning systems; and determining electrical requirements.

It is considered good policy for the design professional to include a *design narrative* and an *outline specification* with DD phase deliverables. The design narrative is often actually a series of documents, as representatives from each design discipline involved in the project will describe their contributions to the design. The outline-specification describes the products to be incorporated in the design.

When the DD phase is complete, the rule of thumb holds that 90% of the design decisions for the project should afterwards be made.

Contract Documents

The design professional prepares the contract documents after the completion of the design development phase. This is the phase of service in which design decisions are fully documented and coordinated in order to facilitate the construction process. Chapter 11, "The Project Manual," discusses the development of the contract documents in detail.

The economic objectives of the owner should be of primary concern to the professional preparing the documents, as an owner who has been well served will likely re-employ or recommend that professional. Thus, serving the owner's best interest is not simply an ethical goal for the design professional. It makes good business sense.

In keeping with the owner's best interests, the contract documents should define, demand, and ensure high quality standards. Using inferior methods and materials to keep costs low is seldom in the best interest of the owner, as the money saved during construction may be lost to excessive maintenance and repair. Experience shows that the construction cost of a building may be only 10% to 15% of the cost to maintain and operate it during its lifetime.

Assistance During Bidding

Depending on the type of project procurement, the design professional may assist the owner during the bidding process. He may attend and take part in any pre-bid, prepare any needed addenda to the bid documents, and reply to *Requests for Information* (RFI) from individual bidders.

Pre-Construction Conferences

The design professional usually participates in at least one pre-construction conference held by the owner or a designated representative and the constructor and his primary subcontractors prior to the start of construction. The pre-construction conference provides opportunity to accomplish the following:

- Review the general requirements and confirm procedures.
- Review the schedule for construction.
- Confirm format for and attendees at regular progress meetings
- Review and accept submittals such as bonds, certificates of insurance, schedule of values, list of subcontractors and material producers.
- Review and confirm local jurisdiction requirements, safety procedures, temporary job site accommodations, utility access and consumption during construction, and site access restrictions.

Services During Construction

The owner is well served when the design professional's work includes services during construction. The designer of the project will almost always have the best understanding of the full intent of the contract documents, and is therefore the best representative of the owner's interests. Most standard contracts, such as those published by the AIA or the EJCDC, state that the designer should be the interpreter of the contract documents.

Although some projects demand the design professional to serve as a full-time representative of the owner during construction, many require only periodic observation.

Observation of Construction

There has been some confusion in the construction industry regarding the responsibility, or more specifically the *liability*, of the design professional for supervision of the construction process. It should be made absolutely clear that under most forms of agreement, the design professional's role during construction is simply to administer the owner's interest. For this reason, most contracts intentionally avoid the word "supervise" when describing the professional's role. The responsibility for administration and supervision of the construction process belongs to the contractor.

Some have argued that, because the design professional is in a supervisory position as the owner's representative, he should be responsible if the contractor fails in any way to meet the intention of the contract documents. This should not be the case. The design professional is not a party to the contract between owner and contractor, and should not be expected to conduct an exhaustive investigation of the contractor's work at the job site.

To rule out the possible misconception that the architect or engineer is responsible for the contractor's performance, the language of contract agreements must be very specific. Both the professional's responsibility to the owner and relationship to the contractor should be made explicit. AIA and EJCDC standard forms of contract documents make statements similar to the following:

> *The Design Professional shall be a representative of and shall advise and consult with the Owner during the construction process and until final payment to the Contractor is due.*

Some forms of agreement add even stronger language to describe the design professional's responsibility to the owner:

> *The Design Professional shall have authority to act on behalf of the Owner only to the extent provided in this agreement unless otherwise modified by written instrument.*

The design professional's duties may be further described by statements like this one:

> *The Design Professional shall visit the site at intervals appropriate to the stage of construction or as otherwise agreed on by the Owner and Design Professional in writing in order that the Design Professional become generally familiar with the progress and quality of the Work, the completeness of the Work, and to determine in general if the Work is being performed in a manner that is consistent with the Contract Documents.*

Or this one:

> *The Design Professional shall not be required to make exhaustive or continuous on-site inspections to check the quality or quantity of the Work. On the basis of on-site observations, the Design Professional shall keep the Owner informed of the progress and quality of the Work, and shall endeavor to guard the Owner against defects and deficiencies in the Work.*

Finally, the contract should contain language similar to the following:

> *The Design Professional shall not have control over nor charge of, and shall not be responsible for, construction means, methods, techniques, sequences, or procedures, or for safety precautions and programs in connection with the Work, since these are solely the Contractor's responsibility under the Contract for Construction. The Design Professional shall not be responsible for the Contractor's schedules or failure to carry out the Work in Accordance with the Contract Documents. The Architect shall not have control over or charge of acts or omissions of the Contractor, Subcontractors, or their agents or employees, or of any other persons performing portions of the Work.*

Most construction contracts include a separate document called the *General Conditions* that sets forth in detail the architect or engineer's administrative role. The General Conditions are designed to complement the language of the Design Contract. It is very important that the two documents be consistent with one another. In the AIA and EJCDC forms, much of the language in the Design Contract is repeated in the General Conditions, and the standard form of General Conditions is incorporated by reference into the Design Contract (although, as noted above the architect or engineer is only a party to the latter). Chapter 9 discusses general conditions in more detail.

Technical Services Provided During Construction

The constructor, under the General Conditions and under the *General Requirements* and technical sections of the specifications, is required to disclose the materials, equipment, methods of construction, and other components he will furnish under the Contract for Construction. These disclosures, which include shop drawings and manufacturer's product data, are called *submittals.* As interpreter of the design intent, the design professional should review the submittals to confirm that the constructor's plans are in conformity with the contract documents.

In order to clarify the design professional's obligations regarding submittals, the Agreement Between Owner and Design Professional may include language similar to the following:

> *Services of the Design Professional assume that the Owner will acknowledge that the processing of shop drawings and other submittals are directly impacted by the clarity, completeness, and accuracy of said documents. It shall be the Contractor's responsibility to (1) review and coordinate each submittal with all other related or affected work and (2) approve each such submittal before submitting same to the Design Professional for approval. As a part of the Basic Services, the Design Professional will review a first submission and, if required, a second submission of all submittals required by the Construction Documents at no additional cost to the Owner. However, if the Architect is required to (1) review a third or later submission of any submittal due to no fault of the Design Professional; (2) review more than the number of copies of each submittal specified in the Construction Documents; (3) review submittals in addition to those required by the Construction Documents; or (4) review submittals for Contractor-proposed substitutions for previously approved items, such services shall be deemed Additional Services. The Construction Documents shall include a provision that will permit the Owner to back-charge the Contractor for any additional fees paid to the Design Professional under the provisions of this paragraph.*

The design professional may offer additional technical services during construction, including:

- Assistance to the owner in the selection of qualified testing services, the review of those tests, and the determination whether further testing is needed.
- Preparation of change orders to the Contract for Construction to correct inconsistencies in the documents. Changes requested by the owner and unanticipated site conditions will constitute additional service.
- Review of the constructor's applications for payment.

The design professional may also be called on to respond to Requests for Information (RFI) to clarify an aspect of the contract documents or the design intent. This additional responsibility may be articulated in the Agreement Between Owner and Design Professional as follows:

> *As a Basic service, the Design Professional shall review and respond to reasonable requests for information (RFIs) submitted by the Contractor on a timely basis. However, the Owner acknowledges that the request for information process may be susceptible to abuse by contractors, subcontractors, suppliers, producers, and other members of the construction team. For these reasons, the Owner also acknowledges that responding to requests for information or clarification for members of the construction team often requires extensive and time-consuming reviews by many individuals. To the extent that the Design Professional may be required to respond to RFIs*

that result from (1) the Contractor's failure to diligently research and review the Construction Documents, (2) the Contractor errors or omissions, or (3) related causes beyond the control and without the fault or negligence of the Design Professional, such services will be deemed Additional Services.

The construction documents should include a provision that permits the owner to back-charge the constructor for additional fees paid to the design professional for excessive or unusual administration of submittals, Requests For Information, or clarifications that exceed the intent of the contract documents.

Field Services During Construction
Field services provided by the design professional during construction include periodic observational visits to the job site. The Agreement Between Owner and Design Professional should spell out the requirements for these visits. Bimonthly visits may be specified, for instance.

When the project nears its end, the design professional should conduct a site visit to determine whether *substantial completion* of the work has been achieved. At this time, he should also prepare a report for the owner that includes a *punch list* of items that require replacement or are not yet complete. If the design professional deems that work is not sufficiently complete, he may be requested to return to the site for a second visit. However, the Design Professional should not be required to make excessive visits without additional compensation, as this excerpt from a typical Agreement Between Owner and Design Professional makes clear:

> *If the Design Professional determines that the work is not substantially complete after the performance of a second Substantial Completion site visit (should a second visit be required), either because of major items not completed or an excessive number of "punch list" items, subsequent site visits for the purpose of determining Substantial Completion of the work shall be deemed Additional Services. The Construction Contract shall include a provision that will permit the Owner to back-charge the Contractor for any additional fees paid to the Architect under the provisions of this paragraph.*

Once the design professional feels that construction is substantially complete, he usually issues a written statement of such called a *Certificate of Substantial Completion.*

Project Closeout
Once the project is complete, the design professional will review the constructor's final submittal documents, including operations and maintenance manuals and data, and last application for payment. He will also supervise the preparation of the *project record documents,* a collection of documents, plans, specifications, and other materials that serve as the owner's guide to the finished building.

The contract documents that the design professional developed at the outset of the project were intended to describe the building to be completed in great detail. However, they may not be accurate enough to serve the owner's needs for future maintenance. Many of the drawings, particularly those that depict pipes, ducts, mechanical and electrical equipment, are schematic in nature and will not always provide the information needed to locate important elements for maintenance or replacement. Because of this, the General

Requirements of the Specifications may require the constructor to keep accurate records of the locations of embedded items for the owner's benefit. A new set of drawings and specifications, based on the original contract documents, may also be prepared for clarification. This information is presented to the owner at project completion as part of the project record documents.

Other documents furnished for the owner's permanent records include manufacturers' product literature, instruction manuals and maintenance data, along with warranties and guarantees on materials and equipment.

Post Construction Services

In most projects, the design professional's basic services are completed when the owner accepts the finished project and a date of final completion has been established. The constructor generally warrants the finished construction to be free of defects and operational flaws or failures for at least one year after it is accepted. Many elements of the project may have guarantees and warranties that extend for longer periods. The owner may find it advantageous to have the design professional confirm that the constructor has done the work to meet the terms of those guarantees and warranties.

A Word on Perfection

The English poet and playwright George Bernard Shaw once observed that "English speaking peoples are often separated by a common language." Shaw's humor reminds us that technical documentation, specifications and drawings are subject to interpretation. It is unrealistic to expect perfection in the documents created by the design professional.

Standard-of-care is a legal concept that sets reasonable expectations for the services delivered by professionals like lawyers, physicians, and design professionals. Common law in the United States recognizes that much of the value of a professional's service depends on subjective judgment borne of education and individual experience. Just as it is unreasonable to expect the subjective judgment of two professionals to be exactly the same, it is also unreasonable to expect the subjective judgement of a particular professional to be perfect. According to the courts, the quality of a professional's service should not be expected to exceed the profession's common standard-of-care. Chapter 6, "Legal Concerns and Insurance" discusses the subject in more detail.

The legal standard of care does not require perfection in contract documents. A number of studies have been conducted by professional societies, academic and government authorities, and other groups in the construction industry to establish benchmarks of quality in design and construction. In one study, the National Research Council determined that errors and omissions in the design resulting in change orders of not more than an upper range of 5% of the contract price should be an acceptable standard of care for the services of the design professional. A similar study was conducted and published by the Construction Industry Institute in 1987. Based on studies like these, it is reasonable to establish design error and omission standards in the range of 2% to 3% of the contract price for many projects. This translates to a benchmark of a 97% to 98% level of perfection in contract documents for those projects.

At the start of any project, the owner and design professional should discuss and define an acceptable standard of care for the project. In accordance with that standard, a percentage of the contract price should be carried within the owner's contingency fund to cover change orders that result from inconsistencies in the contract documents. This text recommends a contingency of no less than 2% for projects of more than $10 million in value and no less than 5% for projects under $5 million in value. (For renovation or restoration of existing buildings, and other particularly complex objects, higher contingencies may be appropriate.)

Chapter Four

The Constructor

Since they first stood upright, humans have been trying to increase their control over the environment. They quickly learned to construct shelters, which enabled them to adapt to a wide variety of climates and become a global species. Their shelters were simple at first and often lasted only a few days or months, but gradually humans built more enduring structures that led to permanent communities. Early buildings were solely for habitation, but soon structures were built for other functions, such as food storage and ceremony. Some structures began to have symbolic as well as functional value, marking the beginning of the distinction between architecture and building.

The history of building construction is marked by evolving technology. Early building materials, including leaves, branches, and animal hides, were perishable. Later, more durable materials, such as clay, stone, and timber, were used. Finally, synthetic materials like brick, concrete, metals, and plastics were introduced. As the knowledge of structure and the strength and properties of materials grew, the size of structures increased. The desire to control the interior environment of buildings eventually brought the ability to regulate light and ambient conditions. Finally, electricity and fuel-powered machinery brought wholesale changes to how, and how quickly we can build.

Today, building construction is remarkably complex. The world of construction professionals includes manufacturers of building products and systems; craftsmen or tradesmen who assemble products and systems on the building site; contractors who employ and coordinate the work of the craftsmen; and consultants who specialize in such aspects as construction management, quality control, and insurance. A wide variety of building products and systems are available, with each targeted primarily for a specific application or market. Building design is a highly ordered process and draws upon sophisticated research. Code officials adopt and enforce safety standards, to which design professionals must adhere as they determine user needs and then design structures to meet those needs.

Building construction contributes significantly to the global industrial culture and reflects the diversity and complexity of our world. More than anything else, it provides a measure of our ability to master the natural forces of our environment.

The Business of Building Construction

In the United States, construction is usually carried out by a specialized team of experienced professionals. Building services are normally performed separately from those of the design professional, although some large organizations may combine both functions. (Chapter 7, "Project Delivery," discusses design/build, where a contractor provides both design and construction services to an owner.) Figure 4.1 shows the typical organization of resources required to engage in the business of building construction today.

A constructor who enters a contract for construction with an owner and is responsible for the entirety of the project is generally referred to as a *general contractor*. In addition to taking on the role of coordinator, the general contractor may perform some of the actual construction work on the building. However, the majority of the work will likely be done by a group of specialty *subcontractors* under contract to the general contractor. Each subcontractor provides and installs one or more of the building systems. The subcontractors in turn buy the system components from *producers* often the manufacturers or assemblers of such systems. During the construction process the design professional acts as the owner's representative, making sure that the executed building conforms to the contract documents and that the systems and components meet the specified standards of quality and performance.

Specialized Contracting

As building design grows increasingly complicated, more and more constructors are specializing in certain types of buildings or building components. Specialized constructors may function as a prime contractor or as a subcontractor to a general contractor. Their work can include installation of mechanical systems to provide controlled environments; plumbing systems to provide delivery of water, gas and other elements; electric power and lighting; and systems electronics for security and surveillance. Other specialties include:

- Site preparation, including earth work, grading and paving, and storm water management systems.
- Concrete placement and construction.
- Masonry construction.
- Structural steel erection.
- Curtain-wall erection.
- Drywall construction.
- Ceilings and cornice work.
- Carpentry and millwork.
- Painting and wall covering.

Construction Project Management

Managing a construction project is a challenging endeavor. The work must follow a logical sequence of events, yet maintaining that sequence can be difficult as some materials and equipment require long lead times for ordering and fabrication. The work of subcontractors and specialty constructors must be carefully coordinated. Safety procedures and local, state and federal codes must be followed at all times. The premises must be kept clean, with materials and equipment adequately protected and stored. Records must be kept for accounting purposes, and the schedule of completion must be managed.

The Project Manager

The project manager is ultimately accountable for the successful completion of the project responsible for the overall direction of the work. He relies heavily upon the superintendent, as we shall see. The project manager usually handles the executive duties related to

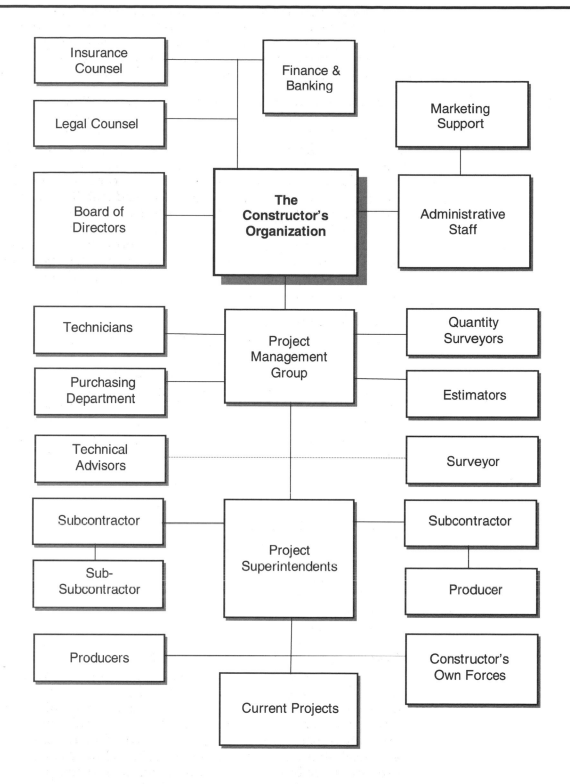

Figure 4.1 The Constructor's Resources

the project, handles record-keeping duties, and communicates regularly with the owner and design professional.

The Superintendent

The superintendent spends most of his time and resources coordinating the various trades, subcontractors, and other collateral activities of a project on a day-by-day basis. The first lieutenant to the project manager, he usually presides over progress meetings; handles the ordering and scheduling of materials, equipment, and other resources; and is accountable to project management for the progress of the work.

The Estimator

The estimator may perform three distinct jobs during the construction process. His primary duty is to study the contract documents, conduct a quantity survey of materials and methods, and prepare estimates of cost for the bidding process. During construction, he may also assist in reviewing accounting records and monitoring general progress of the work. Finally, he often prepares and coordinates the documentation for pay requests and any necessary change orders.

Training and Qualifications

The typical principal manager of a construction company in the United States is a college graduate with both business and engineering acumen. Many colleges and universities in the United States offer degrees related to building construction, including Architectural Engineering. A student in such a program receives basic education in the sciences and engineering with some exposure to architectural design and the history of building construction. Sometimes constructors are civil engineers with a specialty in structural engineering and material behavior.

Specialized constructors are often graduates of a trade school. Some may have studied at a community college to master such skills as plumbing, HVAC, masonry, and woodworking. In many ways, the modern community college has filled the void left by the trade guilds of yesteryear, where an individual could learn from a master craftsman.

Licensing

Many states of the fifty United States now require constructors to be licensed, offering an important safeguard for owners worried about constructor qualifications. Although requirements vary, most state licensing procedures require a licensed trade contractor to:

- Demonstrate proficiency in his particular trade by education and examination.
- Demonstrate understanding of local codes and construction law by examination.

In order to become a licensed *master* of a trade, one must first be licensed as an *apprentice*, then as a *journeyman*. Advancement is achieved through written examination.

Producers who own patented or copyrighted processes often require *process licensing* for constructors who install their systems. Candidates for a process license usually receive extensive training in the application of the process. In requiring the license, producers are, of course, looking to maintain the integrity of their process. Many offer extensive warranties and guarantees, so it is also financially prudent that they control the installation as best they can.

Financial Concerns

Modern building construction is extremely capital intensive. The possibility exists that a contractor may become insolvent during the process of construction. In this event, the potential loss to the owner can be very high. While the owner may recover damages for breach of contract, a money judgment against a financially irresponsible contractor is, at best, an inadequate remedy. For the owner's protection, a system has been established using bonds purchased by the contractor from a surety (at the insistence of the owner) to protect the owner in the case of loss through the contractor's failure to perform. Both private and public owners often require that contractors provide performance bonds in amounts equal to 100% of the contract price. The *surety*, the individual who provides the bonding and assumes legal responsibility for the debt often requires a pledge of substantial collateral in return for the risk inherent with the bond. The surety may also require that the constructor file a financial statement that assures liquidity in the net worth of the company. It is not unusual for the surety to require that the constructor's net worth amount to several times the total amounts of bonds issued at any point in time.

Chapter 6, "Legal Concerns and Insurance," deals in some detail with bid bonds, performance bonds, and payment bonds.

Legal Concerns

Individuals in most countries are held legally liable to others for harmful acts or omissions, and may be required to pay appropriate damages. Legal liability exists when an individual commits an act that causes injury or wrongly encroaches on another person's rights. Examples include slander, assault, and *acts of negligence* where the failure to behave in a responsible manner causes financial loss or injury to others. An act may be considered negligent even if it is unintentional.

Negligence may be imputed from one person to another. For example, a constructor may be liable not only for his own acts but also for the negligent acts of employees, subcontractors, or others legally representing him. In addition, statutes may impute liability on individuals when none would exist otherwise. A constructor may thus be legally liable for the acts of an individual operating a vehicle or piece of equipment owned or leased by the constructor.

Based on the terms of their contracts with owners, constructors are also exposed to claims related to performance. For instance, an owner may claim damage if a project is not completed within the time allowed under the contract. If any portion of the work is not in accordance with the contract documents, the owner may also have a legitimate claim.

Finally, the constructor has exposure to claims from third parties— that is, from parties who are not in a contractual relationship with the constructor, but who claim damages due to an act, or failure to act, by the constructor. If a constructor fails to provide adequate safety procedures on a job site, for instance, and an injury occurs to a pedestrian who ventures on the premises, the constructor may be held accountable.

Liability insurance may be purchased to cover contingencies like these. See Chapter 6, "Legal Concerns and Insurance," for more information.

The Contract Price

The contract price is often a pre-established lump sum, although cost-plus-fee contracts are sometimes used on large projects where construction begins before the contract documents are complete and the building scope is fully defined. (Several alternative means of project delivery are examined in Chapter 7.) The contract price for a project is usually settled during a bidding process.

Public owners are usually mandated by law to engage competing constructors in public bidding, with the contract for construction awarded to the lowest qualified bidder. Private owners are not subject to the same scrutiny, but most also rely on the competitive process to select a constructor.

The process of bidding and negotiating a project price is the primary focus of the constructor's management group. Winning work in highly competitive bidding processes is critical to the constructor's ability to remain in business. For this reason, the constructor will focus its prime senior resources toward such activities. Any mistake made in preparation of the bid price could seriously affect a constructor's economic well-being. Figure 4.2 illustrates a typical constructor's bidding response team.

Project Procurement Methods

The bidding process is expensive, time-consuming, and often intense. The form it takes is dependent on the procurement method in which the project will be carried out. Chapter 7 carefully examines the various methods available to the owner, but we will cover them briefly here to understand the complexity of hiring the constructor who does the work.

Design/Bid/Build

Design/Bid/Build is still considered the traditional method for project procurement. The owner first hires the design professional, who prepares *bidding documents* that include both the contract documents and a schedule of bidding information. Usually, the owner will next create a *defacto* competition between candidate constructors by advertising his intention to solicit bids, issuing the bidding documents, and then selecting the constructor by the lowest responsible bid. Alternatively, the owner may restrict his invitation to selected bidders, or simply select a constructor and negotiate a contract price. In such cases, the owner will first issue a *Request For Qualifications* (RFQ) to find candidates with the best experience, financial strength, ability to provide knowledgeable staff, and similar attributes.

Design/Multiple Bid/Build

A variation of the traditional method, *Design/Multiple Bid/Build* is often mandated by law in public work. Under this methodology, certain aspects of the construction work are bid separately and awarded as separate contracts. Mechanical work, including plumbing and HVAC, may represent as much as 30% to 40% of the total contract price. Electrical work might represent another 20% to 30%. By isolating these high cost components of the construction project,

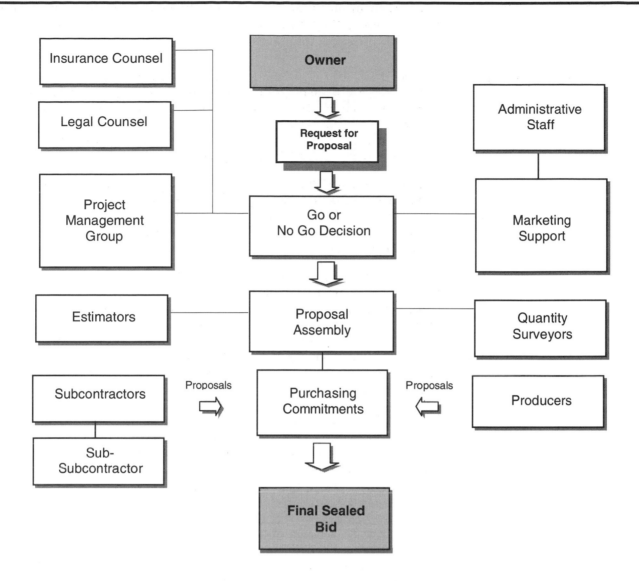

Figure 4.2 *Constructor's Proposal Response Team*

an owner can often maintain a tighter control over the overall cost. Complications may arise in coordinating the work, however, which can lead to a need for a supervisory *construction manager*.

Design/Construction Management/Build

Design/Construction Management/Build, a variation of the Design/Multiple Bid/Build approach, offers the most reasonable method of project procurement where multiple bids are involved. It also allows a project to be *fast-tracked,* where certain parts of the work are awarded before the contract documents are complete. The construction manager (CM) who plays a coordinating role in this approach comes in two forms: the *CM at risk* and the *CM advisor*. The CM at risk awards and is responsible for completion of all contracts. He seldom simply "brokers" the work, and is often required to complete a substantial portion of the project with his own forces. The CM advisor acts as a representative to the owner, is paid a fee to represent the owner's interest, and manages the multiple-bid process. The Agency CM advisor may actually be the permanent employee of an owner who procures new projects annually. The CM is most often selected after the owner issues a RFQ and subsequent RFP.

Program Management

The *program management method* is usually used for large projects with multiple components. The owner hires a *program manager* (PM) to oversee the entire procurement process, including the selection of one or more design professionals. The PM hires constructors using a combination of RFQs, RFPs, and competitive bidding.

Design/Build

The *design build approach,* which involves a single contract for project procurement, has grown significantly in popularity during recent years. The owner selects the designer/constructor by issuing an RFP, just as he selects the design professional under the traditional approach. Chapter 7 includes a complete description of the design/build process.

The Bidding Process

Once the owner makes his project needs known, interested constructors respond to the owner's invitation or advertisement and offer with their contract price sealed in a bid envelope. At a *bid opening,* the offers of competing constructors are revealed and tallied. It is not unusual for the "bid spread" to be as much as 10% between the high bidder and the low bidder.

While the contract for construction generally goes to the low bidder, the owner retains the right to award the contract to whomever he sees fit in a document known as the *instructions to bidders*. If all bids exceed the project budget, the owner has the right to withdraw the offer and make no award. If the lowest bid is substantially lower than the others, the owner may need to take extra steps to confirm that it is adequate to execute the work.

Competitive bidding in other countries often takes a different form. For instance, some European owners award the contract for construction to the candidate whose bid is closest to the mean average of the proposals of all bidders. Similarly, some owners eliminate the highest and lowest bids and award the contract to the constructor whose proposal is closest to the average of the remaining proposals. Proponents of these approaches insist they tend to produce results that are both beneficial to the owner and fair to the competitors. According to these individuals, a selection strategy that focuses only on the low bid forces contractors to produce projects by inferior means and methods.

Other Considerations

The prudent owner will prefer constructors who have successfully completed a project of similar scope to his own. He will also ask that constructors under consideration disclose their financial conditions, the names and resumes of key personnel, and a list of owners for whom they have worked in the past. The American Institute of Architects offers the "Contractor's Qualification Statement," an excellent and comprehensive form that helps owners to determine and compare the qualifications of the constructors.

Chapter 11, "The Project Manual," discusses the bidding documents and the process of bidding and negotiation in detail. Chapter 8, "The Construction Contract," focuses on the contract between owner and contractor. Chapter 9, "Conditions of the Contract" reviews the obligations of Owner, Constructor and Design Professional.

Summary

Survival in the field of building construction has become a game of wit and ingenuity as well as an art requiring great business acumen and daring. The ability of the American building contractor, as the low bidder, to take on a project and produce that project on time and profitably has become one of the absolute wonders of the world. The key to this phenomenon has been innovation. With advances like "tilt wall" construction, component prefabrication, labor-saving tools, and computerized scheduling, it has been the American contractor who has taught the rest of the world how to get a tough job done profitably and on time.

Chapter Five
Labor and Government

When humans began to live in permanent communities, they quickly learned that the overall community benefited when individuals developed specialized skills. Some would gather and distribute food, others made clothing, and still others prepared and maintained shelters. They also learned the value of leadership in maintaining order in the community. There came into being the chief, who carried the authority to make decisions and rules by which all citizens were bound to live.

In this way, labor and government evolved simultaneously. Both institutions would change drastically over the centuries, but they would remain essential pillars of community. This chapter will look briefly at several of the ways in which labor and government have affected the built environment.

The History and Influence of Labor

Before the dawn of the machine age in the 18th century, the primary issue in building construction was not the time required for completion of the structure, but rather the quality of its workmanship and the degree of its ornamentation. Master builders of the past could afford to use time to their advantage, as competition among the trades and guilds was not as keen as it would become in later years. Burgeoning populations provided an excess of workers and the master builders could pick and choose, hire and fire, and set wage rates at levels that suited the budget, if not the needs of the worker.

The many technological advances of the past few hundred years have fundamentally changed building construction. They have not only allowed us to build larger structures and more quickly, but have also drastically changed the availability and value of man's labor. Before the discovery of labor-saving, energy-intensive devices, building construction relied chiefly on man's brute strength to extract, refine, transport, and place the materials. The common laborer, more in demand for his brawn than for his brain or skill, was long the mainstay of the building construction industry. With the advent of increasingly specialized machinery, however, brute force is no longer the chief qualification of the laborer in construction.

Trade Specialization

Organized labor as we know it today seems to have had its beginnings in the *collegia opificum*, which were committees that emerged in the early days of the Roman Empire. According to Plutarch, the Greek historian of the first century, the Roman emperor Numa Pompilius organized the various trades into companies or guilds called *collegia* or *corporia*. By the beginning of the 3rd century AD, there were at least 30 of these guilds. Their existence was based upon statutory authority known as the *lex collegii*, and they were subject to the administration of *magistri*. Thus we see not only the beginnings of labor organization, but also the origins of such institutions as the college, the corporation, and the magistrate. The fate of the *collegia* and the *corporia* after the fall of the Western Roman Empire in 476 AD is largely unknown. Still, there seems no doubt that these Roman institutions were the forerunners of the medieval guild systems that predominated in Europe from the fourth through the early 18th century.

The Labor Movement

The first labor unions and labor laws developed in the beginning of the 18th century, when the ability to harness natural energy led to manufacturing and employment opportunities for great masses of skilled and semiskilled workers. The so-called "Machine Age" came to the United States just as masses of immigrant workers were pouring into a "new land of opportunity." With the machines came employment, and with employment came abuses of employees by their employers.

The term "Industrial Revolution" was first popularized by Arnold Toynbee in the late 19th century. He referred to the explosion of technological, economic, social, and cultural changes that accompanied the development of improved spinning and weaving machines, the steam engine, and the factory. The Industrial Revolution had its roots in the 18th century in England, but it is generally thought to have taken hold in the United States in the early 19th century. With it came new means of mass manufacture and the ability to exploit natural forms of energy, such as coal and natural gas. Electricity could be produced with natural energy, and it soon changed forever the focus upon manpower as a basic source of energy.

Industry's need for large numbers of workers and the corresponding abuses by greedy and unsympathetic employers brought the need for some form of collective bargaining by employee organizations. The history of labor organizations began when groups of tradesmen possessing a similar craft began to band together into groups that were called "guilds," "brotherhoods," or "mechanics societies." The initial objective of these organizations was to provide sickness and death benefits, which were unavailable from employers, to the widows and children of members. In addition, members developed proficiency standards that defined achievement levels in their trade, such as "apprentice," "journeyman," and "master."

Because of employer opposition to any form of organization that might threaten their interests, many of these early trade organizations were forced to operate in secret. As a result, they were often viewed as unlawful, conspiratorial groups that posed a danger to society. From the 1840s until the New Deal era in the early 1930s, the history of labor organizations was a continuing saga of confrontation between labor and management.

Until Samuel Gompers organized the *American Federation of Labor (AFL)* in 1886, semiskilled and unskilled workers had little or no alternative but to work in "sweat shop" manufacturing plants. Labor was not collectively coordinated or organized, as only small, independent trade organizations existed, and aside from much active rhetoric, it had little effect in improving the plight of the average worker. The AFL was the first successful attempt to unite skilled craftworkers, such as cabinetmakers, blacksmiths, and leather tanners. The building trades department of the AFL, organized in 1908, became the "umbrella" organization for the craft unions of the construction industry.

At the start, the AFL sought to bring the existing labor organizations under its influence, rather than allow rival groups to threaten its own existence. Inevitably, groups that represented less skilled workers did not receive the same distinction as those with skilled workers. The resulting friction brought about the creation of the *Congress of Industrial Organizations (CIO)* in 1935. It was a move made without the approval of the AFL board of directors, who branded the CIO a treasonous organization and expelled it from the AFL. The CIO acted independently until 1955, when personal and philosophical differences were put aside and it merged with the AFL. Today, the AFL-CIO remains as the major labor entity in the United States.

Labor unions could impose on management the threat of a *strike*, where union workers would stay away from their jobs unless their demands were met. Portions of annual union dues paid by workers were set aside as a special fund, out of which benefits to striking workers could be paid. This fund provided workers with considerable "staying power" during prolonged strikes and disputes. Since the AFL-CIO included a great majority of trades and crafts, it was very effective in improving the situation of the average worker. The unions brought about many benefits other than increased wages. Among them were retirement benefits, insurance coverage, and cost of living increases. Their efforts also led to the creation of blanket contracts for the conditions and time periods under which members would work. This practice continues to this day.

The Influence of Government

Regulation by the United States federal government began in 1887, when Congress established the *Interstate Commerce Commission (ICC)* to oversee the nation's railroads. During the New Deal of the 1930s, the government set up a number of regulatory agencies, including the *Federal Communications Commission (FCC)*, the *Federal Deposit Insurance Corporation (FDIC)*, and the *Securities and Exchange Commission (SEC)*. A new wave of government regulation occurred during the 1970s. Public interest in controlling pollution spurred the establishment of the *Environmental Protection Agency (EPA)*. Concern for industrial and public safety led to the formation of the *Occupational Safety and Health Administration (OSHA)* and the *Consumer Product Safety Commission*.

Landmark Legislation
Over the past century, the federal government has instituted a number of regulations that have directly affected labor and, by extension, building construction.

The *Sherman Anti-Trust Act* of 1890 was enacted in order to check the growth of big business and to prevent industries from creating monopolies in certain areas of commerce. At that time, the oil and steel companies had joined together by forming giant *cartels* that regulated prices and output. A cartel serves as a "union" of sorts for producers in that it seeks to provide control of a market for self-gain. Many argued that the Sherman Anti-Trust Act should also be applied to labor unions since labor, once organized, could fix prices and therefore monopolize and control the wage level. In 1908, the Supreme Court agreed, and management used the provisions of the ruling to gain judicial injunctions against unions. In this way, the labor movement was prevented from organizing and thereby growing.

In 1914, Congress enacted the *Clayton Act*, which tried to offset the negative effects of the Sherman Anti-Trust Act by allowing labor to organize and negotiate with a single employer. However, management countered that unions were actually organized and controlled by outsiders, rather than those actually seeking employment, and the terms of the Sherman Act continued to be applied.

In 1931, during the height of the Great Depression, a piece of legislation was enacted that would have a profound effect on many industries, including construction. The *Davis-Bacon Act* provided that wages and fringe benefits on all federal or federally funded projects should not be less than the prevailing rate for each particular trade as set by the Secretary of Labor of the United States. To ensure that these rates were paid, the bill further provided that a certified accounting of payrolls be submitted to the agency of contract for auditing.

The Davis-Bacon Act created a major advantage for union contractors because the rates set by the Labor Secretary were usually the highest of current union rates for a particular geographic area. Non-union contractors would usually not be allowed to compete under such circumstances.

In order to avoid hiring union members, some employers began to strong-arm workers with the use of *"yellow dog" contracts*. A yellow dog contract was a statement, signed by a prospective employee as a condition of employment, that he was not, and would not subsequently become, a member of a labor union. Under the contract, the employee would be subject to immediate dismissal for participating in any activity related to the organization of a union.

The *Norris-LaGuardia Act* in 1932 was the first piece of major legislation that would diminish the power of management over labor, accomplishing what the Clayton Act could not. Sometimes referred to as the Anti-Injunction Act, it specifically stated that the courts could not intercede on the part of management to prevent formation of labor organizations. It also protected the rights of employees to strike and picket peacefully, and declared yellow dog contracts unlawful.

The *National Labor Relations Act (NLRA)* of 1935, also known as the Wagner Act, defined and forbade unfair practices by management. Among other provisions, it made it unlawful for an employer to discriminate against a union employee for any reason. The NLRA provided a standard framework by which management-labor relations were to be conducted.

Perhaps most significantly, the NLRA established the *National Labor Relations Board (NLRB)*, a committee appointed by the president to serve as a "clearing house" for management-labor disputes. The act also established the concepts of the *closed shop*, where only union members were hired, and the *open shop*, where non-union personnel could be employed as well. As we shall see, legislation would soon amend the closed shop concept.

In 1938 came the *Fair Labor Standards Act*, commonly referred to as the Minimum Wage Law, which established a minimum wage for all workers except agricultural workers. It also established a maximum workweek of 40 hours, with a rate not less than one-and-one-half times the normal hourly rate for work beyond the 40 hours. The act has been amended over the years to reflect the current purchasing power of the dollar.

As organized labor became more powerful, a disreputable element began to infiltrate the union ranks. In response, Congress enacted the *Hobbs Act*, sometimes called the Anti-Racketeering Act, just after World War II. This legislation was designed to protect employers from having to pay "kickbacks" to unscrupulous union "bosses" in order to ensure that employees would report for work. To demand such bribes was declared a felony, punishable by time in prison.

The Taft-Hartley Act

To complement the National Labor Relations Act, Congress passed the *Labor Management Relations Act*, more commonly known as the *Taft-Hartley Act*, in 1947. It continued the NLRA's basic guarantees of workers' rights, outlawed certain union tactics, and expanded the act's concept of unfair labor practices to include practices of labor organizations. Taft-Hartley also allowed the president to delay for 80 days the start of a strike that might cause a national emergency.

The act significantly weakened the labor union. It forbade unions from using force or discriminating against individuals during organizing campaigns. It also prohibited unions from using dues collected from members for political contributions in national elections. Finally, it outlawed certain coercive union activities, including the *secondary boycott*, where striking employees bring pressure on a party not involved in the dispute so that the party will stop doing business with their employer; the *sympathy strike*, where one union calls a strike in support of another striking union; and the *jurisdictional strike*, where rival unions strike in dispute over which one has the right to work on a job.

Perhaps most importantly, Taft-Hartley outlawed the closed shop, in which only members of a labor union may be hired, and gave states power to restrict the *union shop*, in which employees must join a union after being hired.

Taft-Hartley once more reversed the swing of the pendulum. It still left labor in a position of power, but brought the balance of power closer to center. It was designed to clean up certain practices carried out by the management of organized labor. The act also restructured the make-up of the National Labor Relations Board in an attempt to give management a stronger voice to counter that of labor. Finally, it established the *Federal Mediation and Conciliation Services* group to act as a third party in mediating disputes and empowered the president to invoke a 90-day "cooling off" period that restricts any action by either side.

More Recent Legislation

In the 1950s, there was evidence of widespread graft and corruption among union executives. The *Landrum-Griffin Act* of 1959 subjected labor management to audits for the management of funds collected from members. This act and several federal tax laws have had a significant impact on the administrative procedures of American business.

In 1970, Congress passed the *Occupational Safety and Health Act (OSHA)*, sometimes known as the *Williams-Steiger Act*, to improve job safety. Under this legislation, the U.S. Department of Labor may impose fines and penalties for non-conformance to specific safety standards. OSHA set regulations for protective clothing, tools, equipment, procedures, and other aspects of building construction. Nicknamed the "Hard Hat Law," it made the wearing of construction helmets common practice on the job site.

Civil Rights Legislation

As we discussed in Chapter 2, the Civil Rights Act of 1964 established the concept of equal employment opportunity. It expressly forbids discrimination by an employer on the basis of race, color, religion, sex, or national origin, and applies to hiring, discharge, conditions of employment, and classification of workers. In 1965, President Lyndon Johnson amplified the act with an executive order that mandates affirmative action requirements regarding equal employment on all federal or federally funded construction projects. This rule is administered by the *Office of Federal Contract Compliance (OFCC)*, which has been instrumental in ensuring minority contractor participation and opportunity in bidding for federal contracts. A subsequent executive order extended the minority contractor consideration to specifically include women.

Affirmative Action

Affirmative action refers to policies that aim to increase the numbers of people from certain social groups—including women, minorities, and the disabled—in employment, education, business, government, and other areas. In general, affirmative action is intended to benefit groups who have suffered from discrimination. Critics argue, however, that some groups benefit from affirmative action as a result of their political influence.

In 1995, the United States Supreme Court ruled that a federal program requiring preference based on a person's race is unconstitutional unless the preference is designed to make up for specific instances of past discrimination. This meant that affirmative action could no longer be used to counteract racial discrimination by society as a whole, but instead must be aimed at eliminating specific problems. In 1989, the court made a similar decision regarding state and local programs.

Americans with Disabilities Act

In line with previous Civil Rights legislation, Congress passed the *Americans with Disabilities Act (ADA)* in 1990 to protect handicapped people from discrimination by private employers. Because the law also requires that public buildings and transportation systems be accessible to the disabled, it has had sweeping effect on the work of design professionals.

Chapter Six

Legal Concerns and Insurance

Scholars have concluded that people began to formulate laws in prehistoric times. Insurance, although not a modern concept, has a more recent origin: the 7th century AD. Today, the construction industry relies upon both the law and insurance for contracts between the participants in the OPC relationship. This chapter will discuss concepts of both law and insurance, and how they apply to the construction industry.

Development of Law

Law is defined as the set of enforced rules under which a society is governed. Law is one of the most basic and necessary social institutions. No society could exist if all people acted without regard for the rights of others. Nor could a society exist if its members did not recognize that they also have certain obligations toward each other.

The first civilizations and first systems of writing appeared between about 3500 and 3000 BC. The invention of writing enabled people to assemble codes of law. The term *code* is defined as a system of laws organized in a clear and accessible manner to be useful in society. The development of written codes made the law a matter of public knowledge and so helped advance the rule of law in society.

The first known law codes appeared in ancient Babylon. King Ur-Nammu assembled the earliest known code during the 22nd century (2100) BC. Four hundred years later, King Hammurabi drew up more complete codes during the 18th century (1700) BC. Hammurabi's code laid down the law for such matters as the unfaithfulness of a wife, the theft of a farm animal, and the faulty work of a house builder. Many of the punishments are harsh by today's standards. For example, a son found guilty of striking his father had his hand cut off.

From the 11th century through the 5th century BC, the Israelites (Hebrews) of the Middle East assembled both religious and social laws into a common code. The code reflected the teachings of Moses, a great Israelite leader of the 13th century BC, and is called the *Mosaic Code* or the *Law of Moses*. It became a key part of the first books of the Hebrew Bible and later of the Christian Bible. The Ten Commandments given to Moses by God, as described in the Bible, have had considerable influence on the moral content of the law in western civilization.

In the 7th century BC, ancient Greece made the law a purely human institution. The Greek city-state of Athens became the chief center of the development of Grecian codes of law. The Greek politician Draco drew up Athens' first law code in 621 BC. The Greeks considered respect for the law to be the mark of the good citizen.

The principal of law reached a high degree of development under the Romans. Roman law included all the main branches of public and private law that exist today. The Romans designed their laws not only to govern the people of Rome but also to build and hold together a vast empire. The first known Roman law code, known as the *Laws of the Twelve Tables*, was written about 450 BC. Eventually, the whole body of Roman law became extremely complex. The task of interpreting this great mass of laws fell to a group of highly skilled lawyers called *juris prudentes*, a Latin term for experts in law. *Juris prudentes* is the source of the modern term *jurisprudence*. Beginning with Julius Caesar, a long line of Roman rulers tried to organize the laws of the empire into an orderly code. Emperor Justinian I finally completed this task in the 6th century AD. Justinian's code, which was known as the *Corpus Juris Civilis* (Body of Civil Law), went into effect in 533 and 534. The modern term *justice* comes from the genius of Justinian 26 centuries ago. The *Corpus Juris Civilis* covered the field of law so completely and skillfully, that it became a model for the first modern law codes. Today, the codes of most civil-law countries such as the United States have basis in Roman law.

By the 9th century (800) AD, Europeans had developed a political and military system known as *feudalism*. Under *feudalism*, people owed allegiance to individual lords rather than to a central government. Feudal law remained the basic law in Western Europe until the 14th century (1300) AD. Western Europeans had begun to establish improved legal systems. The economy of Western Europe had begun to grow rapidly during the 11th century (1000) AD and reached a peak during the 13th century. Scholars believed that concepts of ancient Roman law, if revived, could meet the need of individuals. In the 12th century (1100) AD, the University of Bologna in northern Italy trained law students from many parts of Europe in the principles of the *Corpus Juris Civilis* which had been established by Justinian 600 years before. Interest in the code soon spread to other European universities. Revived Roman law thus gradually began to replace feudal law throughout mainland Europe.

England already had a strong, unified legal system by the 13th century (1200) AD. While Roman law was beginning to spread across Europe, England did not rush to adopt the Roman system. England's legal system grew out of the country's courts. English courts had long based their decisions on the customs of the English people. In the early 12th century (1100) AD, strong English kings began to set up a nationwide system of royal courts. Judges in these courts applied the same rulings in similar cases. The courts soon established a body of *common law* that applied equally anywhere in England. Judges could change the law as the nation's needs and customs changed, but any change applied in all common-law courts.

As English common law developed over the years, it established many precedents that limited the powers of government and protected the rights of the people. These precedents even made the monarch subject to the law. The common law thus assisted the growth of democracy in England. The right known as *habeas corpus* was one of the safeguards of personal freedom. Habeas corpus is a Latin term that means, *"you are ordered to have the body."* *Habeas corpus* means that a person cannot be held in prison without the consent of the courts. The founders of the United States considered this right so essential to human liberty that they wrote it into the United States Constitution (Article I, Section 9).

Every independent country in the world has its own legal system. The systems vary according to each country's social traditions and form of government. Most systems can be classed as either *common-law systems* or *civil-law systems*. The United States, Canada, Great Britain, and other English-speaking countries have a common-law system. Most other countries have a civil-law system. Some countries combine features of both systems.

Common-law systems are based largely on case law, that is, on historical court decisions made over years. The common-law system began in England more than 500 years ago. Civil-law systems are based mainly on statutes created by legislative acts. The majority of civil-law countries have assembled their statutes into one or more carefully organized collections called *codes*, a term first recognized 55 centuries ago.

When the American colonists declared independence from England in 1776, they based their claims, in part, on ancient Greek and Roman law coupled with common-law principles. Common law, thus, became a driving force behind the writing of the Declaration of Independence. Common-law principles also influenced the development of the United States Constitution and the Bill of Rights.

The United States adopted the basic ideas, but not the whole body, of English common law. Many parts of the common law were impractical for the new, rapidly expanding nation. English property law was particularly unsuited to American needs. Land was scarce in England, and the law heavily restricted the transfer of land from one owner to another. In stark contrast, however, much of the land in the United States was unsettled, and the nation was constantly expanding its frontiers. To ensure the nation's growth, people had to be free to buy and sell land. American property law therefore began to stress the rights and obligations involved in land transfers. The English laws that restricted such transfers were discarded.

Over the last century, however, the public's attitude toward the law has changed greatly. The belief that the private interests of some members of society should not deprive others of their rights has led to legislation that stresses the social aspects of contract law. For example, Congress and state legislatures have passed laws to help ensure the fairness of employment contracts. Some of these laws regulate working conditions and workers' wages and hours. Other laws guarantee the right of workers to organize and to strike.

The "no fault" principle common to the insurance industry emerged as a result of the need to protect workers in cases involving injury. During the 1800s, for instance, law held that a person could only collect damages for an injury if another person could be proved at fault. But with the development of private and public insurance programs came the idea that a person should be paid for accidental injuries suffered on the job regardless of who was at fault. This "no fault" principle has led to the development of worker's compensation insurance which made it unnecessary for injured workers to sue for damages in many cases involving injury.

Private Law

Law in the United States is divided into two main branches: *private law* and *public law*. Private law deals with the rights and obligations people have in their relations with one another. Public law concerns the rights and obligations of members and citizens in society.

Private law can be divided into a number of major branches. This chapter will discuss *contract and commercial law, tort law, property law,* and *corporation law.*

Contract and commercial law deals with the rights and obligations of people who make contracts. A contract is an agreement between two or more persons, enforceable by the law. Many businesses, including those in the construction industry, depend on the use of contracts. (See Chapter 8, "The Construction Contract".)

Tort law deals with the rights and obligations of persons involved in cases in which an action by one party may cause bodily harm; damage to another person's property, business, or reputation; or make unauthorized use of a person's property. A *tort* is defined as a wrong or injury a person suffers because of the action or negligence of the person or persons responsible.

Property law governs the ownership and use of property. Property may be categorized as real property (such as land and buildings) or personal property (such as an automobile and clothing).

Corporation law governs the formation and operation of business corporations. It deals mainly with the powers and obligations of management and the rights of stockholders. Corporation law is often classed together with contract and commercial law and may be described as *business law.*

Law and the Construction Industry

Below are several scenarios in which law enters the construction industry:

- A construction worker is permanently injured from a fall off a scaffold when an erection clip, welded to the face of a steel column and supporting one end of the scaffold, fails. Because of the accident, a man is confined to a wheelchair for the rest of his life. Who is responsible and how is the workman compensated for the loss of the use of his legs?
- At a high school under construction, thieves break in and steal valuable laboratory equipment. Who pays for the loss? Does it come out of the contractor's profit? Does the owner have to pay for the equipment twice?
- A school child contracts lung cancer. Lung cancer is a disease now associated with exposure to asbestos, a material once used in quantity to provide fire protection in the structure of elementary schools. Should the school board have known about the dangers associated with the existence of asbestos in its school buildings?

These kinds of problems and many others can occur in the modern building construction process. Many have dramatic financial or physical effects both on the parties to the Construction Contract and on others directly or indirectly related to the project.

The responsibilities surrounding the activities of the many components in, and the complexity of the construction industry, under the rule of common law, are of no small concern to owners, design professionals, contractors, subcontractors, material suppliers, manufacturers, skilled workers, and other employees of the industry. Because of the vulnerability of the components in the OPC relationship to law suits, there now exists a body of law which has come to accommodate and offer definition to the complex legal relationships of the construction industry.

The Agreement, or *Contract for Construction,* deals with the direct or voluntary legal responsibilities of the involved parties. The *Contract Documents* define the *Work* to be done. The contractor agrees to do the *Work,* and the owner agrees to pay. The contractor places purchase orders for materials and arranges subcontracts for defined work within his responsibility. These direct agreements are made on a voluntary basis and the covenant between the parties while they may be reasonably clear, may be enforced by Contract and Commercial Law.

A construction project can also involve legal responsibilities that are indirect or involuntary. Many of these types of responsibilities are a matter of state law. Take the case of the permanently injured construction worker. All 50 of the United States now require employers to purchase Worker's Compensation Insurance. Insurance compensates—by a third party agreement—an injured worker for medical expenses and loss of income as a result of injury on the job. The third party in this case is an insurance company. If the injury is proven to be the result of some form of negligence on the part of someone other than the injured worker's employer, such as another contractor, his employees, or subcontractor(s), the responsible party may be liable under tort law for all the legal damages sustained by the worker, including payments made to or on behalf of the worker by the worker's compensation insurer.

If the worker cannot regain his ability to work in the manner to which he was accustomed, the contractor's liability may extend to compensation *equal* to the loss of income and ability suffered by the worker for an extended period of time, as well as compensation for such intangible losses as pain and suffering. This liability on the part of the contractor is an involuntary legal responsibility.

Likewise, if some part of a building fails to properly function, and that failure results in a loss to the owner or a third party, the contractor and/or others may become involuntarily responsible. In many cases, the so-called negligence may be proved a contributing factor. That is, others involved in the construction process might be shown to have contributed in some part of the failure of the erection clip that caused the fall of the injured worker.

In this case, the steel fabricator, under purchase order from the contractor, assembled and fabricated the structural steel components of the building. The erector, under subcontract to the contractor, erected the fabricated steel components and performed the welding of the erection clip to the face of the column flange. The testing laboratory, appointed by the owner, was commissioned to perform periodic testing of welds performed on the job and in the shop. Perhaps it can be shown that all of the parties to the construction process had some responsibility for the failure of the erection clip, and the ensuing injury to the worker. In such a case, the injured worker may seek to enforce his claim against any or all of the responsible parties. In most states, a party that pays more than its pro rata share of damages may seek "contribution" from the other parties responsible for the injury.

The amount of compensation finally paid to the injured worker could be a substantial sum. What is the value of a man's earning ability in the future? How much advancement would he have made in the course of years? How long would he remain able to work at capacity? What is a proper amount of compensation for those years, whatever the number? What is fair compensation for a permanent injury and a lifetime of pain and suffering? Agreement on these questions is not easily reached by the parties directly involved. In the case of commercial disputes involving contractual relationships, liability claims involving personal injury often result in costly and time consuming lawsuits that expose the responsible parties to substantial and even ruinous damage awards following a jury trial. Such cases are frequently settled by the parties before a formal trial is convened. If the defendant is covered by insurance, it is likely that such settlement will be made within the limits of the insurance coverage. Arbitration which is discussed elsewhere in this chapter is another option to a formal court trial that is available for resolution of claims.

Statutes of Limitation

Federal or state law limits the period during which legal action may be taken against those responsible for specific acts under tort and contract law. In general, tort actions must be instituted within 2 or 3 years after the accident or injury. Contract claims must generally be commenced within 5 or 6 years after the breach. However, if the claimant's damages are due to a latent defect, the commencement of these time periods may be delayed until the defect is actually discovered. To protect designers and contractors against being sued long after the completion of construction, some states have adopted statutes of repose, which cut off tort and/or contract claims some length of time (usually 6 to 10 years) after project completion. Statutes of limitation and repose vary widely from state to state, and all parties in the OPC relationship must consult with their legal counsel to identify and manage post-construction risks.

Risk Management

The capitalist economy of the United States is based in large part upon risk. Risks can take a variety of forms, below are just a few examples:

- A farmer risks the cost of seed, equipment, employees, and his own labor against the forces of nature in order to produce a profitable crop.
- An owner risks his capital to build a commercial building in hopes that future tenants will prosper there, bringing a profitable return on investment in the form of increased rents and service charges.
- A constructor studies the Contract Documents prepared for an owner who has advertised for receipt of competitive bids. In preparing his bid, and in order to achieve the favored position of being the "low" bidder, the constructor takes a risk on profits and gambles on his ability to manage according to his estimate of cost and labor.
- The construction worker, injured in the fall, takes a calculated risk to work on a scaffold high in the air, though he does have a right to trust the tools provided by his employer.

• A school board takes a calculated risk in awarding the Contract for Construction based on trust of the contractor's ability to construct and protect the property during construction.

Insurance for the Construction Industry

Insurance is not only essential to the construction industry in the modern century, but it can be thought of as an essential ingredient in the "glue" that holds together the OPC relationship described in Chapter 1, "The Construction Industry."

Insurance may be defined more formally as a system under which the insurer, for a consideration usually agreed upon in advance, as a condition of the policy, promises to reimburse or render services to the insured under the event that certain accidental occurrences result in losses during a given period. The primary purpose of insurance is to replace uncertainty for certainty. It provides an individual with compensation for loss sustained by some unforeseen accident; disaster, catastrophe, or other act or circumstance causing measurable loss. Insurance also spreads the cost of loss that would be sustained by the individual to the many who share the potential for such loss, in a manner that is affordable to all.

The construction industry could not sustain the costs of its involuntary responsibility without the insurance industry. Insurance companies offer, for a fee, to sustain the cost of certain unforeseen incidents that may occur during the process of construction. While not all conditions may be insurable, the most common risks can be covered under insurance. An insurance company will issue an agreement, or *policy* in which covered risks are described. Specific exclusions, or items not covered, are also named and described. When and if the insured, in this case, the contractor, experiences a loss, he makes a claim to the insurance company. If the cause and conditions meet the terms of the policy, the contractor is compensated for the loss by the insurance company.

History and Development of Insurance

The insurance industry had its beginnings in Europe in the late 1700s and early 1800s. The first known life insurance policy was written at the beginning of the Industrial Revolution 200 years ago. This period saw the world economy change from one based on individual production and agriculture, to one based on mass production, mass markets, and rapid transportation. The first insurance companies were more like associations than specific business ventures. These companies were first formed as trade associations for the mutual protection of individual members against losses sustained from elements of risk which were shared by all. For example, entrepreneurs engaged in the shipping business formed associations to manage funds—the mutual contributions of all—in order to compensate the losses of cargoes at sea by a few members. This concept became known as *mutual insurance.* The contributions of the members became known as *premiums* and the basis by which claims were compensated became known as the *policy* of the association, which was known as the *company.* Thus, a contributing member of the trade association could rely upon written assurance that his investment was protected to the extent of the policy of the company. With these protective associations, there came into being what has come to be known as *marine assurance.* When transportation of goods over land came to match that of transportation by ships, another form of insurance known as *inland marine assurance* came into being. The famous Lloyd's of London Insurance Company is one of those European establishments that remains a major insurer in the modern world. For more than 200 years, Lloyd's, has been willing—for a price—to insure almost anything or anybody against anything.

In Colonial America, it was the building owner who ultimately inspired the creation of fire and casualty insurance companies. Most early structures in the United States were built of wood, and losses from fire were great, frequent, and often involved large segments of the early American villages. In early 18th-century New England, building owners joined local fire companies which extracted an annual "premium" from them. In a fashion similar to the European model of associated marine insurance associations, premiums went to sustain the cost of a fire station which housed firemen and steam-powered, horse-drawn fire engines capable of carrying and pumping large amounts of water. Each fire company had a symbol, or "fire-mark," which the member was entitled to prominently display on his house or place of business. When a fire alarm was sounded, the fire company responded with the common equipment. If the building had the proper fire-mark, or the fire threatened a building with such a fire-mark, the company would endeavor to extinguish the flame. If there was no fire-mark, often the company would return to the station and the victim, who did not have the foresight to pay an annual "premium" into the common fire protection "policy," would suffer his loss alone.

Insurance Today

Over the years, two major types of insurance companies have emerged. The mutual company of today is still organized as a cooperative enterprise and based on the "mutual" assurance of earlier associations. The other type of company, known as the stock company, is organized as a private enterprise which includes individual underwriters, syndicates of underwriters, and corporations or joint-stock companies whose ownerships and control are based on corporate stock ownership.

In today's economy, the premiums paid to insure one's life, property, business venture or potential liabilities are relatively inexpensive when compared to the potential losses that the policy may cover. In a widespread economy, the *law of averages* works to the advantage of the insurer. Insurance companies are continually basing annual premiums, or fees for coverage, on relatively predictable mathematical models of probable loss, which are based on well-documented databases of actual statistics. For example, the probability of death to a young person 20 years of age during the policy period is less likely than that of a person who is 80 years old.

The insurance industry of today has four major components to make insurance affordable to individuals and businesses. The insurance industry consists of:

- The insurers—Mutual or Stock Companies whose principal function is to assume risk and provide coverage.
- The field organizations or agencies—organizations whose primary function is to maintain contact with the public for the writing of insurance and settlement of losses.
- Inter-company associations or bureaus—entities that establish standards, make rates, conduct research, do institutional advertising, disseminate information, influence legislation and other activities to promote the interest of the insurers.

- Associations or boards—organizations of agents and brokers that perform many of the same functions as the bureaus, except in the greater interest of the agents and insurance people who make their living in the field.

The fire insurance companies no longer maintain the fire stations and equipment, which have become the responsibility of local subdivisions and municipalities. Now cities and counties, in order to provide uniform protection to all citizens of the community, have assumed the responsibility of maintaining the fire companies, equipment, and personnel. In the interest of protecting the public, laws and mandatory regulations have been enacted by the various branches of government in an attempt to prevent loss to the community through catastrophic events.

Liability Insurance

The potential for loss to businesses and individuals from alleged claims has become great. The whole issue of liability is becoming a matter of national concern among professionals, legislators, and insurers. Professionals, contractors, manufacturers, owners, corporations and proprietary businesses are all being threatened by the devastating cost of malpractice lawsuits. Liability insurance, once commonly available and inexpensive, is in serious danger of becoming unaffordable to individuals and companies engaged in certain "high-risk" activities. Such a development would be damaging to the construction industry as well as to other segments of the economy.

Liability became a concern in the much-publicized collapse of a pedestrian bridge in a major hotel. As a result, several hundred persons were injured or killed, and a net liability claim of more than $3 billion was filed against owner, architect, engineer and contractor. In another instance, the apparent failure of code-required fire dampers in the supply ducts of a major hotel caused the death, by smoke inhalation, of a number of hotel guests. These are large-scale examples of building-design and construction-related calamities.

These kinds of incidents involving liability have caused the construction industry, the insurance industry, the legal community, and legislative bodies to look to more responsible building designs, more stringent legislation and code requirements, and more rigid field enforcement of building codes. The implications of increased liability can be seen in the case of the widespread use of asbestos in building construction. This large-scale problem emerged when asbestos was discovered to be hazardous; and subsequently required massive abatement procedures.

When asbestos was discovered in the 19th century, it was heralded as a major scientific achievement against fire loss. Shortly thereafter almost every school, public building, and many private sector developments used asbestos materials for ceilings, floors, and cladding of exterior walls and roofs. Asbestos was also used to insulate steam and hot water lines in major environmental systems, as fireproofing on structural systems, and even in clothing for firefighters and combat troops. When scientific evidence linked asbestos exposure to cancer, asbestos companies were faced not only with the costly removal of asbestos from existing structures, but also with liability claims forcing the asbestos companies into receivership. Governments and private owners alike were forced to spend many times more than the original cost of the building to either remove or encapsulate exposed asbestos fibers. Lead, once a common ingredient in petroleum fuels such as gasoline, and a base ingredient in paint has been found to be hazardous as well. As a result, a new hazardous material abatement industry has sprung up and prospered in just a few years.

History may record the last two decades of 20th century America as the generation of *run-away litigation*. As a result, tomorrow's professional will have to be a student of science and technology, and have some knowledge of law and the environment.

Insurance to Protect the Owner's Interests

The owner's legal responsibility under the various agreements, and his/her liability as a proprietor are two separate issues. For example, the owner of a proposed new commercial building may go to great trouble and expense to find an extraordinary or "signature" architect who goes on to produce an award-winning design for a building the community recognizes as a landmark.

The weak point of this landmark may not be recognized until one rainy winter morning when the surface of the specially designed Italian marble plaza becomes slippery with ice that has melted perhaps because of the heat from the mechanical equipment room below the surface. A pedestrian may be injured and possibly suffer a lifelong disability. The cost of the resulting lawsuit and the potential for another similar accident emphasize the importance of liability insurance. Who must pay? In all likelihood it is both the owner and the architect. The pedestrian may sue the owner who has primary responsibility, but the owner and the injured person may have an action against the architect because of the choice of the terrazzo paving. The architect may, in turn, have an action against his engineering consultant because of the transference of non-dissipated heat through the plaza deck. The potential for liability in the construction of a modern building often extends to multiple defendants each of whom must carry liability coverage to protect against just such an event as the failure of a simple pane of glass.

Another situation in which liability may be a concern emerges when an owner experiences severe budget limitations and must borrow funds in order to build. The lender may wish to limit his exposure to loss, and therefore place restrictions on the amount of money he is willing to advance for the project. The potential is great for "saving" money by overlooking or eliminating a construction feature that might prevent an accident or damage to a building. Following this course, however, can be a common "trap" for the owner, lender, and design professional alike.

All members of the OPC relationship and those who serve each of them must be vigilant about the hazards during the planning process and should periodically advise the other members accordingly. This in no way implies that the design professional should presume to give legal or insurance advice to his client, or that the owner or contractor should give design advice to the design professional. Quite the contrary! The design professional, through his participation in continuing education seminars sponsored by professional societies, through study of professional and trade journals, and through his own experience and the "shared" experience of others, must continually educate himself on potential claims. The owner, on the other hand, should avail himself of the advice of competent legal, financial, and insurance counsel in order to create the best available "umbrella" of protection for his circumstances. The contractor should also seek competent counsel, and should view current building and safety codes as protective tools not bureaucratic obstacles.

Professional Liability Insurance

Professional offices often employ by subcontract a number of different specialists commonly called *consultants* who help create construction documents. The office structure may be such that an architect or engineer may be assigned the task of *project manager*, and charged with administering several projects at the same time. The project manager must not only deal with each client and his needs and issues individually, but must also direct the activities of the office staff and of consultants located elsewhere. There are also building code issues to be settled with the municipality, land use issues to be resolved with the zoning commission, and environmental issues to be resolved with the overview of the Federal Government. These are just a few of the daily complications faced by today's design professional.

As much as half of the project manager's time is taken up with meetings, most of which may take place outside the office. The other half of his time goes to decision-making and the administration of his own organization. The job captain, usually an architect is responsible for managing the completion of the Contract Documents. He may have several subordinates under his direct supervision. The civil, structural, mechanical and electrical engineering design are commonly executed by other departments in the case of an architectural/engineering practice. In the case of a sole architectural practice, the work of the engineering disciplines under sub-contracts with the architect may be executed by consultants in another location. The Project Manual is usually prepared by the specification writer, and specialized portions of the design may be prepared by a variety of persons making up the project team. (The Project Manual is the subject of Chapter 11.)

In today's medium-to-large professional office, there may be a number of other specialists involved in a project. A landscape architect, an interior designer, a specification writer, and a cost estimator might each be involved. With an increase in the number of individuals involved comes a higher potential for errors and omissions, the risk of inconsistencies between drawings and specifications—*and* the necessity for professional liability insurance.

There are hundreds of circumstances that can lead to potential liability on the part of the design professional. The specification writer, for example, may assume that an item to be included is in the drawings. The engineer may fail to take into consideration the depth of a beam when locating ducts and lighting fixtures. There may be mathematical mistakes in preparing dimensions. A typographical error in preparing the specifications may completely change the meaning of an item of work. On the other hand, the design professional might simply make an error in judgment. A type of waterproofing that has proved satisfactory in a number of projects might fail when used in new work that is subjected to marginally different soil conditions. Alternatively, an item may simply and inadvertently be left out of the documents. Perhaps the language used to describe a particular requirement is written unclearly and may be misunderstood by those preparing a bid under competitive circumstances. The primary issue to be decided when considering professional liability is negligence and application of judgment related to what is the reasonable *standard-of-care* for design professionals.

A specific example of professional responsibility is demonstrated in the case of the collapse of a brick veneer exterior wall as a result of unusually high storm winds. Laboratory testing after the collapse found that the mortar used in the construction did not meet the specified strength requirements. Further, the wreckage revealed that an insufficient number of structural ties had been used in constructing the wall (as measured by the requirements of the specification for masonry accessories). To complicate matters, both the building's contractor who had constructed the building and the masonry subcontractor had gone out of business and could not be found to account for the deficiency. Searching for a source of compensation, the owner's counsel decided that the architect who designed the building and "supervised" the construction might be liable. The courts held that the architect had properly designed the building, specified the proper mortar strength and had called for a proper number of wall ties, and since he was not required to make "exhaustive or continuous on-site inspections to check the quality or quantity of the work," the architect should not be held accountable for the failure of the brick wall.

Like members of other professions such as medicine and law, the design professional must protect himself with liability insurance coverage if he is to survive this age of "runaway" litigation. Lawyer's fees can become substantial, and the cost of defense in court can easily surpass the design professional's total fee for the project. *Professional liability insurance* commonly called "Errors and Omissions" insurance is available to prudent design professionals who recognize their vulnerability to law suits during the life of professional practice. The insurance company, by virtue of its covenant to protect the insured, is obligated to allocate funds to defend claims based upon alleged *negligence* on the part of the design professional. Many insurance companies will fund the cost of legal services to defend the insured from a list of approved attorneys. Others will allow the insured to select his own attorney. Most professional liability policies provide for a *deductable* which establish an amount that the insured will pay for the first costs of defense in liability law suits. Other provisions of the policy will describe *limits of liability* covered and will establish limits on the *aggregate of all claims* for which the insurance carrier will be responsible.

We suggested earlier that this period in history will be known for its enormous number of lawsuits. Indeed, many claims against design professionals can be called "frivolous," to a large degree because the design professional's responsibility has been misunderstood. In the early development of such documents as the General Conditions, the term "supervise" was commonly used to describe the activity of the design professional in pursuing his obligation as the owner's representative. Litigation and the quest to determine responsibility for "what went wrong" after the fact changed the implications of the term, "supervise." This term came to suggest responsibility on the part of the design professional for the sequences and means and methods of construction. Lawsuits naming the architect became common when owners or contractors' bonding companies sought relief from the cost of a major building failure. Such lawsuits, albeit not frequently filed, remain as a potential threat to the design professional. To a large degree, the design professional's responsibility remains misunderstood. The judgement related to the expectation of perfection in the Design Professional's work is discussed under the section titled *The Professional Standard of Care* in this chapter and in Chapter 3, "The Design Professional."

In recent years, the word "supervise," when used in describing the design professional's responsibilities during construction, has come under close scrutiny. A legal argument has been made that those who "supervise" also "manage" or that the term "supervise" infers management responsibility. Seeing this weakness in the recommended language of typical contract documents, and seeing that the design professional was vulnerable to law suits filed by third parties including injured workers, the American Institute of Architects (AIA), and the Engineers Joint Contract Documents Committee in collaboration with other institutions related to the construction industry, brought about changes in the language describing the limit of the design professional's role in the OPC relationship. In the modern document, the design professional is described as the "Administrator" (not Supervisor) of the Contract for Construction and has *the authority to act on behalf of the owner to the extent provided by the Contract Documents.*

Historically, in the United States, it has been the intent of the contract documents that the contractor have the ultimate responsibility to construct the building according to the contract documents drawn up by the design professional. Likewise, historically, it has been the intent of the contract documents that the design professional not be required to be present at the job site on a continual or full-time basis, and "is generally not held to be responsible for control over construction means, methods, techniques, sequences or procedures, or for safety precautions and programs in connection with the Work." This statement, usually found in institutional versions of General Conditions, made with the cooperation of professional, industry, and construction institutions, has stood the test of time and the courts. The courts have, in fact, ruled consistently against claims that the design professional is responsible for the overall quality of the contractor's work.

The term "supervise" has been omitted from most institutionally prepared standard forms of contract between owner and design professional. It has been recognized that the word "supervise" may be misunderstood to mean that quality assurance and conformity with the Contract Documents are somehow insured by the design professional when, in fact, they are not! There have been occasions where an owner may bring a lawsuit against the design professional on the basis that the design professional's responsibility to provide adequate *supervision* allegedly caused a failure in the construction of the project. Because there remains a current misconception among some owners, attorneys and insurance companies that the design professional shares responsibility with the contractor for the quality of construction, it is important that the language of the agreement between owner and design professional leave no doubt that the contractor, and only the contractor is responsible for construction. Likewise, the language should leave no doubt that the design professional, and only the design professional is responsible for design.

It has been suggested that the words "observe" and "observation" be substituted for the words "supervise" and "supervision" in contract language. Such changes in language do not relieve the design professional of responsibility for negligence that leads to any failure in the design of a building. In the case of negligent errors and omissions in the preparation of the Contract Documents, depending upon the law in the state of jurisdiction, he can be held responsible to both owner and contractor, and if found to be negligent in a court of law, be ordered to pay for damages.

The design professional's ultimate protection from excessive liability comes from a combination of professional competence and continuing education, as well as the competence of personnel, consultants, and legal counsel. The other essential element is the purchase of professional liability insurance as it continues to be available. The days are gone when the architect or engineer is able to survive purely on competence, talent, training and sharpness of wit.

The design professional's ultimate protection from excessive liability comes from a combination of professional competence and continuing education, as well as from the competence of personnel, consultants, and legal counsel. The other essential element is the purchase of professional liability insurance as it continues to be available. The days are gone when the architect or engineer is able to survive purely on competence, talent, training and sharpness of wit. The emphasis upon *continuing education* throughout the career of the design professional cannot be stressed strongly enough.

Insurance to Protect the Contractor
The contractor is the member of the OPC triad who bears the ultimate responsibility for safety, performance, quality of workmanship, organization of the construction process, payment for equipment, materials and labor, taxes, transportation, non-conforming work and labor, insurance, miscellaneous fees, and any other cost that is required or implied by the Contract Documents.

Job safety has become not only a matter of law and propriety, but a science requiring considerable experience, knowledge, and special training. The potential for loss of life or limb during the process of construction is great, as is the risk of other serious injury. In a highly competitive atmosphere where only the "low" bidder wins the Contract, the potential expenditure for safety precautions naturally becomes a low priority in the quest for potential profit. Because of this tendency, substantial changes have been made in the "system," including the adoption of laws requiring protection of the worker in the workplace. Chapter 5 addresses labor issues and points out the fact that frequent abuses on the part of employers brought about organized labor and the now powerful labor unions. By the same token, the failure of contractors to make necessary safety preparations has brought about such laws as mandatory Worker's Compensation insurance, and such federal organizations as the Occupational Safety and Health Act (OSHA) and the Environmental Protection Agency (EPA). OSHA, for example, has brought about numerous changes to the procedures of construction including mandatory protective helmets (hard hats), the use of safety equipment (goggles and shoes), temporary safety railings, and improvements to lighting, graphics, and signs. OSHA makes periodic inspections of the workplace and is empowered to levy heavy fines on employers who do not conform to its regulations.

Imposed safety regulations and the requirement of certain types of insurance still do not absolve the constructor of responsibility for many types of loss or damage claims. The role of the constructor is fast changing from "tradesman" to professional; that is, one who pursues an art requiring special training and talent. Today's constructor must constantly improve himself by means of experience, training, continuing education, and participation in construction-oriented institutions and organizations.

The Professional Standard of Care

Chapter 3, "The Design Professional," under the topic *Professional Standard-of-Care*, addresses the quality of professional practice in the construction industry. In the triad relationship of owner, design professional (architect and/or engineer) and constructor which we have called the OPC relationship, each party is related to the other by separate, legally binding agreement. In the OPC relationship, the design professional (prime architect or engineer) is responsible for providing fair and impartial judgments in interpreting the intent of the contract documents.

Errors and Omissions

There is always a potential for law suits against design professionals over alleged "errors and omissions" in the contract documents for which the design professional was both author and interpreter. There has been a parallel misconception that somehow it is reasonable to expect that the contract documents prepared by the design professional will be free of "errors and omissions." The design professional, like the physician, the dentist, the lawyer and any other classic professional who offers advice and a remedy to a client's problem or his need often dispenses *subjective opinion* based on a combination of education, experience, and skill acquired over years.

It is unreasonable for the professional's work or advice to be judged by the same criteria as the work of a silversmith, a jeweler or a mason. The work of the silversmith, the jeweler and the mason for centuries has been judged for centuries by *objective opinion*. Two or more silversmiths are capable of producing nearly identical silver goblets given the same design is followed by each. The object is the goblet and the basis is the design documentation. Similarly, with the Contract Documents as his guide, the contractor's work is objective and is based on the Contract Documents as interpreted by the design professional.

If the Design Professional is accused of an "error" or an "omission," it is appropriate that the judgement of that fact be based on whether or not a *negligent* act has been committed. *Negligence* is defined legally as the lack of proper care or attention; the failure to exercise reasonable care required by the circumstances; the lack of reasonable care in doing something; the failure to do something; or indifference or inattention to a matter of responsibility. The degree of perfection that is reasonable in the work under the contract for construction is comparative to the degree of perfection that is the norm of each individual trade's peer group. The silversmith, the jeweler and the mason have the right, both morally and legally, to expect an objective judgement of perfection in his work by his peers comparing his work to that of a recognized master of his trade or guild. The word *masterpiece* comes from the term used by the guild system of the

Middle Ages to describe the work of an apprentice craftsman that is judged to be on a par with that of his master. The Design Professional, the physician and the lawyer have the right, both morally and legally, to expect a subjective judgment of the quality of service provided by comparing it with the standard of care that is consistent with the work of his peers.

The Two-Percent Rule

Chapter 3, "The Design Professional" discusses the concept of "Standard of Care" in mitigating the expectations of perfection in the work of the design professional. It is prudent that the contract between owner and design professional make some provision to recognize the fact that it is unreasonable for owners to expect perfection in the documents prepared by the design professional. It is entirely reasonable that an amount, say two percent (2%) of the contract price, be established as part of the owner's contingency to sustain the cost of change orders that (may) become necessary to execute the full intent of the contract documents as interpreted by the design professional after the execution of the contract for construction.

In reaching an assessment of what is reasonable in judging what is an appropriate *standard of care* in the product of a particular Design Professional this text offers the following example. Consider a project with construction value of $5 million. If, after award of contract, certain inconsistencies in the Contract Documents result in Change Orders amounting to less then 2% of the cost of construction, then the Design Professionals work meets the usual standard of care that is reasonable for projects of that magnitude. Before a claim of negligence is levied toward the Design Professional, apply the following test to the situation:

- Consider the Design Professional's opportunity to interpret the intent of his design. Was the Design Professional asked, or allowed to address the issue of an apparent "error" or "omission" upon discovery and to express his intention for the design?
- In the case of discovery of an apparent "error" or "omission" after the contract price has been established, and if the discovery results in a Change Order as the Contract Documents are adjusted, then apply the 2% rule. If the amount is equal to or below 2% of the construction cost, then the reasonable standard of care has been met.

General Liability Insurance

Most mutual and stock insurance companies offer policies that provide insurance against claims brought by third parties for property damage or personal injury. In this type of general insurance, the provisions of the policy are written to be exclusionary rather than inclusive. The term "exclusionary" means that the policy will be interpreted to cover all forms of potential loss, up to the amount of money named as the limit for coverage for each separate incident, (unless a particular risk is specifically excluded from the coverage in writing). Inclusive coverage, by the same token, means that only specific acts, which are specifically included or described in the policy, are covered to the limits named. General liability may exclude acts of nature, coverage under Worker's Compensation, acts of war, and similar specific acts or related events.

Vehicle Liability

No construction project in the United States could be accomplished without the use of vehicles. Much of the actual work, as well as material delivery and worker transportation, involves the use of various vehicles. While the motor-operated vehicle has changed the means and magnitude of modern construction, the use of vehicles has also created a special element of risk requiring specialized liability coverage. Vehicular liability coverage usually covers any form of injury to persons or property, operator of or passengers in a vehicle to certain limits. Vehicle insurance is mandatory coverage as a matter of statute in most states.

Property Insurance

It is in the mutual interest of both owner and constructor that either the owner or the constructor carry insurance designed to cover the premises of the project (for the time of construction). Sometimes called "Builder's Risk Insurance," this coverage protects owner, contractor, subcontractors and sub-subcontractors as their interests appear and includes possible perils such as fire, windstorm, hail damage, and other inclusive risks. It also provides compensation for itemized perils common to construction work. Under special endorsements, additional coverage may be written to include other items commonly excluded such as damage from falling aircraft, and from rising floodwaters, lightning, and other natural phenomena.

Theft from construction sites has become such a common occurrence in recent times that many insurance companies exclude compensation for theft of materials. Insurers, however, are willing to insure against theft of materials and equipment that have been actually installed into the job. Materials simply stored on the job may be excluded as a condition of the builder's risk insurance coverage.

All Risk Insurance

In some states, it is possible for general liability coverage, vehicle liability, and property insurance to be combined into one single policy commonly called "All Risk" insurance. By creating one policy, the cost is somewhat less than the individual policies. This type of coverage is written almost exclusively for contractors and may not be available in all locations in the United States.

Owner's General Liability

It is advisable that the owner carry coverage against general liability during the process of construction. Risks such as injury to a pedestrian or to someone who wanders into the construction site are a possibility on any construction project, and the owner is likely to be named in a lawsuit because of property ownership. Generally, the design professional is also named in such coverage. The contractor may be required by the Contract to provide additional liability coverage for the owner and the design professional.

Bonds

A bond is defined as a sealed agreement or promise by a surety to take certain actions at a specified time, or to make a payment in case of certain events. Certain types of bonds are required for the owner's protection in case of default by the contractor. These bonds offer a "sure" guarantee of the covenant, or the "fruit" of the agreement between two parties. Bonds may be offered with some form of security by one or more parties to the agreement. Generally, a surety (a financial institution or an insurance company), as a third party, agrees to be financially responsible for the fulfillment of the covenants of the agreement at no loss of time or expense to the first party. Three common types of bonds are usually required of the contractor for the benefit of the owner. They are the *Bid Bond*, the *Performance Bond* and the *Payment Bond*.

Bid Bonds

When competition is keen for the award of the construction contract, bids are sealed and confidential. When the other proposals are eventually revealed, any constructor submitting a bid or proposal may wish to withdraw his low bid for any number of reasons. The bid bond, submitted to the owner along with the proposal, guarantees that the bidder will honor his proposal as a firm Contract Sum, and if asked by the owner to do so, will faithfully enter an Agreement between Owner and Contractor for the construction of the project, according to the Contract Documents. The consequence of failure of the bidder to enter a contract can result in the forfeit of the amount of the bid bond to the owner as liquidated damages for failure to meet the conditions of the Invitation to Bid. Bid bonds are discussed in more detail in Chapter 5, "Labor and Government."

Performance Bonds

The Performance Bond usually comes in the form of an agreement, parallel to the Contract for Construction. In this agreement, a third party surety, acceptable to the owner, guarantees that the contractor will faithfully perform the Work of the Contract Documents in all respects with no loss of time or money to the owner. Under this agreement, if the contractor, for any reason, should default on the agreement with the owner, the surety will take full responsibility for the performance of the Contract or for reimbursing the owner for the additional cost of such performance.

Payment Bonds

The third type of bond usually required of the contractor is a guarantee by a surety that all costs of construction, labor, materials, and equipment and all related incidentals will be paid by the contractor. The owner is subject to significant vulnerability in the Contract for Construction. He pays the contractor for work accomplished as certified by the design principal, but without the payment bond, he
has no guarantee that the contractor will in turn pay those who do the Work or provide materials or equipment. There are statutes, now enacted by all 50 states that protect the "mechanic" who does work on the property or premises of an owner. Essentially, these statutes allow a subcontractor or supplier to file a lien against the value of the owner's property to protect their right to be paid for work done or materials supplied. A *mechanic's lien* is filed with the clerk of the county or parish where the property ownership is recorded in the official property records. This filing of lien effectively prevents the owner, thereafter, from conveying title, or giving a Deed of Trust (mortgage) to that property until such time as the mechanic has been satisfied and agrees to release the lien. In other words, if an employee, subcontractor, material supplier, or other party, engaged by the contractor, but with no direct contractual relationship with the owner were to remain unpaid, that person could, under the law, protect himself by filing a

lien against the owner's property. With a lien against the property, the owner cannot, without paying the mechanic (thereby having to pay for the work twice), convey clear title to the property—either to a buyer or a lender (in the case of establishing a mortgage on the property). The Payment Bond assures the owner of the following: in the event that the contractor defaults on payments to others, the surety will satisfy all obligations to the relief of the owner. This is true provided the owner meets the obligation of paying the contractor for the Work. There are instances where liens that are filed against the owner may prove to be invalid and have the potential of causing some actual damage or loss to the owner. Such cases often result from an unsettled dispute involving a third party to the Contract for Construction such as a subcontractor or a vendor. In the event that the point of Substantial Completion has been reached and agreed upon, and the contractor is unable to produce lien waivers from all of his subcontractors, sub-subcontractors, vendors and others (as required by the Contract Documents), the contractor should be required to post additional bonds to protect the owner. This is true regardless of how the dispute or other issue may be eventually settled. In the case of an arbitrary and groundless lien, the owner may also have the legal recourse for damages against the party filing the invalid lien.

Settlement of Disputes

The case of fair and equitable compensation for a permanently injured worker is but one example of the type of problem that can arise during the construction process. Disputes can arise for any number of reasons over the complicated relationships that exist in the construction process.

An example of this complexity is demonstrated in the case of a faulty roof. Sometime after a building is completed, a severe roof leak causes considerable damage to the interior of the building and its contents. The owner looks to the contractor to compensate him for the damage and loss of use, and to repair the leak. The contractor, in turn, looks to the roofing subcontractor who installed the Work surrounding the apparent failure. The roofing contractor points out that the leak happened because of damage done to his work by the mechanical subcontractor who installed the rooftop mechanical equipment after the roof was in place. The mechanical contractor claims that his work meets all the requirements of the Contract Documents prepared by the design professional. The design professional looks to his consultant engineer who designed the system that was installed on the roof. Which individual was at fault? Did both subcontractors contribute to the problem? Was the building design somehow inadequate? Was the contractor's superintendent careless in not discovering the problem as the Work was being done? Perhaps the mechanical contractor was at fault, but has since died or declared bankruptcy; what then? What if the general contractor was no longer in business?

Arbitration

One of the two methods of solving a dispute over who is responsible, who pays and how much is to be paid is the process of *arbitration*. Under this method of dispute resolution, a panel is convened of knowledgeable, outside, third parties to the dispute. The parties agree to be bound by the findings and determinations of the arbitrators. The facts of the case, the various contracts by which each is related to the other, the claims made by each and other issues pertinent to the case are then studied and debated. Sworn testimony of witnesses is given and other evidence is presented by a variety of methods. Through this procedure, the opportunity is given to present all the facts surrounding the issue. Once the facts are disclosed, each arbitrator privately presents an opinion to the panel. A common opinion is then arrived at among the panel of arbitrators, and a legally binding award is rendered. Without a contract provision requiring arbitration, the parties to a dispute always have litigation in the courts as a final resort. However, many favor the arbitration process and tend to discourage litigation because of the time, expense, and likelihood that the results of any settlement derived from the courts would vary substantially from that found by a panel of unbiased experts.

Litigation

A second option in settling disputes is *litigation*. Litigation is determined by the filing of lawsuits and is decided in a court of law. This process is carried out according to the court rules of the state or other local jurisdiction. The court renders a judgment, which is binding by law and can be enforced by officers of the court. A jury may be convened to hear the evidence and render a decision, or verdict. The judge in the case accepts the verdict of the jury and renders a judgment according to the law. If both parties so agree, some cases are heard by the judge alone, who then renders a judgment.

The advantages of arbitration over litigation are that:

- First, litigation is much more expensive than arbitration.
- Second, in most jurisdictions, the court dockets are overcrowded and it may be years before the case is actually heard by the court.
- Third, there is no guarantee that the judge who presides over the case or the jurors who decide upon it will be at all knowledgeable of construction technology or the unique established relationships in the construction industry.

In litigation, the initial burden of "educating" those who will judge construction-related issues is both time-consuming and expensive. Each side to the dispute must parade a host of "experts" before the jury to present opinions on the issues. Obviously each party to the dispute will select experts whose testimony will support their position. Quite often the testimony is contradictory and confusing, and because of this, the results may be less than satisfactory to one or both of the disputants.

Compensation for Involuntary Responsibility

The process of achieving the Contract Sum for the construction of a modern building or other construction project is obviously not an exact science. The process of bidding and negotiating for the Contract for Construction is discussed in Chapter 8. The implications of such procedures are addressed elsewhere in this chapter. The constructor, who bids or negotiates the Contract Sum, may add a contingency in order to protect himself from unknown factors for which he may become responsible. Obviously he cannot include a contingency adequate to cover every possible unforeseen circumstance for which he may have an involuntary responsibility. Coverage of such unforeseen expenditures can be lessened to some degree by the purchase of insurance. Insurance is an agreement made by a third party that promises to pay unforeseen but designated misfortunes that may become the insured party's responsibility through a variety of predictable causes. Insurance, a necessary service in the construction and other businesses, has become a major industry in itself.

Summary

Owners, Design Professionals, and Constructors should be acquainted with the law; particularly the law as it affects contracts, liability, and the responsibility that each participant bears for the other in the OPC relationship. However, neither this text nor common sense would advocate that some knowledge of law is a substitute for the services of an attorney, a member of the local bar, who is trained to represent and counsel his clients on the law during the process of building construction. The participants of the OPC relationship should all be represented by competent legal counsel before entering into any agreement, either written or oral. Chapter 8, "The Construction Contract" discusses the contractual relationships of the OPC relationship in more detail.

Chapter Seven
Project Delivery

The 20th century saw more construction in the U.S. than any preceding century. The "tried and true" methods of project procurement used during this time will continue to serve the needs of some owners well into the 21st century. But as technology and commerce have changed and evolved over the years, alternative project delivery systems have emerged, and will continue to spring up from an informed, highly creative, and competitive construction industry.

While previous editions of this text dealt with the traditional project delivery method known as *design/bid/build* in some depth (with several alternatives to design/bid/build mentioned in the first and second editions), this edition will review and expand upon alternative methods of project procurement and delivery. These methods will most likely become commonplace in the new millennium.

Factors that Drive the Owner's Decision

The term *alternative* when used to describe project delivery methods suggests there are a number of choices available to the owner interested in procuring a new project. The key to choosing the "right" alternative is understanding the factors that drive the decision process during project delivery. This text will identify three primary objectives or decision "drivers" common to any project delivery process.

- *Cost* is defined as total project cost: the total of "hard" cost and "soft" cost. Hard cost is defined as the cost of construction including the contractor's overhead and profit and any modifications to the contract for construction. Soft cost is defined as the cost of land, professional fees, owner's contingencies, and other incidental costs.
- *Quality* is defined as the combination of attributes, properties, life value, and other characteristics of a particular material, system, or element of equipment preferred according to comparative excellence and degree of perfection in workmanship, manufacture or attractiveness. The term *life value* is discussed under the topic *Value Engineering* later in the chapter.
- *Time* is defined as the period required to do all that is necessary to bring the project to completion. Completion includes the time required to establish the program of design plus the work of the Design Professional leading to the preparation of the Contract Documents and, finally, the work of the constructor required to complete the construction process.

It is important to understand that these three primary factors, cost, quality, and time, when identified in the decision process are mutually exclusive. That is to say that *any one* of these three factors can be the primary basis for decision, but not all three equally.

When *cost* is identified as the primary goal in the project delivery process, it usually means lowest possible cost with quality and time becoming results of the decisions made to achieve the goal related to cost.

With a cost-driven process, the period for bidding or negotiating with candidate constructors will require added time for the competitors to:

- Study, the Contract Documents in considerable detail.
- Strategize a cost-effective methodology to accomplish the work.
- Seek, receive, and evaluate cost of materials from competing producers.
- Evaluate bids from competing subcontractors.

The process of construction will require added time because:

- Overtime and extended workweeks are not appropriate.
- The lowest material cost often means longer lead times for delivery.
- The lowest subcontract cost may mean longer delivery periods for the reasons listed above.
- It is seldom possible, in most projects, for the factors of cost and time to be controlled with equal priority.

When *time* is the primary decision driver then quality to some extent and cost will be the result of subsequent decisions made in order to deliver the project in a predetermined time frame.

The period for bidding or negotiation, if it is arbitrarily shortened, may not provide candidate constructors sufficient time to:

- Study in considerable detail, the Contract Documents.
- Strategize a cost-effective methodology to accomplish the work.
- Seek, receive, and evaluate cost of materials from competing producers.
- Evaluate bids from competing subcontractors.

The result of a limited bidding period often results in inflated costs as contingencies are included to cover unknowns that cannot be thoroughly evaluated for economy.

The process of construction will be more costly because:

- Overtime and extended workweeks drive up the cost of labor that may be required to meet deadlines.
- Material cost may be higher because of the impact of expedited delivery demands.
- The cost of subcontracts may be higher because of expedited delivery demands and the reasons listed above.

It is not possible, in most projects, to achieve lowest possible cost when time is the primary decision driver in the project delivery strategy.

When *quality* is the primary decision driver, both cost and time required to deliver the project will be determined by subsequent decisions that assure the highest possible quality. The most effective control of quality as the primary objective requires that:

- The Design Professional is selected more for his ability to provide unusual or award winning so-called "signature" design than for cost-related reasons such as competitive fees.
- Selection of materials is made on the basis of quality selection rather than by competitive price and availability.
- Note: It is not possible, in most projects, to achieve lowest possible cost within a foreshortened time frame when highest available quality is the primary decision driver in the owner's priorities.

Once the owner has made a primary choice of either cost, time, or quality, then one of the remaining decision drivers can be selected as the secondary project priority. It is unreasonable to approach the project procurement process with an expectation of being able to control cost, time, and quality equally.

A process called *Value Engineering* or *Value Management* is often applied to projects in their early stages to address the conflicts that often surround the establishment of priorities between decisions made relative to cost, quality, and time.

Value Engineering

Value Engineering (VE) is an effective methodology of project management. It is a process that identifies and presents methods to the procurement process that will sustain value while at the same time respects the owner's priorities between cost, quality, and time. Value Engineering related to building arose in the mid-20th century out of the common needs of the participants in the OPC relationship. Value Engineering recognized that owners often expect the procurement process to deliver a project of greatest value, although the factors of cost, quality, and time must be prioritized.

The Value Engineering process includes the formation and presentation of proposals that will:

- Measure the probable life cycle value of critical building components—the life cycle of a material, system, or piece of equipment is defined as the probable time that the particular item will function until it fails, and requires replacement.
- Consider design alternatives that will improve the quality of the completed project.
- Consider design alternatives that may save cost without a sacrifice of value.
- Consider design alternatives that may reduce time of delivery without a sacrifice of value.

Value Engineering Methodology

The methodology for Value Engineering as recommended by the Society of American Value Engineering International (SAVE International) includes conducting user attitude surveys, function analyses, implementing recommendations, financial reporting, life-cycle cost analyses—all delivered by a multi-disciplined team. Steps in the Value Engineering process include:

Step 1—Information Gathering and Review
Review by the VE team of all available information upon which the owner and design professional have based the design.

Step 2—Function Assessment
Development of an independent assessment of the function of the project and all of its components. The objective is to identify functions that are basic and essential to the project, separating functions that may be desirable, even mandated, but that are not essential to the basic function.

Step 3—Creative Component
Examination of ideas and drafts proposals that could improve the design under the premise that there is always a "better" way to accomplish the desired result.

Step 4—Evaluation
Examination of the creative phase products, elimination of creative ideas proposed in Step 3 that do not add significant value, and elaboration on proposals that add significant value to the project. Evaluation may focus on factors of cost, quality, and time that have been prioritized in the approach to the project design.

Step 5—Development
Expansion of proposals identified in Step 4 and preparation of data describing cost, function, and quality related to each proposal with an assessment of advantages and disadvantages of each proposal. When appropriate, assessment of impact on time of project delivery are included.

Step 6—Presentation
The VE team makes a formal presentation of each proposal. A final VE report is generated that accumulates and documents the VE process and the recommendations that have been developed.

Step 7—Acceptance
The final VE report is reviewed by owner and design professional. The owner may accept some VE proposals and reject others—there is no mandate that the owner must either accept or reject any VE proposal.

The value of the VE process is that (regardless of the outcome) both owner and design professional obtain an improved perspective on the project that will improve the decision-making process during project development and execution. It also includes a process of observation that focuses attention on all attributes of materials, systems, and equipment that will be incorporated into the design of the project. This portion of VE is often developed by a third party, a highly qualified team. Often, the third party brings an unbiased point of view to the process. This provides the owner with a greater degree of assurance and understanding of the issues and decisions that finally define the project.

The underlying principal of VE is that there is always a "better" way to achieve the primary objectives of a project. The VE proposals, developed by peers of the design professional, or by the design professional's own staff have been shown to consistently identify ways to improve the design, save cost, and preserve higher quality.

Value Engineering is most effective if it is applied before the typical design development phase of a project is completed. The advantages of Value Engineering applied early during the design process often include:

- Higher flexibility on the part of the design professional—since design changes that may not affect cost can still be made at this point.
- Substantial savings for the owner in both initial cost and life-cycle cost during useful life, plus improved quality in his project with little or no impact on the time required for project delivery.

In a cost-driven project, decisions related to cost take priority over considerations related to time (and considerations related to time often mean that quality has the least priority in the process). When the VE process is applied early in the design process, the result often introduces proposals that may improve quality without penalty to contract price. Figure 7.1 illustrates the impact of Value Engineering on the typical *cost-driven* project.

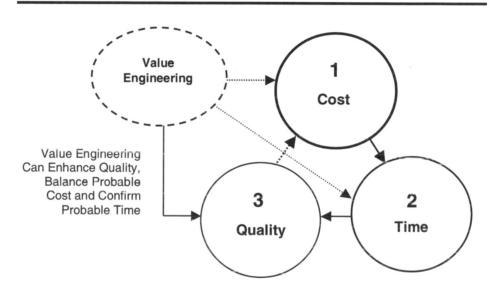

In the Cost-Driven Project
Cost Typically Drives Time and Time Typically Drives Quality

Figure 7.1 *VE Applied to the Cost-Driven Project*

In the *time-driven* project where the second priority of the owner is cost of construction, it can be shown that time drives cost, and cost drives quality. The VE process applied early in the design process often introduces proposals that both enhance quality and balance cost without penalty to the time required for building construction. It is not unusual for the VE process to provide a number of proposals that enhance quality (and life-value) which are balanced with other proposals that will save significant cost with little or no impact on time.

Figure 7.2 illustrates the impact of Value Engineering on the typical *time-driven* project.

In the *quality-driven* project where the second priority of the owner is either cost of construction or time required for project delivery, it can be shown that quality design drives both cost and time. When the VE process is applied early in the design process of the quality driven project, the result often introduces proposals that both save cost and balance quality without penalty to the time required for building construction. It is not unusual for the VE process to result in proposals that suggest cost savings and are balanced with other proposals that may insure little or no delay of the construction process. Figure 7.3 illustrates the impact of Value Engineering on the typical *quality-driven* project.

Partnering in the Project Delivery Process

In the last 25 years, the construction industry has actively sought to remedy the all-too-frequent breakdown of cooperation and trust among participants in the traditional OPC relationship. Out of this search has come a process called *partnering.* Partnering is a process that seeks to reduce the incidence of distrust among participants, eliminate the incidence of claims and litigation, and implement a general improvement in communication among participants in the OPC relationship. The partnering process depends on a commitment of the participants to find "common-ground" in a process in which owner, design professional, and constructor(s) pledge to support the objectives and welfare of the others as "partners" in the decision-making process that leads to delivery of the project. The partnering process may involve any or all of the following procedures:

- One or more pre-bid conferences between the owner, the design professional and candidates for the contract for construction in which the goals of the owner are explained and the expectations of project delivery and roles of the participants are explained in detail. The pre-bid conference is an opportunity for the design professional, as interpreter of the intent of the contract documents, to explain and amplify the decisions that are written in the execution of the contract documents.
- One or more pre-contract conferences between the apparent successful bidder and bidders, with the owner (or owner's representative), and the design professional. The pre-contract conference is an opportunity for the owner and design professional to again explain the owner's primary objectives, and to review the candidates choice of subcontractors and any required documents such as Project Delivery Schedule, Schedule of Values, and Certificates of Insurance.
- At least one pre-construction question-and-answer conference between contractor(s), major subcontractors, and providers. The pre-construction conference is an opportunity for the design professional to review the General Requirements (Division 1 of the Specifications) and to explain the procedures of document control and approval to be utilized during the construction process.
- Frequent progress meetings between owner, design professional, and contractor(s) to discuss the progress of the project, performance of the participants, compliance with schedule of delivery and the responsiveness of the participants to execute actions essential to successful project completion. Essential to the

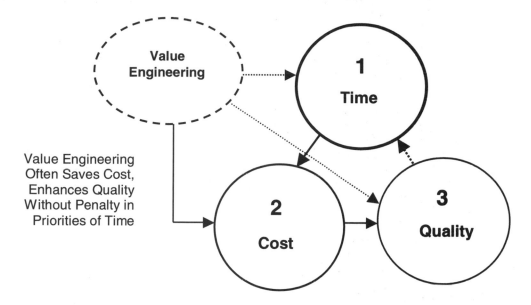

In the Time-Driven Project
Time Requirements Typically Drive Cost and Time, in Turn, Drives Quality

Figure 7.2 VE Applied to the Time-Driven Project

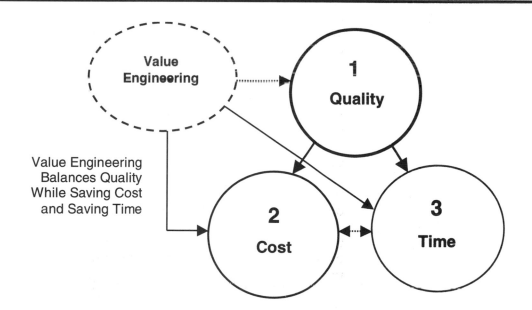

Quality Typically Drives Both Cost and Time

Figure 7.3 VE Applied to the Quality-Driven Project

partnering concept is the commitment of the participants to be accountable to each other for their respective responsibilities.

The partnering process, to be effective, should seek to apply principals of organizational and group dynamics that have been proven in other industry organizations such as the Society of American Value Engineers International (SAVE), with emphasis upon honoring the individual goals of all participants, not just the goals of the owner. The use of a neutral facilitator, a knowledgeable professional who is not associated with the project, to facilitate, or to lead the partnering process, is often useful to facilitate proven communications procedures and conflict resolution strategies. Figure 7.4 illustrates the ideal partnering session and the lines of communication that should take place in the partnering process.

The Advent of Construction Management

The advent of Construction Management came in the middle of the 20th century when the design/multiple-bid/build tactic and the need to compress the time of construction began to appear as a common project procurement methodology. With the emergence of Construction Management came the need for the *Construction Manager* (CM). The CM is defined as one selected by the owner for the express purpose of managing the process of construction.

In the traditional design/bid/build methodology, the contractor was both builder and manager of the construction process. When the concept of multiple contracts was introduced, the problem became identifying who would manage the work of separate contractors, who generally fell into the categories of (1) General Construction; (2) Plumbing; (3) Mechanical HVAC, and (4) Electrical.

Typically, a CM is employed to manage multiple contracts under the design/multiple-bid/build project delivery system. (Figure 7.8 illustrates the design/multiple-bid/build organization.) Since the 1960s a number of distinctive types of Construction Management methods have appeared. Among the most prominent types of Construction Management that have become commonplace near the end of the 20th century are:

The Construction Manager as Advisor
Under this construction management approach, the CM may serve in an advisory role to the owner, and be compensated in the form of fee without risk. As illustrated in Figure 7.5, the CM acts as an extension of the owner, serving as the owner's agent, managing one or more prime contracts that are made between owner and prime contractor.

The Construction Manager at Risk
Under this construction management approach, the CM may act as contractor, awarding and managing one or more prime multiple contracts under a single Construction Management contract with the owner. As illustrated in Figure 7.6, the CM-at-Risk may accomplish portions of the work with his own forces, but he is responsible for the completion of the project, therefore he is at risk for either profit or loss depending on his ability to manage the work of multiple-prime contracts.

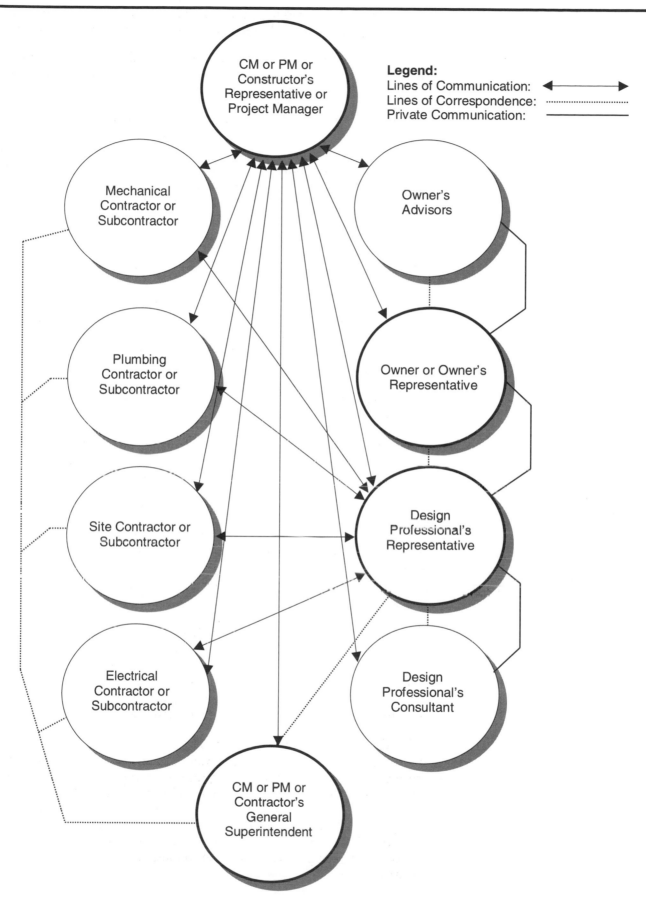

Figure 7.4 The Partnering Process

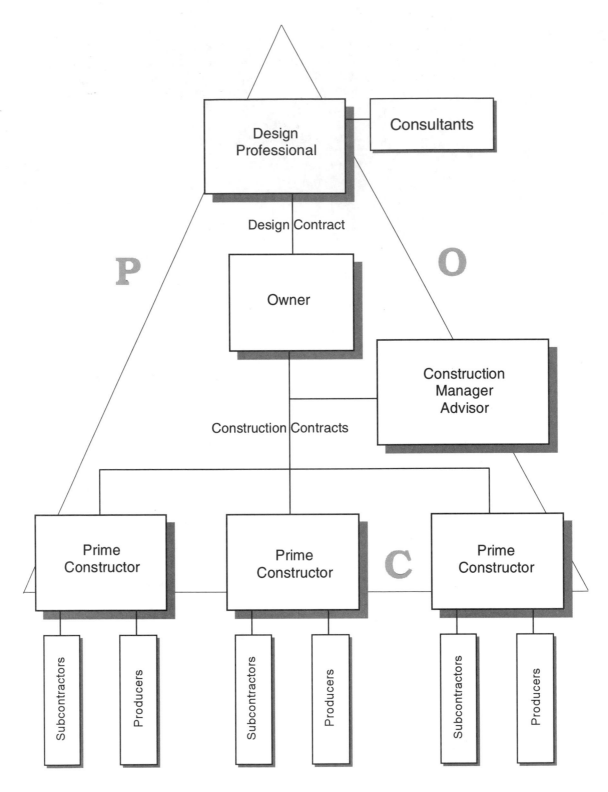

Figure 7.5 *The Construction Manager as Advisor*

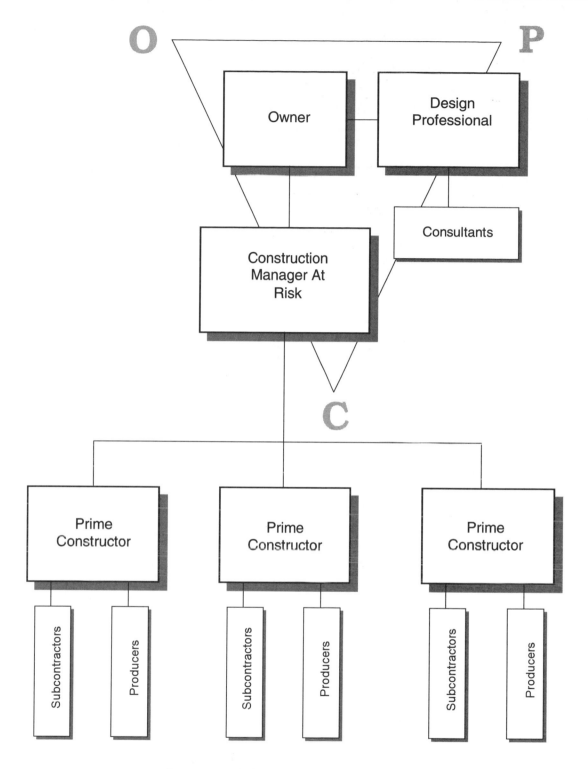

Figure 7.6 The Construction Manager at Risk

The Advent of Program Management

Program Management as it is used in the construction industry today means different things to different people. This text defines *Program Management* as the services of an individual or a company, retained by the owner who acts as the owner's representative and who is responsible for the entire process of project development. The Program Manager selects and hires the design professional(s), selects the constructor(s), and awards the contract(s) for construction and supervises the total project development from beginning to end, as illustrated in Figure 7.7.

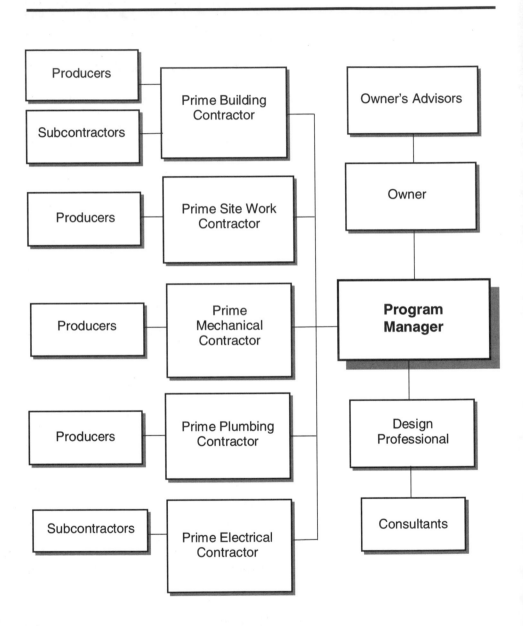

Figure 7.7 *The Program Management Organization*

"Fast-Track" Methods of Construction

In recent years, a construction method known as "fast track" has evolved to accommodate the time-driven project. This technique is based on allowing the construction process to begin before the Contract Documents are complete. The owner's need for early delivery is achieved because the normal time required for construction is compressed. However, since the primary decision driver is time, the process may not realize a savings in cost. In fact, it is likely that the fast-track process may require additional cost.

The methodology of construction contracting consists of a series of related but limited-scope contracts which phase the construction, *or* a series of multi-prime contracts, as discussed in subsequent paragraphs. The fast-track method requires dynamic scheduling and coordination and may be organized in a series of phases as follows:

- **Phase one** may involve site preparation and other related work that can be accomplished while the design professional is preparing Contract Documents for the substructure, foundation, and superstructure construction.
- **Phase two** may involve the construction of the building substructure and foundation while components of the superstructure are being shop-fabricated. Meanwhile, the design professional is preparing Contract Documents for the building envelope, special equipment, and mechanical and electrical systems design.
- **Phase three** may involve the construction of the building envelope, rough-in of special equipment, and mechanical, and electrical systems. Meanwhile, the design professional is preparing Contract Documents for interior construction, finish work, and landscaping.
- **Phase four** and subsequent phases of the Work may involve the final work required to complete the building.

The fast track method involves a much higher risk factor for the owner than any of the other more conventional methods of contracting. When there is, however, a high degree of professionalism, integrity, experience, and skill, there is a potential for financial benefits that can be highly rewarding to all members of the OPC relationship.

In a competitive economy, the selection of contractor is fundamental to the fortunes and objectives of the owner. The process of competitive bidding, although time consuming, has been the most universally accepted method, as it gives the owner reasonable assurance of the lowest possible cost. Because of restraints and the relationship of cost to time, the direct selection method is becoming popular among private owners and, to a lesser degree, public owners.

Project Delivery Alternatives

The expectation by an owner to obtain his project at the lowest possible *cost*, with the highest *quality*, and the expectation that the project be delivered in a fixed *time* frame has been shown to be unrealistic and a probable formula for disappointment if not failure.

As we have seen, an owner in the 21st century can choose from a number of well-established alternative project delivery systems —each of which has distinct advantages and disadvantages. From the owner's perspective the process may begin by deciding an appropriate priority to apply the three decision drivers we have identified as cost, quality, and time.

Traditional Method (Design/Bid/Build)

For most of the 20th century, owners relied heavily upon the education, skill, and experience of the design professional to guide their objectives through the selection of the third member of the OPC triad, the constructor. The traditional system of project procurement under the OPC relationship is what this text will refer to as the *design/bid/build* project delivery system.

As we have seen, the term design/bid/build characterizing the traditional project delivery may be the methodology of choice when the owner identifies the decision drivers to be cost, quality, and time, in that order. The design/bid/build method is executed and delivered in a two-step process. First, the design professional is selected. Under agreement with the owner, the project is designed and contract documents are produced. Next, the bidding or negotiation process is evoked, which results in the selection of a constructor. The second step begins with the award of contract construction after which the process of building takes place.

Under the design/bid/build method, the owner selects the design professional by direct selection, or more commonly by comparative selection. Then, with the design professional's assistance, the contract for construction is executed between owner and contractor. The contractor may be selected either by competitive bidding or by a selective process, followed by negotiation for price.

In the traditional design/bid/build delivery system, the professional and the contractor have no direct contractual relationship with each other. The design professional contracts with, and is responsible for, any subconsultants he may employ to enhance his service to the owner. The contractor, in turn, awards subcontracts for portions of the work that may include such specialties as mechanical (HVAC) systems, plumbing systems, and electrical systems. Either the contractor or the subcontractor may purchase materials, systems, or equipment for the project from the entity this text defines as the producer (manufacturers or suppliers). Figure 7.8 illustrates the relationships of the parties under the design/bid/build method of project delivery.

Design/Bid/Build Project Delivery

Advantages:
- Initial project investment is limited to design professional's fee.
- Design professional is advocate for design intent.
- Owner selects design professional on basis of ability.
- By competitive bidding, owner, assisted by design professional is assured of reasonable project cost by a qualified contractor.
- Contractor is responsible for coordination and management of construction process.

Disadvantages
- Assurance of contract price and date of project delivery is established late in process.
- Constructor is selected on basis of contract price, not on managerial ability.

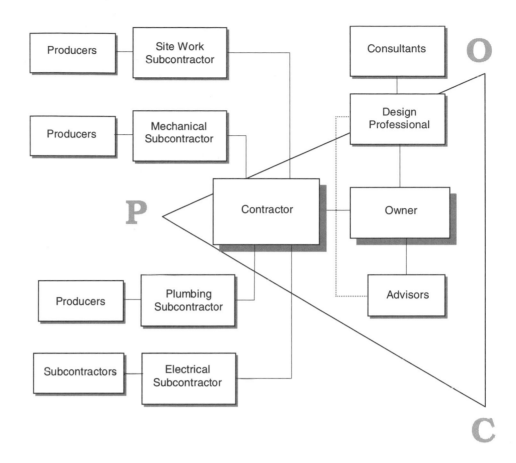

Figure 7.8 Design/Bid/Build Organization

- OPC relationship has potential for becoming adversarial and may be subject to costly claims and disputes.
- Design/bid/build may require more time than alternative methods of project procurement.

Design/Multiple-Bid/ Build Project Delivery

In the 1950s, an alternative we shall identify as *design/multiple-bid/build* began to emerge as a viable project delivery methodology. With technological advances, the work of certain traditional subcontractors changed dramatically. The mechanical systems constructor (HVAC Contractor) and the energy systems constructor (Electrical Contractor) not only became more specialized but the combined value of these two major subcontracts began to equal the value of the "general" construction. Factors of competition, ethics, and legislation related to government procurement led to the evolution of design/multiple-bid/build contracts. The effect of multiple contract legislation makes mandatory, in certain jurisdictions that in public works projects, contracts are awarded separately for (1) general construction, (2) mechanical systems construction, and (3) energy delivery systems construction.

The term design/multiple-bid/build characterizes a system similar to design/bid/build, with the exception that the project is sub-divided and awarded to two or more prime contractors. In some jurisdictions, projects that exceed a certain value or scope of work are awarded to multiple prime contractors as a matter of law. Under this arrangement, some of those contractors who enjoyed subcontract status under the single general contract of design/bid/build are awarded separate prime contracts usually with the owner acting as the coordinator/manager of multiple contracts. For example, all the general (building) construction may be awarded to a general contractor. The mechanical (HVAC) systems may be awarded to a contractor who specializes in heating, ventilating and air-conditioning systems. The plumbing systems may be awarded to a plumbing contractor and the electrical systems may be awarded to an electrical contractor. The advantages and disadvantages of Design/Multiple-Bid/Build follow:

Design/Multiple-Bid/Build Project Delivery

Advantages
- As in design/bid/build, design professional works directly for owner and owes no allegiance to, nor derives any benefit from, work of contractors, subcontractors, or manufacturers.
- As in design/bid/build, the owner/design professional relationship during design provides owner with reasonable assurance of a balance between economy and quality.
- By competitive bidding, owner is assured of reasonable project cost by qualified contractors.
- Owner/design professional relationship during design provides owner with reasonable assurance of economy and quality.
- Owner/design professional relationship during construction provides owner with reasonable assurance of contractor conformity with Contract Documents.
- Owner/design professional relationship during warranty period provides owner with reasonable assurance of identification of construction defects for contractor remedy.

Disadvantages
- No single contractor is responsible for over-all coordination. Owner is burdened with determining who will be responsible for coordination of multiple contracts.
- Cost of design may be higher because of requirement of implementing documentation for multiple contracts.
- Coordination of multiple prime contracts during construction is difficult and has potential for delays and additional cost.
- Multiple-contractors will probably have separate bonding companies. Opportunity for dispute as to limits of individual contracts means less protection for owner should one or more contractors default.

Figure 7.9 illustrates the design/multiple-bid/build organization.

Construction Management Project Delivery

The three forms of Construction Management that have emerged in the United States have been discussed in the section *The Advent of Construction Management* earlier in this chapter. The Construction Manager usually becomes the owner's primary representative during construction when multiple contracts are involved. Figure 7.5 illustrates the Construction Manager-as-Advisor organization. Figure 7.6 illustrates the Construction Manager-At-Risk Organization. Figure 7.7 illustrates the Agency Construction Manager Organization.

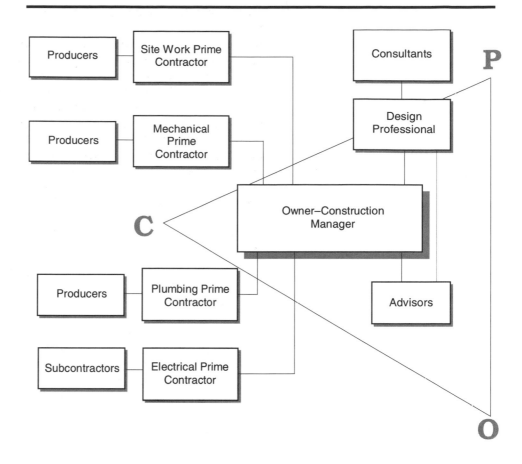

Figure 7.9 *Design/Multiple-Bid/Build Organization*

Under the CM method of project procurement, the design professional retains his position as the primary authority on design issues. In the absence of a sole responsibility for the construction process, however, the Construction Manager becomes responsible for construction coordination and scheduling. Typically the Construction Manager will mediate conflicts, determine payment, and decide the acceptability of work from the various separate contracts.

The Construction Manager-as-Advisor is usually compensated under a fee arrangement with the owner. Advantages and disadvantages of the Construction Manager-as-Advisor follow:

Construction Manager-As-Advisor Project Delivery
Advantages
   • In similar manner to the traditional design/bid/build delivery method, design professional works directly for owner and owes no allegiance to, nor derives any benefit from, work of construction manager-as-agent, prime contractors, sub-contractors or manufacturers.
   • Owner/design professional relationship with assistance of the construction manager-as-agent being hired before or during the design process provides owner with an additional "layer" of

expertise in achieving more reasonable assurance of balance between economy and quality.
- Owner may opt to employ fast-track method of project delivery in order to take maximum advantage of time.
- By competitive bidding among multiple contractors owner is assured of reasonable project cost by qualified contractors with work of all prime contractors to be coordinated by construction manager-as-agent.
- Owner/design professional relationship, in coordination with the work of the construction manager-as-agent during construction provides owner with even more reasonable assurance of contractor conformity with contract documents.
- Owner/design professional relationship coordinated with work of the construction manager-as-agent during the warranty period provides owner with reasonable assurance of identification of construction defects for contractor remedy under the general first year unconditional warranty period, provided such warranty is required by the contract documents.
- Owner has reasonable assurance of adequate coordination of multiple contractors.
- Potential for delay claims and disputes are minimized as compared to the design/multiple bid/build method.
- Option to subject the project to VE is to greater advantage to the owner's objectives when CM-as-agent is directly involved in VE process.
- Option to utilize partnering may provide an extra degree of "claims avoidance" if CM-as-agent is skilled in the practice.

Disadvantages
- Added burden of construction manager's fee means cost of project may be higher than project delivery by traditional OPC methods.
- Small projects may not be able to justify additional cost of construction manager-as-agent.
- Services of construction manager-as-agent may not be bonded and may not offer protection of errors and omissions liability insurance.
- CM-as-agent does not assume any risk in establishment of contract price with multiple-prime contractors. Owner is entirely dependent upon the experience and integrity of CM-as-agent.
- CM-at-risk is usually compensated out of total contract price under which CM has agreed to deliver the project. Owner may acquire services of CM-at-risk either by competitive bid or in the case of private owner, by negotiation.

The advantages and disadvantages of CM-at-risk follow:

Construction Manager-at-Risk Project Delivery
Advantages
- In similar manner to traditional design/bid/build delivery method and CM-as-agent method, design professional works directly for owner and owes no allegiance to, nor derives any benefit from, work of construction manager-at-risk, prime contractors, sub-contractors or manufacturers.
- Owner may opt to award CM-at-risk contract by competitive bid and therefore may be reasonably assured of lowest reasonable contract price.

- Owner may opt to employ fast-track method of project delivery in order to take maximum advantage of time.
- By competitive bidding among multiple-prime-contractors, owner is assured of reasonable project cost by qualified contractors with work of all prime contractors to be coordinated by construction manager-at-risk.
- Owner has reasonable assurance of adequate coordination of multiple contractors.
- Option to utilize partnering may provide an extra degree of "claims avoidance" if CM-at-risk is skilled in the practice and conduct of partnering process.

Disadvantages
- Small projects may not be able to justify additional cost of construction manager-as-agent.
- Owner does not have same assurance of professionalism from CM-at-risk he has with CM-as-agent methodology.
- If CM-at-risk is awarded a contract by competitive bid, CM will not be part of project design process and therefore owner does not have added "layer" of expertise to assist in guiding project's decision process.

Program Management Project Delivery

It is not unusual in recent years for some projects to be large and complicated. Such projects may involve unusually high cost, and may require the services of multiple design professionals and multiple prime contractors who must work under conditions of phased construction with multiple and sometimes overlapping schedules. In other cases, a project may have an unusual time restraint for delivery, or the owner may wish to occupy certain portions of the project while others are still under construction. For projects of this nature, the owner may hire a *Program Manager* for purposes of managing the entire project delivery process. In this instance, the Program Manager becomes the sole representative of the owner and may be responsible for selecting the design professional(s), and multi-prime contractors as well as managing other procurement methods in concert with project completion. Under this method of project delivery, the program manager establishes and manages the lines of communication between all the participants. The program manager establishes the scheduling of work and manages the payment of the participants as the project is completed. Figure 7.7 illustrates the Program Management Organization.

Program Management Project Delivery
Advantages
- Program manager obtains competitive bids from all participants, including design professional(s), giving owner optimum advantage of capturing lower costs.
- Single responsibility of program manager, including control of design professional, gives ability to fast track design by creating multiple bid packages with phased construction that have potential to save time compared to other delivery systems.

Disadvantages
- Design professional does not have an independent relationship with owner.

- Owner may not be able to rely directly upon design professional's advice in matters of quality of materials and methods during construction.

Design/Build Project Delivery

As we shall see, the time required for delivery of the completed project has become increasingly important to owners. In the past 50 years, more owners require that their projects be fast tracked or be delivered in unusually short time frames. Some owners have need for "high-tech" or highly specialized buildings, which require specialized expertise on the part of both design professional and constructor. Other owners have limited or fixed budgets and need to employ a delivery strategy that establishes early on a *guaranteed maximum price* (GMP) for the completed project. This need to mandate control of either cost, or quality or time in the delivery of a project has given rise to a project delivery methodology we know today simply as *Design/Build*.

The design/build process in the United States today can be defined as "one-stop shopping" for the owner. The process requires the owner to award a contract to a single entity who becomes responsible for designing the project as well as constructing the project under a single contract. Although the design/build process has come in favor in recent years in the United States, it may be the oldest project delivery system. Many of the world's monuments, such as the Great Pyramid of Egypt, have been products of a design/build team centuries ago. While the process may seem to be simplified in comparison to other project delivery systems, design/build is not without the potential of risk to all parties, including the owner.

Over the course of two centuries of building construction in the United States, as much as 90% of projects constructed have been delivered under the traditional design/bid/build method. This method has usually assured the owner that his project will be delivered for a very competitive price. A second area of assurance of this method is that the design professional—acting on behalf of the owner, and being independent of the contractor or the construction process and its potential rewards, can assure that the owner will receive a quality project at the end. Neither of these traditional safeguards may be fully available to the owner in the design/build process. It should be noted, however, that with design/build there are performance specifications and requirements that serve as a safeguard because the design-builder is contractually bound to perform. In approaching the design/build process, an owner is advised to conduct a fair degree of risk analysis.

The design/build process, by its definition, places both the design process and the construction process under a single contract responsibility. Figure 7.10 illustrates the typical arrangement of the parties in a design/build project.

Organization of Design/Build Team

As the technique of design/build methodology has begun to achieve higher demand among private and public owners, D/B teams have assembled themselves in various ways. Typical arrangements may include:

- A design/build team assembled to respond to a specific project or series of similar projects. Typical teaming in this circumstance

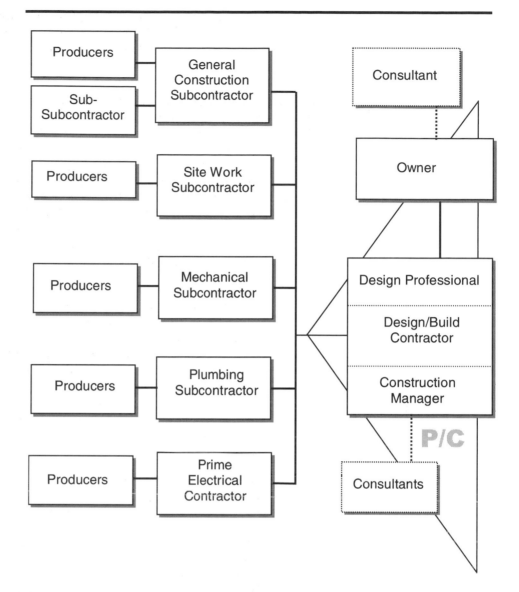

Figure 7.10 *Design/Build Contract Organization*

has been between an independent constructor, (either a construction management firm or an independent general contractor) who agrees to join an independent design professional (either an architect or an engineer or an architect/engineer) in response to an owner for a specific project. Typically the constructor becomes the Prime Entity of the association and the design professional becomes a Subcontractor to the Prime Entity.

• A design/build firm assembled to specialize in the design/build process as its primary business. The design/build firm is staffed with both constructors and design professionals under one system of management, or it may be a joint venture between a constructor and a design professional.

An owner may select a design/build team through *direct selection* or *competitive selection*. His choice of method of selection will depend in large part on the owner's identified primary objective—be it cost, quality, or time as we shall see.

101

Direct Selection of the Design/Build Team

The direct selection method is a process whereby the owner selects his D/B team by judging of credentials, experience, and response. The owner first documents his project objectives then makes a statement of acceptable credentials and experience expected of respondents. This document is called a *Request for Qualifications* or more commonly, an RFQ. Secondly, the owner may prepare a *Request for Proposal* or more commonly an RFP. The RFP process may have two or more successive steps in the selective process.

The One-Step D/B Selection Process

The one-step selection process relies solely on a candidate's response to the RFQ for selection and subsequently a design/build contract. The one-step process is particularly appropriate for the owner who chooses *quality* or *time* as his first priority for project delivery. The quality-oriented owner will look for the candidate who presents significant evidence of *tenure*, that is, years of relative experience in delivery of projects that have similar *attributes* to the project the owner anticipates and secondly, evidence of *availability*, that is, evidence that the candidate has the ability to pledge sufficient human resources, management skill, and financial ability to accomplish the design and construction of the project in an acceptable time frame for delivery. Once the tentative choice of D/B contractor is made, the cost and schedule for delivery of the Contract Documents and subsequently the construction of the project will be negotiated and a design/build contract is executed with the successful candidate. The one-step selection process is useful and valid when the owner is willing to risk the following:

- Sufficient time for the process of design and development of Contract Documents to occur in, with an adequate process of review and approval by the owner.
- Paying a satisfactory, mutually agreed upon amount for the design work even if a satisfactory price for the project delivery fails in subsequent negotiations.

A second alternative to the above may be attractive if the owner and the selected design/build team are each willing to accept certain risks wherein:

- The owner risks sufficient time for the process of design and development of Contract Documents to occur in, with an adequate process of review and approval by the owner, and with the uncompensated design submission the Design/Build team offers a GMP.
- The design/build team is willing to risk the cost of the process of design and development of Contract Documents to the owner's satisfaction and the additional risk that an acceptable GMP may be exceeded in the project completion.

The second alternative may be more attractive to the Design/Build team if:

- The owner is willing to share a percentage of any savings or difference in the final cost of project delivery and the amount of the GMP.
- Subsequently, the Design/Build team is willing to make a full accounting of the actual cost of construction which would

include a pre-established fee for the Design/Build team and an agreeable allowance in the cost for normal overhead for the project's management and incidental costs.

Obviously in choosing the single-step direct selection of a Design/Builder, the factors of cost and time must be of secondary importance to quality in the owner's priorities. If, however, the owner must choose either cost or time as his primary objective, then the single step direct selection method alone is not a satisfactory procurement method.

The Two-Step D/B Direct Selection Process

A second step in the D/B selection process is necessary if the owner's primary objective is assurance of competitive cost (with time being of secondary importance). The two-step process of D/B selection involves first determining a "short-list" of finalists based upon response to a published RFQ (much as is described in the one-step selection process above). The second step is a selection process which is focused on an RFP. The finalists of the first step (usually no more than 5 candidates) are then invited to make a second-step response to the RFP. The RFP may ask respondents to make an offer of price for the delivery of the design and construction of the project. The combination of first-step selection by qualification and second step selection by competitive price is particularly suited to the owner who has decided that *cost* is the primary objective of his project. There is considerable advantage to the owner in selecting the two-step process of D/B team selection, however there is considerable financial risk for the design/build team, particularly the Design Professional component of the D/B team.

In order for the D/B team to determine a price for the project, the design professional must first produce Construction Documents to a high degree of completion in order that the Work be sufficiently described to allow subcontractors and producers to offer competitive bids upon which a competitive price is based. This usually translates to the Design Professional being required to risk as much as 60% to 70% of his potential fee in order to comply with the requirements.

For the two-step selection process to be attractive to potential Design/Build teams and therefore to be of any consequence to the owner's objectives, several alternatives in the development of the owner's RFP may be considered:

- The owner may elect to include documentation that defines certain design criteria, sometimes called *bridge documents*, be included in the RFP. These offer a program of design and a well-developed set of concept drawings for the proposed building and site sufficient to provide a basis of competitive bid for price. These are prepared by an outside consultant at the owner's expense. While this option reduces some of the risk for the D/B team, there remains a significant amount of financial risk for the competitors because of the risk in offering too low a price for both design and construction based on incomplete Construction Documents.
- The Owner may offer a *cash incentive* to all "short-listed" candidates during the preliminary design phase in order to "share" the risk with the remaining field of candidates. This option, however, may limit the number of candidates who will be "short-listed" because of the outlay of cash that must be paid to non-successful candidates.

If the two-step process yields a satisfactory Design/Build team based on final selection by price, a contract between owner and the successful candidate is agreed upon. This process includes negotiating a schedule for delivery, and agreeing upon an amount for liquidated damages per day should the project be delayed beyond the agreed-upon date for final completion.

The Three-Step D/B Direct Selection Process

The three-step D/B selection process is similar to the two-step process, except the second step requires one or more D/B teams to present well-detailed design proposal. The third step requires subsequent disclosure of a price for the project delivery. The three-step process works to an owner's advantage because he may be able to choose between two or more designs at the end of the second step with the proposal for price being disclosed in a later step. To decrease the potential financial risk of the D/B candidates in the three-step process and to make the competition more attractive to more candidates, the owner may include in the RFP portion of the process, the following:

- Bridging documents prepared at the owner's expense consisting of program of design, concept drawings of site and building, and outline specifications that set quality standards for critical portions of the project, and/or …
- Offer of minimum compensation for candidates who do not survive the second step of the three-step process.

Competitive Selection of the Design/Build Team

The two-and three-step direct selection processes are particularly suited to the owner's project budget when it is sufficient to offer the additional expense of the various risk reduction incentives suggested in order to attract viable D/B candidates who are, themselves, willing to assume some risk in order to survive elimination at any step for award of the contract.

The competitive selection process for identifying a satisfactory Design/Build contractor is a little more straightforward in terms of defined risk for the candidates, and offers defined risk containment for the owner. Before the competition begins, viable potential candidates may be narrowed to a manageable number by invoking the RFQ process described in step-one of the direct selection process. Once a slate of potential candidates have been identified through the RFQ process, the candidate D/B teams are invited to respond to a design competition by RFP which identifies the following:

- A detailed program of design which describes the owner's project requirements.
- Description of the site including a recent boundary and topography survey, a geo-technical report, a Phase 1 Environmental Report made to federal environmental standards, and any requirements for site development required by local ordinances.
- A monetary prize for the design submission judged by a jury of peers to be most responsive to the owner's program of design and local ordinances.

Approaching the Competitive D/B Team Selective Process

The design competition as a means of project procurement has been a recognized methodology in the design community since the mid-1900s in the United States. The American Institute of Architects (AIA) has long established procedures for design competitions that have been used for many years. The rules of competition as endorsed by AIA have held that the owner does not have an obligation to award the contract for design to the winning submission as judged by an independent jury as long as a monetary prize is offered and paid to the apparent winner as offered in the solicitation. The submissions become the property of the owner and the owner has the right to select the design professional of his choice for execution of the project, regardless of the jury's judgement.

The recommended procedure for competitive selection of design/build team follows the general guidelines of the design competition process. The competitive process for design/build award may generally include the following:

- The owner prepares and advertises an invitation to design/build contractors or associations to submit a proposed design solution. Design competition rules have generally held that the owner should not unnecessarily restrict the competition to a "short listed" group of candidates. However, if the project, by its character, requires considerable specialized skill, the owner may find advantage in using the RFQ solicitation as a preliminary step to identify a group of contestants.
- The competition solicitation explicitly states how the submission should be presented and be very clear as to how candidate submissions will be judged, as well as describe the prize or prizes offered to the competition winners. The solicitation should provide a highly developed package of information about the project including, but not limited to a fully developed description of the site, a detailed program of design, and disclosure of any restrictive conditions that would limit the design approach including appropriate local ordinances related to zoning or building codes. The competition should allow a sufficient amount of time before the due date for submissions to allow candidates to react to the solicitation and prepare a well-developed candidate design solution.

The Two-Step Competitive D/B Team Selective Process

In the first step, the competition is held, the submissions judged, the winners announced and otherwise advertised, and the promised prizes awarded. In the second step, the owner may enter negotiations with one or more of the candidates he selects for that purpose. The owner should not be restricted to those companies who were judged winners of the design competition. Candidates should be prepared to offer a price for the project delivery and a schedule based on time for its delivery.

The Three-Step Competitive Process

The owner may elect to individually negotiate a more thoroughly developed design, and a price offering with schedule between two or more candidates as a second step in the process and then as a third step in the process, request that each of the finalists submit a Best and Final Offer (BAFO) for the owner to consider after award of the Design/Build contract.

Design/Build Project Procurement

Advantages

- The owner's procurement process is simplified to a "one-stop-shopping" experience. Time that is otherwise expended in the selection of a design professional, negotiating a contract for design, preparation of the design through the Contract Documents Phase and the subsequent competitive bidding or negotiating for selection of a constructor is considerably reduced.
- Project cost and schedule of delivery is identified early in the process. Although some time is required for the design to be produced before a final price and schedule can be expected, the time required to reach a basis for contract is much less than would be expected in more traditional design/bid/build approaches. For example, it is not unusual for the traditional design/bid/build approach to require 9 to 12 months for the preparation of Bidding Documents. The bidding or negotiation process may require a minimum of 2 months, for a total of 14 months or more. In the design/build approach, a satisfactory price and schedule for project could be reached in as few as 4 months, and at most 6 to 8 months.
- Design documentation is simplified; less detail may be required in completing the construction documents because of the elimination of the traditional bidding or negotiating process that is part of the traditional design/bid/build approach.
- Delivery of completed project may occur much earlier than by traditional methods. We have seen that the process leading to contract award can yield a time savings of 6 to 8 months. There is also the probability that the project can be fast-tracked for an additional and significant savings of time.
- The total cost of the project as reflected in the agreed contract price, may be lower than the total of design fees plus contract price that might be expected of the design/bid/build approach, however there is no expedient way to provide absolute assurance of that fact.
- In general, the design/build method of project procurement may be an ideal choice for the owner who has identified *time* as the primary objective in his project decision process. While the *cost* of the project may be lower, there is no clear assurance of that fact which is available.

Disadvantages

- The owner has limited opportunity to assure himself that the contract price for his project has had the full advantage of a wide range of competition in the marketplace.
- The owner has little or no advanced approval opportunity over the quality of materials, equipment, and methodology employed to produce his project.
- The owner cannot rely upon the design professional's independent advice or assurance that the design professional component of the D/B team will act as the owner's advocate in the project delivery process.
- "One-stop-shopping" heavily favors the D/B contractor's interests; therefore, the owner's interests rely upon both the integrity and the professionalism of the selected D/B team.

Financial Risk The foundation of capitalism is the right of individuals to accumulate capital and use it in competing for more business. Competition in the free-market atmosphere of capitalism means continual risk for all participants. In the Construction Industry, there are significant risks by owner, design professional, and constructor alike. The consideration of project procurement alternatives must finally consider the elements of risk taken by the various parties in order to be complete.

Risks of the Owner

The owner takes certain calculated risks regarding the capability, experience, and integrity of the design professional he chooses. (See Chapter 3, "The Design Professional" for methods of procuring the services of an architect and/or engineer). Depending on the skill and advice of the design professional during the development of the project, the opportunity to control the cost of the project diminishes rapidly as the phased services take place. As the process continues from schematic design through the creation of Contract Documents the savings opportunity diminishes from a high of about 20% to about 5% at the completion of Contract Documents. During bidding/negotiations it is conceivable that savings of up to 2% may be realized. After bidding/negotiations, changes in the design may result in additional cost if expensive Change Orders are required. As a result, the curve dips below the 0% line.

The owner takes certain calculated risks regarding the credibility and integrity of the constructor he chooses. (See Chapter 4, "The Constructor," for methods of procuring the services of the Constructor). To offset these risks, the design professional acting as the agent and representative of the owner, must thoroughly investigate the experience, financial resources, and capability of the candidates for contractor. The American Institute of Architects (AIA) and the Engineer's Joint Contract Documents Committee (EJCDC) and others have developed forms usually called the *"Contractor's Qualification Statement"* which have been designed to record detailed information about the prospective contractor, enabling the owner to make an informed decision on whether to award the Contract to that candidate.

Risks of the Design Professional

The primary risk of the design professional in the process of project procurement lies in two definable areas of professional practice. The competition among design professionals for desirable commissions is intense and increasingly expensive. Recent statistics revealed by the AIA and a number of engineering societies indicate that the most successful firms have a reasonable expectation of winning only 15%–20% of the projects they compete for. Marketing expenses are very high and often represent up to 15% of the annual earned income of the firm. Considering that profits on earned fees seem to average 10% or less, the financial risks associated with normal business practice are indeed high.

Of the alternative project procurement methods mentioned in this book, the design/build method of project procurement poses the highest financial risk to the design professional. Depending upon the owner's choice of selection methodology, when the design professional must offer a substantial amount of design work as part of a competitive offering, the financial risk is seen by many practicing professionals to be prohibitive.

Risks of the Constructor

Recent statistics report that the business failure rate of companies engaged in general contracting is extremely high, and that many general contracting companies in the United States declare bankruptcy or are forced into receivership by creditors. In recent history, it has not been unusual for the contractor to become insolvent during the process of building construction.

The process of competitive bidding requires the constructor to study the construction documents, estimate the total cost of building the project, factor in a profit, and be prepared to pay all costs (foreseen and unforeseen) that are included in the Contract Documents. To "win" the award of the Contract for Construction, a bid must be lowest among all other bids submitted by competitors. The bidder's work includes computing quantities, discerning exactly what is required by the documents, and anticipating changes in wage rates. Mistakes in any of these areas or the unforeseen failure of a subcontractor or material vendor to deliver as promised can result in losses to the constructor who wins the bid.

Alternative Bidding Rules

The risks to the participants in the OPC relationship might be reduced if alternative bidding rules were to be used in the United States. In many European countries, such as England, the process of competitive bidding includes "rules" requiring the owner to disregard, or "throw out" the amount and name of both the highest and the lowest bidder. The amounts of the remaining bidders are then averaged, and the bidder whose bid amount comes closest to the average of all is selected and awarded the Contract. This process has at least two distinct advantages. Since the final contract price is near the average of those proposed by all who have studied the project, the owner has some assurance that the Work will be done properly, while the constructor is assured a reasonable profit. This approach may mean that the owner will pay several percentage points more for the Work than he would under the low bidder system. Both private and public owners in the United States would be well served if they would consider the advantages offered by the Europeon method described above.

Chapter Eight
The Construction Contract

Building construction has become a complex undertaking that requires the coordinated efforts of many trades and professions. Today's building projects involve sums of money and a commitment of skills, material, and equipment that would have astonished our predecessors just two or three generations ago. The successful administration of both work and money calls for considerable management skills, planning, and documentation. An owner can no longer rely on verbal agreements, or leave work requirements, quality of construction, and matters of cost to trust or chance.

A written, legally binding agreement or contract has become a necessity, and should provide:

- Maximum detail and disclosure of the Work to be done.
- The extent of services required.
- The quality of materials to be employed.
- Other commitments that must be established in order to complete the project in an orderly manner.

Contracts Defined

A contract is an *agreement* between two or more parties. It represents a specified promise or series of promises to be performed, for which consideration is given. Common law recognizes performance under such an agreement to be an enforceable duty. A contract can be oral—made by spoken agreement, or it can be written—defined in writing and signed by the parties to the agreement. Oral contracts can be legally binding, but difficult to enforce because of the confusion that often occurs when the parties to the agreement must recall the exact specifications of the original agreement. Today's building owner requires documentation, not only to describe the work requirements for completion of the building, but for legal and financial protection as well. In order to be a complete or valid agreement, any contract must contain *identification* of the parties, a description of the *covenants*, a statement of the *consideration,* and *acceptance* by the parties.

Identification of Parties
The parties to the agreement must be named by the most appropriate legal identification. They can be individuals, partnerships, joint ventures, or corporations or any combination thereof. Each party is represented by the name by which it is most commonly known. The address of each party serves as further identification.

Covenants

A covenant is a clause in an agreement. It is a pledge to take, or refrain from taking, certain specified actions. The covenants form the "body" of the agreement for the Work of construction.

Consideration

Consideration is a recompense or payment for work done. In the legal sense, consideration is the element that makes a promise legally binding and usually something of value given in exchange for the promise. In the Contract for Construction, the Contract Sum is the consideration paid by the owner to the constructor for the Work of construction.

Acceptance

Acceptance is generally expressed with a signature attached to a legal document, representing the authority of the individual party to the agreement. By placing his signature on the agreement, each party indicates that he is not a minor, understands the content and terms of the agreement, and is duly authorized to bind his company, corporation, or other organization to the terms of the agreement.

Figure 8.1 shows a view of the Contract for Construction in terms of a common set of requirements. This list shows the elements that should be included in a valid contract from the standpoint of quality and preparation.

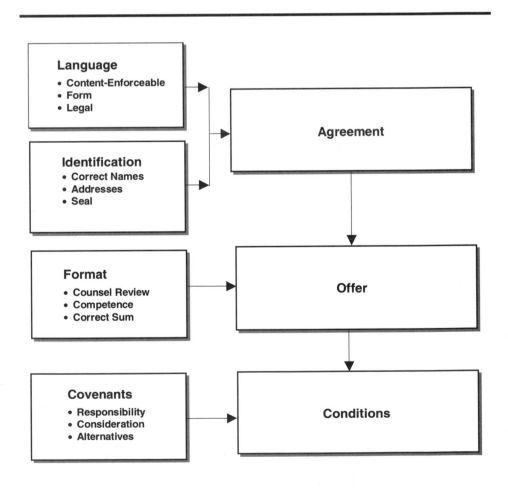

Figure 8.1 Elements of a Valid Contract

Agreement Between Owner and Contractor

The key component for the Contract for Construction is the *Agreement Between Owner and Contractor*. In order to be effective, the agreement must incorporate in the covenants, a complete definition of the Work to be done. It must also describe materials, skills, and other services to be used in the construction. The complex and interrelated responsibilities of the parties to the Contract must be outlined. The agreement should also illustrate how the building will be constructed. For the sake of convenience, the Contract for Construction is usually a single document. It names and sets forth the basic covenants between the parties; states the method of payment; establishes the Contract Sum; states the date of expected completion, and sets forth the conditions under which final completion; and acceptance will be accomplished.

So that the Contract for Construction can be properly drawn up and the Work defined, the prudent owner commissions a design professional (architect or engineer) and an attorney to advise him how best to achieve his needs. As a part of this service to the owner, the design professional will create documents that describe the design of the project, and create further documentation needed to carry out the requirements of the Contract for Construction. Once the project has been fully defined and documented, the design approved, and a budget committed for the anticipated cost, the owner is prepared to enter an agreement with a qualified constructor. Once chosen, the constructor is thereafter referred to as the *contractor*.

In order for the Work to be completely defined, the Contract must be accompanied by a number of other documents that (for the sake of convenience and propriety) are prepared separately from the body of the Contract. This collection of documents is generally known as the Contract Documents. The contract document lists these documents as:

- All Addenda (issued prior to the execution of the Agreement).
- The Agreement.
- The Conditions of the Contract, (General, Supplementary, and other Conditions).
- The Drawings.
- The Specifications, and Modifications (Issued During Constructions).

Figure 8.2 illustrates the various components of the Bidding Documents. These components may be thought of as "building blocks" designed to fit together in a particular way. Figure 8.3 shows the process by which these basic "building blocks" are assembled. Together, they form the basis for the bidding or negotiating process. An additional "building block," the Addenda, may be added to the package prior to the execution of the agreement. Once a Contract Sum and other pertinent conditions (such as the number of days allowed for construction) have been agreed upon, the Agreement can be executed. Figure 8.3 also illustrates the completed Contract Documents package. The Agreement between Owner and Contractor serves as the cord that ties the components together.

Components of the Contract Documents

Figure 8.2 illustrates that the Contractor's Qualification Statement, the Invitation to Bid and the Bid Form (all shown shaded) precede the Agreement, and are not part of the Contract Documents.

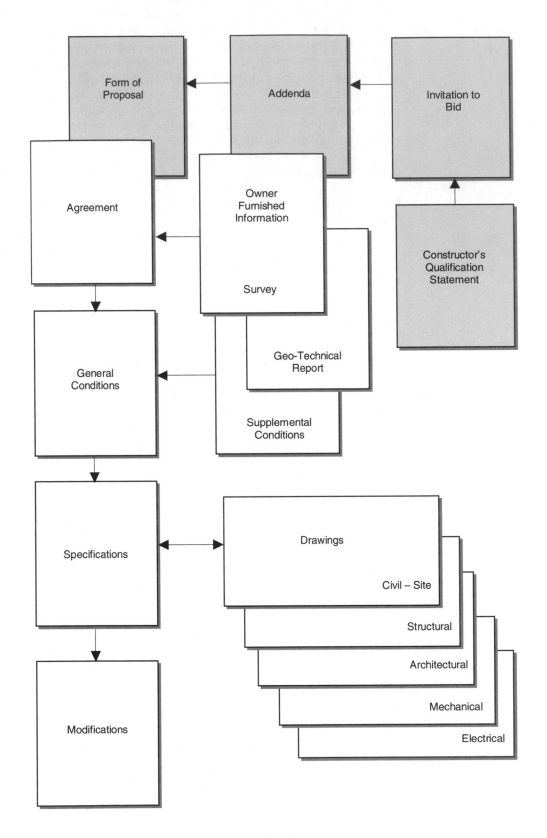

Figure 8.2 Bidding Documents

Figure 8.3 indicates that Bidding Requirements are not part of the Contract Documents, but rather, supplemental information furnished to explain the constructor selection process. If appropriate, the Bidding Requirements establish the rules for competitive bidding or negotiation for the award of the Contract. The bidding documents generally consist of the advertisement or invitation to bid, instructions to bidders, bid forms and other information that may be made available to bidders or selected constructors with whom negotiations are being conducted. Once the Contract is executed, the bidding documents are of no further value and are not a part of the main "package" of data.

It often becomes necessary or desirable to modify the Contract for Construction once the agreement has been executed and construction begun. Figure 8.3 shows the assembly of the Contract Documents together with additional modifications. In this illustration, the Agreement is represented by a "C" clamp which, when loosened, allows for the insertion of an additional "building block," the Modifications to the Contract for Construction. Notice that the bidding documents (represented by the tag) can now be removed as they are no longer needed.

Addenda

The Addenda are periodic publications that are modifications to the contract documents issued by the design professional on behalf of the owner during bidding or project procurement. They are issued prior to execution of the Agreement between Owner and Contractor for the purpose of modifying or clarifying the intent of the Contract Documents. Addenda may contain changes or corrections to the Work in addition to general information, answers to questions, and statements intended to clarify the general intent of the Contract Documents. Constructors bidding the Work are usually encouraged to point out any errors or inconsistencies they have discovered in the documents during the bidding or negotiating period. The design professional may use the bidding period to conduct a detailed "check" of the documents for his own benefit.

Conditions of the Contract

Because of the complexity of the OPC relationship (See Chapter 1) and other contractual relationships, it has become convenient to establish a definitive document accompanying and clarifying the Agreement. This document is often called the *General Conditions of the Contract* (between Owner and Contractor) for Construction, or simply the General Conditions. (See Chapter 9, "Conditions of the Contract.")

The General Conditions serve as the definitive or explanatory document among the Contract Documents. Therein, the parties are defined and their mutual responsibilities are set forth. The General Conditions outline the responsibilities of the owner, the design professional, the contractor and subcontractors. The Work of the Contract may also be defined. Work by the owner or separate contractors may also be defined. The General Conditions also contain miscellaneous provisions to define time, and include matters pertaining to payments and completion, protection of persons and property, insurance requirements, changes in the Work, uncovering and correction of the unacceptable work, and termination of the Contract.

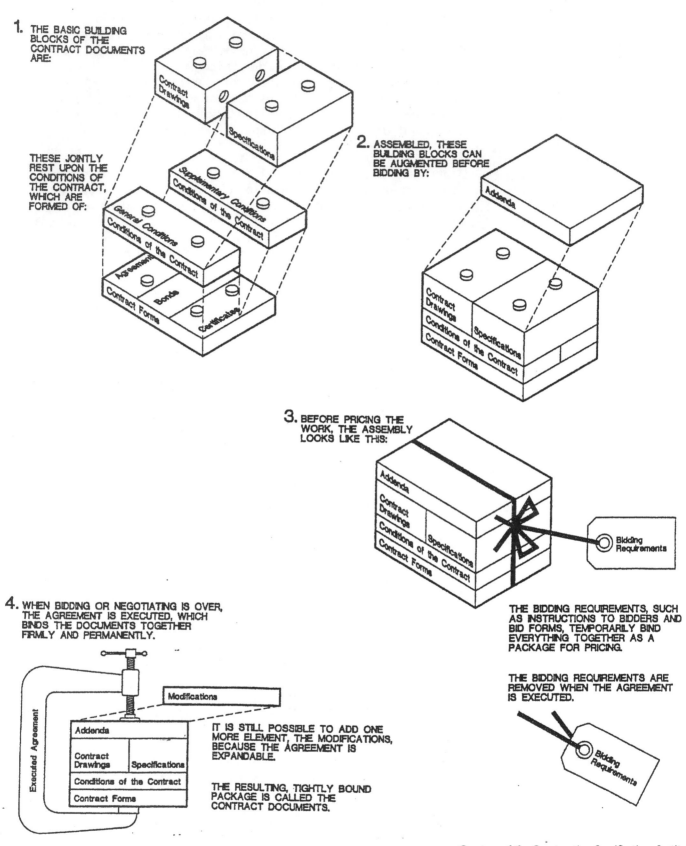

1. THE BASIC BUILDING BLOCKS OF THE CONTRACT DOCUMENTS ARE:

Contract Drawings

Specifications

THESE JOINTLY REST UPON THE CONDITIONS OF THE CONTRACT, WHICH ARE FORMED OF:

Supplementary Conditions of the Contract

General Conditions of the Contract

Agreement

Contract Forms

Bonds

Certificates

2. ASSEMBLED, THESE BUILDING BLOCKS CAN BE AUGMENTED BEFORE BIDDING BY:

Addenda

Contract Drawings

Specifications

Conditions of the Contract

Contract Forms

3. BEFORE PRICING THE WORK, THE ASSEMBLY LOOKS LIKE THIS:

Addenda

Contract Drawings

Conditions of the Contract

Specifications

Contract Forms

Bidding Requirements

THE BIDDING REQUIREMENTS, SUCH AS INSTRUCTIONS TO BIDDERS AND BID FORMS, TEMPORARILY BIND EVERYTHING TOGETHER AS A PACKAGE FOR PRICING.

THE BIDDING REQUIREMENTS ARE REMOVED WHEN THE AGREEMENT IS EXECUTED.

Bidding Requirements

4. WHEN BIDDING OR NEGOTIATING IS OVER, THE AGREEMENT IS EXECUTED, WHICH BINDS THE DOCUMENTS TOGETHER FIRMLY AND PERMANENTLY.

Modifications

Executed Agreement

Addenda

Contract Drawings

Specifications

Conditions of the Contract

Contract Forms

IT IS STILL POSSIBLE TO ADD ONE MORE ELEMENT, THE MODIFICATIONS, BECAUSE THE AGREEMENT IS EXPANDABLE.

THE RESULTING, TIGHTLY BOUND PACKAGE IS CALLED THE CONTRACT DOCUMENTS.

Courtesy of the Construction Specifications Institute

Figure 8.3 *The Agreement*

Supplemental Conditions of the Contract

Supplemental Conditions of the Contract are modifications of and additions to statements made in the General Conditions. In professional practice, the Supplemental Conditions are most often prepared as a separate document. This document details changes and additions to be made to the language of the General Conditions in order to meet the requirements of an individual project. Supplemental Conditions may address matters of local law, custom, and taxation. Equal Opportunity hiring requirements, minimum wage laws, and payment of local sales tax are examples of the kinds of laws and codes that may have jurisdiction over the project and the owner. The owner's own unique insurance requirements should also be spelled out in the Supplemental Conditions, as should the use of any tax exemption status. Information should be included regarding record keeping and other administrative procedures that may be required by others outside the OPC relationship. More specific administrative matters—the observation of certain project procedures, for example—will be discussed in subsequent chapters relating to Division 1 of the Specifications. (See Chapter 10, "Project Definition.")

Specifications

Specifications are generally defined in the American Institute of Architects' *Handbook of Professional Practice* and The Construction Specification Institute's *Manual of Practice*: The following is a definition from the CSI *Manual of Practice*:

> *Specifications define the qualitative requirements of products, materials, and workmanship upon which the Contract (for construction) is based.*

The full intent and content of the Contract for Construction cannot be fully expressed by words or drawings that act independently of each other. Specifications and Drawings are complementary and for that reason must be created as parts of equivalent value to the whole.

Drawings

The CSI *Manual of Practice* defines the Drawings as follows:

> *The drawings are a graphic representation of the Work to be done. They indicate the relationships between the components and materials and should show the following:*
>
> - *Location of each material, assembly, component, and accessory.*
> - *Identification of all components and pieces of equipment.*
> - *Dimensions of the construction and sizes of field-assembled components.*
> - *Details and diagrams of connections.*

As with the writing of Specifications, well-prepared drawings should be orchestrated to be in harmony with the other Contract Documents, but designed with an organization and logic that makes the material easily accessible to the user in the field.

Modifications

The Contract for Construction should be flexible enough to allow for changes, clarifications, additions, or deletions in the OPC relationship. Such alterations are often necessary, even desirable, and usually inevitable in such a complex undertaking as the construction of a modern building. The change order is the instrument by which modifications are made to the Contract for Construction.

Figure 8.4 illustrates a Means Contract Change Order, a form often used for documenting such modifications.

Types of Contracts

The forms of agreement used in the construction process are usually identified based on the method of payment to the Contractor. The American Institute of Architects (AIA), the Engineer's Joint Contract Documents Committee (EJCDC) and others have developed pre-printed forms of contracts. These forms are based on years of experience and considerable legal advice, and are commonly used and accepted throughout the construction industry.

Single Prime Contracts

The majority of building projects in the United States today are organized under a single prime contract. A single prime contract is a contract or agreement between owner and constructor wherein the contractor, for consideration (the Contract Price) agrees to become the prime party responsible for the construction of the project. The project is defined by construction documents prepared by the design professional. The contractor is responsible for providing all materials, labor, tools, equipment, and methods necessary for the completion of the Work defined by the Contract Documents. The word "prime" is used to distinguish the contractor from other constructors the owner might hire to perform certain portions of the work, or subcontractors which the contractor might contract for designated portions of the work.

In the Single Prime Contract for Construction, there is no direct contractual relationship between the owner and the subcontractor, nor between the contractor and the design professional. In most cases, the design professional acts as the owner's representative during the construction process and performs a number of services known as the Administration of the Contract. (See Figure 8.5). The various consultants employed by the design professional may assist in technical services during construction, but they are directly related only to the design professional who bears the total responsibility for professional services to the owner.

The subcontractor is related to the project by a separate agreement with the contractor. This agreement is known as the Subcontract. The subcontractor (defined in Chapter 1), usually a specialist in performing a particular portion of the building construction, serves the project at the discretion of the contractor. The contractor assumes total responsibility for the subcontractor's work and payment. Occasionally, the subcontractor requires a sub-subcontractor to perform portions of the subcontract work. In this case, the subcontractor is responsible for the sub-subcontractor's work and payment.

The producer may be either a manufacturer or distributor of materials, assemblies, or equipment. The producer is directly related to the contractor either through a separate contract or a contract for the purchase of certain items, known as the Purchase Order.

Means
CONTRACT
CHANGE ORDER

FROM:

_____
_____
_____
_____

TO:

_____
_____
_____
_____

CHANGE ORDER NO.	
DATE	
PROJECT	
LOCATION	
JOB NO.	
ORIGINAL CONTRACT AMOUNT	$
TOTAL PREVIOUS CONTRACT CHANGES	
TOTAL BEFORE THIS CHANGE ORDER	
AMOUNT OF THIS CHANGE ORDER	
REVISED CONTRACT TO DATE	

Gentlemen:

This CHANGE ORDER includes all Material, Labor and Equipment necessary to complete the following work and to adjust the total contract as indicated;

☐ the work below to be paid for at actual cost of Labor, Materials and Equipment plus_____percent (_____%)

☐ the work below to be completed for the sum of_____

_____ dollars ($_____)

_____
_____
_____
_____
_____
_____
_____
_____
_____
_____
_____
_____
_____
_____
_____
_____
_____
_____
_____
_____
_____
_____

CHANGES APPROVED

The work covered by this order shall be performed under the same Terms and Conditions as that included in the original contract unless stated otherwise above.

By_____

By_____

Signed_____

By _____

Figure 8.4 Contract Change Order Form

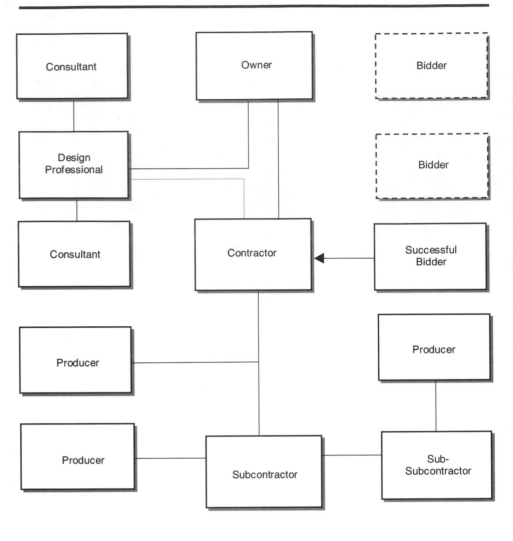

Figure 8.5 *Single Prime Contract*

The single prime contract may be used in project procurement methodologies (further described in Chapter 7, "Project Delivery") as follows:

Multiple Prime Contracts— Construction Management Contracts

Increasing numbers of construction projects involve two or more prime contractors doing work on the same project under related contracts. These contracts are usually referred to as "Multiple Prime Contracts." Chapter 7, "Project Delivery," refers to multiple-prime contract methodology as design/multiple-bid/build contracts.

In the traditional approach to project construction, the owner must first select the professional (architect or engineer) and finalize the acquisition of the building site. He then contracts with the professional to design the building, secures any required financing, arranges for the creation of Contract Documents, and selects the constructor (see Chapter 7, "Project Delivery"). In the case of major projects, this process may require a year, or more, before any construction can begin. The expense sustained by the owner during this period is substantial.

The outlay for land acquisition, professional fees, the cost of surveys, soil tests, zoning, and planning reviews and approvals are all costs that must be borne prior to construction. These costs can amount to a significant percentage of the total project development cost. Occasionally, the owner must also sustain certain ancillary off-site improvements such as construction of access roads, extension of utility lines, flood control structures, demolition of existing improvements and other preliminary work before any construction of the actual project can begin. If the owner borrows any funds to develop his project, interest must also be applied to the sums that are expended during both the pre-construction and the construction periods.

If the factors of time and expense are to become substantial (30% or more of the total project development cost) prior to the start of the actual project construction, the owner may wish to utilize an approach called the *fast track* method of project procurement. Simply stated, the fast track method involves awarding a series of Multiple Prime Contracts, each of which accomplishes a subsequent phase or stage of the building construction (see Figure 8.6).

The owner has the option of contracting with a Construction Manager to coordinate and otherwise manage the construction process. The first option, the Construction Manager/Advisor (CM/A) serves the owner's needs as an advisor with compensation on the basis of a fee. The CM/A takes little or no risk in the process, which may be a definite disadvantage to the owner. The second option is for the owner to contract with a Construction Manager/Constructor (CM/C). In this option the Construction Manager is responsible for the project delivery but may obtain separate constructors to complete the work. The CM/C takes certain risks if the Owner/CM/C agreement requires project delivery for a stipulated price. An alternate method to the stipulated sum contract provides for project delivery whereby the Owner/CM/C agreement states a Guaranteed Maximum Price (GMP) and defines a fee for the CM/C. The CM/C earns a defined fee, and is at risk only if the project cost exceeds the defined GMP. Often it is to the advantage of both Owner and CM/C if the Owner/CM/C agreement offers a percentage of any savings between final cost and GMP as a bonus that the CM/C may earn, over and above his stipulated fee, through superior management and cooperation among the multiple-prime constructors.

The basic principle of the fast track method is that time (and often, money) can be saved if the construction can begin before all the traditional pre-construction functions are completed. The fast-track method may be used under CM/Adviser, CM/Constructor, Program Manager or Design/Build contracts.

As an example, consider the first phases of the construction of a medium sized multi-story building in a busy commercial neighborhood. The design professional's work is phased and is time-related. In this example, the design professional's contract begins on day 1 and the CM/C contract begins on day 1. The design professional's schedule for production of construction documents as follows:

Phase 1—Schematic Design
Requires 30 days to complete. Allowing two weeks for presentation and owner approval, Schematic Design is complete on day 44. Schematic Design is to include establishing a final site design. The

contract documents for site clearing and demolition begin on day 1 and require 14 days to complete. Site clearing and demolition can begin as early as day 20. The contract documents for site grading and excavation begin on day 15 and require 21 days to complete. Site grading and excavation can begin as early as day 45.

Phase 2—Design Development

Requires 45 days to complete. Design Development begins on day 44 and continues through day 89. Allowing two weeks for owner review and approval, phase 3 may begin on day 103. Design Development is to include finalizing the building design. The contract documents for foundation begin on day 44 and will require 40 days to complete. Foundation work can begin as early as day 92. The contract documents for steel superstructure begin on day 93 and require 52 days to complete. Steel structural shop drawings requiring 14 days can begin as early as day 145. Steel fabrication can begin as early as day 159. The first fabricated components of the superstructure will be available at the jobsite as early as day 170.

Phase 3—Contract Documents

Requires 90 days to complete. The Contract Documents phase begins on day 103 and continues through day 193.

The construction of the building may be broken down into multiple-prime, time-related contracts as illustrated in Figures 8.7a, 8.7b, and 8.7c.

By utilizing the fast track method, the owner has realized completion of his project in 392 days, or 13 months.

The same project, delivered under the traditional design/bid/build procurement method would require the following schedule:

- A/E Design through completion of Contract Documents—begins on day 1 and is complete on day 193.
- Bidding and Negotiations—begins on day 223 and ends on day 265.
- Contract for Construction—is awarded on day 295.
- General Construction—begins on day 300 and is complete on day 720 (14 months).

The traditional methodology generally requires 24 months to complete. The fast track multiple contract method saves 11 months or almost one full year in comparison.

While this example of the fast track method compared with traditional methods has been simplified for purposes of explanation, the potential time savings are evident. Though subject to the perils of human error, misunderstanding, and coordination, the fast track method can save time that would otherwise be spent by professionals in preparing fully implemented and complete Contract Documents and Bidding Requirements. This savings of time, and thereby money, as well as the accelerated date of owner occupancy, is often worth the risks. The chief risk is that an error might be introduced to the construction documents. Such an error might result in the unforeseen cost of modifications to the various Prime Contracts as the project is being completed.

The fast track method of construction (by separate Multiple Prime Contracts) is becoming more and more common as a method of economical phased construction. In the fast track, each phase relates to

Fast-Track—Multiple Contract Methodology

Contract 1—Site Clearing and Demolition

- Phase 1a—Demolition requires 20 days to complete. Demolition begins on day 1 and ends on day 20.
- Phase 1b—Site Clearing requires 60 days to complete. Site Clearing begins on day 20 and ends on day 80.

Contract 2—Site Work

- Phase 2a—Rough grading and excavating can begin 30 days after site clearing and demolition begins, and requires 30 days to complete. Rough grading begins on day 50 and ends on day 80.
- Phase 2b—Structural base for foundations requires 10 days to complete. Placement can begin on day 81 and end on day 91.
- Phase 2c—Paving and site improvements.

Contract 3—Structural Construction

- Phase 3a—Foundation and substructure requires 80 days to complete. Foundation can begin on day 92 and will be complete on day 172.
- Phase 3b—Superstructure requires 120 days to complete. Superstructure construction can begin on day 175 and be complete by day 295.

Contract 4—Plumbing

- Phase 4a—Underground plumbing must be coordinated with Phase 2a. Underground plumbing must begin after day 50 and be complete before day 80.
- Phase 4b—Superstructure plumbing rough-in must be coordinated with Phase 3b. Plumbing rough in must begin after day 175 and be complete by day 255.
- Phase 4c—Placement of plumbing fixtures.

Contract 5—Construction of Building Envelope

- Building shell must be coordinated with Phase 3b. Building envelope can begin when superstructure is 50% complete. Building envelope must begin after day 232 and be complete by day 365.

Contract 6—Heating, Ventilating and Air Conditioning

- Phase 6a—HVAC rough-in must be coordinated with Phase 3b. HVAC rough-in can begin after day 175 and be complete by day 255.
- Phase 6b—HVAC equipment and start-up must be coordinated with Contract 8. HVAC equipment and start-up can begin after day 332 and end before day 392.

Contract 7—Electrical Power and Lighting

- Phase 7a—Underground electrical and site rough-in must be coordinated with Phase 3a and 4a. Underground electrical can begin after day 50 and must end before day 92.
- Phase 7b—Superstructure electrical rough-in must be coordinated with Contract 3. Electrical rough-in can begin after day 175 and be complete by day 255.
- Phase 7c—Place electrical equipment and fixtures must be coordinated with Contract 8. Electrical equipment and fixtures can begin after day 332 and end on day 390.

Contract 8—Interior Construction

- Phase 8a—Construction of all public and common space must be coordinated with Contract 5. Building envelope will be "dried-in" when Contract No. 5 is 70% complete. Interior construction can begin after day 332 and end on day 390.
- Phase 8b—Interior finishing must be coordinated with Contract 5 and Phase 8a. Interior finishing can begin after day 332 and be complete before day 392.

Contract 9—Landscaping

- Contract 9 can begin any time after "dry-in" on day 332 and be complete by day 392.

Figure 8.6 Fast-Track Methodology

others in a vertical type of progression with some parallel overlapping. "Parallel construction" is another construction method. It utilizes Multiple Prime Contracts, but is more horizontal in nature. "Parallel construction" applies to projects such as a Planned Unit Development (PUD)—a project with major components requiring specialized pre-fabrication of major component parts that are built in a shop or a controlled manufacturing facility and shipped to the site at an appropriate time for installation. Examples are a tract housing project utilizing prefabricated or panelized components, and a jail which uses prefabricated inmate cells. Each of these projects is apt to require specialized components and equipment that can be fabricated in a time frame parallel to other basic construction operations. Such projects are therefore appropriate projects for multiple prime contracts.

Like the "fast track" approach which uses time-phased contracts in order to save time and money, the parallel method also provides certain economic advantages. The parallel method may save time and expense in terms of the contractor's overhead and profit. By utilizing parallel prime contracts the owner does not depend on a single contractor to subcontract specialty items. The owner may save money by separately contracting and coordinating the Work himself or with the assistance of a Construction Manager/Advisor. Figures 8.7a, 8.7b, and 8.7c illustrate the relationships that are created for multiple-prime contracts.

Multiple prime contracts may be used in project delivery methodologies (further described in Chapter 7, "Project Delivery").

Design/Multiple-Bid/Build
- Design professional is contracted by owner under owner/prime design professional agreement. Design professional, at his option, contracts with one or more sub-consultant.

CM Advisor alternative to Contract(s) for construction
- Owner, at his option, may contract with Construction Manager-Adviser. Owner contracts with two or more constructors under separate owner/prime constructor agreements. Each constructor is charged with designated responsibility by owner. Each constructor at his option, (with owner approval) may contract with subcontractor, under contractor/subcontractor agreement. Subcontractor at his option, may contract with one or more sub-subcontractors. Constructor, subcontractor and sub-subcontractor each obtain materials, assemblies, and equipment from the producer by purchase order.

CM Constructor alternative to contract(s) for construction
- Owner contracts with Construction Manager-Constructor. CM contracts with two or more constructors under separate agreements. Each constructor is charged with designated responsibility by CM. Each constructor at his option, (with Owner/CM approval) may contract with subcontractor under contractor/subcontractor agreement. Subcontractor at his option, may contract with one or more sub-subcontractors. CM constructor, multiple constructors, subcontractor and sub-subcontractor each obtain materials, assemblies and equipment from the producer by purchase order.

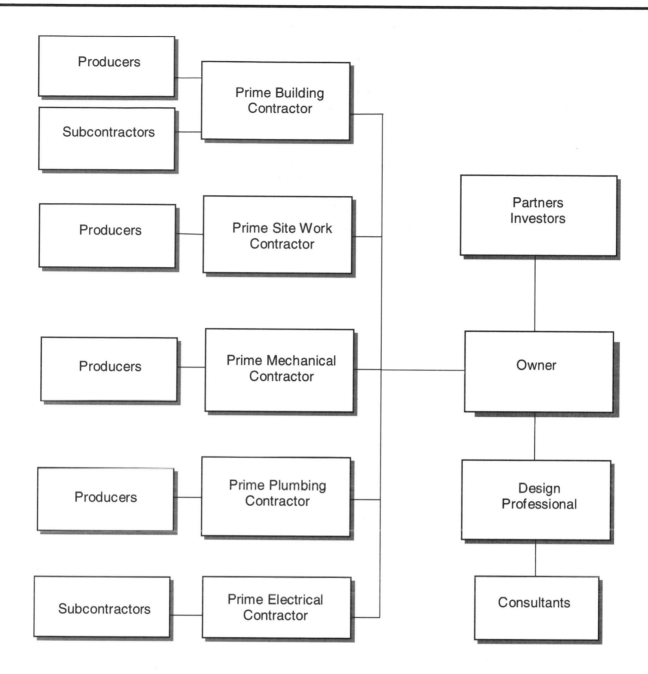

Figure 8.7a *Contractor-Owner-Multiple-Prime Contracts*

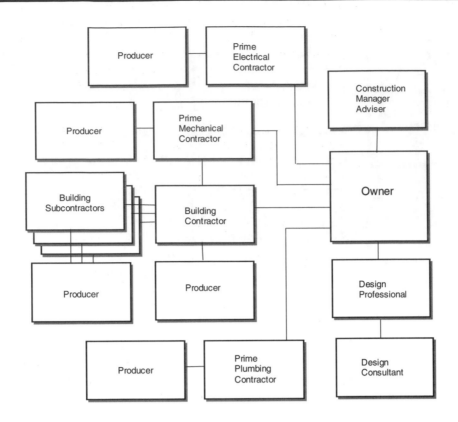

Figure 8.7b *Multiple-Prime Contract for Construction Manager Advisor*

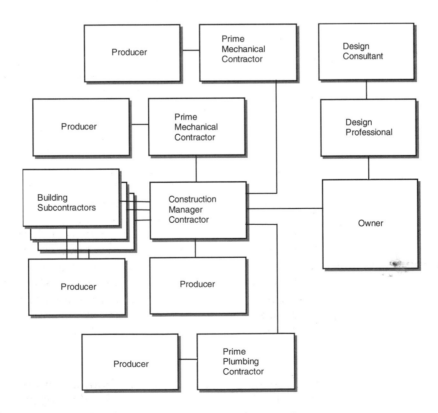

Figure 8.7c *Multiple-Prime Contract for Construction Manager/Constructor*

Turn-Key Contracts

The term "turn-key" has commonly been applied to projects where the owner may accept (and pay for) the project at the time when he is able to "turn his key" in the lock of the main entrance and take possession of a completed project. In the typical turn-key project, the constructor provides the construction financing. The owner accepts the completed project at "closing," as may be agreed by previous contract for sale.

A common example of a turn-key contract approach is the business of a home-builder operating in any number of new residential subdivisions. Some builders find it economically advantageous to design several "prototype" homes, repeating these models over and over again with minor variations of exterior material, color and texture—an approach which seems to appeal to a "mass" market of American home buyers. Other builders contract with a prospective homeowner to build what is now commonly referred to as a "custom" home. In this case, the owner has considerable influence over the design. He may or may not employ a design professional, but arranges what is called a "stand-by" mortgage commitment for the long term financing of the project. The owner, together with the lender, accepts the building according to a contract of sale with the builder once the construction work is complete.

There is a growing element within the established construction industry—constructors who are looking to other contracting methods to overcome the many disadvantages of the competitive process. Although the traditional OPC relationship (described in Chapter 1) continues to serve the majority of projects constructed in the U.S., there is an increasing desire among owners, design professionals and particularly constructors, to find more profitable ways to carry out design and construction.

Design/Build Contracts

There is a growing demand to consolidate the functions of ownership, professional design, and construction under a more predictable, if not controllable, atmosphere for survival and profit. The design/build method of organizing and implementing the construction process may be one of several answers to such a quest.

In the design/build approach to project completion, the owner presents his needs, program, and budget. The constructor assembles a "team" of specialists. Among them may be the architects and engineers, together with traditional major subcontractors and others who will work together under the control of the contractor to satisfy the owner's needs according to a pre-established budget. In this process, a Contract Sum is negotiated, and the role and compensation of each team member is defined. This system often lends itself to the fast-track method of construction. In addition, each participant in the process may share in the final profit (or loss) that is achieved once the project is constructed. Figure 8.8 illustrates the relationships that may exist in the design/build process. Chapter 7, "Project Delivery," covers the design/build contract in more detail.

Methods of Payment

Regardless of the contracting method, experience has proven that the preferred method of payment should employ checks and balances in the best interest of both parties to the Contract for Construction.

There are several terms that should be understood prior to a discussion of contract payment provisions.

- *The Contract Sum*: the total value of the Work, defined by the Contract Documents; the amount that is to be paid to the contractor according to the terms of the Agreement between Owner and Contractor.
- *The Schedule of Values*: a listing or schedule of monetary values. Each item on the schedule represents a proportionate value for a definable portion of the Work. The total amount is equal to the Contract Sum.
- *Retainage*: a percentage (set forth in the agreement) which the owner retains or withholds from the total periodic payments according to the terms of the agreement. Retaining a portion of the contractor's earnings gives the owner some leverage in enforcing compliance with the requirements of the Contract Documents.

The Schedule of Values is usually determined by the contractor, reviewed, and approved by the design professional and accepted by the owner at or very near the beginning of the construction process. Having been predetermined and agreed to by each party in the OPC

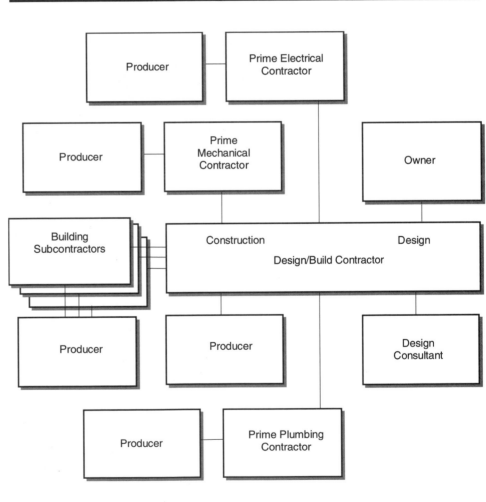

Figure 8.8 Design/Build Contract

relationship, the Schedule of Values is then used as a guide to determine amounts of incremental payments. These payments are made in proportion to the Work completed on a monthly or other periodic basis. The contractor periodically prepares an Application and Certificate for Payment and makes adjustment to the Contract Sum for any Modifications or Change Orders that have been approved by each owner, contractor, and design professional. Once approved by either the design professional or the construction manager, payment by
the owner is made to the contractor. The mechanism of payment procedures and the use of various forms for application and approval are discussed more fully in subsequent chapters.

Definite or "Lump Sum" Contracts

The most common form of provision for payment is the "lump sum" or definite sum contract. The definite sum contract may be achieved by any of the various contracting methods described in this chapter. It may be derived by competitive bidding or by negotiation, and the contract(s) may be awarded to single or multiple prime contractors. Definite sum contracts may be applied to projects with a traditional OPC relationship, or to a variety of design-build projects which may or may not use the traditional relationships. Payment may be made periodically according to a percentage of work completed or in a single payment at completion of the entire project, as in the case of the turn-key type of contract.

Advantages of the definite sum contract are as follows:
- The owner can accept or reject the proposed Contract Sum according to his budget constraints.
- The Contract Sum is fixed thereby offering some protection to the owner from cost escalation due to outside economic factors.
- The cost of contract administration is included in the design professional's fee. Generally, there is no additional expenditure required to achieve project completion.

Disadvantages of the definite sum contract are listed below:
- The owner and/or design professional may be liable for extra cost because of errors and omissions in the Contract Documents.
- Modifications to the Contract may cost more than if such changes had been incorporated originally.
- The contractor may sustain heavy losses due to error in estimating or cost changes due to economic factors.

Unit Cost Contracts

Unit cost contracts are most commonly used for projects involving heavy construction: highways, streets, roads, bridges, underground and above ground utilities, drainage structures, and dams. The Contract Documents are similar to those of the definite cost contract, except that the value of each item of work is defined by an agreed unit price applicable to basic units or measurable quantities of work. Because the drawings for these types of contracts tend to be diagrammatic, and are not always measured drawings drawn to scale (as in the case of building construction drawings), the payments to the contractor must be determined by measuring the Work completed in the field. The amount of work completed to date is established by actual measurement in terms of units of work, and the total value of work is determined by multiplying the units completed by the pre-agreed unit prices stated in the agreement.

Occasionally there is need to supplement a determined sum contract with provision for payment for certain portions of the Work by unit prices. A typical example is a building that requires excavation for a basement, with the expectation that there will be considerable amounts of stone or rock strata. Leaving to guesswork the total cost of excavating solid rock could result in a higher cost to the owner, or a loss to the contractor because of unknown quantities. To avoid either of these repercussions, the Contract for Construction may provide a reasonable unit cost for rock removal based on units measured during the actual work. Payment is then made on the basis of actual work required, rather than on a nebulous estimate that may prove to be incorrect. Other items that may vary from the anticipated quantities in building construction should be treated in a similar manner.

Another use of unit pricing is in determining the final length of structural piling that may be required for the substructure of a building where the upper strata of soil is not suitable to bear the weight of the structure. Soils data gathered before construction may not be sufficient to determine the actual depth to which structural piles must be constructed or driven in order to reach suitable bearing. In this case, unit prices can be established before any work is done. This is a suitable method for determining equitable payment due the contractor should the piles exceed the anticipated depth. This method is also useful for deciding the appropriate amount of credit to be given to the Contract Sum if pilings are not required to the depths originally anticipated.

The use of stipulated unit prices may be convenient for finish and other items if the owner wishes to postpone some design decisions.

The owner may prefer to make these selections when the building has begun to take shape and he has a better perspective on budgetary adjustments.

Cost of Work Plus a Fee

For various reasons, an owner may not be satisfied with a determined sum in a contract derived by the competitive bidding procedure. Since a contractor's contingency for unforeseen cost and profit margin is not usually disclosed by the competitive bidding process, there is always the lingering question that perhaps the contract price is more to the advantage of the contractor than it is to the owner. The negotiation process is sometimes more agreeable to both parties to the contract in that the actual cost of the Work as well as the contractor's mark-up for overhead and profit are often disclosed. Contracting on the basis of cost of work plus fee helps to overcome any doubts the owner may have as to "excessive" profits of the contractor. In the cost of the Work plus a fee type of contract, a schedule of values is established representing the contractor's best estimate of the actual cost of each item of the Work. The Contract Sum is derived either by adding a pre-established percentage mark-up to each item in the schedule, or by applying a fixed pre-determined fee for overhead and profit. This fee is added to the total cost. Periodic payment is made to the contractor when an accounting of the actual cost is submitted, along with proof that these costs have been paid for.

Advantages of the cost-plus-fee contract:
- Hidden contingencies that may otherwise be concealed in the Contract Sum may be avoided.
- Savings are possible through careful management and coordination.
- Many of the risks that the contractor takes in the fixed sum contract method may be eliminated in the cost-plus-fee contract.

Disadvantages of the cost-plus-fee contract:
- Some costs may escalate in the course of the project, causing the Contract Sum to be greater than if it were fixed in the beginning.
- The Work of the design professional may be greatly increased, thus the professional fees may be larger.

Guaranteed Maximum Price (GMP) Contracts

The cost-of-work-plus-fee contract will often specify what is sometimes called an *up-set-price* or the guaranteed maximum price (GMP). The GMP is an agreed-upon maximum Contract Sum not to be exceeded. This agreement is established as a condition of the Contract. Should the final cost exceed such stated amount, the contractor pre-agrees to pay any such excess. It is to the owner's benefit that the contractor be given some substantial profit incentive in the GMP Contract. In this way, the contractor is more likely to make every effort to reduce the owner's cost—through good management of labor and supervision, competitive subcontractor award techniques, thrifty purchasing methods, and by maximum available discounts obtained from suppliers (e.g., for early payment during the construction process). This arrangement provides excellent protection for the owner against possible cost overruns, but may be unreasonable to the contractor unless some reciprocal benefit or incentive is provided if he is able to complete the construction at a total cost plus fee which is *less* than the guaranteed maximum Contract Sum. This contingent amount may be set as a percentage, either fixed or on a *sliding* scale, based on the difference between actual cost plus fee and the guaranteed maximum sum. Or, it may be a percentage of the apparent savings with a fixed upper limit. In any event, this continuing method offers advantages to both parties.

Advantages of GMP contracts:
- The owner has a definite possibility of reducing costs, unlike the fixed sum method.
- The contractor's risk is reduced and he has a chance to increase his profit by exercising creative management of the project.

Disadvantages of GMP contracts:
- The design professional's work, and thereby his fee, may be increased.
- The contractor is vulnerable to loss if management techniques fail to produce the project for the guaranteed price.

Bonus and Penalty Provisions

Many times the Instructions to Bidders will state that "time is the essence of the Contract . . ." That is to say, the bidder's pledge for the number of calendar days and a definite Contract Sum is of vital consideration to the owner's objectives. The time required for construction is often as valuable to the owner as is a determined price that is within the owner's budget. There was a time when it was not unusual for the conditions of the Contract to set forth a penalty clause. This clause made provision for the owner to assess a charge to be deducted from the Contract Sum for each calendar day that the contractor was late, beyond the date for substantial completion established in the Contract. There is considerable argument that such penalty provisions may be arbitrary, unfair, and may not be enforceable in a court of law. The argument follows that if the owner will be damaged by late delivery of a project, then he may be equally benefited by an early delivery of the project. In other words, if there is to be a penalty for late delivery, then there should also be a corresponding bonus for early delivery. But many owners are not willing to agree to corresponding bonus provisions in construction contracts as they have been to demand penalties. When penalty provisions have been tested in the courts, owners have often been required to offer substantial proof of actual damage in order to prevail in such lawsuits.

Liquidated Damages

While the matter of penalty and bonus provisions can be argued, the courts also held that the covenant of the Contract which promises a certain date for substantial completion is not without certain binding legal consequences. Over time, in an effort to eliminate contract language which has high potential for dispute, it has become commonplace for contract language to include specifications for *liquidated damages.* The term *liquidated* is generally associated with discharge of a debt by agreement or litigation. It means to turn an asset into money rather than to distribute the asset in kind. For example, the assets of an insolvent debtor in bankruptcy may be *liquidated* by a court-appointed receiver by selling the assets of the debtor and distributing the proceeds; in general, assignments for the benefit of creditors.

The owner may establish in the contract language an amount per day in the form of *liquidated damages* to be assessed for each day, or other period of time that a project is delivered after the established date for completion. This amount should represent the owner's potential loss if completion is substantially delayed. By agreeing to establish such an amount in the conditions of the Contract, the parties may obviate the need to litigate the issue of damages for delay. The owner can be compensated by the terms of the agreement if the contractor cannot establish that the delay was caused by factors beyond his ability and control.

Profit Sharing Provisions

Just as there are methods to give the contractor incentive to complete the Work quickly and economically, it follows that savings can also be more readily achieved with similar incentives for those who work under the contractor. There is a growing tendency for general contractors to subcontract large portions of the Work, leaving little or no work to be accomplished by the contractor's own forces. In these cases, it is unlikely that the contractor will earn bonus provisions for early completion or for *savings* unless maximum cooperation is achieved from the subcontractors. A prudent contractor, striving to earn bonus provisions under the Contract will make a similar provision in the agreements with key subcontractors allowing the subcontractors to share in any bonus or extra profit that the contractor may realize. Even without a specific proposal for a bonus or share in the savings the contractor stands to gain substantial benefits from the maximum cooperation of subcontractors as well as his own employees. Thus, it is not unusual for the contractor to reward the superintendent and key employees with a bonus or a share of profits realized from a project that has been completed on time and at a profit.

Summary

In a perfect world, populated by perfect people, all of whom are dedicated to the mutual best interest of one and all, a perfect contract would be . . . well, it would be unnecessary. But, the world is not a perfect place and its inhabitants are not only imperfect, but most, if not all are prone to act in self interest, particularly in a highly complex construction project fraught with multiple interrelationships, actions and reactions, where the factors of time, quality, and cost are often adversarial.

The contract for construction should be written so that:

- The language is simple and straightforward.
- The vocabulary is familiar and the syntax skillful.
- The individual responsibilities of each party are clearly and completely stated.

All parties to the contract for construction should seek the advice of competent counsel no matter how simple the language, how familiar and straightforward the intent, how accessible the vocabulary, and how skillful the syntax.

The application of proprietary contract forms such as those published by the AIA and EJCDC is entirely appropriate and often advised. Such documents, however, are designed to serve a broad number of applications and therefore may be incomplete without the review of a skilled and competent attorney.

The Family of Standard Construction Contracts

Single Prime Contract for Construction:

- Owner/Constructor—Stipulated Price
- Owner/Constructor—Cost plus a Fee with GMP
- Owner/Constructor—Unit Cost

Multiple Prime Contract for Construction:

- Owner/Constructor Agreement—Designated Work—Stipulated Price
- Owner/Constructor Agreement—Designated Work—Cost plus a Fee with GMP
- Owner/Constructor Agreement—Designated Work—Unit Cost
- Owner/Construction Manager—Constructor Agreement

Parallel Separate Contracts—Multiple Prime Constructors:

- Owner/Design Professional Agreement—Stipulated Fee
- Owner/Design Professional Agreement—Cost plus Fee
- Owner/Design Professional Agreement—Percentage of Construction Cost
- Owner/Construction Manager/Adviser Agreement
- Construction Manager/Constructor Agreement—Designated Work—Stipulated Price

Program Management Contracts:

- Owner/Program Manager Agreement—Stipulated Price
- Owner/Program Manager Agreement—Cost plus Fee with GMP

Parallel Separate Contracts—Program Management:

- Program Manager/Design Professional Agreement—Stipulated Fee
- Program Manager/Constructor Agreement—Cost plus Fee with GMP

Design/Build Contracts:

- Owner/Design—Build Agreement—Stipulated Price
- Owner/Design—Build Agreement—Cost plus a Fee with GMP

Parallel Separate Contracts:

- Constructor/Design Professional—Design/Build Team
- Design Professional/ Single Prime Constructor—Design/Build Team
- Design Professional/Designated Work Prime Constructor—Design/Build Team

Figure 8.9 *Standard Construction Contract Forms*

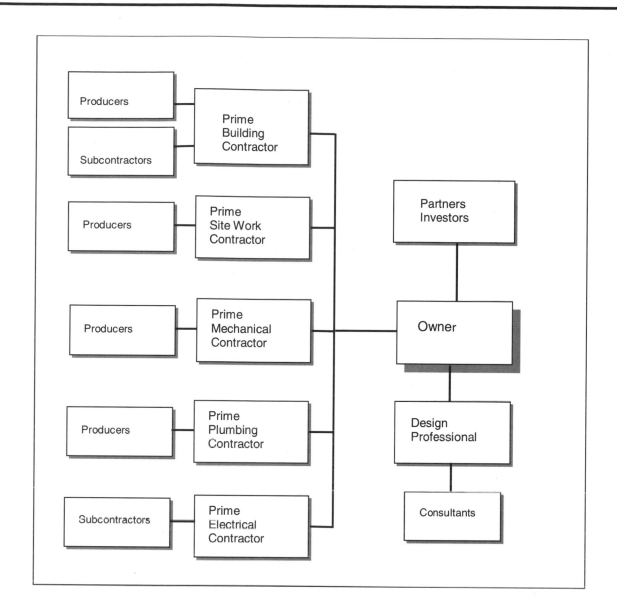

Figure 8.10 *Owner Acting as Contractor*

Chapter Nine
Conditions of the Contract

The Contract for Construction, described in Chapter 8, is the keystone in the series of legal instruments described as the *Contract Documents*. In order for any agreement to be complete, the following information must be recorded:

- A complete and legal identification of all involved parties.
- The mutual responsibilities of those parties to one another.
- The rights of each party.
- Other anticipated definitions, relationships, conditions, procedures, requirements, and alternatives that will help in avoiding disputes when misunderstandings arise.

A typical construction project requires the services of parties who are *indirectly* related to the contract, employed by one of the parties to the Contract. For example, the design professional is employed by the owner, and the subcontractor is employed by the contractor. The design professional has no *direct* contractual agreement with the contractor; nor does the subcontractor have a direct agreement with the owner. The identities and roles of parties indirectly related to the Contract must be described in no less detail than the roles of the parties directly related by the Contract. Potential misunderstandings and disputes between all parties must be anticipated and remedies described.

The object of the Contract for Construction is the *Work,* or the project as defined in the Contract. The most convenient way to describe the Work is to prepare drawings and technical specifications. These drawings and specifications become part of the Contract for Construction by reference and attachment.

In view of the countless disputes that have taken place over contract arrangements, the language of the Contract for Construction has become more and more explicit and detailed. It has become necessary for the design professional preparing the contract documents to anticipate situations that could lead to costly disputes. The most common approach to preventing such problems (in addition to seeking the advice of an attorney) has been the preparation of additional explanatory documents which, like the drawings and specifications, are complementary, referenced, and attached to the Contract for Construction. One of these explanatory documents is the *Conditions of the Contract for Construction,* the subject of this chapter.

The Evolution of Standardized Documents

Early in this century, joint committees comprised of architectural and engineering societies, ownership groups, construction industry organizations, interested individuals and others met and discussed mutual problems and objectives related to construction contracts. Each group made compromises and together produced language, which was published as a document called Conditions to the Contract for Construction.

Over the years, improvements have been made periodically, resulting in a number of familiar forms of contract conditions. Some of these documents have become standards in the construction industry and are used to avoid, adjudicate or provide a mechanism by which to resolve disputes. The American Institute of Architects publishes *The General Conditions of the Contract for Construction*. The Engineer's Joint Contract Documents Committee (EJCDC) publishes the *Standard Conditions of the Construction Contract*. Many ownership agencies of state and federal government prefer to use their own proprietary forms of Conditions of the Contract written to suit particular types of public works projects and political objectives. Among these are the Corps of Engineers of the United States Army, the United States Navy, and the United States Postal Service. Whichever "standard" is used, each is intended to achieve the same goal: to facilitate the successful administration of the Contract for Construction.

AIA General Conditions

Since its inception over a century ago, the American Institute of Architects (AIA), in collaboration with other industry organizations such as the Construction Specifications Institute (CSI) and the Associated General Contractors of America (AGC), has dedicated itself to establishing and honing an interrelated series of published documents. The aim of these documents is to facilitate all contractual relationships in modern building construction.

The AIA has produced a number of standard documents and contracts, such as agreements between owner and contractor, owner and design professional, contractor and subcontractor, and others. The *Conditions of the Contract for Construction* (or any one of several variations of the Conditions of the Contract) published by AIA can be used to supplement, interrelate, or otherwise expand on the purposes, agreements, covenants, and responsibilities between and among the parties to the various types of contracts.

EJCDC Conditions

While the architects have tended to organize themselves into one or two national organizations, the AIA being the most prominent, engineers have tended to organize themselves by engineering discipline. As a result, there are many nationally recognized engineering societies and institutes such as the American Society of Civil Engineers (ASCE), the Institute of Electrical and Electronic Engineers (IEEE), and the National Society of Professional Engineers (NSPE) to mention a few. In the middle of the 20th century, several of the professional engineering organizations that were engaged in building design and related fields organized the Engineers Joint Contract Documents Committee (EJCDC) to create and publish a library of proprietary contract documents that serve the needs of the wider and diverse engineering community. The EJCDC is supported by the sale of the documents it publishes with subsidy from a number of professional engineering organizations.

Owner-Generated Conditions of the Contract

Today, it is not unusual for local governments, taxing districts and similar jurisdictions to create and maintain standard contract conditions that they believe better serve the needs of the local community. Washington DC and the Fairfax County Virginia School Board are examples of local public owners who make such a practice.

Contractual Relationships

The Contract for Construction is an agreement between the owner and the contractor. However, there are other issues and relationships that complicate this arrangement. There is usually a distinct and separate agreement relating the services of the design professional to the owner and his objectives. The design professional will often contract with an engineer and other consultants to perform portions of the design. The contractor, in turn, contracts with various subcontractors. Each subcontractor then has the option of contracting portions of his work to others, known as *sub-subcontractors*. Each of the contractors is also related to various producers (suppliers and manufacturers), either by contract or by purchase order. The purchase order is, in effect, a contract wherein the contractor agrees to purchase materials or services for use in executing the work.

Figure 9.1 shows some of the possible contractual and implied relationships involved in the construction of a modern facility. In his or her responsibility to the owner, the design professional has an indirect and implied relationship to the contractor, as well as to the various subcontractors, sub-subcontractors, suppliers, and manufacturers assigned by the contractor to portions of the work.

Because the relationships of parties in the construction process can be so complex, disputes are possible when any of the involved parties do not agree on how specific work or materials are to be furnished and in what sequence to be installed. Over the years, common solutions have been found for many problems, and certain language has been developed and accepted among most participants regularly involved in building construction. Much of this information, in written form, is commonly included in Contract Documents and the Conditions of the Contract.

The Conditions of the Contract are most often contained in a document separate from, but part of, the Contract for Construction. The Conditions of the Contract uses detailed descriptive language, supportive of, and incidental to, the *Agreement between Owner and Contractor*, recognizing the related work of others acting under separate agreements toward a common goal. The Conditions of the Contract are made a part of the Contract for Construction by reference or attachment. Figure 9.2 illustrates the relationship of the group of documents that are influenced by and dependent upon the Contract Conditions as modified by the Supplemental Conditions.

Advice of Legal Counsel

It should be noted that the architect or engineer who prepares the contract documents is licensed to practice architecture or engineering, but not law, unless of course that person is a member of the bar as well. *Owners, design professionals, and contractors alike should always retain competent legal counsel to review and give advice as to the form and language of the contract documents before agreements are consummated.* Design professionals must also exercise great care in preparing the contract

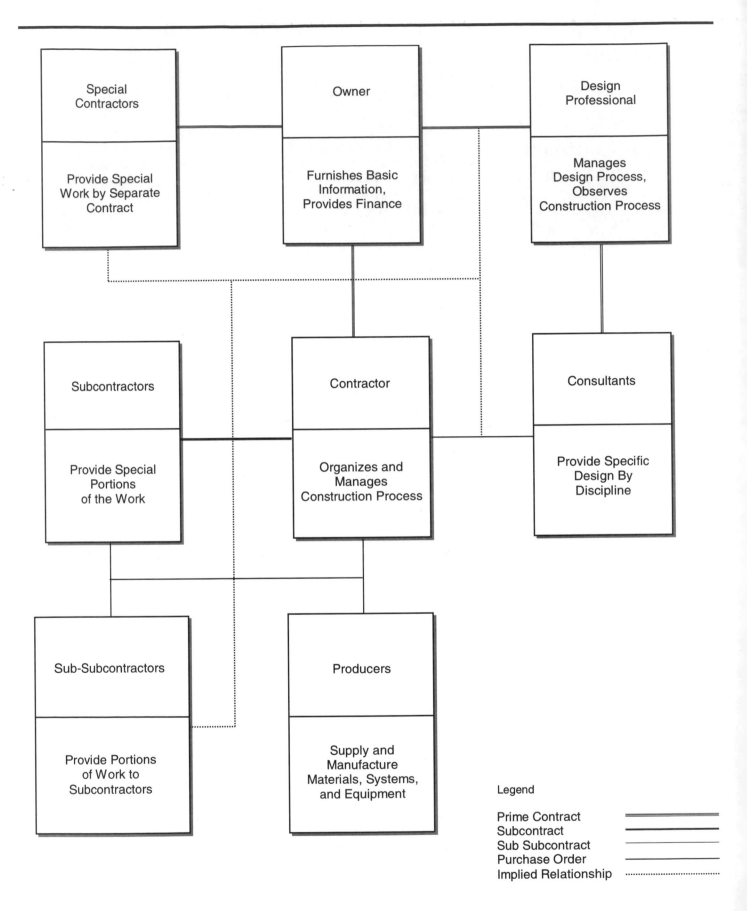

Figure 9.1 *Contractual and Implied Relationships*

documents, lest they inadvertently change a legal relationship or meaning. Changes should only be made following established legal guidelines and advice.

Standard documents, such as those available from the AIA and EJCDC, have all been prepared by design and construction professionals with careful coordination of language and content under experienced legal counsel. These documents have been generally accepted by the design professions, the construction industry, and the courts. *The Conditions of the Contract, or any other prepared documents which are either directly or indirectly related to all of the other published contract forms and contract documents, should never be modified except by creation of a supplementary document, which is written to make any necessary alterations in the language and intent of the Conditions of the Contract. In no case should an alteration or addenda be made to prepared documents without competent legal advice.*

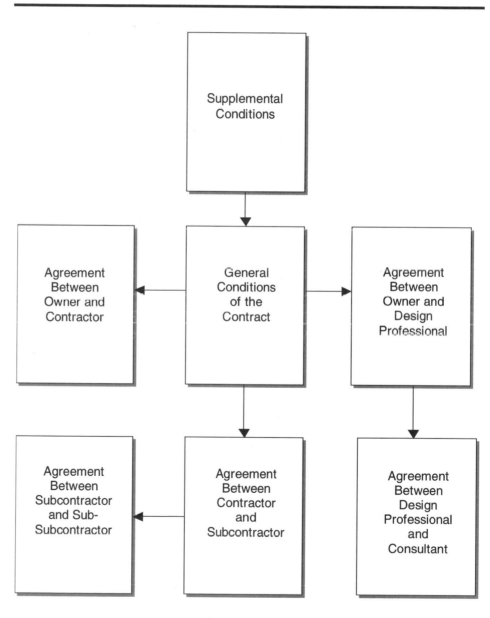

Figure 9.2 Contract Relationships

Writing Conditions of the Contract

The *Conditions of the Contract* (Conditions of the Contract and Supplemental Conditions of the Contract) can be thought of as the foundation supporting the contract documents.

The Agreement between Owner and Contractor, discussed in Chapter 8, generally establishes the following:

- The date on which the agreement was made.
- The parties to the contract.
- The name and location of the project.
- Other parties who may perform services during execution of the Work on behalf of the owner.
- The various components of the Contract Documents.
- Description of the Work.
- The date of commencement of the Work.
- The Contract Sum, or unit prices for components of work, or both.
- Conditions for partial, periodic payments.
- Conditions for final payment.
- Miscellaneous provisions.
- Conditions for termination or suspension of the Work.
- Detailed description of the Contract Documents.

The Conditions of the Contract, as a complementary document appended to the Agreement, may establish or elaborate on the following:

- Expanded provisions of the Agreement.
- Definitions of terms.
- Procedures by which the Work is accomplished.
- The rights of the parties to the contract.
- Methods by which misunderstandings and disputes may be remedied.
- The role, responsibilities, and rights of the owner.
- The role, responsibilities, and rights of the contractor.
- The role, responsibilities and rights of the design professional. Or…
- The role, responsibilities, and rights of those who, on behalf of the owner, provide administration of the Contract for Construction or accomplish other Work by separate contract.
- Procedures for making changes in the Work.
- Definition of time as it applies to completion of Work and mutual responsibilities of the parties to the contract.
- Processes related to payment for Work completed and completion of Work.
- Protection of the various parties by required insurance and bonds.
- Procedures for enforcing provisions of the various contract documents by uncovering and correction of Work.
- Provisions for terminating or suspending the Work.

The Supplemental Conditions of the Contract are written for the individual project to amend or supplement the standard or "master" form of Conditions of the Contract, thereby "tailoring" the contract to the peculiarities of the individual project. Supplemental Conditions of the Contract try to accomplish one or more of the following:

- State the legal address and other descriptions of each of the parties to the contract.

- Name authorized representatives of the parties to the contract.
- Describe additional rights and remedies of the parties to the contract in the event of an alleged breach of agreement by either party, or other respective representatives.
- Describe unusual or unique conditions related to payment or completion of the Work.
- Provide specific conditions of required insurance coverage by describing limits of liability to be provided to the owner and contractor.
- Describe anticipated conditions that would require completed work to be uncovered and corrected.
- Provide supplementary language to add any special or unique provisions.
- Describe procedures to be used if termination or suspension of the Work is required by either party or circumstance.

Supplements to Contract Conditions

Where standardized forms of Conditions of the Contract such as those produced by AIA and EJCDC or other public owners are used, certain modifications are often required to accommodate the unique situations of individual projects. Since the standard document is intended to correlate other contracts and legal relationships, it is best to leave that document intact. A separate document can then be written, supplemental to the Conditions of the Contract, which carefully denotes any appropriate changes, additions, or deletions. Such a custom document is referred to as the *Supplemental Conditions of the Contract*. This technique of "customizing" the primary document is useful in that the intended legal status of any and all parties to the contract for construction remains intact.

For example, if the provisions for insurance coverage are to be altered in the agreement between the owner and contractor, such changes should not be made on the actual Conditions of the Contract as these changes may not apply to the agreement between the contractor and subcontractor, or between the owner and separate contractor. Where the Conditions of the Contract simply describe the type and extent of insurance coverage to be provided, the Supplemental Conditions of the Contract may describe the limits of liability applicable to that agreement. The Supplemental Conditions of the Contract may also spell out any additional requirements related to local laws or the owner's needs without altering the Conditions of the Contract of some other agreement under the "umbrella" of the Conditions of the Contract.

Recently, standard contract forms such as AIA documents and EJCDC documents have become available in electronic format. These allow the user to make changes to the original text and may make supplements as separate documents unneccesary.

Figure 9.3 is a *Special Notice*, a suggested instruction placed at the beginning of the Supplemental Conditions of the Contract. This statement should clearly describe the document that it supplements as well as the intention of the supplementary document. It is helpful if the statement reinforces the fact that the document is not intended to change the general provisions of the document being modified.

For the sake of simplicity, the term "Conditions of the Contract" is intended to apply to any proprietary form of Conditions of the Contract that are generally available to the construction industry. The term "supplementary" or "supplementary statement" generally refers to information that should be contained in the document known as *Supplementary Conditions of the Contract*. The term *Design Professional* refers to the professional entity described in Chapter 1 as the "P" in the "OPC" relationship and may include any or all of the following individuals or firms:

- Architect.
- Architect/Engineer.
- Engineer.
- Professional Partnership.
- Professional Corporation, Limited Liability Company if duly licensed and otherwise qualified under the law, with the experience required to serve the owner in the professional capacity discussed in Chapter 3, "The Design Professional."

SPECIAL NOTICE

This document, called the *Supplementary General Conditions,* amends or supplements AIA document A201—*General Conditions to the Contract for Construction*—1987 Edition (often referred to as the *General Conditions.)* Where any Article of the General Conditions is supplemented by the Supplementary General Conditions, the provisions and intent of that Article of the General Conditions shall remain in effect and the supplemental provisions shall be considered as added thereto. Where any Article of the General Conditions is amended, voided, or superseded by a provision of the Supplementary General Conditions, those provisions pertain only to the Agreement Between Owner and Contractor. Provisions of the General Conditions that are not amended, voided, or superseded by a provision of the Supplementary General Conditions shall remain in effect.

Figure 9.3 Special Notice

General Provisions

The Conditions of the Contract first establish the "ground rules"—both language and intent—of the contract documents as a whole. This is accomplished by:

- A definition of the terms used in the various contract documents.

- A description of each of the contract documents.
- A description in detail of how the work is to be executed.
- The intent of the contract documents as a whole.
- A description of how the various contract documents are related.
- Any specific limitations imposed on interpretation of the documents.

The General Provisions portion of the Conditions of the Contract often establish other basic provisions, such as:

- Ownership and use of the contract documents.
- The meaning and intended use of capitals, italics, bold print, underlines, and other such graphic "highlights" in the text of documents.
- Statements of explanation regarding the intentional omission of common words with broad meanings such as "all" and "any," and articles, such as "the" and "an," for the sake of brevity.

Supplemental language to the general provisions may add:

- Definitions of terms applicable to the specific project.
- Unique objectives of the owner.
- Unusual language related to local ordinances or codes, and other terms frequently used that do not appear in the Conditions of the Contract document.
- Statements of unusual provisions that affect the execution, correlation, or intent of the documents.
- Statements used to reinforce a common understanding or interpretation of responsibilities of the parties to the contract that are unique to the particular project and that may differ from language contained in the "standard" document.
- New language intended to replace language contained in the "standard" document.

Modification Documents

The single most frequent cause of dispute in matters related to the Contract for Construction is misunderstandings about modifications to the Work. A key ingredient in avoiding such problems is proper documentation. While all parties are interested in saving time and avoiding delays, a convenient form of documentation can and should be used to attest to the mutual understanding and acceptance of the modification(s) by both parties to the Contract. The opportunity for disagreement can be avoided if such documents are signed by all parties before any work is altered or expense incurred. Any modification or change to the Contract should be made in writing and agreed to by the parties, and if appropriate, ratified by the design professional or the owner's designated project representative. The ratification by a third party provides an important witness to the document if litigation occurs in the future.

The three basic documents used to modify the contract are *Addenda, Change Orders*, and *Construction Change Directives*. Each of these is described in the following sections.

Addenda

Addenda are modifications to the Bidding Documents made prior to the award, or signing of the contract. Addenda, although issued during the bidding process, are in fact, modifications to the Construction Documents, and therefore become components of the Contract Documents. The Bid Form often requires that the bidder acknowledge receipt or awareness of any and all addenda issued prior to receipt of bids. Such acknowledgment assures the owner that the proposed modifications have been taken into account in determining the bidder's proposed contract price. Since the contract price reflects the modification made by addenda, it follows that the addenda must be part of the Contract for Construction.

Change Orders

Change Orders to the Contract for Construction, on the other hand, are modifications that are made after the contract has been executed and the Work begun. Change Orders, once accepted by signature of the parties and, if appropriate, ratified by the design professional, become part of the Contract Documents.

Construction Change Directive (CCD)

A recent addition to traditional modification documents is the *Construction Change Directive*. This modification instrument is designed to be initiated by the owner, without prior approval by the contractor, then ratified by the design professional or construction manager. Its purpose is to direct a proposed change in the Work without invalidating the Contract by stating a reasonable proposal for adjusting the Contract Sum or Contract Time, or both. The Construction Change Directive is discussed later in this chapter in the section entitled, "Changes in the Work."

It is generally understood in the construction industry that a Construction Change Directive, issued by the owner and ratified by the architect or construction manager, need not require prior acceptance by the contractor, provided "reasonable" compensation is derived by any of several methods which have been agreed as a condition of the contract. The CCD has become useful in avoiding substantial delays or other problems which otherwise may arise during construction when a change in the Work becomes necessary. As is often the case, a "reasonable" value must be negotiated for the proposed change. The contractor may require some time to prepare a proposed price for the additional work or contractor's proposed price for the change may appear unreasonably high; and negotiations must ensue if the change is rejected. In such cases the project may otherwise be delayed were there no ready means, or basis in the Conditions of the Contract by which the parties agree in advance to be able to postpone agreement on compensation, schedule, and other collateral issues which accompany the ordered change.

Importance of Definitions

The terms described in the Conditions of the Contract are commonly used and accepted throughout the construction industry. Their meanings are of primary importance to the legal relationships of the Contract for Construction. Definitions of primary terms are stated in the Conditions of the Contract in order to remove any doubt or misconception as to their exact meaning. Such primary terms may include:

- The Contract Documents.
- The Contract.
- The Work.
- The Project.
- The Drawings.
- The Specifications.
- The Project Manual.

The *Glossary of Terms* at the back of this book offers definitions of these and other terms as they are commonly used and understood in the construction industry.

Supplemental Definitions

The Supplemental Conditions of the Contract often include definitions of frequently used, common words that may have special and unique contractual meaning when used in the contract documents.

Examples of supplementary definitions:

- **Product:** basic and raw materials, assembled or sub-assembled components or parts, complete systems, manufactured items or equipment.
- **Provide:** to furnish and install, complete; in place and ready for intended operation and use.

Defining Execution, Correlation, and Intent

The Contract Documents, particularly the Contract itself, in order to be legally binding, should be signed by the owner and the contractor. The language of the Conditions of the Contract should express intent that identification of all of the Contract Documents, as well as interpretation of the intent of the documents, should be the responsibility of the design professional. It is good policy to make three sets of originals of all of the Contract Documents, signed by the parties to the contract. Each copy should be ratified in original signature by the design professional. Most lawyers will agree that by initialing each page of each document, there can be no doubt as to the content and extent of the Contract Documents on the official date that the Contract for Construction is executed by the parties. In the case of major projects, where the pages of the contract documents could number into the hundreds, this suggestion would be impractical. However, each of the signatories should hold in safe keeping one of the three sets, each of which can act as an official representation of the Contract in its entirety if the need should occur.

By his signature, the contractor indicates that he is familiar with all of the Contract Documents, and has understood all of the requirements for the Work. This includes familiarity with the site and all of its conditions prior to beginning the Work.

The Conditions of the Contract usually leave the contractor no defense in the form of ignorance of obvious site conditions. However, it would be unfair to the contractor if he were to be held responsible for unknown conditions that are discovered only after work begins. If the owner or the design professional anticipates the possible discovery of such unknown conditions, the Supplemental Conditions of the Contract should modify the language of the Conditions of the Contract by referring to a General Requirements (Division 1) section of the specifications (such as Section 01025, "Measurement and Payment,") which would provide for measurement and cost coverage for such conditions as excess rock found in excavations, or for extra length of foundation piles that may be recommended by the design professional's structural consultant.

By providing unit prices in anticipation of such events, work that may vary from the requirements of the Contract Documents can be paid for under prearranged terms. Under this arrangement, both the owner and the contractor are protected from any dispute that may arise over unspecified work discovered after the Contract for Construction is executed. Unit prices, when stated in both the Bid Form and the body of the Contract for Construction, establish pre-agreed compensation for labor and materials that may be applied to any contingent work not covered by the Contract Documents.

Conditions of the Contract should state the overall intent of the Contract Documents to be a *completed project*, which is the essence of the contract. The Conditions of the Contract should provide for the design professional or the construction manager to make a final inspection of the Work and to issue a *Certificate of Final Completion* which determines and provides documentation of such completion.

It is advisable that the Conditions of the Contract also state that the organization of the Specifications into Divisions, Sections, and Articles does not necessarily constitute or imply a division of the work that the contractor may assign to a subcontractor, nor should it establish the extent of work to be performed by any particular trade. A great many disputes have occurred because the contractor fails to fully describe the extent of work that he may expect of a subcontractor. Likewise, many disputes have occurred because the Contract Documents may seem to infer divisions of the Work. It is important that the Conditions of the Contract in concert with the General Requirements make it perfectly clear that the contractor is totally responsible for all of the Work and any subdivision of the Work. In the case of multiple-prime contracts (See Chapter 7, "Project Delivery," Multiple-Prime Contracts) the scope of work for each prime contractor should be thoroughly described in separate sections of the General Requirements (Division 1 of the Specifications).

In composing the Contract Documents, and particularly in dealing with the Conditions of the Contract, the design professional should always bear in mind that the language of the documents he or she prepares is directed to the relationship between owner and contractor. The design professional must not address notes or language to a traditional trade or subcontractor, nor arbitrarily set the boundaries of work done by particular sub-trades, either directly or indirectly. The coordinated language of the contract documents should leave no doubt that the contractor alone is the party responsible for establishing the limits of those parties to whom he may direct work by separate contract. If the design professional uses proper definitive language, then the organization of the Specifications or the Drawings cannot be used as a defense in a dispute which could cause delays and extra cost to the owner, contractor, or the design professional.

In all probability, there has never been a group of Contract Documents produced for a project that has not contained some errors, inconsistencies, and contradictions. *It is for this reason that the design professional should be the interpreter of the intent of the contract documents when such errors, inconsistencies, and contradictions are discovered.*

Despite the popular argument to the contrary among "knowledgeable" construction people, there simply is no "unwritten law" which states that information shown on drawings takes precedence over the requirements of the specifications, or vice versa. It can and should be said as a condition of the contract that the design professional is named to be the judge of which document should take precedence in the case of error or inconsistency in the documents.

Although it is clear that the contractor is not responsible for errors and omissions in the Contract Documents (which are created by the design professional), it should also be observed that the contractor may be liable for error if he fails to bring any discovered error or omission to the attention of the appropriate parties. The contractor should certainly be encouraged, if not required, by the Conditions of the Contract to immediately report any error or inconsistency in the Contract Documents to the design professional in writing. This procedure, if followed by responsible, ethical construction professionals, will save untold delays, cost, and loss of potential profits to all concerned in the OPC relationship.

Describing Contract Documents

It is important in the discussion of Conditions of the Contract that a differentiation be made between the following terms:

- Contract Documents.
- Construction Documents.
- Bidding Requirements.
- Bidding Documents.

Contract Documents are the "package" of documents that form the Contract for Construction. The Contract Documents usually include the following:

- The Agreement.
- Conditions of the Contract.
- Specifications.
- Drawings.
- Modifications to any of the contract documents.

Construction Documents are the collection of documents produced by the design professional describing or otherwise relating to the Work. Since, in the technical sense, Construction Documents are not Contract Documents until a contract is executed, the term *Construction Documents* is usually applied to the documents "package" prior to the time that a contract is executed between owner and contractor.

Bidding Requirements can be described as the owner's requirements or proposal for attracting a party or parties to bid for the Work. It often includes the following:

- Invitation to Bid, or the Advertisement for Bidders.
- Instructions to Bidders.
- Form of Proposal (Bid Form).
- Bid Requirements.

When the Bid Requirements are added to the collection of Construction Documents, the "package" is often referred to as the *Bid Documents*. The Bid Requirements serve a single purpose, and once the contract for construction has been awarded, usually are not included in the package called *Contract Documents*.

The bidding process results in proposals or bids from candidate constructors in the form specified by the Bid Requirements. Since the proposal shows a candidate's willingness to enter into a contract with the owner, and the basis of the proposal is the Instructions to Bidders, there is some validity to appending selected components of the Bid Requirements to the Contract Documents for informational or reference purposes. When this is done, the contractor's proposal, and sometimes the instructions to Bidders may be appended to the Contract for Construction as an "exhibit" for information and reference purposes.

Figure 9.4 illustrates how the various components of the Contract Documents are "packaged." Note that the Bid Requirements have been discarded from the Contract Documents "package." Figure 9.5 shows the relationship of the various Construction Documents "packages" and components for purposes of bidding or negotiating. It also shows which of these are intended to become Contract Documents upon execution of the Contract for Construction.

Establishing Procedures, Rights, and Remedies

Construction of a modern building is a complex undertaking. It requires much skill on the part of the contractor, combined with the talent and directives of the design professional, to achieve a product acceptable to the owner and suitable for his purposes. The Conditions of the Contract are intended not only to amplify the covenants of the Contract for Construction, but also to provide the means for establishing an orderly construction process, specifying the responsibilities of each party to the contract.

The Conditions of the Contract should also provide the means by which the parties to the contract can establish evidence of compliance with the requirements and intent of the contract. For instance, the Conditions of the Contract may establish conditions for payment to the contractor, including possible instructions for withholding payment depending on the contractor's performance. At the same time, the Conditions of the Contract may also provide protective remedies to protect the contractor if payment is not made by the owner.

Common law, discussed in Chapter 8, provides certain rights that protect the parties to the contract, regardless of the terms of the contract or its general and/or supplemental Conditions of the Contract. If, for instance, the contract were to contain a provision that proved to be unconscionable or unlawful, it could be successfully argued in a court of law that the provision was not enforceable. On the other hand, a contract that does not clearly state the extent of the parties' responsibilities may not be enforceable either. The Conditions of the Contract should establish clear and understandable language that accomplishes the following:

- Defines the owner.
- Describes the services the owner is to provide for the purpose of the project.
- Establishes the rights and remedies of the owner in case of default by the contractor under the agreement.
- Establishes the right of the owner to accomplish other Work by separate contract or other arrangement.

Owner

The owner is a prime party to the Contract for Construction. Since the owner is identified by name in the Contract for Construction, it is not necessary to add a supplemental statement with name identification in the Supplemental Conditions of the Contract. The term *Owner* can also mean the owner's representative if language to that effect is provided.

Owner's Obligations

The duties, obligations, information, and services the owner is obligated to perform or provide include the following:

- Information that is relevant and necessary for the contractor to evaluate, give notice of, or enforce any rights he may possess by law in establishing a lien against the owner's property in case the owner may be in default of the agreement.
- Reasonable evidence that financial arrangements have been made sufficient to fulfill the owner's obligations under the agreement.
- Property descriptions, surveys, and legal limitations of the site.
- Locations of utilities at the site.

The owner is usually required to have secured and otherwise paid for a number of items that are mandated by local authorities prior to construction, and which may include the following:

- Approvals of zoning authorities and any other requirements mandated by law.
- Building permits and fees.
- Easements on the surface of the property required for access, utilities, and the like.
- Assessments required by local ordinance.
- Any permits and approvals that may be required for the use or occupancy of permanent structures or for permanent changes in existing facilities, such as protected historical buildings.

The owner usually pays the reproduction cost for a specific number of sets of Contract Documents that the contractor may use for the construction process. The Supplemental Conditions of the Contract should state the following regarding reproductions of the Contract Documents:

- The number of sets of Contract Documents that the owner will provide at no cost to the contractor.
- A cost to the contractor for each additional set that he may wish to acquire.
- A requirement that the contractor account for and return all sets of Contract Documents upon completion of the Work, with the exception of the contractor's record set(s). Alternatively, the owner may provide the contractor with reproducible versions of the contract documents, in physical or digital form, from which the contractor can make all required copies.

Owner's Limitations

If there are any reasons to suspect that the owner's limitations may prevent him from being able to fulfill his obligations under the agreement, he is advised to include in the Supplemental Conditions statements that would avoid misleading either contractor or prospective bidders. It should be recognized that bidders attracted to the project through the Invitation or the Advertisement are apt to expend substantial sums of money in preparing a proposal in anticipation of being awarded the Contract for Construction. Supplemental language may be required if the owner's ability to execute payment depends, for any reason, on any of the following:

- Statutory approval before award of contract.
- A budget limitation that could be exceeded by the bid proposals.
- Conditions whereby additional financial arrangements or commitments must be made in the event that the contract price exceeds a certain limitation.

The owner's counsel may wish to add supplemental language to protect the owner from claims of nonperformance or damages if the owner decides not to award the contract after bids have been prepared and made public.

Owner's Right to Stop the Work

A basic provision of most forms of Conditions of the Contract gives the owner the right to stop the work and terminate the Contract for Construction if any of the following conditions occur:

- Persistent failure by the contractor to correct portions of the work that do not conform with the Contract Documents.
- Consistent failure by the contractor to perform the work in accordance with the Contract Documents.

It should be noted that the design professional, who is not a party to the Contract for Construction, does not have the direct right to stop the work. Depending upon the provisions of the Agreement between Owner and Design Professional, the design professional often has an obligation to reject work that does not conform to the intent of the Contract Documents. If and when the design professional should discover that the work does not conform to the requirements of the Contract Documents, he or she should make full disclosure of such findings and recommend that the work be corrected or re-performed. In turn, the owner, as a direct party to the Contract for Construction, must officially take action to stop the work, if that action should become necessary for any reason.

To stop the work it is reasonable that the owner first give reasonable notice in writing to the contractor stating that deficiencies exist that must be remedied in accordance with the Contract Documents. Such reasonable notice may be seven days, or no more than ten days. If the contractor, after receipt of such notice, fails to respond or to begin making the necessary corrections or, cannot, or will not, show due cause why such corrections are not being carried out, then the owner may issue a second similar notice. If at the end of the prescribed time, the contractor continues his default without providing evidence of due cause, the owner may correct such work *without prejudice* (i.e., surrendering any other right he may have under the law) to any other remedy he may possess.

Owner's Right to Carry out the Work

The Conditions of the Contract should define the owner's right to carry out the work, in case of the contractor's default. It should be understood that this remedy may not involve termination of the entire contract. Supplemental Conditions of the Contract should provide for assignment of subcontracts to the owner in the event of default or breach of contract by the contractor. Such contingent language should stipulate that in such cases, each subcontract agreement be assigned to the owner provided that:

- Assignment is effective only after termination of the Contract by the owner for cause pursuant to the provisions of the Contract Documents, and only for those subcontract agreements that the owner accepts by notifying the subcontractor in writing.
- Assignment is subject to the prior rights of the contractor's surety, if any, obliged under bond related to the Contract.

Retainage

Retainage is discussed in more detail under the section entitled *Changes to the Work* in this Chapter. In the case of default by the contractor, the Conditions of the Contract may provide that the owner may use any retained sums to correct the Work, and deduct such amount from the Contract Sum by Change Order or Directive, provided he or she has complied with the prescribed legal remedies or the provisions of the Conditions of the Contract.

The contractor is the second party to the Contract for Construction. Since the contractor, like the owner, is a party to the Contract for Construction, it is not necessary to add supplemental language to further identify this individual or entity in the Supplemental Conditions of the Contract. (The term *contractor* may also refer to the contractor's authorized representative.)

The Conditions of the Contract usually expand upon the responsibilities of the contractor and set forth duties and procedures common to, and necessary for, most construction projects. The Conditions of the Contract's description of the contractor's responsibilities covers the following topics.

- Review of and responsibility for provisions of the Contract Documents.
- Review of and responsibility for all reasonably visible conditions at the site.
- Supervision and construction procedures.
- Provision of all labor, materials, and payment for same.
- Provision of general warranty for the Work.
- Payment of all taxes.
- Securing and payment for all required permits, fees and notices.
- Application of allowances.
- Provision of a superintendent.
- Adherence to construction schedules.
- Maintenance of documents and samples at the site.
- Provision of shop drawings, product data, and samples.
- Use of the site.
- Cutting and patching of Work in place or existing work.
- Cleaning of the premises and disposal of refuse.
- Access to the Work by the owner, design professional, or others.
- Responsibility for conforming to requirements and costs related to royalties and patents.
- Indemnification of other parties from liability related to the Work.

Contractor's Review of Contract Documents and Field Conditions

The Conditions of the Contract normally charge the contractor with the responsibility to study the Contract Documents and become thoroughly acquainted with the conditions of the site and its surroundings. The contractor is further required to report any discrepancies to the design professional. The Conditions of the Contract may also state that the contractor is not liable for any damage resulting from errors and omissions on the part of the design professional. However, failure to comply with the requirement of reporting any discovered discrepancies may result in liability for the contractor.

The standard documents contain an intended spirit of trust and mutual cooperation among all parties in the OPC relationship. It is virtually impossible for the design professional to create a perfect, error-free set of Contract Documents, and it is the intent of the Conditions of the Contract that any errors be discovered at the earliest possible time. In most cases, early discovery and disclosure allow the design professional to remedy minor inconsistencies with little or no loss of time or expense on the part of any party in the OPC relationship. The design professional may wish to further protect him or herself from liability by adding language to the Supplementary Conditions of the Contract to the effect that:

> *Under no conditions shall the contractor attempt to accomplish any work without benefit of the Contract Documents as a guide to such accomplishment.*

Here again, we see the vital importance of the Contract Documents in defining, controlling, and illustrating the Work. The contractor incurs significant liability if he deviates from the Contract Documents, but the design professional also must bear significant liability in the responsibility to be thorough, competent, and diligent in creating the Contract Documents. (See *Professional Standard of Care* in Chapter 3, "The Design Professionals.")

Supervision and Construction Procedures

The Conditions of the Contract should clearly establish that the contractor is totally and solely responsible for the Work. This means that he determines and has total control over construction means, methods, techniques, sequences, and procedures used in accomplishing the Work. The contractor alone is responsible for coordinating all portions of the Work described in the Contract Documents, and is responsible for any acts or omissions by his agents or employees, subcontractors and their agents or employees, and anyone directly or indirectly in his employ for purposes of accomplishing the Work.

The contractor is solely responsible for determining that the work performed is in proper condition to receive subsequent work. If the Conditions of the Contract do not make such a statement, it is advisable that the Supplemental Conditions of the Contract contain a statement to the effect that:

> *Any subdivision of the drawings or specifications are not intended to establish a subdivision of the Work, such as the limits of a subcontractor's work or trade jurisdiction.*

It is not uncommon for disputes to arise as to which subcontractor or tradesman is responsible when the work of one trade depends upon, is adjacent to, or must be constructed in sequence with or on the work of another. The intent of the Conditions of the Contract must be extremely clear. *The contractor is responsible for coordination of all trades and subcontracts. He alone determines the means, methods, sequences, and procedures used in accomplishing the Work.*

The Conditions of the Contract should not relieve the contractor of liability for any alleged interference with the Work by the design professional who represents the owner, or by any agent or employee of the owner who may perform tests, inspections, or approvals in the owner's interest.

Labor and Materials

The issues surrounding construction labor and materials are wide-ranging and complex. Chapter 5, "Labor and Government" covers many current issues that influence labor in the construction industry. The Conditions of the Contract usually require the contractor to provide and pay for all labor, materials, equipment, tools, construction equipment and machinery, water, heat, utilities, transportation, and other facilities and services necessary for proper execution and completion of the Work. These items apply whether temporary or permanent and whether or not they are incorporated or will be incorporated into the Work.

It is advisable and appropriate that if not included in the Conditions of the Contract, the Supplemental Conditions of the Contract should stipulate that the contractor make disclosure, in writing, of materials and manufacturers he intends to use for the project. It is important that the design professional and the owner have the opportunity to approve the materials to be incorporated in the Work. (See the discussion later in this chapter in the section entitled "Submittals.")

As detailed in Chapter 10, "Project Definition," the design professional may specify materials and methods of construction in several different ways. A *Descriptive Specification* provides a detailed description of the required properties of a product, material, or piece of equipment, and the quality of workmanship required for its proper installation. A *Performance Specification* describes the required results or performance of a product, material, or piece of equipment, with criteria for verifying compliance. A *Proprietary Specification* describes a product, material, or piece of equipment by its trade name or by naming the manufacturer or manufacturers who may produce products acceptable to the owner and design professional. A *Reference Standard Specification* describes an accepted industry standard by which a product, material, or piece of equipment may be judged, compared, tested, or otherwise evaluated.

Public authorities and elected officials charged with the building of publicly-owned projects have long advocated that the Conditions of the Contract stipulate a requirement for competition in order to achieve the lowest possible price for Work at all levels of the bidding process. In many jurisdictions, competitive bidding is a legal requirement for public sector projects. In such cases, the contractor should be afforded wide discretion in the choice of materials in order to take maximum advantage of the competitive bidding process.

Many argue that the design professional who is charged with the responsibility of enforcing quality standards (by the language of the Conditions of the Contract), should be established as the appropriate judge of whether or not a product, material, or piece of equipment meets the requirement of the specifications. Some design professionals recognize that time spent during the bidding process offering advice and opinion of prospective bidders is generally profitable to all concerned. This investment of time and effort may save even more time during the construction period. Early research and consultation regarding material substitutions may result in a more competitive price without sacrificing quality in the building.

If a bidding constructor wishes to make a substitution, using a material that has not been named in the Specifications, or that may not clearly fit the performance criteria or exactly meet the descriptive criteria or reference standard, he should be required by the Supplemental Conditions of the Contract to apply to the design professional for approval of the product, material, or piece of equipment during the bidding process. The design professional may set certain guidelines and requirements in the Instructions to Bidders wherein he stipulates a "cut-off" date for this sort of application for approval. In this way, the design professional may fairly inform other bidders by Addendum of his approval of a substitute material for which a particular bidder has applied.

It is to the design professional's advantage that the Supplemental Conditions of the Contract contain language setting forth substitution criteria and requiring the applying bidder to provide sufficient information for a proper evaluation in light of the specifications and other contract documents. This statement should be worded such that the burden of proving compliance of a substitution is clearly the responsibility of the contractor.

Substitutions that are requested *after* the Contract for Construction has been executed tend to be met with suspicion by the owner and design professional, who may question the contractor's motive for making such a request. The owner is perfectly within his rights to refuse any substitution unless the contractor can offer a benefit to the owner from using the substituted item. On the other hand, such a request would not be unreasonable if a particular product were unavailable for some reason beyond the contractor's control.

The proper place to establish a procedure for requesting a substitution before receipt of bids is in the *Instructions to Bidders*. The proper location for substitution language with respect to the established contract is in the *General Requirements* of the specifications. (Division 1, Section 01600, "Material and Equipment.") Here the design professional may specify methods and procedures whereby the contractor may propose substitutions for the material, assembly, equipment, or system specified.

It should be noted that some federal bidding procedures do not permit bidders to obtain pre-bid approval of materials, assemblies, or equipment. For example, the Federal Acquisition Regulations (FAR) only permit substitutions to be considered after the bidding period, and then under statutory "or equal" rules.

Warranty
The term *Warranty* is defined as a pledge or guarantee made by the contractor to the owner, which promises that the Work shall be free of defects, that the materials and equipment will be new, and that the Work will conform to the requirements of the Contract Documents. The contractor's warranty includes remedy for any repair or

replacement. It excludes damage from owner's abuse, improper maintenance, and normal wear. These provisions are limited to a specific period of time.

If the Conditions of the Contract are not specific about the time limits of the warranty period, the Supplemental Conditions of the Contract should contain language providing a General Warranty for a specific time period, usually one year from the date of final acceptance of the building. Additional statements may require that the contractor furnish satisfactory evidence as to the type and quality of materials and equipment provided. It should be noted, however, that such warranty periods do not affect applicable statutes of limitation such as those that apply to claims related to breach of contract.

Taxes

The contractor is generally required to pay all sales and other consumer taxes, as well as use, franchise, and other similar taxes for the entire Work or portions of the Work for which he is responsible. Publicly-owned projects are often exempt from the payment of sales and other taxes. In the case of public projects, the Supplemental Conditions of the Contract should identify the procedure under the law by which the contractor should account for or be granted such tax exemptions on behalf of the owner.

Permits, Fees, and Notices

Most jurisdictions in the United States have lawfully constituted building codes and ordinances that regulate the construction of new or remodeled buildings. Each jurisdiction normally requires that public notice be given of the intent to build, and that the contractor apply for a permit or license for construction.

The contractor is responsible for conforming to all such requirements, and must pay all required fees and associated costs. The contractor is not responsible for determining whether the contract documents conform to applicable building codes and regulations, but he does have a duty under the typical provisions of the Conditions of the Contract to notify the design professional if he discovers any variance between the Contract Documents and the law. The Conditions of the Contract should include a statement to the effect that should the Contractor knowingly perform Work that is contrary to applicable laws and regulations, he assumes full responsibility for this action and shall bear any attributable costs and liability that result.

Allowances

Describing certain *Allowances* in the Contract Documents is a commonly used device whereby a material, assembly, appliance, or equipment can be included in the contract, even in cases where the item is not specifically identified or described in the specifications. This is done by specifying a dollar amount to be included in the Contract Price for the item, to be selected by the owner and purchased by the contractor at a future date. In this way, the owner is not restricted by a detailed specification description, but its cost is included or "allowed." To avoid misunderstandings regarding the details of incorporating the allowed item into the Work, the Conditions of the Contract may provide:

- A covenant that the owner shall act promptly in selecting the allowed item(s) so as not to delay the Work.

- A statement that the amount specified as the allowance shall cover only the cost of purchasing the item and the reasonable cost of delivery to the site of the Work.
- The Conditions of the Contract may also stipulate that the contractor anticipate the following costs associated with the allowance items to be included in the Contract Sum:
  - The cost of unloading the allowed item at the site.
  - The cost of assembly and installation of the item.
  - The contractor's cost of overhead and profit, if any.

The amount specified for the allowance may be a lump sum or a unit price. The lump sum applies to the price of an item, such as a special piece of equipment. However, in the case of items that are measured as yard goods, such as carpeting or wall or other surface covering, or material counted by the piece, such as masonry units, the unit price as applied to the measured amount or number of units required for installation is used. Once the actual price or total cost of the allowed item or items is known, a change order is written incorporating the allowed item into the Work, thereby producing an accounting of the actual price of the item, to be compared to the amount of the allowance. If the actual price is less than the allowance, the change order *deducts* the difference from the Contract Sum. If the actual price exceeds the allowance amount, the change order *adds* the difference to the Contract Sum.

In the case of unit price allowances, the Supplemental Conditions of the Contract may require the contractor to calculate and disclose to the owner, in writing, the amount of each allowed item in terms of measured goods and/or the number of units that shall be required for the Work. This must be done prior to purchase under the specified allowance. The contractor should be required to include in his calculation the amount sufficient to allow for waste during installation. In this way, the total amount of each allowance can be calculated on a unit price basis, and the contractor is responsible that a sufficient quantity of material will be purchased to complete the Work.

Since the provision of allowances is an *obligation* of the Contract as well as a *specification*, they should be stipulated in the Conditions of the Contract. However, the description of the various allowances used should be specified under a section of Division 1—General Requirements. It is appropriate and helpful to prospective bidders if the section where allowances are specified is referenced in the Supplemental Conditions of the Contract.

Superintendent

The term *Superintendent* is usually applied to a senior supervisor, who is an employee of the contractor and directs the Work at the job site. The competence and experience of this individual is crucial to the proper administration of the project. (See Chapter 12, "Contract Administration" for a discussion of the superintendent's role in the administration of the Contract for Construction). The following are among the many duties assigned to the superintendent by the contractor:

- Act as liaison between the design professional and the contractor.
- Handle communications and direct the activities of the contractor's employees, subcontractors, producers, and others performing the Work.

- Maintain all required records, samples, and pertinent data for periodic review at the job site.
- Call and conduct periodic meetings on the progress of the Work.

The design professional may wish to add statements in the Supplemental Conditions of the Contract stipulating certain minimum qualifications expected of the contractor's general superintendent and of the superintendents of major subcontractors as well. To assure that there is no interruption in these responsibilities from day-to-day, the design professional may wish to add a statement assuring that the superintendent would not be moved or substituted without good reason, and then only with the design professional's approval.

Contractor's Construction Schedules

Standard forms of Conditions of the Contract usually state that time is the *essence* in the contract. Since the number of calendar days required to complete the Work is usually an obligation of the contract, the contractor is required to forecast the conduct of the Work by providing a calendar of events leading to completion. Chapter 12, "Contract Administration" illustrates common forms of construction schedules used for this purpose. The Construction Schedule must be prepared by the contractor and must be kept up to date with changes, delays, and other events that affect the conduct of the Work. Consequently, it is more appropriate to cover the design, preparation, and implementation of the construction schedule in Division 1 of the Specifications rather than in the Supplemental Conditions of the Contract.

Documents and Samples at the Site

Chapter 13, "Project Completion" discusses in more detail the record keeping process that is usually required by the Conditions of the Contract. The Conditions of the Contract may identify a number of items, generally called *Submittals* that are used for communicating and documenting the owner's approval. The design professional is responsible to be the interpreter of submittals and the intent of the Contract Documents and administrator of the contract. Submittals may include:

- Shop Drawings.
- Samples of materials to be used in construction.
- Mock-ups of materials or equipment assemblies.
- Correspondence and record forms.
- Minutes of meetings.
- Accounting records.

The submittals made during the construction process become essential to the project record and serve a number of purposes, such as:

- Documentation of the quality of the work.
- Assurance of adherence and conformity to the requirements of the Contract Documents.
- Assurance of conformity to the intent of the design.
- Preparation of required Project Record Documents.
- General coordination, execution, and scheduling of the Work.

The Conditions of the Contract provide for submission of records not only to facilitate the administration for the contract, but to provide much valuable information that can be used by the owner during the life of the building. It is recommended that the design professional include a statement in the Supplemental Conditions of the Contract setting forth the responsibility for marking, filing, and otherwise preserving project record documents at the job site, and then, at Substantial Completion, turning these records over to the owner for his or her use. Additional submittal requirements and procedures should be specified in an appropriate section of the General Requirements (Division 1 of the Specifications).

Submittals

The Conditions of the Contract usually establish a procedure whereby the contractor is required to submit shop drawings, product data, and samples to the design professional for approval in keeping with his responsibility as interpreter of the intent of the Contract Documents and design of the project.

Shop Drawings are documentation prepared by or for the contractor in the form of drawings, diagrams, schedules, or other information illustrating the construction of some portion of the Work.

Product Data are illustrations, standard schedules, performance criteria, instructions, brochures, diagrams, and other information prepared by the manufacturer. Their purpose is to illustrate or otherwise describe a particular material or component to be used in the Work. Product data can also be defined as technical information supplied by the manufacturer of a product that is to be incorporated in the work. Product data may consist of specifications describing the character of various ingredients of the product, limitations and recommendations as to use and application, instructions for installation, and manufacturer's recommendations for maintenance of the material once installed. It is clearly very important that the contractor set aside this information, to be turned over to the owner upon completion of the project.

Samples are composed of the actual building materials to be used for a particular application. They are used to illustrate materials, equipment, or workmanship and establish standards by which the Work will be judged. Samples represent the actual physical properties of a material, including construction, texture, color, finish, and other attributes that the design professional will wish to approve before installation or application.

The design professional should include the more detailed information and requirements regarding shop drawings, product data, and samples in the specifications. An appropriate Division 1 section should include a definition of the types of submittals required for approval. It may also establish general requirements and procedures for submittals. The specification sections appropriate to a particular product may contain requirements unique to that product.

It is the intent of the Conditions of the Contract that shop drawings, product data, samples, and other submittal information not be considered Contract Documents, but rather a means of demonstrating the contractor's intent to conform to the requirements of the Contract Documents. Approval of submittal information does not relieve the contractor of the responsibility to fulfill the full intent of the Contract Documents. The contractor is also responsible for any error that may result from information contained in the submission. For example:

- A piece of cabinet millwork fabricated in the shop and delivered to the job does not fit the space intended for its installation.

Consequently, an error in dimensioning is discovered on the shop drawing approved by the design professional. Since the Conditions of the Contract assign full responsibility to the contractor for the coordination and execution of the Work, it is the contractor who must bear the cost of correcting the error, with no financial relief for any time that may have been lost as a result.

- A material fails to perform according to claims made by the manufacturer (as illustrated in submitted and approved product data). The contractor is responsible for all costs associated with repair and replacement. Any recourse that he may have in recovering compensation from the manufacturer is separate from his responsibility to the owner.
- The design professional rules that a certain material installed in the project varies in color and texture from the approved sample and, therefore, is not acceptable. The contractor must remove and replace the unacceptable material and bear all costs associated with the material replacement and loss of time.

Use of Site

The Conditions of the Contract usually state that the contractor must use the site lawfully and only for the purposes of performing the Work, and that he not unreasonably encumber the site with materials or equipment. Although most standard Conditions of the Contract defer to site usage in conformity with local law, ordinance, or permit procedures, the contractor is obliged in any case to conform to the restrictions established by the public jurisdiction over the site.

Depending on the conditions at the particular site, the Supplemental Conditions of the Contract may contain further instructions regarding traffic on adjacent public thoroughfares, or conformance with local code or tradition. Other statements may be necessary to protect against damage to existing improvements or the environment.

Cutting and Patching

The nature of building construction often requires that existing Work be cut to accommodate the access or installation of other Work, or for purposes of inspection or repair of a deficiency. The Conditions of the Contract should properly require that cutting and patching be avoided to the greatest extent possible. They should state that where a necessary alteration *must* be made to an existing condition, the result should be properly repaired or patched to match adjacent work and/or the original condition.

If the design professional anticipates any cutting or patching, he or she should provide a Division 1 section in the specifications that generally describes anticipated conditions and standards of workmanship to be expected in such events. It is also appropriate to elaborate on such general requirements in individual sections of the specifications related to particular products or components of the Work.

Cleaning Up

Building construction creates an accumulation of dust, waste material, debris, rubbish, and other refuse. The Conditions of the Contract properly assign responsibility to the contractor for keeping the premises and surrounding area free of such accumulations. The Conditions of the Contract may also provide that if the contractor fails in his duty according to the Contract Documents, the owner may clean up and charge the cost to the contractor. The design professional may in the Supplemental Conditions of the Contract further define the contractor's responsibility in this regard. Such language would:

- Define the term *clean.*
- Establish removal of waste and debris periodically.
- Establish standards and procedures for cleaning, relative to owner acceptance upon completion.
- Establish standards and procedures for the handling and disposal of hazardous waste and hazardous materials.

More specific requirements and procedures for clean-up should be specified in an appropriate Division 1 Section of the Specifications, and in individual sections as well.

Access to Work
The Conditions of the Contract generally provide that the design professional and the owner shall have access to the Work under all conditions and wherever it may be located.

Royalties and Patents
Building construction often requires the application of a process or use of certain material, equipment, or procedure that may be controlled or its use protected by a patent owned by a party not related to the contract. Since the contractor is entirely responsible for all labor, materials, equipment, tools, construction equipment and machinery, utilities, transportation, and other facilities and services necessary for the proper execution of the Work, it follows that he should be responsible for paying any royalties or fees that may be due to patent rights held by a third party, as well as to defend and hold the owner and the design professional harmless from any claims due to alleged infringement on patent rights claim for payment of royalty.

The Conditions of the Contract may modify the contractor's responsibility regarding patent infringement if a project or process is required by the Contract Documents. If a provision limiting the contractor's liability to patent infringement is included, all parties in the OPC relationship are advised to seek legal counsel regarding any modification statements to be made in the form of Supplemental Conditions of the Contract.

Indemnification
In the case of liability as applied by the law, it is possible that the owner and/or the design professional may be sued if a claim of injury or loss to a third party is filed relative to the construction of a modern building. The contractor's insurance may contain provisions to indemnify the owner and/or design professional in the case of negligence on the part of the contractor. The Conditions of the Contract quite properly include statements regarding indemnification of the owner and the design professional from liability in connection with the construction process. The matter of liability as it may be related to the owner, architect, and contractor is discussed in Chapter 6, "Legal Concerns and Insurance."

In some jurisdictions statutory restrictions or other conditions may be imposed on the contractor indemnifying the owner and, in some cases, the architect. These local restrictions may not agree with the language of the Conditions of the Contract. *The design professional and the owner should seek legal counsel regarding any supplementary information regarding indemnification of the parties in the OPC relationship.*

Administration of the Contract for Construction

Chapter 7, "Project Delivery" discusses a number of alternatives or choices that are available to the owner by which he may procure his project. The owner's choice of procurement methodology establishes how, and by whom, the contract for construction may be administered.

The Role of the Design Professional

Chapter 3, "The Design Professional" discusses the role of the design professional in what we refer to as the *OPC Relationship*. The Conditions of the Contract usually define the design professional (architect, engineer, or other professional practitioner employed by the owner) for purposes that include:

- Design of the project.
- Preparation of the Contract Documents.
- Specified Services During Construction.

Most jurisdictions, on behalf of the public welfare, require that the design professional be lawfully licensed to practice within a particular discipline.

Administration of the Contract for Construction

The party designated as the administrator of the contract acts as the owner's representative during construction, until final payment has been made. The design professional has traditionally fulfilled the role of contract administration, however, that role may be fulfilled by others, depending on the chosen procurement method as illustrated in Figure 9.4. In some cases, depending on the owner, the administrator of the contract may be someone other than the design professional. For example, many agencies of state and local government prefer to have one of the owner's employees perform the duties of administration. In some cases, the owner who wishes more exclusive representation at the project site may prefer to employ a construction manager who can either act alone or in concert with the duties of the design professional.

Contract administration services may be limited, or may continue at the owner's option until and during the time when the contractor makes any corrections that become necessary after completion of construction and final payment.

Administration of the Contract for Construction generally means that the designated administrator will advise and consult with the owner, and will have authority to act for the owner, within the limit of the Contract Documents or other written instructions to the extent allowed by common law.

Chapter 12, "Contract Administration" discusses the duties of the owner's representative and administration of the contract and presents in some detail the various factors that may come into play during the construction process. For our purpose in this discussion of the provision of the Conditions of the Contract, it is sufficient to list the general administrative duties of the contract administrator during construction. These duties include:

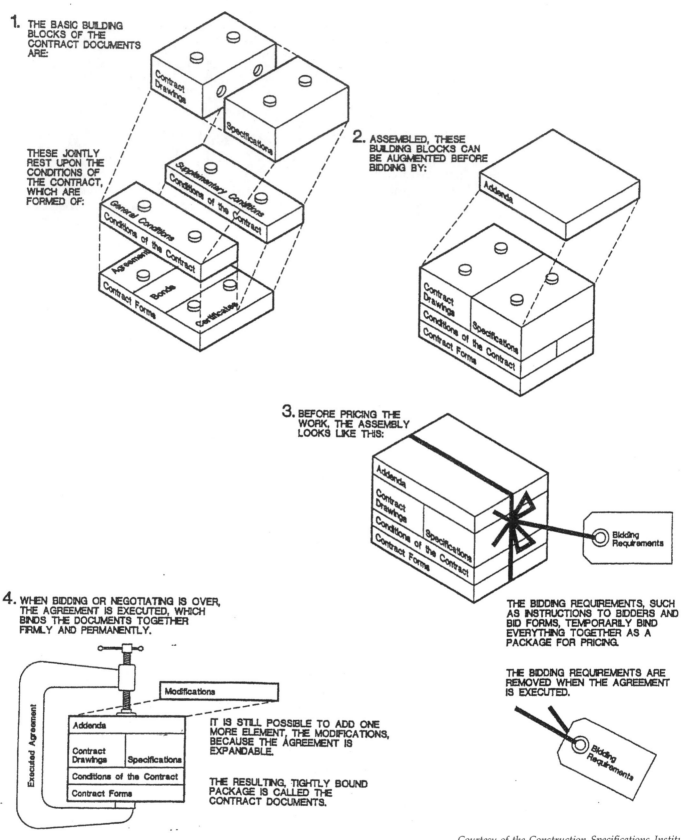

1. THE BASIC BUILDING BLOCKS OF THE CONTRACT DOCUMENTS ARE:

Contract Drawings

Specifications

THESE JOINTLY REST UPON THE CONDITIONS OF THE CONTRACT, WHICH ARE FORMED OF:

Supplementary Conditions of the Contract

General Conditions Conditions of the Contract

Agreement

Contract Forms

Bonds

Certificates

2. ASSEMBLED, THESE BUILDING BLOCKS CAN BE AUGMENTED BEFORE BIDDING BY:

Addenda

Contract Drawings

Specifications

Conditions of the Contract

Contract Forms

3. BEFORE PRICING THE WORK, THE ASSEMBLY LOOKS LIKE THIS:

Addenda

Contract Drawings

Specifications

Conditions of the Contract

Contract Forms

Bidding Requirements

THE BIDDING REQUIREMENTS, SUCH AS INSTRUCTIONS TO BIDDERS AND BID FORMS, TEMPORARILY BIND EVERYTHING TOGETHER AS A PACKAGE FOR PRICING.

THE BIDDING REQUIREMENTS ARE REMOVED WHEN THE AGREEMENT IS EXECUTED.

Bidding Requirements

4. WHEN BIDDING OR NEGOTIATING IS OVER, THE AGREEMENT IS EXECUTED, WHICH BINDS THE DOCUMENTS TOGETHER FIRMLY AND PERMANENTLY.

Modifications

Executed Agreement

Addenda

Contract Drawings

Specifications

Conditions of the Contract

Contract Forms

IT IS STILL POSSIBLE TO ADD ONE MORE ELEMENT, THE MODIFICATIONS, BECAUSE THE AGREEMENT IS EXPANDABLE.

THE RESULTING, TIGHTLY BOUND PACKAGE IS CALLED THE CONTRACT DOCUMENTS.

Courtesy of the Construction Specifications Institute

Figure 9.4 *The Agreement*

- Making periodic visits to the site at appropriate intervals to determine the progress and quality of the Work completed, and then report to the owner.
- Keeping the owner informed of the contractor's general conformity with the requirements of the Contract Documents.
- Endeavoring to protect the owner against defects in the work.
- Issuing or certifying Certificates of Payment, verifying periodic payments to the contractor under the provisions of the Contract Documents.

The Contract Documents assign the contractor total responsibility for construction, safety on the job, and conformity with the Contract Documents. In the traditional OPC relationship, as the owner's representative, the duties of the design professional do not include the following:

- Exhaustive or continuous on-site inspections to check the quantity or quality of the Work.
- Control over or charge of the Work.
- Responsibility for the means, methods, techniques, sequences, or procedures in connection with the Work.
- Responsibility for the contractor's failure to carry out the Work in accordance with the Contract Documents.
- Responsibility for acts or omissions of the contractor, subcontractors, or their agents or employees, or any persons performing portions of the Work.
- Responsibility for any acts or omissions of the building inspector or any representative or authority holding jurisdiction over the job site.
- Responsibility for safety precautions and programs.

In the event of termination of the employment of the designated contract administrator after the contract for construction has been executed, the contractor should be given the opportunity to concur with the selection of a replacement.

Communications in Contract Administration

The design professional is chosen by the owner for a number of reasons in addition to skill in building design. As author of the construction documents, and having a knowledge of building construction, the design professional is well qualified to serve as the owner's surrogate during construction. He is in a position to communicate directly with the contractor to the common advantage of both parties to the Contract for Construction. To avoid confusion, contradictions and miscommunications, the Conditions of the Contract should require that all communications between owner and contractor, or consultant and contractor, be conducted through the design professional or the party designated as contract administrator. For the same reasons, all communications between the design professional and subcontractors, sub-subcontractors, producers, and others should be through the contractor. It is clear that establishing a clear line of communication between these parties limits the opportunity for confusion and disagreement.

Establishing a Claim or Dispute

A claim is a demand by one of the parties to the contract. It seeks, as a matter of right, adjustment, or interpretation of contract terms, the payment of money, extension of time, or other relief with respect to the terms of the contract. The term *claim* may also include other disputes and matters in question between owner and contractor arising out of or relating to the contract. Claims are usually required to be made in writing. It is generally held, as a procedure by law and example, that the party making the claim should also bear the burden of proof of the allegation.

The Conditions of the Contract normally describe procedures for settling disputes by arbitration. There are however, some jurisdictions where a public entity is prohibited by law from submitting to arbitration. The design professional should seek competent legal advice in modifying or omitting this requirement.

The Conditions of the Contract usually provide that any and all claims and other notices be presented to the design professional prior to the date that final payment is due, for action or decision within a specified amount of time. The Conditions of the Contract may require action or interpretation by the design professional as a precedent to the parties' right to arbitration or litigation.

The design professional's initial actions in dealing with a claim may include:

- Requesting additional or specific supporting data from the claimant.
- Submitting a schedule to the parties indicating when the design professional expects to take action, and under what conditions he will do so.
- Rejecting the claim.
- Recommending that the other party accept the claim or make a suggested compromise.

A claim is a potential obstacle to both the progress of the Work and the relationship of the parties to the contract. The Conditions of the Contract must, therefore, be specific as to the provision of time limits for the filing and disposition of claims. Time limits should be imposed based on the latter of the following:

- Number of calendar days after the occurrence of the event that gives a rise to the claim, or
- Number of calendar days from the date on which the claimant first recognizes the condition giving rise to the claim.

In order to assure the parties to the contract that final payment indeed finalizes the covenants of the contract, the Conditions of the Contract should state that final payment constitutes a waiver of claims by either party, except those that arise from:

- Any unresolved liens, claims, security interests, or encumbrances arising out of the contract.
- Failure of the Work to comply with the requirements of the Contract Documents, or
- Terms of warranties or special guarantees required by the Contract Documents.

It is possible, if not common, that conditions affecting the Work, the Contract Sum, or the Contract Time will not be discovered until after the contract is executed and the Work begun. Such conditions often include:

- Subsurface or otherwise concealed physical conditions that differ materially from those indicated or anticipated by the Contract Documents, or
- Previously unknown and unusual physical conditions that differ materially from those ordinarily found to exist and generally recognized as inherent in construction activities of the character provided for in the Contract Documents.

The Conditions of the Contract should provide a procedure for submitting claims, and should state the time limits. If the owner, his advisors, or the design professional have any reason to believe that any unusual concealed condition may be discovered, the contract should provide unit prices for such conditions as may be anticipated. In addition, supplemental language should be included to establish the contractor's compensation for overhead and profit. This is especially valuable in resolving claims for unforeseen circumstances.

If the contractor wishes to submit claim(s) for additional compensation, he may do so, but only by following the general procedures established by the Conditions of the Contract for claims. Only in the case of an emergency that endangers life or property can prior notice be waived before commencing Work where a claim for additional compensation remains unresolved. Reasonable grounds for a claim for additional compensation may arise from, but are not limited to the following:

- Written interpretation, or failure to render timely interpretation by the design professional.
- An order to stop the Work by the owner, where the contractor is not at fault.
- Written order for a minor change in the Work by the design professional.
- Failure to make timely payment by the owner.
- Suspension of the Work by the owner.
- Other "reasonable" grounds.

The Conditions of the Contract generally stipulate that, if the contractor wishes to make claim for an increase in the Contract Time, he shall give written notice within a specific number of days (usually 10 to 20) from the event giving rise to the claim. The Conditions of the Contract should stipulate that the contractor making such a claim estimate any cost as well as probable effect of a delay on the progress of the Work.

The most common events giving rise to a claim for extension of Contract Time are:

- Inclement weather, exceeding any provision of the Supplemental Conditions of the Contract, that requires the contractor to take into account the recorded history of normal weather conditions when submitting his proposal of Contract Sum.
- Delays caused by untimely processing of submittals, claims, and other data remanded to the responsibility of the owner, owner's representative, or the design professional.
- Delays caused by other circumstances that are not the fault of the contractor.

A legitimate claim would arise if either party to the contract suffered injury or damage to person or property due to an act or omission on the part of the other party. The Conditions of the Contract should require either party to the contract to give written notice to the other of any emergency, accident, or event creating potential liability, injury, or damage to person or property. This is true regardless of whether or not such party is legally liable or otherwise responsible, and whether or not insurance may cover the event. The information provided should be in sufficient detail that it allows the other party to thoroughly investigate the matter.

Resolution of Claims and Disputes

The Conditions of the Contract, where there is a separate contract between owner and design professional, anticipate that the design professional shall be the first line of communication regarding alleged claims or disputes. Possible actions of the design professional have been discussed in the section entitled *Decisions of the Design Professional*. If a claim has been resolved by the procedures set forth in the General or Supplemental Conditions of the Contract, the design professional has made a preliminary response within the provision of the Conditions of the Contract, and a claim still has not been resolved, the party making the claim is usually required to:

- Submit additional data as may be requested by the design professional.
- Modify the original claim.
- Notify the design professional that the claim stands as originally presented.

Most forms of Conditions of the Contract provide that the design professional's decision regarding any and all claims is final, subject to mediation and in some instances, if allowed by the General or Supplemental Conditions of the Contract, a process of arbitration. However, action by the design professional may not be required preceding mediation or arbitration in one of the following cases:

- The position of design professional is vacant.
- The design professional has not received requested evidence.
- The claimant has not answered the design professional's preliminary finding within the specified number of days.

As a third party to the Contract for Construction, the contractor's surety has an interest in any modification to the Contract, and deserves to be notified of any pending, yet unresolved claim by either party. Even when not obligated to do so, it is generally recommended that the design professional communicate changes or pending claims to the contractor's surety.

Mediation

In mediation, a neutral third party called a mediator suggests solutions to the dispute. Neither side is required to accept the recommendations, however, sometimes, the parties to the dispute seek help from a neutral third party whom both sides respect and trust to act as mediator. If mediation fails, the two sides may enter into binding arbitration. It is increasingly common for the Conditions of the Contract to require the parties to attempt to resolve disputes by mediation before resorting to arbitration.

Arbitration

The process of arbitration is covered in detail, together with the settlement of disputes, in Chapter 6, "Legal Concerns and Insurance."

Any claim related to the Contract for Construction, or a breach of contract, can be, and often is, settled by arbitration. The Conditions of the Contract should name a mutually acceptable arbiter, such as the American Arbitration Association (AAA), to be used in event of an unresolved claim by either party. To this end, the AAA has developed a widely accepted procedure set forth in the association's "Construction Industry Arbitration Rules." Under the procedure administered by AAA, evidence and testimony is heard before an arbiter or panel of arbiters. A decision or award is reached by the arbiter(s). The award of the arbiter(s) may be entered into the court of law that has jurisdiction over the project. The General or Supplemental Conditions of the Contract may state certain exceptions to the right to demand arbitration. These exceptions may include:

- Claims related to aesthetic effect.
- Claims previously waived as a condition of final payment.

The language of the Conditions of the Contract is such that the owner and contractor agree to exhaust all reasonable efforts to resolve disputes before arbitration. These efforts include the submittal by the aggrieved party of a written claim with supporting evidence to the design professional, who is then obliged to render judgment in a reasonable time. If, having complied with the procedures set forth in the Conditions of the Contract, the claimant is not satisfied by the final decision of the design professional, and if mediation is required, but has not been successful, a written demand for arbitration may then be filed with all parties to the Contract for Construction, the design professional, and the arbitration authority named in the Contract or Conditions of the Contract. The Conditions of the Contract should state a time limit for filing a demand for arbitration. A limit of 30 days from the date that the final decision is rendered by the design professional is not unreasonable.

The Conditions of the Contract should provide that the parties to the contract agree to continue performance under the contract even though arbitration may have been demanded or may be in progress. In this way, the demand for arbitration offers no defense or relief to either party for failure to continue to perform according to the terms of the contract and the Contract Documents.

Consolidation is a legal term that describes a procedure wherein two or more claims by different individuals against a common defendant may be consolidated, for the mutual advantage of the claimants. *Joinder* describes a procedure wherein the claimant may name additional defendants in his claim and request for relief. The Conditions of the Contract may limit unreasonable consolidation or joinder in the process of resolving potential claims and disputes.

Subcontractors

A *subcontractor* is a person or entity having a direct contract with the contractor to perform a portion or portions of the Work. The term *subcontractor* should not be confused with the term *contractor*. (This latter term may be applied to other contractors employed directly by the owner.) The term subcontractor refers to a person or entity who has a direct or indirect contract with a contractor to perform a portion or portions of the Work.

The subcontractor is governed only indirectly by the Contract for Construction. The contractor is solely responsible for the selection of the subcontractor, and the quality and timeliness of the subcontractor's work. The contractor also determines the compensation for, scheduling of, and limits of the subcontractor's work product. However, since a very high percentage of the Work may be constructed by subcontractors and sub-subcontractors, the Conditions of the Contract are obliged to define and identify the subcontractor, and set guidelines and approval mechanisms for the owner's protection.

The Conditions of the Contract may also provide for the exclusion of a proposed subcontractor to whom the owner or design professional may object. The Conditions of the Contract may also prohibit the replacement of an established subcontractor without the approval of the design professional. They may further require the agreement between contractor and subcontractor, as well as the agreement between subcontractor and sub-subcontractor, be written in such manner as to bind the subcontractor to the intent and terms of the contract documents including the Conditions of the Contract.

It has become accepted practice in most U.S. jurisdictions to require that electricians, plumbers, and heating, ventilating and air conditioning mechanics be qualified by licensing. Licensing at the journeyman level usually requires that the license holder have certain educational qualifications as well as a specific number of years of experience or apprenticeship served under a principal holding a Master's License. They must also have passed the Journeyman Examination. Life journeymen, holders of a Master's License, must have attained a certain level of education. In addition, they must also have served a specific number of years as journeyman, and have passed the Master's Examination. These prerequisites, like the professional requirements demanded of the design professional, are established to protect the public health and welfare.

In certain cases, a supplemental statement may require subcontractors and sub-subcontractors to hold a Master's license issued by the municipality (or in some jurisdictions, the state) where the Work is to be accomplished. This provision further ensures that the contractor will have selected qualified subcontractors, which benefits the owner and protects the public welfare.

Construction by Owner or Separate Contractor

The Conditions of the Contract may establish the owner's right to accomplish separate work, or to contract work by separate contractors. This provision allows the owner to accomplish work outside of the Contract for Construction. Such provisions generally require that the owner be responsible for coordination of the separate work, and pledges the contractor to be cooperative.

The Conditions of the Contract generally address the issue of mutual responsibility, and set forth procedural requirements intended to establish harmony among disassociated contractors. It is important that the provision for separate contracts also provide for *reimbursement*, one separate contractor to the other, for any damage to the other's work. In the event of dispute, separate contractors are not likely to be cooperative with each other for any damage to the other's work. In anticipating such events, the stipulations in the Conditions of the Contract may further provide the owner's right to accomplish any necessary clean-up or other adjustment and charge either or both contractors for this expense.

If separate contracts are anticipated, the Supplemental Conditions of the Contract should recognize and name such contracts. The General Requirements (Division 1—Section 01010—Summary of the Work), should further identify the limits of each contract, and the procedures required by each separate contract, with statements properly coordinating the work of each contract.

Making Changes in the Work

The Conditions of the Contract should anticipate the likelihood of adjustments to the Contract after it has been agreed and signed. Such changes in the Work may be desirable or necessary for a variety of reasons. For example: unforeseen field conditions may appear that interfere with the Work as designed, or the owner may wish to alter the Work in some way. Or, a conflict in the Contract Documents may cause a change. The Conditions of the Contract should allow modifications to be made to the contract without invalidating the Contract, by the use of either a *Change Order* or, in some instances, an instrument called a *Change Directive*.

Change Order

A *Change Order* is a written instrument, usually prepared by the design professional, signed by the owner and contractor, and ratified by the signature of the design professional, which states the agreement of the parties to all of the following:

- A change in the Work.
- An adjustment in the Contract Sum, if any.
- An adjustment in the Contract Time, if any.

Construction Change Directive

A *Construction Change Directive* is a written order, initiated by the owner and written and ratified by the design professional. It is used in the absence of total agreement by the contractor, to direct a change in the Work.

The Construction Change Directive is a device generally used to accomplish a directive of the owner, in the absence of a properly executed Change Order. Its purpose is to avoid any claim for delay in the progress of the Work. A Construction Change Directive initiated by the owner should be used with care so as not to cause a dispute involving costly remedies by adjudication or arbitration. A Construction Change Directive should be considered when the following conditions exist.

- Advice of legal counsel has been obtained.
- The Conditions of the Contract or Supplemental Conditions of the Contract clearly define a Construction Change Directive and establish procedures for the issuance of such an instrument in lieu of a Change Order.

If the Construction Change Directive provides for an adjustment in the Contract Sum, the adjustment should be based on one of the following methods:

- A fair and equitable sum, clearly itemized and supported by sufficient substantiating data to permit thorough evaluation.
- Mutual acceptance by the parties to the Contract of a certain sum, such agreement being supported by written acceptance of

the contractor, whereupon the Construction Change Directive becomes an agreed-upon Change Order.

- A sum based on unit prices that were stated in the Contract Documents forming the original Contract, *or* an Allowance in the Contract Documents forming the original Contract.

Provided that the Contract Documents so allow or stipulate, the contractor, upon receipt of a Construction Change Directive, must proceed with the change in the Work. This signed document provides reasonable assurance that a fair and equitable adjustment in Contract Sum or Contract Time, or both, shall be made in time. To further assure that a reasonable and equitable settlement is made, the Conditions of the Contract or Supplemental Conditions of the Contract should require that the contractor respond to the receipt of the Construction Change Directive by stating in writing either his agreement or disagreement with the proposed adjustment in Contract Sum or Contract Time.

In anticipation that the contractor may not respond to the Construction Change Directive promptly, the Conditions of the Contract or Supplemental Conditions of the Contract should allow the design professional to determine adjustments. Such adjustments should be determined on the basis of reasonable expenditures and savings related to the change, and attributable to those performing the Work (including in the case of an increase in the Contract Sum, a reasonable allowance for overhead and profit). On the other hand, the Conditions of the Contract or Supplemental Conditions of the Contract should require the contractor to document on forms prescribed by the design professional an itemized accounting of expenditures related to any changes, together with appropriate supporting data. For these purposes, the supporting data may include the following:

- Cost of labor, including social security benefits, retirement or disability benefits, unemployment insurance premiums or benefits, Worker's Compensation premiums, and any fringe benefits that may be required by agreement, law, or custom.
- Cost of materials, supplies and equipment, including the cost of transportation, whether incorporated or consumed.
- Cost of use or rental of machinery and equipment, exclusive of hand tools, whether owned by the contractor or others.
- Cost of additional premiums for bonds, insurance, permit fees, sales or use tax, and any other expense related to the change in the Work.
- Additional cost of supervision and field office personnel directly attributable to the change.

Concluding Construction Change Directives

Pending resolution and final agreement to provisions established by Construction Change Directives, the Conditions of the Contract may further state the following:

- Undisputed amounts may be applied to current Applications for Payment.
- Credits made for deleting Work which results in a decrease in the Contract Sum shall be actual net cost as confirmed by the design professional.

- When both additions and deletions affect the same item of work, the allowance for Overhead and Profit shall apply to the *net increase* if any, with respect to the change.
- When owner and contractor do not agree with any adjustment in the contract, or the method of determining such adjustment, the method shall be referred to the design professional for determination.
- When owner and contractor come to an agreement on all provisions of a Construction Change Directive, such agreement shall become effective immediately and an appropriate change order shall be issued.

Contractor's Overhead and Profit for Changed Work

Other than contracts that compensate the contractor by an established fee in addition to the cost of the Work, the Contract Sum (whether it is a lump sum or a sum calculated by applying unit prices to a volume of Work) is generally understood to include the contractor's overhead cost and profit (OH&P). In addition to his ability to accurately anticipate the total cost of the Work, the contractor's "edge" in the competition for award of contract is often his allowance for OH&P, an amount that is not generally disclosed. However, where changes in the work are involved, the amount to be applied for the contractor's OH&P can become the subject of controversy and dispute. This is especially true when Construction Change Directives are used. In order to avoid dispute over just compensation "after the fact" (as is most probably the case in the use of the Constructive Change Directive), it is wise to state in the Supplemental Conditions of the Contract certain amounts to be applied for compensation for OH&P to both Change Orders and Construction change Directives. An example of such supplemental language is illustrated in Figure 9.5.

When the type of language as illustrated in Figure 9.5 is incorporated into the bid documents, the formula for calculation of any OH&P is established as a condition of the contract. By his signature to the Contract for Construction, the owner accepts the formula in advance for any change in the Work by either Change Order or Construction Change Directive.

Defining Time & Establishing "Milestones"

Time is defined as the calendar period required for completion of the Work, including authorized adjustments by Change Order or Construction Change Directive. The terms, *Substantial Completion* and *Final Completion* as generally used in the Contract Documents require some explanation. Substantial Completion is usually defined as the stage in the progress of the Work when the Work or a designated portion thereof is sufficiently complete (in accordance with the Contract Documents) that the owner can occupy or utilize the Work for the purpose for which it was intended. Final Completion is usually defined as the stage of the Work (as certified by the design professional) whereby all construction is declared to be fully performed in accordance with the Contract Documents. The terms of the Contract for Construction regarding final payment to the contractor hinge on the mutual understanding of these terms.

Progress and Completion

The Conditions of the Contract usually state or imply that *time* is the essence of the Contract. The legal implications of time have a direct

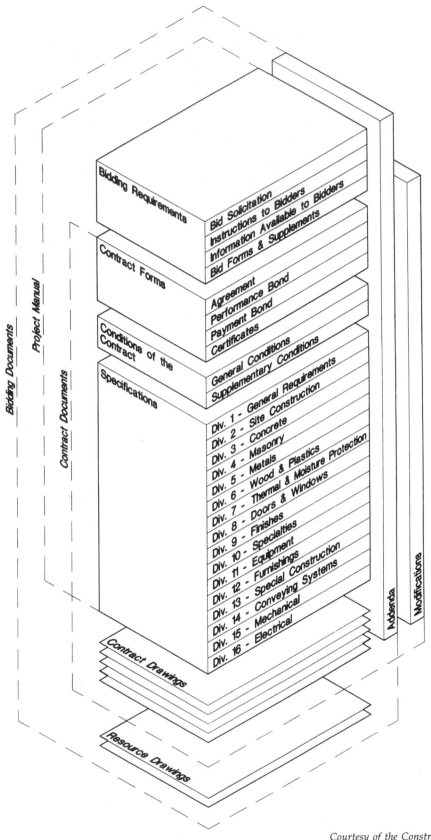

Bidding Requirements
- Bid Solicitation
- Instructions to Bidders
- Information Available to Bidders
- Bid Forms & Supplements

Contract Forms
- Agreement
- Performance Bond
- Payment Bond
- Certificates

Conditions of the Contract
- General Conditions
- Supplementary Conditions

Specifications
- Div. 1 - General Requirements
- Div. 2 - Site Construction
- Div. 3 - Concrete
- Div. 4 - Masonry
- Div. 5 - Metals
- Div. 6 - Wood & Plastics
- Div. 7 - Thermal & Moisture Protection
- Div. 8 - Doors & Windows
- Div. 9 - Finishes
- Div. 10 - Specialties
- Div. 11 - Equipment
- Div. 12 - Furnishings
- Div. 13 - Special Construction
- Div. 14 - Conveying Systems
- Div. 15 - Mechanical
- Div. 16 - Electrical

Contract Drawings

Resource Drawings

Bidding Documents

Project Manual

Contract Documents

Addenda

Modifications

Courtesy of the Construction Specifications Institute

Figure 9.5 Construction Documents

bearing on the responsibilities of the parties to the Contract for Construction, whether or not a completion date is stated in the Contract.

From the owner's standpoint, occupancy and use of the building is the ultimate objective. Any delay beyond either an agreed time of completion or what may be mutually considered to be a reasonable time for completion has definite economic implications for the owner. The contractor also benefits from timely completion, since he accumulates considerable cost for each day that is required to complete the project. Any unanticipated delay in completing the project diminishes the amount of profit he may earn. It is generally held that real damage may occur to either party to the Contract for Construction should the other party fail in some way to fulfill the covenants of the agreement. The contractor's failure to complete in a timely manner may result in a legitimate claim for compensation by the owner.

The owner's failure to compensate the contractor in a timely manner, or the design professional's failure to carry out his responsibilities of documentation and approval in a timely manner may result in a claim for additional compensation by the contractor.

Other considerations concerning time as it relates to the Contract for Construction are addressed in Chapter 8, "The Construction Contract." Please refer to the sections entitled *Bonus Provisions* and *Liquidated Damages*.

It is appropriate for the owner to establish the date for commencement of the Work by issuing a document or letter to the contractor generally referred to as an *Order (or Notice) to Proceed* on a given date. There may be significant legal implications, if not other consequences, regarding work begun prematurely on the site before the official order to proceed is issued. If, for instance, work has begun before the required instruments of insurance are in effect, the contractor and the owner may be exposed to substantial liability. The insurance company could and probably would refuse any coverage where a preexistent condition of liability may exist. In another instance where the owner depends upon mortgage financing to pay for the work, the lender depends upon a clear first lien right on the property as collateral for the loan he will make. (See Chapter 2, "The Owner," *Private Sector Finance*). Under the precedence of law in most states, were the contractor to begin the Work prior to the date of the lender's first lien, the contractor, not the lender, would have prior first lien rights.

Delays and Extensions of Time

Because time required for the construction process has a great impact on the fortunes of both owner and contractor, the matter of agreement on time of completion is of unusual importance. The contractor is normally granted extra time in the completion of the contract when the work has encountered delays that are clearly beyond his control. These "legitimate" delays due to situations such as inclement weather in the early months of construction or labor and transportation strikes (that would delay both labor and material reaching the job site) may be approved.

The design professional, in the best interest of the client, may wish to add certain language in the Supplemental Conditions of the Contract that would expand and describe more specifically the manner in which the contractor can receive credit for delays in the work. For example: the following is a supplemental statement that may be included in the Supplementary Conditions of the Contract. Its purpose is to direct the contractor's marshalling of materials on and to the job site:

> The Contractor shall have all materials delivered to the job site in such quantities as are required for the uninterrupted progress of the Work and the least obstruction of the premises and the adjoining property. No extension of Time will be allowed for failure of the Contractor to order the material in time or in sufficient quantities.

Some owners prefer to stipulate a number of calendar days for completion of a project as a condition of the contract. Others prefer to have bidders do this on the bid form. It is often difficult to enforce this requirement if the contractor is delayed by inclement weather. It may be more reasonable to allow the bidders to stipulate the number of days required for completion for several reasons. When the time requirement is included in the bid offer, the owner has the advantage of selecting a contractor on the basis of time required as well as by contract price. A prudent design professional may see the advantage of publishing in the Contract Documents (by way of the Supplemental Conditions of the Contract), a schedule of historical weather information. This data gives bidders some idea of how many days, during certain months of the year, that the site of the project has been subject to the sort of inclement weather that would prohibit work continuing in similar circumstances. Having alerted bidders to these facts, the owner may be less forgiving regarding approval of weather delays.

Payments and Completion

The term *Contract Sum* is defined as an amount of money which is the total consideration for the Work. Under certain federal and state wage guidelines, there is a legal requirement that employers pay a premium rate per hour for time of non-exempt workers beyond a minimum of 40 hours per week. (See Chapter 5, "Labor and Government," *Labor Legislation*). In order to avoid any indirect liability for overtime wages on the job site, the owner may be counseled or require a statement in the Supplemental Conditions of the Contract as follows:

> The Contractor should anticipate any overtime cost as a result of the Work and shall be responsible for payment of any overtime rates that may be required during the course of the work and should include all such cost in the Contract Sum.

Furthermore, the Conditions of the Contract should provide that the contractor shall hold the Owner harmless from any claims that may arise related to labor matters resulting from the Work.

Schedule of Values

It is common for the Conditions of the Contract to require the contractor to prepare a *Schedule of Values*. A Schedule of Values is a definitive breakdown of the Work into its most basic components, with an approximate value assigned to each component, the total of which equals the Contract Sum. This document, unless objected to by the design professional, becomes the basis for the contractor's payment throughout the project. Provided that the language of the Conditions of the Contract clearly defines and describes the application of the Schedule of Values, there may be no need for supplemental language regarding the Schedule of Values.

Application for Payment

The *Application for Payment* is a formal, written request for partial payment of a portion of the Contract Sum. It contains an accounting of the following:

- The Schedule of Values with allocations of cost per item as approved by the design professional or the owner's contract administrator.
- A schedule of modification to the contract by approved change order. Each change order should be itemized. The amount that results in a net change to the Contract Sum should be indicated.
- A schedule by percentage of Work Completed for each line item of the Schedule of Values, with corresponding amounts for completed Work through the date of the *current* Application.
- A schedule, by percentage of work, completed for each line item of the Schedule of Values, with corresponding amounts for completed work through the date of *previous* Applications.
- A schedule by percentage of work that remains to be completed for each line item of the Schedule of Values, with corresponding amounts for uncompleted work through the date of the current Application.

From this information, the current amount due the contractor can be derived. Using the appropriate formula, retainage, if any, can also be calculated.

Certificate for Payment

A *Certificate for Payment* is a statement, addressed to the owner, and usually written by the design professional or the owner's contract administrator. It evaluates the extent of work completed by the contractor and verifies the amount of consideration due the contractor. The certificate for Payment is issued in response to the contractor's application for payment.

Under the usual procedure, the contractor prepares the Application and submits it to the design professional for approval. The design professional reviews the Application, applies his observations, reviews his records, and then issues a Certificate for Payment certifying an amount that he believes to be appropriate, in proportion to work completed less previous payments. The Application and Certificate for Payment is transmitted to the owner, who then has a specified number of days in which to make payment to the contractor.

The Owners and those who prepare the Certificate for Payment should understand certain implications of liability that are implicit in the process of approving the Schedule of Values and issuing the Certificate for Payment. The design professional or owner's designated contract administrator is expected to be knowledgeable of the cost of construction, and prepared to object to any line item in the contractor's proposed Schedule of Values or application for payment that he or she feels exceeds the current cost of any component in the project. If the contractor defaults and a performance bond is in effect, the bonding company becomes responsible for completion of the Work. In this case, the party preparing the Certificate for Payment may be held liable for any overpayment made to the contractor prior to the date of the default. If it could be shown that the owner had overpaid the contractor as a result of oversight or error in the

Certificate for Payment, the bonding company would have the right to refuse to give the owner credit for the overage. The owner, in turn, could claim that the design professional or other contracted designee had certified the applications for payment, approved the schedule of values and, therefore, must be responsible for the deficit.

The owner may wish to have a definitive statement of the contractor's anticipated monthly payment requests in order to marshal his own cash reserves. This requirement, if not stated in the Conditions of the Contract may be stated in the Supplemental Conditions of the Contract. The following is an example of such a supplemental statement.

> *Prior to the issuance of the Notice to Proceed order by the owner, and in accordance with the requirement for submission of a Schedule of Values, the Contractor shall prepare an estimated Progress Schedule, graphically indicating the probable sequence and percentage of construction that may be expected by the end of each successive month. The Progress Schedule should identify the "milestones" for each state of the Work, indicating the approximate amounts the owner may anticipate on monthly applications for payment up to the point of Substantial Completion.*

Retainage

The Contract for Construction normally allows the owner to withhold an agreed or specified percentage of the contractor's earnings from each payment. The retained sum is usually withheld for the purpose of ensuring faithful performance until the Work reaches the point of substantial completion. A generally accepted retainage amount is 10% of the amounts earned.

Some states have enacted legislation, relative to public work, that governs the percentage of the Contract Sum that may be withheld, without compensation, from a contractor's payment. Many such laws stipulate that the owner may retain up to 10% of the contractor's earnings, but only until the Work reaches the point of 50% completion. Then, the amount retained may be lowered to 5% for subsequent payments. On occasion, the design professional or owner's representative, the owner's financial or legal advisors, or the bonding company may have reason, because of some perceived weakness in the contractor's ability to perform, to insist that the retainage not be diminished at mid-completion, but remain at the same 10% for each payment. In such cases, the intent of the law may, on advice of counsel, be fulfilled, so long as the amounts retained earn interest that will be credited to the contractor once the Work is complete. Where the conditions of payment and retainage may vary from the norm, or from the provisions of law, the Contract Documents must clearly state such conditions and confirm that bidders understand and accept such conditions when proposing the Contract Sum.

Since most proprietary forms of Conditions of the Contract establish procedures for payment and retainage that follow the norm, additional language should be included in the Supplemental Conditions of the Contract to more closely define any specific procedures by which payments are to be made. These supplemental statements further define the formula by which retainage, higher than those considered normal, may be held. In composing such language, the design professional is advised to rely on the owner's legal counsel in determining the amounts and/or percentages to be applied to such retainage and "custom" conditions of payment that can, within the law, be stipulated.

A common solution that is generally regarded as being fair to both owner and contractor is a mutual agreement between the parties whereby retained funds are to be placed in escrow via an interest-bearing account, in the name of both owner and contractor. Under this arrangement, the occurred interest, subject to any applicable usury laws, may be considered fair compensation to the contractor for the retainage held over the construction period. At the same time, the money held in the joint account may be welcome relief to the owner or the bonding company in the event the contractor defaults by failing to complete the Work. If, however, all goes well and the work is completed according to the Contract Documents, the total retainage and accrued interest, less amounts needed to complete the punch list, would be paid to the contractor upon the design professional's certification of Substantial Completion.

Decisions to Withhold Certification

When the design professional (or other designated contract administrator) bears the responsibility to certify payment, his or her administrative duty throughout the construction process comes into focus. The entity preparing the Certificate for Payment, in order to protect the owner, may refuse to certify all or part of any current Application for Payment for reasons that include:

- Defective Work not remedied.
- Claims by third parties, or evidence that such claims may be filed.
- Failure of the contractor to make proper payments to subcontractors or for labor and materials.
- Reasonable evidence that the Work cannot be completed for the unpaid balance of the Contract Sum.
- Damage to property of the Owner or another contractor.
- Reasonable evidence that the Work cannot be completed within the Contract Time, and that the unpaid balance is not adequate to cover actual or liquidated damages for the anticipated delay, or
- Persistent failure to carry out the Work in accordance with the Contract Documents.

When reasons for withholding certification for payment are evident, the entity preparing the Certificate for Payment should notify the contractor and the owner of such reasons in writing, establishing conditions under which these causes (for withholding certification) can be reasonably removed. The contractor should be given a reasonable time to respond. Once such reasons have been remedied to the satisfaction of the owner, withheld funds are accounted for, certified, and paid out in the next Applications for Payment.

Failure of Payment

The Conditions of the Contract usually establish a course of action for the protection of the contractor in the event that the design professional or others should fail to expedite processing of the Certificate for Payment, or in case the owner should fail to pay the contractor in accordance with the agreement. If, for instance, the design professional, through no fault of the contractor, should fail to issue a Certificate for Payment in a reasonable time, or if the owner fails to pay the contractor in a timely manner, the contractor, upon written notice, and within a reasonable time, may stop the Work until such time as payment of amounts owed are made. In this case, it is appropriate to adjust the Contract Time in accordance with any delay that may be caused, and to adjust the Contract Sum to add any reasonable costs that can be justified by the contractor for shutdown, delay, and start-up.

Progress Payments

Unless the Contract for Construction stipulates otherwise, it is customary for the contractor to be paid a proportionate amount of the Contract Sum monthly, based on the Certificate of Payment. The contractor must then promptly pay his subcontractors, material suppliers, and others in his employ the obligation amounts that correspond to the current percentage of completion. Failure to do so may result in one or more third-party claim(s) made to the owner, or in liens being filed against the owner's property.

The contractor may withhold, under appropriate agreement, a percentage from subcontractors that is similar to the retainage withheld from the contractor's earnings by the owner. While neither the owner nor the design professional has an obligation to subcontractors nor to other creditors of the contractor, any of these third parties may request information from the design professional regarding the status of payments made to the contractor. Furthermore, any unsatisfied creditor of the contractor may notify the owner of his situation and intention to seek remedy.

Substantial Completion

The term *Substantial Completion* has been defined under discussion of Contract Time earlier in this chapter. The Conditions of the Contract usually establish that once the stage of Substantial Completion has been reached and certified by the design professional, the contractor shall be paid the following amount: a sum equal to the Contract Sum including any retainage and, if appropriate, any accumulated interest due from deposited retainage, *less* an amount, determined by the design professional, that is sufficient to cover the cost of any remaining minor work to be completed, and amounts related to any unresolved claims or other unresolved issues as may be documented by the design professional.

The Conditions of the Contract usually stipulate a series of administrative procedures that must be carried out prior to such payment upon certification of Substantial Completion. Such procedures may be described in the Conditions of the Contract and the Supplemental Conditions of the Contract and further described in the General Requirements division of the Specifications. Conditions preceding payment at Substantial Completion usually include the following provisions:

- Final, comprehensive inspection by the design professional leading to certification of Substantial Completion (subject to a list of items to be completed).
- Approval of surety to release retainage and commence final payment.
- Approval of jurisdictional authority by Certificate of Occupancy or similar requirement.
- Transitional procedures as specified and required to be completed prior to owner possession and occupancy.
- Satisfactory termination of contractor's responsibility for insurance, temporary utilities, and similar services.

This list of items to be completed as drawn up by the design professional at substantial completion is sometimes referred to as the *punch list*. The term comes from an earlier time, when writing instruments were primitive, paper was scarce, and duplicate lists not readily made. Construction professionals and others customarily made use of paper punch devices that acted as a signature or seal for the purpose of identifying the user. The design professional would prepare the list on paper with pen and ink, and transmit the document to the contractor. The contractor would then signify compliance with completion of items on the list by using his punch to "punch" a small hole at the margin adjacent to the item, using a paper punch or other similar device. The design professional, in turn, would punch another hole, his identifying marks beside the contractor's hole, thereby signifying his satisfaction that the item was, in fact, complete. The final punched list would be forwarded to the owner as a permanent record that the project was complete.

Final Payment

The Conditions of the Contract have the final word on the conditions by which final completion is judged and documented subsequent to final payment and project closeout. Written notice by the contractor to the owner signifying final completion is required, together with the contractor's final Application for Payment. At the time of final payment, the design professional should have made a subsequent inspection of the project to satisfy completion of any unfinished work documented at the time of Substantial Completion.

The requirements of the contractor, leading to final payment at completion, can be more appropriately written into the General Requirements Division of the Specifications. (See Chapter 10, "Drawings and Specifications and the General Requirements (Sections 01700—"Project Closeout," and 0710, "Project Record Documents"). While the requirements for documenting completion are obligations of the contract, they are also administrative and may, therefore, be more clearly specified as such rather than stated only as conditions of the contract.

Protection of Persons and Property

Requirements for protection of persons and property during construction are clearly the sole obligation of the contractor. The Conditions of the Contract properly set forth the contractor's duties and responsibilities for safety and protection of property related to the Work. Among these provisions, the Conditions of the Contract may stipulate, as does the 1997 edition of AIA A201, that the contractor shall immediately stop the Work if he encounters any substance known to be harmful to humans, which requires special handling to remove. Other provisions provide safeguards for the contractor and design professional.

In recent years, a great many local, state, and federal laws have been created concerning life safety requirements. Chapter 6, "Legal Concerns and Insurance" covers some of the broader issues related to codes and standards governing liability, as well as insurance against potential loss. Regardless of any stipulations to the contrary, current statutes require, under penalty of law, that certain specific steps be taken regarding the protection of persons and property.

Although most proprietary forms of Conditions of the Contract, such as the AIA *General Conditions of the Contract*, may properly endeavor to remain current with legally required safeguards, the design professional and the contractor should also stay up to date on published facts regarding health and safety. Clinical evidence has proven that contact with certain substances such as lead, asbestos, polychlorinated biphenyl (PCB), and others are most certainly injurious to the health of humans. Owners and construction professionals alike are strongly advised to avail themselves of the many resources of continuing education available today on hazards related to building construction.

Safety of Persons and Property

The Conditions of the Contract should normally require that the contractor take reasonable precautions and provide reasonable protection for prevention of damage, injury, or loss to:

- Employees on the Work and other persons who may be affected thereby.
- The materials and equipment to be incorporated into the Work, whether in storage on or off the site, under care and custody of the contractor or others.
- Other property at the site or adjacent to the site, including, but not limited to, trees, shrubs, walks, pavements, roadways, structures and utilities not scheduled for removal or relocation.

It is generally held that it is unnecessary for the Conditions of the Contract or the Supplemental Conditions of the Contract to echo requirements that are a matter of law, such as regulations mandated by the Occupational Safety and Health Act (OSHA) and others. Lawyers argue that the law is sufficient requirement which needs no repetition, advertisement, or improvement.

Requirements for Insurance and Bonds

Chapter 6, "Legal Concerns and Insurance" addresses the subject of Insurance, and the extent to which the Construction Industry is dependent upon the insurance industry. Each state of the union, the various political subdivisions within each state, and private owners as well, have differing conditions, regulations, requirements, and needs for insurance against the multiple hazards that exist during the process of building construction. The Conditions of the Contract modified by the Supplemental Conditions of the Contract is the proper vehicle in the contract documents through which to identify the types of insurance, and conditions related to insurance coverage that may be required by the owner. Insurance coverage that should be included in the Contract Price may include the following:

- Claims under Worker's Compensation, disability benefit, and other employee benefit acts which are applicable to the Work performed.
- Claims for damages due to bodily injury, occupational sickness or disease, or death of the contractor's employees.
- Claims for damages resulting from bodily injury, occupational sickness or disease, or death of any person other than the contractor's employees.
- Claims for damages insured by usual personal injury liability coverage which are sustained by a person as a result of an offense directly or indirectly related to the employment of such person by the contractor, or by another person.

- Claims for damages other than to the Work itself, such as damage or destruction to tangible property, including loss of use therefrom.
- Claims for damages because of bodily injury, death of a person, or destruction of tangible property arising out of ownership, maintenance, or use of a motor vehicle.
- Claims involving contractual liability insurance applicable to the contractor's obligations under indemnification provisions of the Conditions of the Contract, Supplemental Conditions of the Contract, or the Contract for Construction.

The details of insurance coverage, the limits of compensation, the extent of coverage required, and other such necessary information are subjects for the Supplemental Conditions of the Contract. In the main, neither the design professional nor the owner is an expert in insurance. Therefore, the design professional should always advise the owner to retain the services of an experienced insurance counselor who will recommend the insurance "package" to be described in the Contract Documents. The insurance counselor will establish the minimum and maximum amounts of insurance coverage that should be made a condition of the contract, and will recommend the types and limits of coverage that should be carried by both owner and contractor during project construction.

Certificates of Insurance

The contractor is required to file with the owner, certificates of insurance prepared by the insurance company providing the coverage. Such documents should state the effective date of coverage, the limits of coverage, and, in terms of dates, the duration of coverage. It is to the owner's advantage that, as a condition of the insurance coverage, the insurance company be required to give the owner at least 30 days notice of cancellation or expiration of any insurance policy carried by the contractor as a condition of the contract Since certificates of insurance are filed with the owner at the beginning of the construction process for projects that require more than a year to construct, it is advisable that the Conditions of the Contract require periodic certification of insurance coverage to be submitted to the owner. In any event, it is advisable that a current certificate of insurance be presented at the time of Substantial Completion and project closeout.

Forms of Insurance Coverage

As to the contractor's insurance requirements, the insurance counselor may provide additional language to be included in the Supplementary Conditions of the Contract. Such statements would provide more specific comprehensive coverage in other major divisions of insurance, which have not been identified in the proprietary form of the Conditions of the Contract. Depending upon the nature of the project, these coverages may include:

- Premises Operations Insurance covering property loss including extended coverage against perils of fire and Acts of God.
- Independent Contractors' Protective Insurance.
- Personal injury liability.
- Liability coverage of contractor-owned, non-owned, or hired motor vehicles of all types and descriptions.
- Separate coverage over and above "normal" liability coverage, generally called "umbrella excess liability" coverage.

Premises Operations Insurance

Premises Operations Insurance is commonly called *Builder's Risk* insurance. It is a broad form of property damage insurance which includes completed operations during the construction process and generally includes risks that could occur from the following:

- Damage resulting from wind, rain storm, or flood.
- Fire in or around the premises.
- Any operation that may occur on or around the job site.
- Acts of vandalism or malicious mischief.

Some types of hazards may be specifically excluded from the basic builder's risk policy. If, in the opinion of owner, design professional, or owner's insurance counsel, such exclusions should be covered, such coverage may be required by endorsement to the basic policy. Such unusual hazards may include:

- Explosion or collapse of structure, either above grade or underground.
- Theft of materials, appliances, or equipment not yet attached to or installed in the building.

Independent Contractors' Protective Insurance

Independent Contractors' Protective Insurance will provide coverage from claims from other (independent) contractors. This coverage would apply in the case of multiple prime contracts or owner-employed separate contractor(s).

Contractors' Liability Insurance

The contractor is usually required by the contract documents to carry general liability insurance which protects him, as well as the owner and design professional, from any loss of property or life due to negligence of the contractor, his employees, subcontractors, sub-subcontractors, and others in his direct or indirect employ during the construction process. Comprehensive motor vehicle liability insurance is normally obtained as a separate policy. It is advisable for reasons of economy and convenience to require that this coverage be carried by the same company which provides the general liability coverage.

Some forms of general liability insurance may exclude medical payments to employees in deference to the legal requirement that an employer such as the contractor be required to carry Worker's Compensation Insurance. The owner's insurance counselor may advise an endorsement that would delete such an employment exclusion. In this way the required insurance will provide for personal injury above and beyond the statutory limits of Worker's Compensation.

Motor Vehicle Liability Insurance is protection against claims resulting from the operation of any motor vehicle. Such occurrences are common hazards that may or may not take place at the job site. Coverage would include injury of persons or property from the operation of motor vehicles related to the work during the construction process.

Excess Liability Insurance

The process of construction may create hazards, the loss from which may exceed the "normal" bounds of most general and motor vehicle liability policies. The term "umbrella," or excess liability, coverage extends the limits of general liability coverage to cover any loss from liability over and above the limits of other forms of liability insurance.

Owner's Liability Insurance

Aside from other insurance requirements that may be the contractor's responsibility, the owner should purchase and maintain liability insurance for self-protection from claims that may arise from operations under the contract. It is not unusual for the owner, particularly public sector owners, to have in effect liability insurance for general purposes. If the owner maintains general liability coverage for purposes other than coverage for the particular project, the insurance counselor should be aware of such coverage in order to recommend special endorsements that name and relate the project to the owner's policy.

Property Insurance

The owner, to further protect his interest, should purchase and maintain what has come to be known as *all-risk* insurance against hazards that may cause damage to the owner's property. All-risk insurance is designed to compensate for loss that may occur from fire and to provide what is generally called *extended coverage*, which includes loss from natural perils such as wind, water, lightning, and other Acts of God. Included in the all-risk feature is coverage of loss that may occur from theft, vandalism, malicious mischief, collapse, and other such potential causes of loss. Such insurance coverage is designed to be available to the owner, on an annual basis of renewal, throughout the life of the building. At the time construction begins, the insurance counselor should be asked to design special endorsements to a basic all-risk policy which would accomplish the following in support of the contract for construction.

- Name the contractor and his assigns, including subcontractors, and sub-subcontractors, as beneficiaries until such time as project closeout has been accomplished and final payment made.
- Include any temporary buildings and contents, contractor's equipment, vehicles, and other appliances located on the site during construction.
- Cover perils that may result from acts of debris removal and demolition during construction.
- Provide just compensation for the services of the design professional in case of loss and necessary reconstruction.

It is generally held that the owner is responsible for the risk of loss of his property. If the owner, for any reason, elects not to acquire property insurance during the construction period, such intention should be clearly communicated to the contractor, either in writing prior to commencement of the Work, or by the language of the bidding documents.

The contractor may obtain insurance coverage similar to that described above, in the form of what is generally called *Builder's Risk Insurance*. By requiring the contractor to maintain builder's risk insurance until final payment, such insurance is paid for by the contractor as part of the Contract Sum. If such insurance coverage is not required by the contract documents, the contractor may have a legitimate claim against the owner for the expense of insurance, necessary for the contractor's protection, but which protects the owner's interest as well.

Deductibility

Insurance companies generally offer policies that provide for specific amounts of compensation for loss to be self-insured by the policyholder. That is, in case of loss, the policyholder sustains a specified amount of the loss, with the insurance company paying for the balance. Such amounts of self coverage are generally called *deductibility*, which means that a specific amount of the loss may be deducted from any compensation made under coverage provided by the policy. Because of the lowered risk factor to the insurance carrier, the premiums for insurance coverage may be substantially lower than the normal premium for 100% coverage. Such deductibility provisions may be available for and applicable to all types of insurance policies.

In writing the Supplemental Conditions of the Contract, the design professional, in coordination with the owner's insurance counselor, should identify in the Conditions of the Contract any such deductibility that may be provided in any of the insurance coverage. The Conditions of the Contract should also name the party to the contract who bears any expense to the other party in event of any deductible amounts not compensated for loss.

If any type of insurance is required by the contract documents to be maintained by the contractor, the language of the General or Supplemental Conditions of the Contract should either disallow any deductible in the face value of the policy or, if the contractor is allowed to take advantage of a reduced premium by the device of deductibility, he should be made responsible to indemnify the owner for any amount deducted from the full value of loss compensated by insurance in case of loss. If, on the other hand, the owner provides any part of the insurance "package," then the Conditions of the Contract should require the owner to indemnify the contractor for any loss he may sustain as beneficiary to the full value compensated by insurance in case of loss.

Boiler and Machinery Insurance

The owner, as a matter of law, may be required to maintain specific insurance coverage against any liability resulting from use of mechanical equipment, such as a boiler or other hazardous appliance that may be part of the building. In defining the insurance "package," the design professional, in coordination with the owner's insurance counselor, should identify any such boiler and machinery insurance to be provided by the owner, and specify in the Conditions of the Contract the requirement for insurance coverage of mechanical equipment during installation and start-up. Such coverage protects the contractor, subcontractors, and any subcontractors against loss until final acceptance of the Work, project closeout, and final payment.

Loss of Use Insurance

If a catastrophe should occur during construction, there may be a significant delay in the completion that may or may not be the fault of the contractor. It is in the owner's interest to purchase and maintain insurance that would compensate him for loss of use in such a case. If the owner does not volunteer to provide such coverage, the contractor may request an arrangement whereby he (the contractor) provides the insurance, paying for it in the form of a reduction in the Contract Sum. In instances where the owner, rather than the contractor, elects to carry insurance related to the Work, the conditions of the contract should require the owner to furnish the contractor with copies of the policy, or certificates of such insurance, with instructions to the carrier to give the contractor 30 days or more notice that such insurance is to be cancelled or renewed.

Waivers of Subrogation

Subrogation is a process by which insurance carriers endeavor to collect from each other, or from third parties, reimbursement for loss paid under the coverage of a policy, when there may be contributory responsibility to the loss by parties other than the named insured. If not the Conditions, then the Supplemental Conditions (under advice of both the owner's legal counsel and the owner's insurance counsel) should provide language creating waivers of subrogation which would protect third parties related to the Contract for Construction. The Construction documents should make clear that the principals to the Contract for Construction and contractor are responsible (by virtue of insurance policies which each is required by the contract to carry) to assure payment of any loss that may occur. This must be done without recourse to third parties who may be related to the Work. Such third parties (who should be protected by waiver of subrogation language) may include:

- The design professional, his agents or employees, consultants and consultant's employees.
- Any subcontractor, sub-subcontractor, and their respective agents and employees.

Bonds

Chapter 6, "Legal Concerns and Insurance" provides a broad discussion of bonds, i.e., Bid Bonds, Performance Bonds, and Payment Bonds, that may be required of the contractor by the Conditions of the Contract for Construction. For the Performance Bond and Labor and Materials Payment Bond, the design professional should seek the counsel of the owner's attorney.

Miscellaneous Provisions

Any complex agreement such as the Contract for Construction is usually organized and subdivided under headings of major importance, as are the headings of this chapter on the Conditions of the Contract. Of no less importance are many less lengthy subjects that may not be conveniently subdivided under major headings. Most proprietary forms of Conditions of the Contract, therefore, place a number of topics under the general heading *Miscellaneous Provisions*. The following subjects are commonly included in this category.

Governing Law

The Conditions of the Contract may establish the project location as the legal jurisdiction, usually the state, which governs the Contract for Construction. This statement is designed to prevent litigation (associated with disputes during construction) from bringing complicated lawsuits filed outside the project jurisdiction. It is not unusual for a project located on the East coast of the United States to be designed by a professional firm from the Gulf coast, and constructed by a contractor from the Pacific coast. It is easy to see that without an agreement as to jurisdiction, any litigation brought in another jurisdiction could be both inconvenient and expensive to both owner and design professional.

If the owner or other parties to the Contract for Construction wish to establish a jurisdiction for the project that is other than the physical location of the project, a supplemental statement naming that jurisdiction may be made in the Supplemental Conditions of the Contract. It may also be appropriate to include in the Supplemental Conditions of the Contract a statement requiring the contractor to conform to all applicable laws, codes, and regulations, whether they be local, state or federal, and which requires the contractor to hold the owner harmless from any violation of any such regulation that may occur. In addition, the statement, by reference, and under the advice of owner's legal counsel, may add applicable statutes, codes, and other regulations, all of which must be properly identified.

Successors and Assigns

Most forms of proprietary Conditions of the Contract indicate certain procedures by which the responsibilities of the various parties to the contract can be assigned to certain successors or designated parties (*assigns*). This is common practice in a variety of forms of responsible agreement between two or more parties. Such statements make provision for the possible demise or incapacity of either party by enabling performance to continue under the terms of the agreement. Covenants may bind any partners, successors, assigns, or legal representatives of the parties to provisions of the agreement. In this way, each party offers the other reasonable assurance that the covenant between themselves will be completed, regardless of any circumstance that may prevent performance by one or the other.

Written Notice

Legal experts generally agree that the Conditions of the Contract should describe procedures requiring written notice between the parties to the contract. These procedures are required for a number of purposes, including claims for damages, and claims to rights and remedies to any disputes that may occur between the parties to the Contract. For the most part, these provisions serve to formally communicate any alleged failure to perform under the contract requirements, and recognize an established procedure for such notice under common law. The Supplemental Conditions of the Contract, under advice of the owner's legal counsel, may specify procedures for serving notice in a variety of situations.

Rights and Remedies

In the language of law, a *Breach of Contract* constitutes substantial failure of either party to perform according to the primary covenant of the agreement. In order that minor disagreements are not interpreted as breach of contract under the law, the Conditions of the Contract or Supplemental Conditions of the Contract ought to contain statements similar to the following.

- Duties and obligations imposed by the Contract Documents and rights and remedies available thereunder shall be in addition to and not a limitation of duties, obligations, rights, and remedies otherwise imposed or available by law.
- No action or failure to act by the Owner, Architect/Engineer, or Contractor shall constitute a waiver of a right or duty afforded them under the Contract, nor shall such action or failure to act constitute approval of or acquiescence in a breach thereunder, except as may be specifically agreed in writing.

Tests and Inspections

Controlled testing of materials, assemblies, chemicals, soils, and other elements related to a modern building project have become the primary method by which the owner can gain reasonable assurance that the critical elements of the project either meet or exceed specified design standards and quality expectations. Modern professional testing laboratories are available near the sites of most building projects in the United States.

By taking sample borings of the soil that is to support a proposed building, and by making a series of laboratory tests, the Soils Engineer (usually a sub-consultant to the design professional) can determine the physical properties of the soil and recommend the type and design of foundation that will be adequate. Experience indicates that the structural capacity of soils can vary greatly from site to site, and even from location to location on the same site. Competent design professionals should never attempt to accomplish any form of structural design of building foundations without first obtaining a reliable soils report.

Concrete is a material common to most modern buildings, particularly in the construction of foundations. The quality of concrete, its structural capability, and other physical properties can vary greatly depending on the type and proportion of ingredients from which it is made. Other factors affecting the quality of concrete include the environmental conditions under which it is mixed, transported, and conveyed to its intended location. The quality of the concrete is vital to the structural integrity of the building. Quality can only be proved by testing.

A number of tests of various building components are generally required by the design professional in the performance of professional duty. For example, the structural base must be tested to determine conformance with moisture and compaction requirements, structural welds should be x-rayed to determine adequacy, fabricated structural components should be submitted to stress analysis, and wood components assessed for compliance with specified moisture and flexure requirements. In accordance with a compendium of new codes and laws regarding environmental safety, finish materials and other surfaces must be tested to determine smoke contribution and flame spread capability as they would affect the occupants of a building in the event of fire.

Most proprietary forms of Conditions of the Contract establish the responsibilities of the parties to the Contract regarding testing. The right of the design professional or the owner to require testing should not be prevented by any legal misconception. Therefore, the owner's legal counsel may recommend additional statements clarifying this issue in the Supplemental Conditions of the Contract.

In careful coordination with the language of the Conditions of the Contract, the Division 1 Sections of the Specifications related to testing should describe in detail the procedures for testing, the required qualifications of the testing laboratory, and other matters of procedure. The various sections of the Specifications should indicate which products and assemblies should be tested, and the types of tests to be administered.

The matter of who should pay for testing is a subject of debate among participants in the OPC relationship. Many forms of Conditions of the Contract suggest that the contractor should pay for all tests. Others state that the contractor should pay for other testing and approvals. Some owners and design professionals prefer that the contractor pay for *all* testing that is required or specified in order that the cost be included in the Contract Sum.

Other owners and design professionals prefer to control the testing as well as to select the laboratory that will perform it. Many argue that the owner and design professional should monitor the testing process to protect their interests and prevent any opportunity for collusion and fraud.

The contractor must also know the type and exact number of tests that will be required, as well as the name of the laboratory that the owner approves, in order to anticipate properly the cost of testing in preparing his proposal of Contract Sum. It would be unfair and inappropriate to expect the contractor to pay for testing unless testing requirements are clearly and completely described by the contract documents. There are three alternatives to requiring and/or specifying testing during construction:

1. The design professional can specify the exact number and type of tests that will be required, and list two or more Testing Laboratories that are acceptable to the owner. Under this provision, the contractor would be expected to have provided for the cost of testing in the Contract Sum. In this case, the Conditions of the Contract language may be modified in the Supplemental Conditions of the Contract to make the contractor responsible for all testing costs.

2. The design professional can specify, in the General Requirements (Division 1 of the Specifications), an *Allowance* to cover the cost of testing. In this case, the contractor is required to pay for testing under the provisions of the allowance, but the owner is allowed to both select and direct the testing laboratory. Under this method, the design professional can require, confirm, or waive testing requirements as the progress of the Work continues. If this method is chosen, a supplementary statement to the Conditions of the Contract may be required in the Supplemental Conditions of the Contract. The design professional must carefully coordinate the Allowance provisions in appropriate sections of Division 1 of the Specifications.

3. The Contract Documents may be written so as to require the owner to select the testing laboratory and pay for all required tests, with the contractor pledged to cooperate with the needs of the testing laboratory at no additional cost to the owner. This alternative gives the owner complete control of the testing. Most if not all of the required testing should be specified so that the contractor can properly anticipate when and where testing will take place. Under this arrangement, the design professional may, with permission of the owner, require additional testing at any time if, in his professional judgment, a system or material may not meet specified standards.

Interest
The Conditions of the Contract should provide instructions for the accrual of interest on amounts due under the Contract for Construction that remain unpaid for any reason, according to the terms of the

Agreement. The intent of this provision is that the contractor be compensated for portions of Work certified complete should the owner, for a reason that is not the fault of the contractor, fail to make timely payment according to the terms of the contract. By compensating the contractor for any delay in payment, costly delay in the Work may be avoided. If, on the other hand, the contractor has failed to perform, or the Work, in the opinion of the design professional does not meet specified standards, any delay in payment to the contractor may not accrue interest.

The owner, under advice of counsel, may wish to modify or supplement this provision. However, the general provisions of such statements regarding the accumulation of interest on amounts due and payable that remain unpaid is a standard right under provision of law in most jurisdictions.

Statutes of Limitation

Many proprietary forms of Conditions of the Contract do not define *Statutes of Limitation*. Nevertheless, time limits within which a law suit can be filed, should be of major concern to all participants in the OPC relationship. Most state jurisdictions place time limits on legal claims. The statutes that prescribe such time limits are called *Statutes of Limitation* and are discussed in Chapter 6, "Legal Concerns and Insurance." With the considerable incidence of major liability claims being filed against owners, contractors, and design professionals alike, it is appropriate that a date be established in the contract from which time the statutory period may be measured. If the Conditions of the Contract do not specify statutes of limitation, the design professional may be advised by both legal and insurance counsel to add supplemental provisions to the Conditions of the Contract to establish such dates.

Commencement of Statutory Limitation Period

The Statutory period is limited by intervals established under the law, as to the acts or failure to act by either party to the contract. This period may be established as follows.

- Any act or failure to act (under applicable statute of limitations) alleged to have occurred during the course of the Work, shall be deemed to have occurred no later than the (relevant date) of Substantial Completion.
- Any act or failure to act (under applicable statute of limitations) alleged to have occurred after the date of Final Certificate of Payment shall be deemed to have occurred not later than the date of any act or failure to act by the contractor. This statement applies within the limits of any warranty period established by the Contract Documents, the date of any correction of Work, failure to correct any work after due notice has been given, or the date of actual commission of any other act or failure to perform any duty or obligation by the contractor or the owner, whichever occurs last.

Other Miscellaneous Provisions

There may be other miscellaneous provisions and obligations of the circumstances surrounding the individual project that are not included in the Conditions of the Contract. Such provisions are appropriately included in the Supplemental Conditions of the Contract. Among them are the following.

Reference Standards:
A number of organizations dedicate themselves to determining, defining, specifying, and publishing standards of quality and performance for generic materials and assemblies commonly used in building construction. Other organizations establish model codes for building. These codes are adopted by governing bodies and become law. In most cases, published standards and model codes are dated when published, and are frequently updated.

Design professionals frequently make use of such reference standards when preparing the specifications. Supplemental language may establish that the reference standards and codes which are in effect on the date that bids are received will govern the Contract for Construction. This provision avoids a dispute during construction in the event that a particular standard was revised after the bid date, thereby changing the contractor's anticipated cost of construction.

Equal Opportunity for Employment: Supplemental language may be required to define laws that affect employment by public sector owners. Public owners have an obligation under federal law to demand certain employment practices by the contractor and his subcontractors. For example, federal statutes establish equal opportunity guidelines for the employment of persons engaged in the work for or by a public owner.

Minimum Wage: Supplemental language may also be required to define laws that affect wages paid by public sector owners. Public owners have an obligation under federal law to demand that the contractor and his subcontractors pay certain applicable wages. For example, federal statutes and policies establish minimum wage guidelines for employment of persons according to trade category. Such wage scales, applicable to the locale of the project, should be included in the Supplemental Conditions of the Contract.

Sales Tax Exemption: In the case of a public owner, the law may provide an exemption from payment of local, state, or other sales tax. In this case, it is appropriate to include a statement in the Supplemental Conditions of the Contract describing the procedure whereby the contractor may apply for sales tax exemption to the benefit of the owner.

Defining Termination or Suspension of the Contract

The General Conditions normally set forth conditions whereby the Contract for Construction can be terminated by either party, for certain stipulated causes and with certain requirements of notice of such action each to the other.

Termination by the Owner for Cause
The owner may terminate the contract if the contractor:

- Persistently or repeatedly refuses or fails to supply enough properly skilled workers or proper materials.
- Fails to make payment to subcontractors for materials or labor in accordance with respective agreements between the contractor and the subcontractor.

- Persistently disregards laws, ordinances, rules, regulations, or orders of a public authority having jurisdiction or is otherwise guilty of substantial breach of a provision of the Contract Documents.

When any of the above reasons exist, the owner, upon certification by the design professional that there is sufficient cause to justify such action, may terminate the contract. This is done without prejudice to any other rights or remedies of the owner and after giving the contractor and the contractor's surety (if any) adequate written notice (usually seven days). The owner may (subject to any rights of the surety):

- Take possession of the site and of all materials, equipment, tools, and construction equipment and machinery owned by the contractor.
- Accept assignment of subcontracts, subject to contingent assignment provisions provided in the Contract Documents.
- Finish the Work by whatever reasonable method the owner may deem expedient.

An owner contemplating such action is advised to seek legal counsel (as to circumstances and notice). When the owner terminates the contract for one of the causes stated above, payments to the contractor (for work already completed) may be suspended until the Work is finished. If the unpaid balance of the Contract Sum exceeds the owner's actual cost of finishing the Work (including compensation for additional required services by the design professional), such excess amount shall be paid to the contractor. If such costs exceed the unpaid balance, the contractor shall pay the difference to the owner. The amount to be paid to contractor or owner, as the case may be, should be certified by the design professional. The termination provisions should also stipulate that any adjusted payments to the contractor or owner that may be due after termination of the contract shall survive the termination in any event.

Suspension by the Owner for Convenience

The General Conditions should state that the owner may for any reason order the contractor by written notice to suspend, delay, or interrupt the Work in whole or in part for such period of time as the owner may determine. In the event that such right of owner is provided, a parallel statement to benefit the contractor should also be included. This protects the contractor in the event that such suspension, delay, or interruption results in increased cost in performance of the contract, thereby reducing the contractor's expected profit. Exceptions may include:

- A suspended, delayed, or interrupted performance for which the contractor is responsible, or
- A situation in which equitable adjustment is made or denied under another provision of the Contract.

In order to avoid any potential disagreement that may arise due to suspension of the Work by the owner, it is recommended that the Supplemental General Conditions establish a mutually agreed fixed or percentage fee that would apply to any and all adjustments in the contractor's compensation.

Chapter Ten

Project Definition: Drawings and Specification Preparations

While there is no record of the first architectural or engineering drawing, it is clear that some form of graphic illustration must have been used to guide some of man's earliest construction projects. The term "drawing" implies much more than just the process of placing lines on a writing surface. In many languages (e.g., Latin, French, and Italian), the word for drawing also means designing. The Greeks and the Chinese use the same word to mean drawing, painting, and writing. Samuel Johnson's *Dictionary of the English Language*, printed in 1755, describes a drawing as a "delineation, representation, sketch or outline." Architects' or engineers' drawings have long been the basic means by which the ideas and instructions of the design professional are communicated to those who accomplish the Work of construction.

A specification on the other hand, is simply defined as a statement of particulars that describes something to be defined. Project definition, then, is accomplished by the use of drawings and specifications.

Engineering and Architectural Graphics

With the dawn of the Machine Age came what we know today as *engineering drawing.* By the early 18th century, building construction was a well-developed industry involving the coordination of many trades under the architect's supervision. The architect used simple geometric drawings and details to establish the basic principles of the architectural design, and personally coordinated and supervised the construction work. The mass production of industrial machines, on the other hand, required highly detailed and measured drawings to communicate the exact shape, size, material, and assembly of the machine's components. In response to this need, the art of "mechanical" drawing was developed by engineers who gave meaning to such terms as "scale" and "descriptive geometry." Soon such graphic techniques as *orthographic, axonometric, oblique,* and *perspective projection* were developed. Using these principles, an object to be constructed could be "built" on paper, and the drawing used as an exact pattern to guide the technician who would make the machine. Architects soon adopted many of these engineering techniques to produce drawings that would faithfully depict a building and its component parts. These improved drawings significantly reduced the time required of the architect to actually direct the detailing at the job site during construction.

Reproduction of Drawings

Modern building construction and modern manufacturing require that the drawings of the design professional be reproduced in quantity for distribution among the many related trades and crafts required for the project. The simple ability to economically reproduce quantities of architectural drawings has had a significant impact on building construction and manufacturing in the modern age.

Graphic Media

The design professional's drawings were once created on waxed linen cloth using carbon ink as the medium. Today, design professional's drawings are prepared either by hand or by computer, on _vellum_, or more frequently on thin but sturdy, dimensionally stable _mylar_ (plastic) sheets. Mylar is translucent, which allows for reproduction, and has a surface that is particularly adapted to ink lines produced by modern drafting pens. Plastic pencil "lead" has been developed specifically for the mylar surface which allows for hand work that is relatively free of graphite dust and smearing that sometimes occurs with conventional graphite leads. The tough plastic surface allows for machine erasures with a minimum of the kind of damage that may occur on the surface of paper or linen.

Blueprints

The process of blue printing was discovered by Sir John Herschel, an Englishman, in 1842. His discovery was a means of reproducing drawings and was not substantially improved until the middle of the 20th century when the "whiteprint" came into general use.

The term _blueprint_ was once a familiar expression used to describe reproductions of the design professional's drawings. True blue prints, once used exclusively for drawing reproduction, are seldom used in construction today. The blue printing process owes its discovery to the development of photography. It requires an original drawing on transparent media, commonly called a _tracing_. The tracing is placed directly over a second sheet, called the "print," which has been sensitized with a mixture of ferric ammonium citrate and potassium ferricynide. The "sandwiched" combination is then exposed to a strong light source which, by the sensitivity of the chemical emulsion, creates a reverse or negative image of the tracing on the print. The lines of the drawing, being opaque, are not exposed, and thus appear as white (or the color of the print paper) on a background of blue.

In the early days of blue printing, the prints were produced in flat glass frames and exposed to sunlight. The chemical emulsion was applied by hand to the print media, and after exposure washing in water was all that was necessary to produce the print. Later it was found that a bath of potassium dichromate would darken the exposed emulsion and greatly improve the contrast between the light and dark areas of the print. Once developed and dried, the blue print exhibits a remarkable "life," seldom fading, thus providing use for many years. As the demand for blue prints increased, a machine was developed to reproduce them.

White Prints

The *white print* unlike the blue print, is a positive image, dark lines on a light background. The white print process was first developed by Gustav Kogel in 1917. Like blue printing, white printing is also a photoreactive process. Because white printing involves a chemical process that produces a dye in the image, it is possible to create a number of different line colors and use a number of different textures, colors and weights of paper as the base of the print. Common, commercially available colors include black, blue, brown (sepia), green, and red. The flexibility and color range in the use of white printing expands the creativity of the design professional's presentation.

Electrostatic Copying

Electrostatic copying was invented in 1938 by Chester F. Carlson, an American physicist. Unlike earlier methods, which require liquid developers, Carlson's process is completely dry. It became known as *xerography*, a term that comes from two Greek words meaning "dry" and "writing."

In xerography, a drum, belt, or plate coated with the element selenium or some other light-sensitive material is charged with static electricity. Light reflected from the original (the document or illustration to be copied) then passes through a lens. The light strikes the light-sensitive surface, forming on that surface a positively charged image corresponding to the dark areas of the original. The remainder of the surface loses its charge. Next, negatively charged toner (powdered ink) is dusted onto the surface. Because oppositely charged materials attract each other, toner sticks to the image. The inked image is then transferred to positively charged paper and heated for an instant. The toner melts, creating a permanent copy. Some electrostatic copiers project the image from the original directly onto specially coated paper, rather than onto a drum, belt, or plate.

Digital Copies

A digital copier scans a document, converting the document into an electronic digital "code," which is stored in the copier's computerized memory. The electronic "image" once "stored" in the copier's memory, can be used for reproduction by xerographic means. The user may also be able to edit the document, merge multiple documents and produce images at different scales. The copier may be able to transmit documents to other digital devices, such as facsimile (fax) machines and personal computers.

"Working Drawings"

The term *working drawings* is often used to refer to the construction drawings, which are part of the Contract Documents. Construction drawings serve to illustrate portions of the Work that are difficult to describe in any other way. Drawings show the relationship of the materials, including sizes, shapes, locations, and connections. The drawings may include schematic diagrams showing such elements as mechanical and electrical systems. They may also include schedules and details of structural elements, equipment, finishes, and other similar items.

Figure 10.1 illustrates a professional service/phase matrix involving as many as ten phases of service, giving a sense of the design professional's responsibilities.

Typical Services of the Design Professional

1	2	3	4	5	6	7	8	9	10
Pre-Design Services		Basic Services					Additional Services		
Pre-Design Services	Site Analysis Services	Schematic Design Services	Design Development Services	Preparation of Contract Documents	Assistance During Bidding or Negotiation	Administration of the Contract for Construction	Field Observation of Construction	Project Closeout Services	Post Construction Services
Special Services Administration	Special Services Administration	Project Administration	Project Administration	Project Administration	Project Administration	Project Administration	Project Administration	Special Services Administration	Special Services Administration
Discipline Coordination	Discipline Coordination	Discipline Coordination	Discipline Coordination	Discipline Coordination	Evaluate Constructor Qualifications	Evaluate Schedule of Values	Pre-Bid Conference	Review Approval O&M Manuals	Warranty Inspections
Agency Review & Approval	Document Checking	Document Checking	Document Checking	Document Checking	Discipline Coordination	Monitor Insurance & Bond Certificates	Coordinate Construction Observation	Prepare Project Record Documents	First-Year Inspection
Coordination of Owner's Data	Agency Reviews	Agency Reviews	Agency Reviews	Agency Reviews	Document Checking	Agency Reviews Permit Approvals	Progress Meetings	Interpretations and Decisions	
Functional Programming	Coordination of Owner's Data	Confirm Program	Confirm Program	Confirm Program	Review Insurance Coverage	Review Insurance Coverage	Schedule Evaluation	Furniture Furnishings Equipment Installation	Subsequent Year Inspections
Functional Diagramming	Site Analysis & Planning	Site Design SD Level	Site Design DD Level	Final Site Design	Responses to RFI	Supplemental Documents	Reports to Owner	Systems Commissioning	
Space & Flow Diagramming	Utility Service Analysis	Architecture SD Level	Architecture DD Level	Final Architecture	Addenda Coordination	Testing Agency Coordination	Testing Agency Coordination	Dispute Resolution	
Existing Facility Surveys	Environmental Analysis	Structure SD Level	Structure DD Level	Final Structural Design	Substitution Response	Submittal Review Administration	Change Order Administration		
Marketing Studies	Zoning Analysis	Mechanical SD Level	Mechanical DD Level	Final Mechanical	Bidder Qualifications Review	Pay Request Review	Review Testing Agency Reports		
Economic Feasibility	Project Scheduling	Electrical SD Level	Electrical DD Level	Final Electrical	Attend Bid Opening	Inspection Coordination	Final Payment Review		
Financing Strategy	Budget Development	Interior SD Level	Interior DD Level	Final Interior Design	Evaluate Bids	Progress Meetings			
Project Scheduling		Specialties SD Level	Specialties DD Level	Final Special Design	Permitting Assistance	Construction Change Directives			
Budget Development		SD Level Cost Estimate	DD Level Cost Estimate	Detailed Cost Estimate	Contract Negotiations	Change Order Administration			
Presentations and Reports	Programming	Schematic Design Report	Outline Specifications	Final Specifications	Notice To Proceed	Document Interpretation			

Figure 10.1 *Design Professional's Services*

The design professional normally approaches the project by preparing drawings and specifications to describe the design of the building. Construction drawings are developed in a systematic way during the process of project development.

The basic five phases of service, considered by most to be the minimum requirement of any project, are generally characterized as follows:

- The Schematic Design Phase.
- The Design Development Phase.
- The Contract Documents Phase.
- The Bidding Phase.
- The Construction Phase.

The Schematic Design Phase

The Schematic Design Phase of the design professional's service is sometimes referred to as the Preliminary Design phase. The project's general design and budget parameters are determined at this level. The program of design stipulating the space and functional requirements is also confirmed and evaluated at this stage, and budget requirements and other limiting factors are addressed. The design professional may determine several design alternatives, each of which requires drawings in the form of sketches. Once the owner and design professional have agreed on a design approach, preliminary sketches are prepared, and generally consist of the following:

- Site plan(s).
- Diagrammatic floor plans of building(s).
- Diagrammatic cross section(s) through buildings.
- Building Elevations.
- Notes and explanations.
- Perspective sketches (Optional, usually provided as an extra service).
- Architectural Model (Optional, usually provided as an extra service).

A preliminary cost estimate may be prepared based on available current square foot and systems costs. An appropriate contingency may be included to allow for variations and unanticipated costs, fees, and expenses. Owner's approval and acceptance of the schematic phase is desirable before the next phase of the Work begins.

The Design Development Phase

The Design Development Phase, may be thought of as the study phase of the project development. At this point, the design professional studies and refines all aspects of the project design by establishing the materials and methods of construction and the environmental and other systems to be used. He also identifies regulatory conditions and other requirements. During this phase, most of the critical decisions regarding size, shape, and function are finalized, as well as the selection of materials, systems, applications, and modifications. The drawings produced at this phase consist of the following:

- Site plan(s).
- Final grading and extent of site improvements.
- Paving and drainage structures.
- Schematic utility locations and connection to building.
- Diagrammatic floor plans of building(s).

- Major dimensions.
- Structural features and requirements.
- Schedules of finishes, windows, and doors.
- Finished carpentry, millwork, and similar features.
- Equipment.
- Furnishings (if applicable).
- Major wall sections with dimensions and material indications.
- Exterior elevations with finish and material indications.
- Notes and explanations.
- Material samples as applicable.
- Interior perspective sketches (optional and extra service).

Subsequent phases of service, which follow, may include:

- The Bidding or Negotiating Phase.
- The Contract Administration Phase.

Figure 10.2 illustrates the progression of documents that are usually created in the design phases of the project development. Figures 10.3 through 10.7 illustrate a set of drawings of a small office building. These drawings are typical of those that might be produced at the design development phase of the design professional's service. These figures are for illustrative purposes only. An actual project might require more drawings and much more detail.

At this stage, a second, more detailed cost estimate may be prepared based on current unit and systems costs, with ample contingency for current construction costs, fees and other anticipated expenses. The owner's approval and acceptance of the design development phase is desirable before the next phase of the Work is begun.

The Construction Documents Phase of Service

The Construction Documents Phase involves just what the title implies. It is during this phase that the design professional and his consultants (if any) prepare the final version of the Contract Documents which include the final construction ("working") drawings. The contract documents created at this phase may include the following:

- Title Sheet (of the Drawing Set) identifying the project, legend of abbreviations, and symbols.
- Site Design including civil engineering, underground utilities, and environmental engineering design including storm water management and erosion control.
- Structural Engineering Design including foundation and below-grade structure, framing plans, and structural details, schedules, and notes.
- Architectural Design including floor and roof plans, exterior elevations, wall sections, interior sections, and details, other architectural features.
- Mechanical Engineering of Plumbing Systems, Heating, Ventilation, and Air Conditioning systems design.
- Electrical Engineering of Lighting and Power distribution systems.
- Specialty Design (if any).
- Interior Design including tenant's build-out, furniture, fixtures and equipment (FF&E), other interior details and schedules.

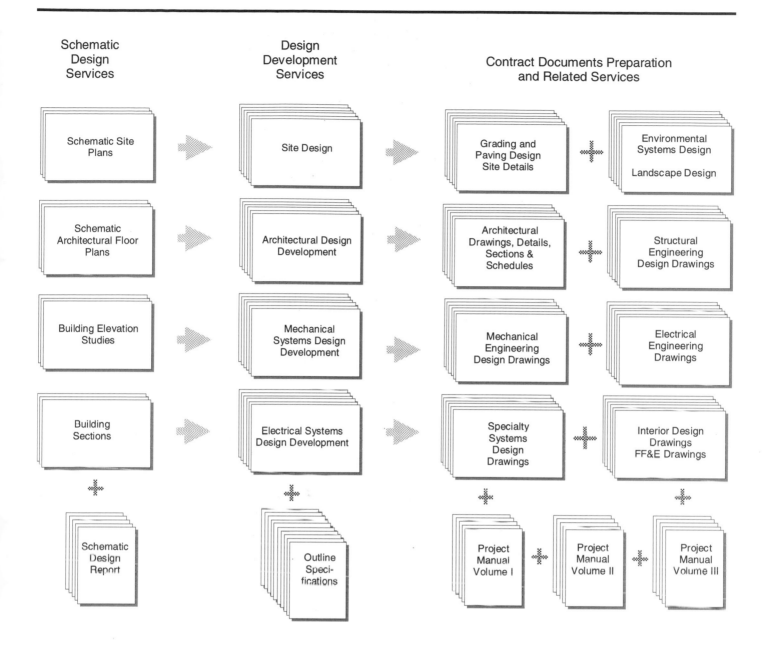

Schematic Design Services

- Schematic Site Plans
- Schematic Architectural Floor Plans
- Building Elevation Studies
- Building Sections
- Schematic Design Report

Design Development Services

- Site Design
- Architectural Design Development
- Mechanical Systems Design Development
- Electrical Systems Design Development
- Outline Specifications

Contract Documents Preparation and Related Services

- Grading and Paving Design Site Details
- Environmental Systems Design / Landscape Design
- Architectural Drawings, Details, Sections & Schedules
- Structural Engineering Design Drawings
- Mechanical Engineering Design Drawings
- Electrical Engineering Drawings
- Specialty Systems Design Drawings
- Interior Design Drawings FF&E Drawings
- Project Manual Volume I
- Project Manual Volume II
- Project Manual Volume III

Figure 10.2 Progression of Design Documents

199

Organizing the "Set" of Construction Drawings

The number of drawings and kind of information required in the final set of drawings vary with the type, character, size, and complexity of the project type. The organization of the "set" may also vary depending on the size and composition of the prime design professional's staff. Many major design firms employ staff professionals representing most of the major design disciplines that are required to produce the final work. Medium-sized firms tend to maintain one or more of the required disciplines on staff and hire others as outside consultants according to the needs of the individual project. Regardless of how the prime design professional maintains or assembles the various disciplines required to finally design the project, the organization of the construction drawings should follow a logical, organized, interdisciplinary format. In this way, it is relatively easy and convenient for the constructor(s) to find information and determine the scope, sequence, and full extent of the Work. Certain "rules of thumb" and guidelines apply to the basic organization of the set as follows:

- Determine the various design disciplines that will be employed to complete the Contract Documents. The disciplines may include, without being limited to the following:
  —Architecture (A).
  —Civil Engineering (C).
  —Landscape Architecture (L).
  —Structural Engineering (S).
  —Plumbing Engineering Design (P).
  —Mechanical HVAC Engineering (M).
  —Electrical Engineering (E).
- Observe the probable sequence of the Work and generally organize sub-sets of drawings along the lines of the various disciplines and the sequence of the Work:
  —Create two distinct page numbering systems.
  —The primary system should number drawings as they occur sequentially within the primary set, each recognizing the placement within the primary set. (i.e., Drawing No. 10 of 40). Note: This system requires that the primary numbering system not be applied until the entire set of drawings is complete.
  —The secondary system should use a prefix letter denoting the sub-category or sub-set and the drawing number within the sub-set (i.e., S4 of 10S).

The procedures outlined above have certain distinct advantages in organizing and preparing the drawings to be included in the primary set. Among these benefits are the following:

- Sub-sets can be prepared independently of other sub-sets involving other disciplines.
- Drawings within the sub-set can be assigned a sub-set number at an early date for purposes of cross-referencing as the drawings are completed.
- Drawings are organized in a consistent and uniform way into sub-sets with clear divisions based on design discipline. This approach tends to reduce the time required for bidders, estimators, subcontractors, material suppliers, and other users who must search for and use pertinent information.
- Being able to determine the position of the individual drawing within the primary set and sub-set allows the user to re-assemble

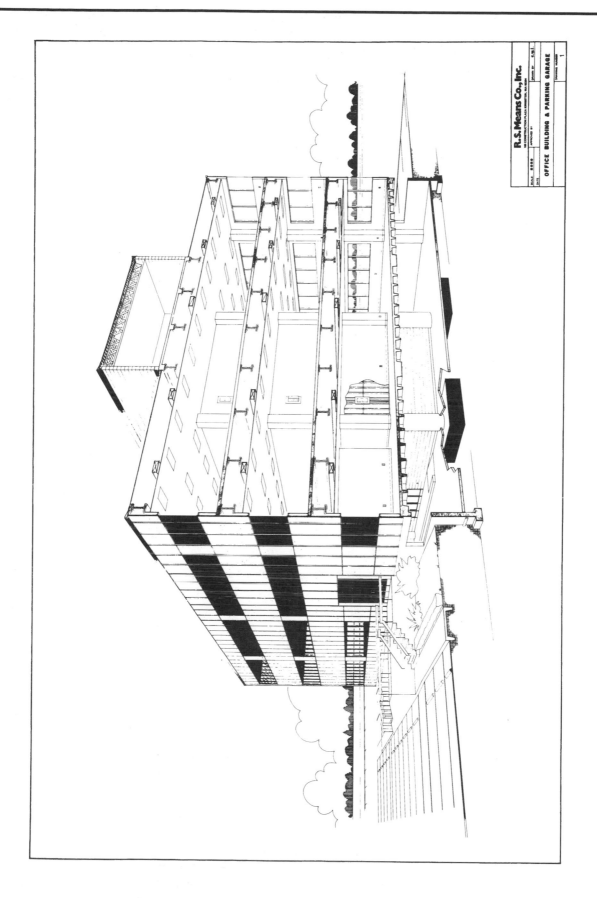

Figure 10.3 *Perspective of three-story building*

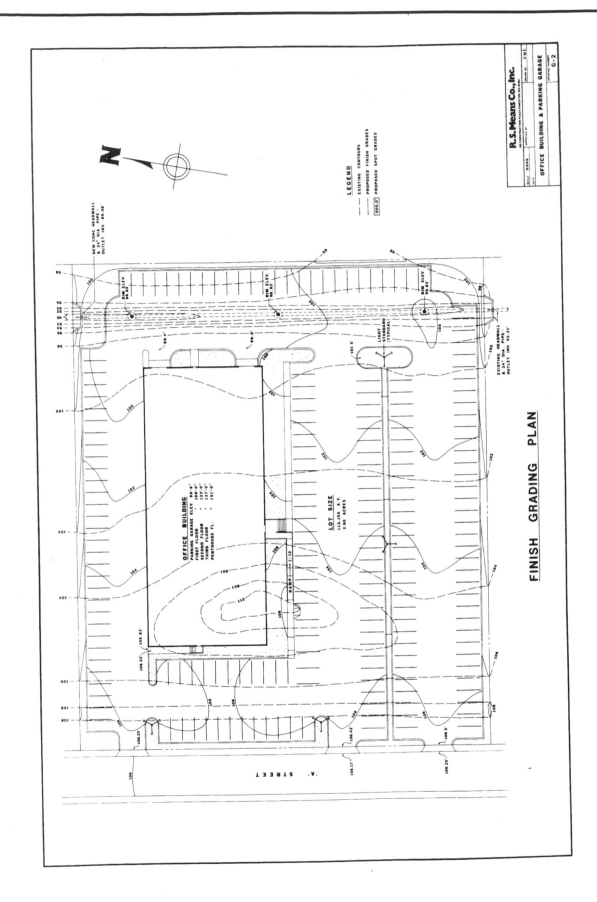

Figure 10.4 *Site plan of office building*

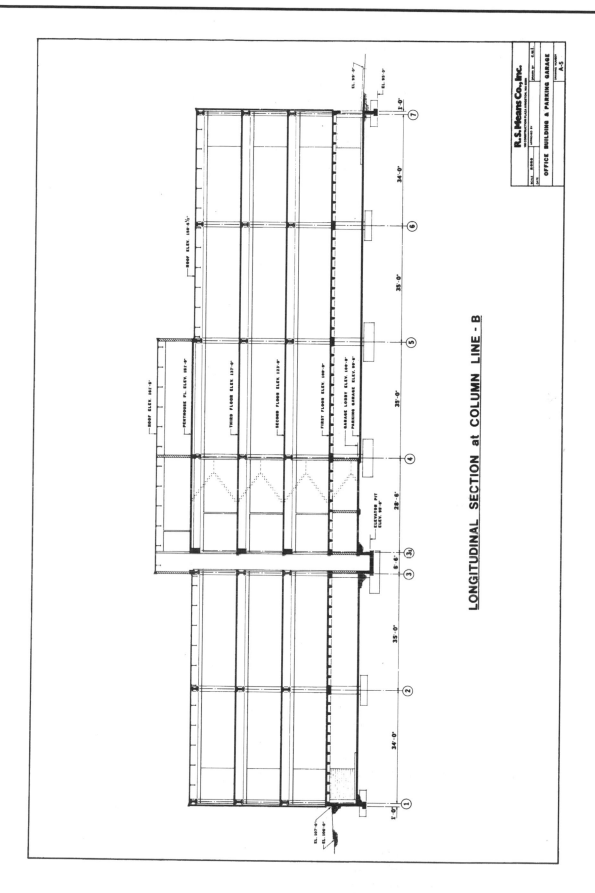

Figure 10.5 Longitudinal Building section of office building

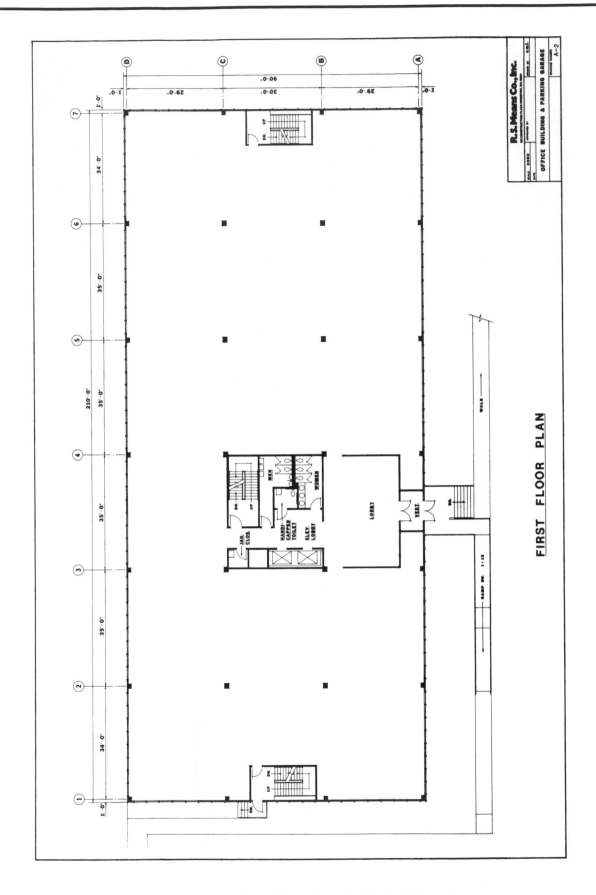

Figure 10.6 First floor plan of office building

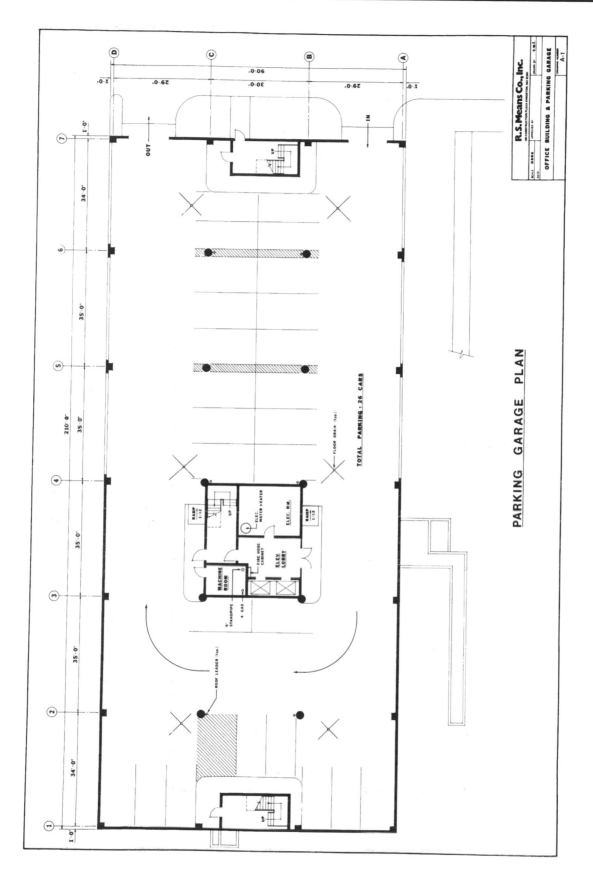

Figure 10.7 Parking: Garage plan of office building

drawings that may be disassembled during the bidding or negotiation processes. It is easy to discover if a drawing is missing.

- Cross-referencing within the sub-set tends to reduce the potential for error, omission, and confusion when unforeseen changes are made or additional sheets added to the sub-set.

Figure 10.8 illustrates an example schedule of Contract Drawings that may be appropriate to the example Mid-Rise Medical Office Building illustrated in Figures 10.3 through Figure 10.7.

Figure 10.9 is a typical drawing sheet that may be used by the design professional. The design of title blocks may vary considerably from office to office. Many design professionals consider the graphic design of such sheets as part of the "logo" expressing the identity or personality of the design professional.

Systems Production of Drawings

The preparation of drawings required for a modern building complex is the single most costly requirement the design professional must consider when negotiating his compensation with the owner. Advancements in the technology of reproduction (including printing, lithography, and photography) have all contributed to reduce the time and expense required to produce professional drawings.

Printing

The plastics and plastic adhesives available today have had a major impact on the production of professional drawings. Among these innovations is the thin mylar transparent sheet backed with a transparent film of adhesive. This process enables the design professional to create and stockpile a library of construction details, title blocks, general notes, schedule forms, symbol and material legends, and other graphics that are repeatedly used in the drawings he creates. These items can be placed on the drawing by use of the adhesive backing. Since they no longer need to be individually re-drawn, significant manhours are saved. Modern lithography also allows for the pre-printing of drawing sheets with borders, title blocks, design professional identification, and other common but repetitive features.

Diazo Reproducibles

The diazo reproduction on transparent media, commonly called a "sepia" because of its familiar brown color, has expanded the design professional's ability to save production time. This process can be used to "model" drawings that serve as a base for other drawings. For instance, the floor plan of the building is common to much of the diagrammatic work and layout of the mechanical and electrical disciplines. The diazo reproducible on a stable mylar base provides a handy "footprint" of the basic building floor plan, site plan, or building section. Other disciplines can use this basic plan to complete their work.

Process Camera Work

The modern process camera was developed as a natural adjunct to the photo-based lithographic printing process. This process has made an "antique" of the direct application printing press used since the 16th century. The photographic preparation necessary for the lithographic process requires little if any sensitivity to intermediate tone. When shades and shadows need to be printed, the effect is accomplished by the use of

Schedule of Drawings

Mid-Rise Medical Office Building

Dwg. No.	Seq. No.*	Description of Drawing
1	G-1	Title Sheet—Schedule of Drawings—Schedule of Abbreviations—Symbol Legend
2	G-2	Building Code Requirements—Life Safety Design—Security Systems Design
3	C-1	Site Plan and Site Details—Civil Engineering Notes and Schedules
4	C-2	Grading and Paving Plan—Site Utilities—Site Construction Details
5	C-3	Storm Water Management Systems Design—Erosion Control Systems Design
6	L-1	Landscaping Design—Planting Schedule
7	S-1	Excavation Plan—Foundation Plan and Details
8	S-2	Basement Plan—Foundation Wall Sections and Details
9	S-3	First Floor Framing Plan and Details—Column and Beam Schedule
10	S-4	Second Floor Framing Plan and Details—Column and Beam Schedule
11	S-5	Third Floor Framing Plan and Details—Column and Beam Schedule
12	S-6	Roof and Penthouse Framing Plans and Details—Column and Beam Schedule
13	A-1	Basement Floor Plan—Architectural Details
14	A-2	First Floor Plan—Architectural Details
15	A-3	Second Floor Plan—Architectural Details
16	A-4	Roof and Penthouse Plan—Roof and Flashing Details
17	A-5	North and South Building Elevations—Exterior Architectural Details
18	A-6	East and West Building Elevations—Window Schedule
19	A-7	Exterior Wall Sections—Wall Construction Details
20	A-8	Enlarged Plan Building Core—Basement and First Floor—Parking Equipment
21	A-9	Door Schedule—Door Types—Door Frame Types—Head Jamb & Sill Details
22	A-10	Interior Partition Types—Interior Walls Sections and Details
23	A-11	Room Finish Schedule—Color Schedule—Interior Casework—Interior Elevations
24	P-1	Basement Plumbing Plan—Plumbing Symbol Legend—Plumbing Notes
25	P-2	First Floor Plumbing Plan—Plumbing Fixture Schedule
26	P-3	Second Floor Plumbing Plan—Plumbing Riser Diagram
27	P-4	Third Floor Plumbing Plan—Plumbing Details
28	P-5	Roof and Penthouse Roof Drainage Plan
29	FP-1	Basement Fire Protection Plan—Fire Riser Diagram
30	FP-2	Typical Floor Fire Protection Plan—Fire Protection Notes and Schedules
31	M-1	Basement HVAC Distribution Plan—Mechanical Symbol Legend—Mechanical Notes
32	M-2	First Floor HVAC Distribution Plan—HVAC Riser Diagram
33	M-3	Second Floor HVAC Distribution Plan—HVAC Equipment Schedule
34	M-4	Third Floor HVAC Distribution Plan—Mechanical Details
35	M-5	Penthouse Equipment Room Plan—Mechanical Details
36	M-6	HVAC Enlarged Equipment Rooms—HVAC Details
37	E-1	Electrical Site lighting Plan—Site Power Plan—Exterior Light Fixture Schedule
38	E-2	Basement Lighting Plan—Basement Power Plan
39	E-3	First Floor Lighting Plan—First Floor Power Plan
40	E-4	Second Floor Lighting Plan—Second Floor Power Plan
41	E-5	Third Floor Lighting Plan—Third Floor Power Plan
42	E-6	Penthouse Lighting Plan—Penthouse Power Plan
43	E-7	Emergency Power

* Sequence letter indicates discipline, e.g. G=general, L=landscaping, M=mechanical

Figure 10.8 *Typical Schedule of Drawings*

Typical Drawing Sheets

D = 22", E = 33", F = 44"

1/2"   1/2"

1 1/2"   20", 31", or 42"   1/2"

1/2"   1/2"

14 1/2", 23", or 31 1/2"

Large Size
Working Drawing Sheets

D - E - F

D = 17", E = 25 1/2", F = 34"

Border Line ⟶

Trim Line ⟶

1 1/2"   1/2"   1/2"

NORTH	SCALE:		DWG. NO.	SHEET NO.
	DESIGNED:			
	DRAWN:			
	CHECKED:			
	APPROVED:			OF:

Architect's or Engineer's Description ⟶

PROJECT NAME:			

Architect's or Engineer's Seal ⟶

PROJECT NO.		DATE:	
DRAWING TITLE:			

NO.	REVISION DESCRIPTION	DATE	NO.	REVISION DESCRIPTION	DATE	

Figure 10.9 Typical Drawing Sheets

"half-tone" screens mounted at the image area of the camera. The camera with greatly enhanced lighting, optics, and exposure control allows the design professional to create drawings photographically in a number of ways. Details can be rapidly drawn at large scale and reduced for final reproduction. Appropriate supporting graphics such as maps, tables, drawings, and photographs can be incorporated into the professional drawing photographically. Double and triple exposures allow composite graphics to be combined into one drawing.

Overlay Drafting

The overlay system of drawing production first became popular in the late 1960s and continues to be of significant value to the design professional. The basic concept is to separate the various types of information and graphics normally placed on a single drawing onto different layers which when overlaid and printed together in register, makes a reproduction of all of the information contained on each layer. The floor plan of a building is either drawn or reproduced many different times within a set of drawings. By using the overlay system, the floor plan, drawn but one time, becomes the "footprint" or background for other drawings. The "footprint" becomes the base layer for a number of other drawings. A second layer may contain all dimension lines and nomenclature. Many of the other drawings using the base "footprint" do not require that the dimensions be reproduced. A third layer may contain symbols that are unique to only one of the disciplines; another layer may incorporate the room titles, door and window symbols, and other nomenclature. By printing the different layers in various combinations and utilizing either the camera or the diazo reproducible or both, much of the basic information common to a number of different drawings can be drawn once, and used again and again for parallel purposes.

Assuring exact register (one layer aligned with the other) is essential. There are two basic methods by which register can be accomplished. In the first more "primitive" method, register marks are strategically placed in identical locations on each sheet so that the draftsperson can register the layers visually by imposing one directly over the other. The second method, commonly called the "pen-graphics" method requires that a series of uniform sized holes, uniformly spaced, be punched into the top of each drawing sheet. Pins, or short posts of similar diameter and spacing are firmly and securely placed at the top of the drawing board, and as each drawing is uniformly placed over the posts, exact register is achieved. By using clear plastic posts in the diazo reproduction machine, reproductions can be made of combined layers, assuring complete register in the printing process as well.

Computer Aided Design and Drafting

The computer as a production tool for creating Contract Documents revolutionized the art of drawing as well as the production of written documents. The primary advantage of the computer is its ability to accomplish a number of operations with tremendous speed and accuracy. The second major advantage is the computer's ability to "remember" and reproduce a series of commands.

Computer aided design (CAD) has been available to the design community since the early 1960s. Originally developed as a tool for industry to assist with the design and manufacture of automobiles and aircraft, CAD has become increasingly affordable to the design professional. CAD utilizes the computer's ability to remember the coordinates of points, each with a specific location on a geometric grid. A line can be described between any two points and then drawn by a computer-driven plotter or similar device. In the earliest application of the technique, the programs required to produce even simple drawings on the computer required large amounts of electronic storage. Thus, only large, mainframe computers were capable of running the program. The technological advancements of the past two decades have allowed CAD programs to be run on both "micro" and "mini" computers. Now, 95% of all of the drawings by design professionals are being produced with the assistance of a personal computer.

Three-Dimensional and Perspective Drawings by CAD

With the development of more "user friendly" computer operating systems such as Microsoft Corporation's "Windows," CAD software systems such as Autodesk Corporation's "AutoCad," and Intergraph Corporation's "Microstation," design professionals now have the ability to create three-dimensional and perspective drawings of their designs.

The Personal Computer—The Design Professional's Tool of Choice

The Personal Computer (PC) has made remarkable advances just in the period in which the three editions of this book have been published. The first edition of this book (titled *Plans, Specs, and Contracts for Building Professionals*) published by R. S. Means in 1987, was written in 1986 on a tabletop model IBM-PC using DOS and Microsoft Word® 1.1 and recorded on 5 1/2 inch "floppy" disks. The second edition utilized MS Word® 5 for DOS. This edition written in on a portable notebook computer utilizing MS Windows® and the MS Office® family of software which allow the creation of many of the drawings and illustrations used in the book.

Graphic Standards

It is not the purpose of this volume to attempt to teach the art of preparing professional drawings, a subject best learned in the workplace. However, this text does endeavor to list and discuss the many attributes of drawings, and the most valuable techniques and resources. Certain standards have been developed so that the "language" of drawings can be understood by all. These standards help establish consistency and uniformity in the industry. For drawings, graphic symbols provide a method for such understanding by representing what otherwise would require a great deal of text. Graphic symbols are a common resource or tool, used to represent, illustrate, direct, emphasize, and abbreviate information conveyed throughout the drawings. Figures 10.10 and 10.11 show many of the typical graphic symbols used among today's practitioners.

Schedules

The use of schedules on the drawings and in the specifications is an excellent way to place a volume of information in a limited space with a minimum of words. The primary schedules used with the architectural drawings are the Finish Schedule, as illustrated in Figure 10.12 and the Door Schedule, as illustrated in Figure 10.13.

Relating Drawings and Specifications

The coordination of information in the drawings and the specifications is a critical responsibility of the design professional. The object of the Contract Documents is to describe, as completely as time and economics will permit, the requirements of the Work needed to complete the building or project. By definition, drawings are graphic illustrations of the Work to be accomplished. Drawings should illustrate the relationships between materials and indicate the following:

- Location of each material, assembly, component and accessory.
- Identification of all components and pieces of equipment.
- Dimensions of the construction and sizes of field-assembled components.
- Details and diagrams of connections.

Specifications, on the other hand, describe requirements for the physical qualities, (composition—both physical and chemical), of materials, assemblies, equipment, and other components. Specifications also establish a minimum standard for workmanship in both the manufacture and installation of these items.

The question is constantly raised in the field as to which takes precedence—the drawings or the specifications? The answer is that drawings and specifications are complementary, and neither implies information that is more important than the other. The General Conditions of the Contract usually imply that all Contract Documents are complementary and may establish the design professional as the interpreter of the designer's intention as the author of the contract documents. The Supplemental General Conditions usually require the contractor to report to the design professional any inconsistency, conflict, omission or error in the documents.

There are several "rules of thumb" for coordinating the information (primarily the drawings and specifications) contained in the Contract Documents. Some guidelines are listed below:

- Drawings illustrate; specifications describe. The design professional should avoid placing information on the drawings that could contradict statements made in the specifications. Example: A note attached to a wall section should call out "Metal Flashing." The corresponding specification found in Section 07600—Flashing and Sheet Metal, should state "32 oz. copper flashing with seams locked and soldered."
- Specifications describe, drawings illustrate. The design professional should avoid statements in the specifications that may contradict the drawings. Example: In Section 05500—Metal Fabrications, there might be the following statement: "Anchor bolts, ASTM A 36 steel." A note on the drawings should state "1/2 inch diameter anchor bolts, placed on 36 inch centers."
- Avoid statements such as "see specifications" on the drawings, or "as shown on the drawings" in the specifications. Imagine the confusion if Section 05500 of the specifications stated, "Anchor bolts, size as shown on the drawings" and the corresponding note on the drawings stated, "Anchor bolts, see specifications."
- Provide the primary information *once* in the most appropriate and conspicuous location. Secondary or repetitive information should be provided by reference to the primary note or location of the note on the drawings or statement in the Specifications.

Architectural Symbols in Section

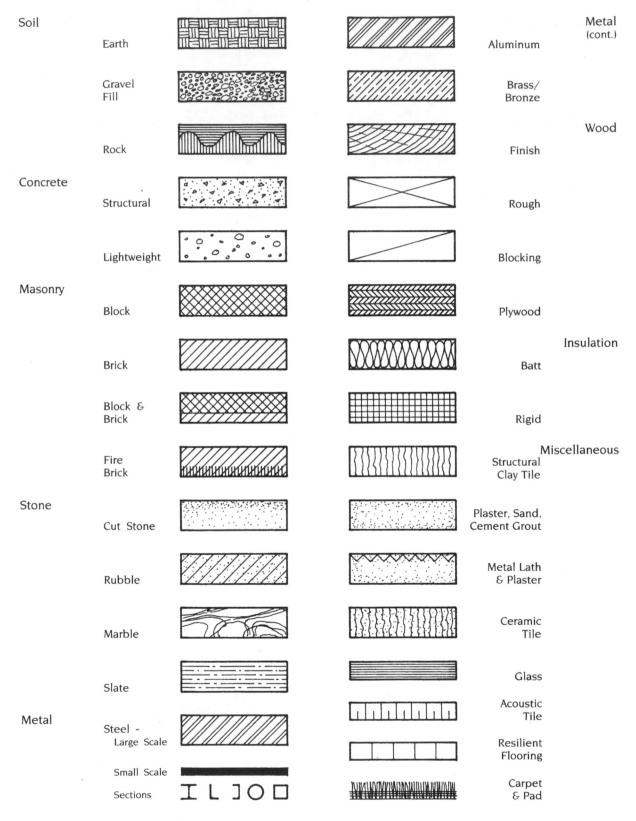

Soil — Earth, Gravel Fill, Rock

Concrete — Structural, Lightweight

Masonry — Block, Brick, Block & Brick, Fire Brick

Stone — Cut Stone, Rubble, Marble, Slate

Metal — Steel - Large Scale, Small Scale, Sections

Metal (cont.) — Aluminum, Brass/Bronze

Wood — Finish, Rough, Blocking, Plywood

Insulation — Batt, Rigid

Miscellaneous — Structural Clay Tile, Plaster, Sand, Cement Grout, Metal Lath & Plaster, Ceramic Tile, Glass, Acoustic Tile, Resilient Flooring, Carpet & Pad

Figure 10.10 *Architectural Symbols in Section*

Architectural Drawing Symbols

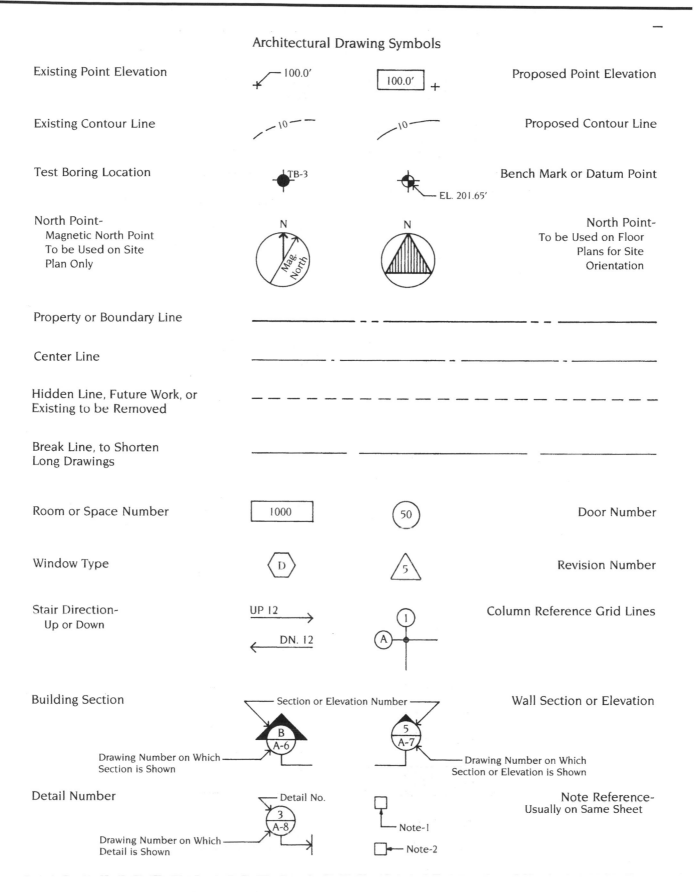

Existing Point Elevation — 100.0' / 100.0' + — Proposed Point Elevation

Existing Contour Line — 10 / 10 — Proposed Contour Line

Test Boring Location — TB-3 / EL. 201.65' — Bench Mark or Datum Point

North Point-
Magnetic North Point
To be Used on Site
Plan Only — N Mag. North / N — North Point-
To be Used on Floor
Plans for Site
Orientation

Property or Boundary Line

Center Line

Hidden Line, Future Work, or
Existing to be Removed

Break Line, to Shorten
Long Drawings

Room or Space Number — 1000 / 50 — Door Number

Window Type — D / 5 — Revision Number

Stair Direction-
Up or Down — UP 12 / DN. 12 / A 1 — Column Reference Grid Lines

Building Section — Section or Elevation Number — B A-6 / 5 A-7 — Wall Section or Elevation
Drawing Number on Which Section is Shown / Drawing Number on Which Section or Elevation is Shown

Detail Number — Detail No. / 3 A-8 / Note-1 / Note-2 — Note Reference-
Usually on Same Sheet
Drawing Number on Which Detail is Shown

Figure 10.11 Architectural Drawing Symbols

Repeating information again and again is not only redundant, but may lead to confusion, and errors when changes made in one location are not made in all the others.
- Be consistent with the use of terminology in both drawings and specifications. A "service sink" shown on the drawings should not be referred to as a "janitor's sink" in the specifications. A "bituminous surface course" in one location should not be an "asphalt topping" in another.
- Establish office standards, preferably in a printed manual distributed to each member of the professional team. Such a manual should contain standards for terminology, symbols, abbreviations, graphic representations of textures and materials, style of hand lettering, (font in the case of CAD produced drawings) uniformity of line weight, and other attributes should be clearly established and enforced as to general use.
- CAD standards should be established with the same degree of detail and conformity as with hand-drawn graphics. Establish common commands for pen (line) weight and "layering" in CAD files.

In summarizing the discussion on drawings, it is important to emphasize the need for care and coordination in the planning and preparation of all of the Contract Documents. Each document has a special purpose, content and intended use. The complete and properly prepared package is required to serve as a proper basis for bidding and construction.

Preparation of Specifications

To specify is to name or to describe in detail a material or a process. Construction Specifications are the requirements for products, materials, and workmanship upon which the Contract for Construction is based. As part of the Contract Documents, the Construction Specifications have a definite legal implication, as well as a more common practical purpose.

Specification Language

From early times, most building projects were constructed from materials which were of local origin and were well known by practitioners of the trades. It was necessary for the plasterer, for example, to know:

- How to mix and apply the material.
- Which tools and accessories to use.
- How to attend the curing and "set" of the material once applied.

As manufacturing processes have improved, and transportation and advertising have evolved, the designers' options for choosing and specifying materials and methods has broadened. As a result, the language and content of construction specifications have become more exact in establishing the designers' choice of materials and methods. At the same time, the designer has come to depend less upon the knowledge and skill of the tradesman in properly selecting and applying the material. Growing competition among materials manufacturers as well as contractors requires the specifier to spell out the performance requirements of materials and assemblies in great detail. The materials and processes selected by the designer must be described in a way that

Means Forms
ROOM
FINISH SCHEDULE

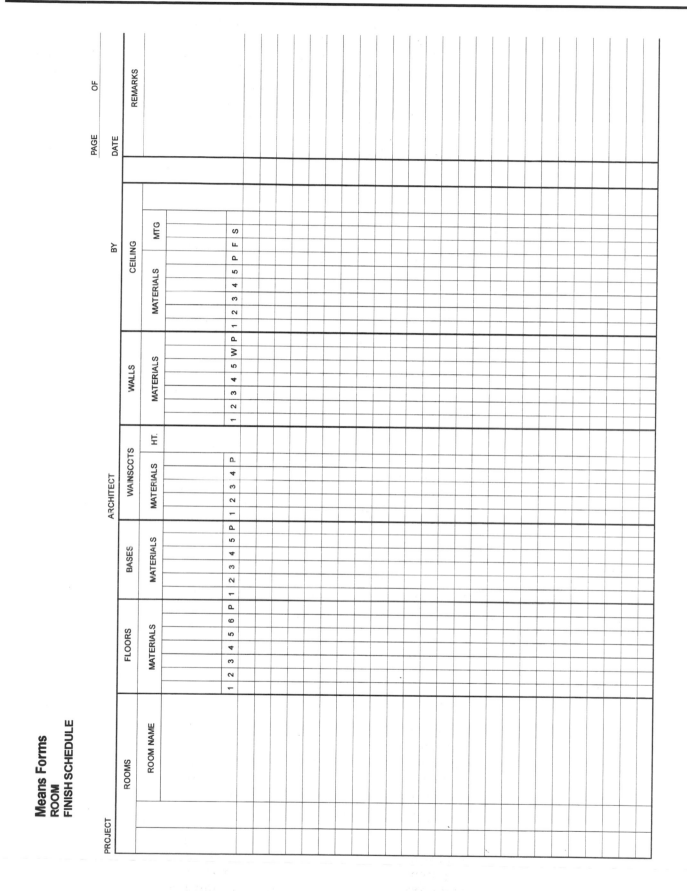

Figure 10.12 *Means Form, Room Finish Schedule*

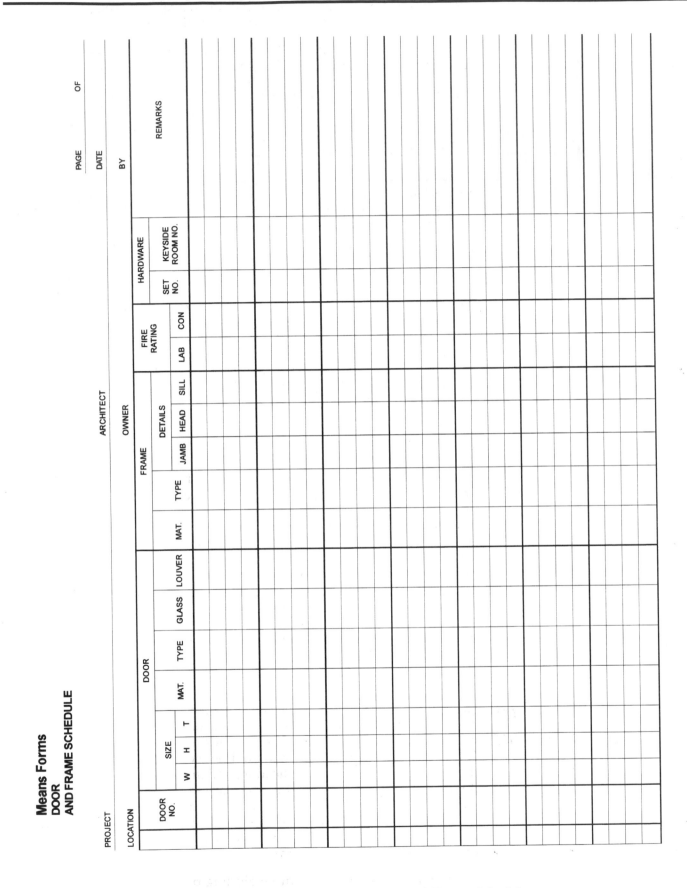

Figure 10.13 *Means Forms, Door and Frame Schedule*

the designer's full intention, as well as the reliability of the product or system can be upheld in case of dispute or litigation.

Ben John Small, in his book *Streamlined Specifications Standards*, describes the specification writer's responsibility in the following way:

> *We are not lawyers, yet by indirection we are compelled to compete with them in the sense that should there exist any shortcomings in our specifications, the lawyers unearth them, waving claims in our face. We are not seers, yet in the event of a dispute, should we have had the good fortune to have written the right thing in the right place we become a 'good man.' If not, we are labeled a 'you know what.'*

In an effort to enforce equal opportunity in publicly funded building construction, as well as to ensure the lowest possible cost by maximizing competition in bidding, the government has entered the process of construction specifying. (See Chapter 2, "The Owner," Public Owners). The use of generic language is required by many public owners to describe materials and processes used in the Contract documentation for public work. The term *generic* is defined as (1) of, in, or referring to a *genus*, or family of similar origin, (2) applicable to a family, class, or group of similar kind, or (3) not protected by a trademark. As new materials and methods have evolved over the years, manufacturers have tended to protect their products from use or duplication by competitors by obtaining patents, registering trademarks, and trade names under copyright laws. (See Chapter 6, "Legal Concerns and Insurance,"— Patents and Trademarks). Such trade names for popular products have tended to become the common description or identification of the product. As a result, the term "generic" has a critical impact as well as legal implications on the language used by the specifier.

In the "common" language of construction, there have been, over the years, many inconsistencies in the meaning and application of terms and in the organization of data. The Construction Specifications Institute (CSI) together with many other professional and industry organizations have responded to this problem, improving, and making universal the language, coordination, content, format, and usefulness of Contract Documents. Special emphasis has been placed on construction specifications. Because of these efforts and the contributions of committee work over many years by dedicated professionals, an understanding now exists whereby the specifier can describe requirements to inform the various segments of the construction industry.

The Three-Part Section Format

Competition in the marketplace and constant technological developments have forced design professionals to use a more and more detailed approach to the language and format of specifications. In the 17th century, the specifier had to do little more than generically name the product, describe the application, and indicate the surfaces to which it would be applied. Today, it is necessary to specify procedures, state administrative requirements, and establish quality standards, as well as describe the product and its accessories, methods of application and workmanship requirements. Specifications have always been intended to serve the following functions:

- To equalize the competitive bidding process.
- To act as a reference guide to the constructor in the field.

- To provide assurance of acceptable quality standards.
- To establish a simple methodology for measuring or determining quality standards in the case of a challenge or a dispute.

In order to successfully carry out these functions, specifications must be highly structured and stated as briefly as possible in an outline format. As time becomes increasingly valuable, it is even more important that the specifications are as organized and consistent as possible. As more uniformity is achieved in the format, outline, placement and sequence of specification data, the response to that data becomes more efficient—both in estimating and in accomplishing the Work. These goals have come of age in the techniques and standards that have been developed under the leadership of the Construction Specifications Institute. The CSI 16 division organization of data, coupled with a standardized three-part section format for specifying segments of work has greatly improved the economy and utility of information in the workplace.

The three-part format as discussed below, is an industry-accepted standard for listing specification information. This format aids both writer and user in locating information quickly and efficiently. Since the location of information is consistent and pre-defined, it serves as a checklist for verifying compliance with written requirements. Both the coordination of design decisions, and the Work of professional staff and consultants are enhanced and facilitated. Use of this format minimizes duplication, errors, and omissions.

Part 1—General
Part 1 is intended to contain specific administrative and procedural requirements unique to the item or items of work. As a minimum, *Part 1—General* should introduce the subject matter, relate the subject to other sections and describe any coordination with other work specified elsewhere. Part 1 can also refer the reader to applicable general requirements found in Division 1, state any reference information that would be helpful in establishing quality and performance standards, and list any requirements for shop drawings, manufacturer's literature, samples and other data that must be submitted for the approval of the design professional. Finally, Part 1 should include any project, site, or environmental restraints as well as scheduling and sequencing requirements, guarantees, warranties, and maintenance requirements.

Part 2—Products
Part 2 deals exclusively with the material or product, or related products, including (if applicable) the manufacturer or manufacturing process. The design professional's requirements for composition of the materials and fabrication should also be described along with quality control standards acceptable to the design professional and regulatory authorities.

Part 3—Execution
Part 3 addresses issues involving the incorporation of the products into the Work. The requirements of the Execution direct the contractor to verify conditions that must be properly accomplished prior to installing or applying the product. The requirements for erection, installation or application are specified in terms of special techniques, tolerances, interface with other products, tests, and inspections related to quality control in the field. Part 3 should also deal with final adjustments, cleaning, and protection during construction, as well as any other requirements leading to final acceptance at substantial completion.

Definitions

Included in the three-part section format are certain definitions. These definitions are part of the specification format concept and define the use, location, and outline of specification information. Examples of such definitions are listed below.

Division: A standard category of information organized as a general topic. There are 16 divisions which together cover the scope of information required to describe the Work.

Section: A basic unit of the specification. Each section concentrates on an item or category of items that constitutes an element of work. Sections are grouped under any one of the 16 divisions.

Part: A further subdivision of a section. A part divides a section into three related groupings of information.

Article: A subdivision of a part. An article consists of a few paragraphs covering a major subject.

Paragraph: One or more sentences that deal with a particular item or point of information within an article.

Part 1—General

1.01 Requirements Included:

A. What items of work are described by the section?

B. What generic types of work, products, or requirements are to be included in this section?

Note: The intention of this paragraph is to allow the reader to quickly assess the section content and not to "scope" the overall work requirement in a way that would imply trade jurisdiction. The specifier should bear in mind that the entire specification is addressed to the (general) contractor, who is a principle party to the Contract for Construction. Although the actual work may be part of divisions that are commonly assigned to a subcontractor, it is the contractor who bears the responsibility for accomplishing the Work specified in any section, and it is to the contractor and the contractor alone that the information is addressed.

1.02 Related Requirements

A. What is the relationship of this work specified in other sections?

B. Where is the other related work specified?

C. Are any requirements specified elsewhere to be erected, installed, or applied under provisions of this section?

D. Are any products specified in this section but installed under the provisions of other sections?

Note: Related requirements should include sections that deal with work related to this section and requiring coordination, previous preparation, adjacency or interface. Question C may refer to owner-furnished items which are normally specified in an appropriate Division 1 section. Question D may refer to a material such as glazing that is specified under Section 08800—Glass and Glazing, but installed by the manufacturer under the provisions of Section 08500—Metal Windows.

1.03 Allowances and Unit Prices

A. Are any items of work to be furnished under cash allowances specified in Section 01020—Allowances? If so, is the allowance limited to purchase of material only, or does it include labor and accessories specified in this and related sections also?

B. Are unit prices specified in Division 1 applicable to overages or underages of materials or labor provided? If so, what system or authority for measuring is to be used?

1.04 References

A. Are there any published, industry-accepted standard specifications, testing requirements or other written standards that should be listed for reference purposes—to complement the requirements of the section or to anticipate challenges involving quality or performance considerations?

B. Does the design professional or the specifier own or have access to a copy of the standard listed?

C. Does the standard state any provisions that contradict, obviate, or otherwise confuse the requirements of this section?

Note: The specifier is cautioned that commonly used reference standards (such as those provided by organizations listed in Chapter 8) should be readily available and well-known to the specifier. It is not unusual for such standards to list multiple types of materials, some of which may not be acceptable for the use intended. Moreover, some standards may contain statements that could change the relationships established either in the Conditions of the Contract or the General Requirements (Division 1). Such misleading or incorrect provisions must be omitted or made inapplicable in this paragraph when appropriate. Specifiers should never list a reference standard unless absolutely certain of its content and possible impact on the intentions established by the Contract Documents.

1.05 Definitions

A. Are there any terms, trade names or processes specified in this section that may be unfamiliar to the reader and which have not been defined elsewhere?

B. Is there any coordination with other sections or requirements specified elsewhere that could be clarified by a definition placed in this particular section? Does the owner's option to contract portions of the Work separately have any bearing on the work of this section?

1.06 System Description

Note: This article should be restricted to statements describing the performance or design requirements and tolerances of a complete system. Descriptions should be limited to composite and operational properties needed to link multiple components of a system or to interface with other systems.

1.07 Submittals

A. Does the design professional require that manufacturer's literature, installation instructions, disclaimers, guarantees, warranties or other statements be submitted for information or approval purposes?

B. Are shop drawings of the scope or work, method of erection, assembly, or application required for submittal and approval?

C. Are samples of materials required? If so, specify number and size if appropriate.

D. Are design data, quality control standards, test reports, certificates, or manufacturers' field reports required?

E. Are contract closeout submittals, project record documents, operational instructions, maintenance data, and warranty submittals required? If so, this information must be coordinated with provisions of Section 01700—Contract Closeout and Section 01710—Project Record Documents.

Note: Section 01300—Submittals deals with the detailed requirements of submissions that are called for in individual sections. Careful coordination is required between submittal requirements and this section.

1.08 Quality Assurance

A. What standards of quality are expected?

B. What credentials, and how many years of experience, if any, must manufacturers and mechanics exhibit?

C. What regulatory and code requirements is the Work expected to meet? It is not necessary to name local building code ordinances which are generally known, but it is necessary to name codes and regulations that may not be known.

D. Are there any certifications of quality and compliance required?

E. Is the material or assembly mock-up required for approval and/or to serve as the model for quality and workmanship? If so, specify the size required, the location, and the length of time during which protection and maintenance is expected. State whether or not the sample can be incorporated into the Work once approved.

F. Are pre-installation meetings required in order to coordinate and ensure the quality of the Work?

1.09 Delivery, Storage, and Handling

A. How should the product be protected, packaged, and shipped?

B. Are there any unusual site conditions that may require special attention to methods of storage and protection during construction?

Note: Statements should supplement the general requirements of product protection stated in Section 01600—Material and Equipment (Division 1).

1.10 Project/Site Conditions

A. What environmental considerations apply to storage and application of the product?

B. Does adverse temperature affect the storage of application of the product? If so, state limits of temperature.

C. Are there any existing conditions at the site that must be considered?

Note: This information may require coordination with "Information Available to Bidders" stated in the Bidding Requirements.

1.11 Sequencing and Scheduling
Do the requirements of this section require special sequencing and coordination with work of another section, or contract, or with work done by the owner?

Note: Section 01010—Summary of the Work, in Division 1, normally contains statements concerning overall sequencing and scheduling. Any statement made here must be coordinated with Division 1 requirements.

1.12 Guarantee and Warranty
A. Are there any guarantee and/or warranty provisions required of the manufacturer or contractor?

B. Are there any provisions required that would exceed the provisions of guarantees or warranties as established in the Conditions of the Contract?

Note: It is important that the specifier coordinate the requirements specified in this section with the provisions of the Conditions of the Contract so as not to void one or the other because of conflict. Guarantees and warranties are difficult to enforce at best, and any conflict between the provisions of a particular section and the Conditions of the Contract is almost sure to give the purveyor an "out," thereby making the owner vulnerable and the design professional liable.

1.13 Maintenance
A. Does the nature of the work specified in this section require special maintenance during and after construction?

B. Should the contractor be required to maintain a paid-up service policy during the construction period?

C. Has consideration been given to requiring the contractor to provide extra stock for the owner's initial maintenance and replacement purposes?

Note: The requirements of C should be coordinated with Section 01700—Contract Closeout.

Part 2 — Products This part is governed mainly by the type of specification that is intended. Recognized specification types are:
- Descriptive Specifications.
- Performance Specifications.
- Specifications based on Reference Standards.
- Proprietary Specifications.
  —Closed Proprietary Specifications.
  —Open Proprietary Specifications.

Specification applications include:
- Restrictive Specifications.
- Non-Restrictive Specifications.

The type and application of specifications determines the approach and application of the various articles of Part 2.

2.01 Products and Manufacture

This article is applicable to the proprietary type of specification. It can be used for either open or closed application where the product can be described by naming one or more manufacturers and the acceptable products. The Instructions to Bidders should deal with procedures that enable bidders to propose substitutions and seek approval prior to the receipt of bids. Section 01600—Materials and Equipment should provide a procedure whereby the contractor can propose substitutions after the execution of the Contract for Construction. Reference to these provisions should be made if the non-restrictive application is to be upheld.

    A. Has the design professional selected a particular product produced by a manufacturer to fulfill the requirements and intent of this section?

Note: If the Closed Proprietary method is used, no further information is necessary. If the Open Proprietary method is used, the following questions are applicable.

    B. Can two or more similar products produced by other manufacturers also meet the requirements of this section so as to be equally acceptable to the design professional?

    C. Have the products named above been recently researched to determine if they are currently available as specified?

2.02 Materials

This article is used where the Descriptive, Performance, or Reference Standard type specification is applicable. The specifier should name each material and describe its attributes according to the type of specification. In the case of the descriptive specification, the specifier should state in detail the minimum acceptable features of the material. In the case of performance specifying, the specifier should describe the end results to be achieved by the use of the product. In the case of reference standard specifying, the specifier should name the standard specification to be followed.

2.03 Accessories

This article is intended to provide requirements for subordinate or secondary items which aid, assist, or are required to complete, prepare, or install the primary products or materials that are the subject of the section. The article is not intended to specify basic options available for manufactured units and equipment. Accessory options should be named together with the product or material.

2.04 Mixes

This article should provide proportions and procedures for mixing materials, and is unique to descriptive specifying of such materials as asphalt paving, concrete, mortar, and plaster.

2.05 Fabrication

This article is intended to describe items that must be shop-manufactured, fabricated, or assembled before they are delivered to the job site. The specifier should specify any required factory-applied finishing and should specify acceptable tolerances or variations from specified requirements.

2.06 Source Quality Control

A. Are any tests and/or inspections required of the product or material before it leaves the source of manufacture or assembly?

B. Is verification of performance required before the product or material is shipped to the job site?

Note: Any testing or inspection that is required at the source of the product or material should be coordinated with Section 01400—Quality Control.

Part 3—Execution

3.01 Examination

A. Does the installation of the product or material depend upon the Work of another section? Must an existing condition be properly prepared before erection, installation, or application can take place?

B. Are any preparations required under this section involving the surface area, surrounding materials, or the site? Are such preparations needed in order to properly incorporate the primary products or materials specified in this section?

3.02 Preparation

A. Does the nature of the Work require any special protective measures to ensure that adjacent surfaces, equipment, or installations are not damaged?

B. Does the Work require any special preparation at adjacent locations before it can be incorporated into the project?

3.03 Erection, Installation, or Application

Note: Only one of the titles listed above is applicable.

A. What actions are required to accomplish the specified unit of work?

B. Are products specified in other sections installed under this section?

C. Can or does the manufacturer provide complete instructions as to the proper erection, installation, or application of the unit of work?

Note: In instances where a guarantee or warranty is required, erection, installation, or application of the unit of work must be specified in strict accordance with the manufacturer's instructions in order to ensure compliance with guarantee and/or warranty provisions.

D. Does the unit of work require any special procedures prior to incorporation into the project?

E. Does the interface of the unit of work with other elements require any process, accessory, anchorage, special separation, or bonding?

F. What are the acceptable tolerances, and variations from plumb or form allowed when the unit of work is erected or installed?

G. What is the required wet or cured thickness of a unit of applied work?

3.04 Field Quality Control

A. Are any tests or inspections required during or after the specified unit of work is erected, installed or applied?

Note: Coordination with Section 01400—Quality Control, or Section 01410—Testing may be required.

B. Does the nature of the unit of work require the manufacturer to provide any service in the field such as instruction or supervision?

3.05 Adjusting and Cleaning

A. Does the erection of the unit of work require adjustments and/or cleaning prior to acceptance?

B. If temporary protective coatings or coverings have been specified in Part 1, when is it acceptable to remove such protective coatings or coverings?

Note: The requirements of this article may involve coordination with one or more Division 1 sections such as Section 01500—Construction Facilities and Temporary Controls and/or Section 01700—Contract Closeout.

3.06 Demonstration

A. Does the nature of the unit of work require that the manufacturer or contractor perform demonstration of the operation and maintenance for the owner's benefit?

3.07 Protection

Are any special procedures required to protect the unit of work subsequent to erection, installation or application?

3.08 Schedules

Note: The specifier may find it convenient to create a schedule to be included in the specification at this point.

Page Format

Figure 10.14 shows the recommended page outline format now commonly used by specifiers who choose to follow the guidelines of the CSI *Manual of Practice*. There are a number of advantages in using this format to organize the specification material; some are listed below:

- Parallel documents such as other specification sections, addenda, and other Contract Documents can easily refer to specific items that have an "address" in the outline. Example: "... as provided in Article 2.04, paragraph A, item 2 of Section 07900—Joint Sealants ...".
- The specification is more easily "scan" read when the user is searching for an item of interest.
- The document is effective in outline form as the provisions stand out for the user rather than being buried in a mass of verbiage difficult to spot.

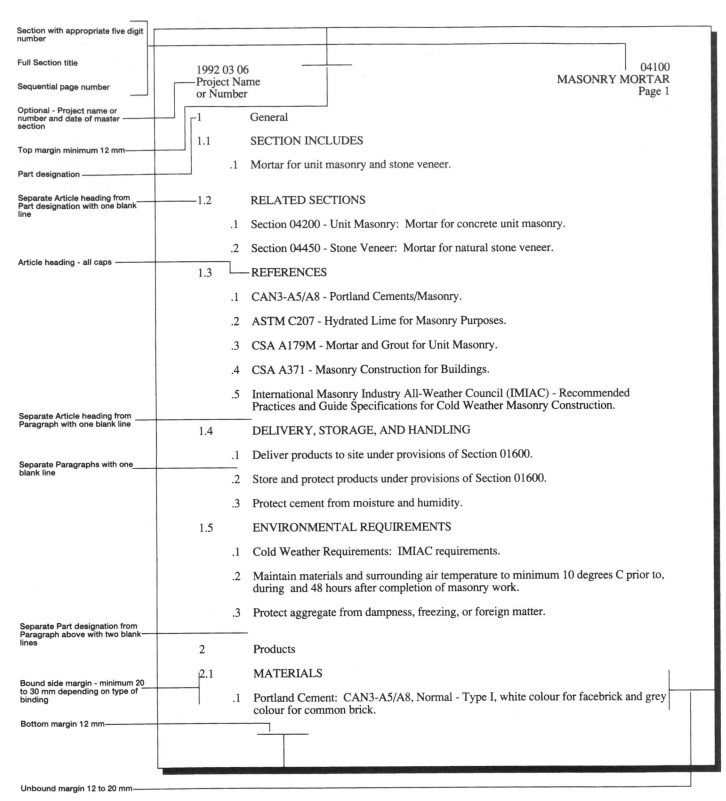

Section with appropriate five digit number

Full Section title

Sequential page number

Optional - Project name or number and date of master section

Top margin minimum 12 mm

Part designation

Separate Article heading from Part designation with one blank line

Article heading - all caps

Separate Article heading from Paragraph with one blank line

Separate Paragraphs with one blank line

Separate Part designation from Paragraph above with two blank lines

Bound side margin - minimum 20 to 30 mm depending on type of binding

Bottom margin 12 mm

Unbound margin 12 to 20 mm

1992 03 06
Project Name
or Number

04100
MASONRY MORTAR
Page 1

1   General

1.1   SECTION INCLUDES

    .1   Mortar for unit masonry and stone veneer.

1.2   RELATED SECTIONS

    .1   Section 04200 - Unit Masonry: Mortar for concrete unit masonry.

    .2   Section 04450 - Stone Veneer: Mortar for natural stone veneer.

1.3   REFERENCES

    .1   CAN3-A5/A8 - Portland Cements/Masonry.

    .2   ASTM C207 - Hydrated Lime for Masonry Purposes.

    .3   CSA A179M - Mortar and Grout for Unit Masonry.

    .4   CSA A371 - Masonry Construction for Buildings.

    .5   International Masonry Industry All-Weather Council (IMIAC) - Recommended Practices and Guide Specifications for Cold Weather Masonry Construction.

1.4   DELIVERY, STORAGE, AND HANDLING

    .1   Deliver products to site under provisions of Section 01600.

    .2   Store and protect products under provisions of Section 01600.

    .3   Protect cement from moisture and humidity.

1.5   ENVIRONMENTAL REQUIREMENTS

    .1   Cold Weather Requirements: IMIAC requirements.

    .2   Maintain materials and surrounding air temperature to minimum 10 degrees C prior to, during and 48 hours after completion of masonry work.

    .3   Protect aggregate from dampness, freezing, or foreign matter.

2   Products

2.1   MATERIALS

    .1   Portland Cement: CAN3-A5/A8, Normal - Type I, white colour for facebrick and grey colour for common brick.

Courtesy of the Construction Specifications Institute

Figure 10.14 *Specifications Page Format*

226

1992 03 06
Project Name
or Number

04100
MASONRY MORTAR
Page 2

.2 Mortar aggregate: CSA A179M, standard masonry type; clean, dry; protected from dampness, freezing, or foreign matter.

.3 Hydrated Lime: ASTM C207, Type S.

.4 Water: Clean and potable.

2.2 MORTAR COLOUR

.1 Mortar Colour: Mineral oxide pigment; chocolate brown colour; "Great Stuff" manufactured by Acme Manufacturing Co. Ltd.

2.3 MIXES

.1 Mortar for Load Bearing Walls and Partitions: CSA A179M, Type S.

.2 Mortar for Non-load Bearing Walls and Partitions: CSA A179M, Type N.

2.4 MORTAR MIXING

.1 Thoroughly mix mortar ingredients in quantities needed for immediate use in accordance with CSA A179M.

.2 Add mortar colour in accordance with manufacturer's instructions. Provide uniformity of mix and colouration.

.3 Do not use anti-freeze compounds to lower the freezing point of mortar.

3 Execution

3.1 INSTALLATION

.1 Install mortar in conjunction with Sections 04200 and 04450.

3.2 FIELD QUALITY CONTROL

.1 Field testing will be performed under provisions of Section 01400.

END OF SECTION

Courtesy of the Construction Specifications Institute

Figure 10.14 *Specifications Page Format (continued)*

The 16 Divisions

The Masterformat is the outgrowth of the 16 Division Format created by the Construction Specifications Institute (CSI) and Construction Specifications Canada (CSC). It is a logical, complete, and uniform system for organizing building construction information. This system has professional and industry acceptance and has been adopted by most professional organizations as well as by most manufacturers and information services associated with the construction industry. Under this system, Division 1—General Requirements deals with the procedural and administrative requirements specified for the individual project. Divisions 2 through 16 contain technical specifications each section of which may contain provisions dependent in some way on the administrative provisions of Division 1.

Masterformat has allocated descriptions and 5 digit numbers to elements of the *Project Manual* including the 16 divisions of the technical specifications. Figure 10.15 offers a summary of the sixteen divisions and commonly used section numbers under each division with subject descriptions of each section. The Masterformat system of information description and numbering has received almost universal acceptance by the construction industry. This acceptance can be seen in manufacturers' literature, information systems libraries, and government specifications. Specifiers are encouraged to follow this system for the sake of uniformity and coordination when writing the individual specification section as well as when creating, organizing, and publishing the Project Manual, and creating an estimate of Probable Cost. (See Chapter 11, "The Project Manual" and Chapter 12, "Construction Cost").

Division 1—General Requirements

The General Requirements of the project (allocated by the 16 Division Format to be contained in Division 1 of the specifications) is one of the key components of the Contract Documents. Division 1 specifications establish the administrative requirements, procedural requirements, restrictions, and other pertinent requirements that define the parameters under which the contractor shall conduct the Work. The General Requirements have a fundamental relationship to all of the other Contract Documents including Divisions 2 through 16 of the specifications. Figure 10.16 illustrates the relationships between Division 1 and the other Contract Documents. Figure 10.17 illustrates a list of sections typical of Division 1 topics with descriptions of information that should be contained in each section of Division 1.

Division 1 sections should be organized and written in the three-part format, in like manner to any of the sections in Divisions 2 through 16. Administrative provisions may not require Part 2 and Part 3 provisions. In any case, the specifier should write the provisions for Division 1 sections in careful coordination with the provisions of the General Conditions of the Contract, the Supplementary General Conditions, and the Part 1 provisions of sections contained in Divisions 2 through 16.

Divisions 2 through 16

Divisions 2 through 16 of the specifications are often referred to as the "Technical Specifications." Beginning with Division 2—Site Work, and ending with Division 16—Electrical. The technical specification are broken down into individual sections, describing specific units of work. These descriptions stipulate the Work to be done, as well as

MASTERFORMAT™

LEVEL TWO NUMBERS AND TITLES

Introductory Information

00001	Project Title Page
00005	Certifications Page
00007	Seals Page
00010	Table of Contents
00015	List of Drawings
00020	List of Schedules

Bidding Requirements

00100	Bid Solicitation
00200	Instructions to Bidders
00300	Information Available to Bidders
00400	Bid Forms and Supplements
00490	Bidding Addenda

Contracting Requirements

00500	Agreement
00600	Bonds and Certificates
00700	General Conditions
00800	Supplementary Conditions
00900	Addenda and Modifications

Facilities and Spaces

	Facilities and Spaces

Systems and Assemblies

	Systems and Assemblies

Construction Products and Activities
Division 1—General Requirements

01100	Summary
01200	Price and Payment Procedures
01300	Administrative Requirements
01400	Quality Requirements
01500	Temporary Facilities and Controls
01600	Product Requirements
01700	Execution Requirements
01800	Facility Operation
01900	Facility Decommissioning

Division 2—Site Construction

02050	Basic Site Materials and Methods
02100	Site Remediation
02200	Site Preparation
02300	Earthwork
02400	Tunneling, Boring, and Jacking
02450	Foundation and Load-Bearing Elements
02500	Utility Services
02600	Drainage and Containment
02700	Bases, Ballasts, Pavements, and Appurtenances
02800	Site Improvements and Amenities
02900	Planting
02950	Site Restoration and Rehabilitation

Division 3—Concrete

03050	Basic Concrete Materials and Methods
03100	Concrete Forms and Accessories
03200	Concrete Reinforcement
03300	Cast-in-Place Concrete
03400	Precast Concrete
03500	Cementitious Decks and Underlayment
03600	Grouts
03700	Mass Concrete
03900	Concrete Restoration and Cleaning

Division 4—Masonry

04050	Basic Masonry Materials and Methods
04200	Masonry Units
04400	Stone
04500	Refractories
04600	Corrosion-Resistant Masonry
04800	Masonry Assemblies
04900	Masonry Restoration and Cleaning

Courtesy of the Construction Specifications Institute, Masterformat

Figure 10.15 *Summary of Sixteen Divisions*

Division 5—Metals

05050	Basic Metal Materials and Methods
05100	Structural Metal Framing
05200	Metal Joists
05400	Metal Deck
05400	Cold-Formed Metal Framing
05500	Metal Fabrications
05600	Hydraulic Fabrications
05650	Railroad Track and Accessories
05700	Ornamental Metal
05800	Expansion Control
05900	Metal Restoration and Cleaning

Division 6—Wood and Plastics

06050	Basic Wood and Plastic Materials and Methods
06100	Rough Carpentry
06200	Finish Carpentry
06400	Architectural Woodwork
06500	Structural Plastics
06600	Plastic Fabrications
06900	Wood and Plastic Restoration and Cleaning

Division 7—Thermal and Moisture Protection

07050	Basic Thermal and Moisture Protection Material and Methods
07100	Dampproofing and Waterproofing
07200	Thermal Protection
07300	Shingles, Roof Tiles, and Roof Coverings
07400	Roofing and Siding Panels
07500	Membrane Roofing
07600	Flashing and Sheet Metal
07700	Roof Specialties and Accessories
07800	Fire and Smoke Protection
07900	Joint Sealers

Division 8—Doors and Windows

08050	Basic Door and Window Materials and Methods
08100	Metal Doors and Frames
08200	Wood and Plastic Doors
08300	Specialty Doors
08400	Entrances and Storefronts
08500	Windows
08600	Skylights
08700	Hardware
08800	Glazing
08900	Glazed Curtain Wall

Division 9—Finishes

09050	Basic Finish Materials and Methods
09100	Metal Support Assemblies
09200	Plaster and Gypsum Board
09300	Tile
09400	Terrazzo
09500	Ceilings
09600	Flooring
09700	Wall Finishes
09800	Acoustical Treatment
09900	Paints and Coatings

Division 10—Specialties

10100	Visual Display Boards
10150	Compartments and Cubicles
10200	Louvers and Vents
10240	Grilles and Screens
10250	Service Walls
10260	Wall and Corner Guards
10270	Access Flooring
10290	Pest Control
10300	Fireplaces and Stoves
10340	Manufactured Exterior Specialties
10350	Flagpoles
10400	Identification Devices
10450	Pedestrian Control Devices
10500	Lockers
10520	Fire Protection Specialties
10530	Protective Covers
10550	Postal Specialties
10600	Partitions
10670	Storage Shelving
10700	Exterior Protection
10750	Telephone Specialties
10800	Toilet, Bath, and Laundry Accessories
10880	Scales
10900	Wardrobe and Closet Specialties

Courtesy of the Construction Specifications Institute, Masterformat

Figure 10.15 *Summary of Sixteen Divisions (continued)*

Division 11—Specialties

11010	Maintenance Equipment
11020	Security and Vault Equipment
11030	Teller and Service Equipment
11040	Ecclesiastical Equipment
11050	Library Equipment
11060	Theater and Stage Equipment
11070	Instrumental Equipment
11080	Registration Equipment
11090	Checkroom Equipment
11100	Mercantile Equipment
11110	Commercial Laundry and Dry Cleaning Equipment
11120	Vending Equipment
11130	Audio-Visual Equipment
11140	Vehicle Service Equipment
11150	Parking Control Equipment
11160	Loading Dock Equipment
11170	Solid Waste Handling Equipment
11190	Detention Equipment
11200	Water Supply and Treatment Equipment
11280	Hydraulic Gates and Valves
11300	Fluid Waste Treatment and Disposal Equipment
11400	Food Service Equipment
11450	Residential Equipment
11460	Unit Kitchens
11470	Darkroom Equipment
11480	Athletic, Recreational, and Therapeutic Equipment
11500	Industrial and Process Equipment
11600	Laboratory Equipment
11650	Planetarium Equipment
11660	Observatory Equipment
11680	Office Equipment
11700	Medical Equipment
11780	Mortuary Equipment
11850	Navigation Equipment
11870	Agricultural Equipment
11900	Exhibit Equipment

Courtesy of the Construction Specifications Institute, Masterformat

Figure 10.15 Summary of Sixteen Divisions (continued)

Division 12—Furnishings

12050	Fabrics
12100	Art
12300	Manufactured Casework
12400	Furnishings and Accessories
12500	Furniture
12600	Multiple Seating
12700	Systems Furniture
12800	Interior Plants and Planters
12900	Furnishings Restoration and Repair

Division 13—Special Construction

13010	Air-Supported Structures
13020	Building Modules
13030	Special Purpose Rooms
13080	Sound, Vibration, and Seismic Control
13090	Radiation Protection
13100	Lightning Protection
13110	Cathodic Protection
13120	Pre-Engineering Structures
13150	Swimming Pools
13160	Aquariums
13165	Aquatic Park Facilities
13170	Tubs and Pools
13175	Ice Rinks
13185	Kennels and Animal Shelters
13190	Site-Constructed Incinerators
13200	Storage Tanks
13220	Filter Underdrains and Media
13230	Digester Covers and Appurtenances
13240	Oxygenation Systems
13260	Sludge Conditioning Systems
13280	Hazardous Material Remediation
13400	Measurement and Control Instrumentation
13500	Recording Instrumentation
13550	Transportation Control Instrumentation
13600	Solar and Wind Energy Equipment
13700	Security Access and Surveillance
13800	Building Automation and Control
13850	Detection and Alarm
13900	Fire Suppression

Courtesy of the Construction Specifications Institute, Masterformat

Figure 10.15 Summary of Sixteen Divisions (continued)

Division 14—Conveying Systems

14100	Dumbwaiter
14200	Elevators
14300	Escalators and Moving Walks
14400	Lifts
14500	Material Handling
14600	Hoists and Cranes
14700	Turntables
14800	Scaffolding
14900	Transportation

Division 15—Mechanical

15050	Basic Mechanical Materials and Methods
15100	Building Services Piping
15200	Process Piping
15300	Fire Protection Piping
15400	Plumbing Fixtures and Equipment
15500	Heat-Generation Equipment
15600	Refrigeration Equipment
15700	Heating, Ventilating, and Air Conditioning Equipment
15800	Air Distribution
15900	HVAC Instrumentation and Controls
15950	Testing, Adjusting, and Balancing

Division 16—Electrical

16050	Basic Electrical Materials and Methods
16100	Wiring Methods
16200	Electrical Power
16300	Transmission and Distribution
16400	Low-Voltage Distribution
16500	Lighting
16700	Communications
16800	Sound and Video

Courtesy of the Construction Specifications Institute, Masterformat

Figure 10.15 *Summary of Sixteen Divisions (continued)*

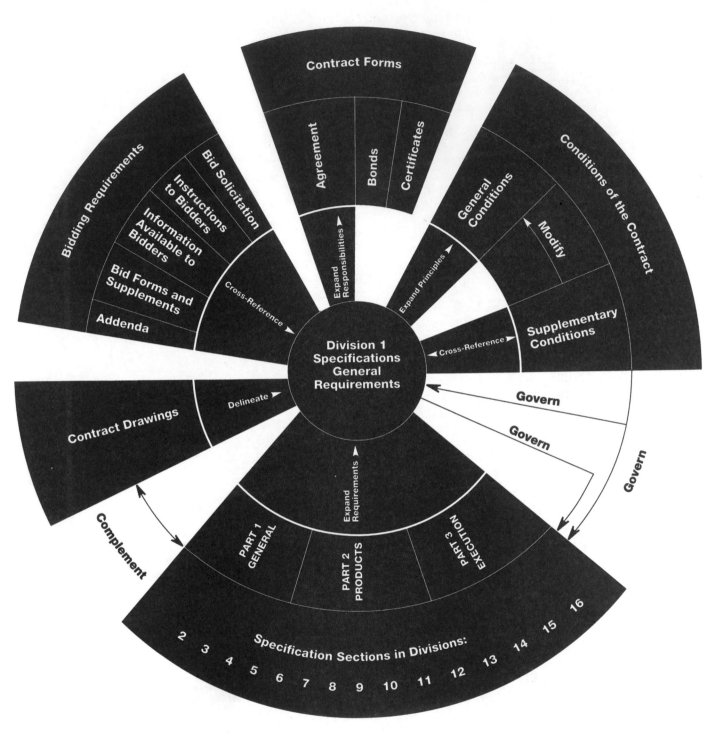

Courtesy of the Construction Specifications Institute, Masterformat

Figure 10.16 *Relationships between Division 1 and Other Contract Documents*

SECTION 01010 - SUMMARY OF THE WORK

This section describes the scope and extent of the work covered by the Contract Documents, denotes work to be accomplished by others, the sequence of the work, restrictions on use of site, coordination of the work, regulatory requirements and similar items related to the conduct of the work.

SECTION 01020 - CASH ALLOWANCES

This section itemizes and describes allowances in terms of lump sum cash amounts that are specified to be included in the Contract Sum for providing items of materials and/or work that shall be selected by the owner.

SECTION 01028 - CHANGE ORDER PROCEDURES

This section describes procedures to be followed in the probable event that changes in the contract will occur.

SECTION 01030 - ALTERNATES

This section describes bidding procedures required to propose itemized alternates to be added or subtracted from the Contract Sum at the Owner's option.

SECTION 01031 - ALTERATION PROCEDURES

This section describes special procedures that are required for projects which involve the work of additions and/or alterations to existing facilities.

SECTION 01040 - CONTRACT COORDINATION

This section describes the procedures required for coordination of the work, including separate contracts, work or items furnished by the owner as well as coordination of work under this contract.

SECTION 01045 - CUTTING AND PATCHING

This section describes the restrictions and procedures required for cutting and patching of existing work, correction of contract work, or for accommodation of related work.

SECTION 01050 - FIELD ENGINEERING

This section describes requirements of contractor furnished engineering for building location and layout, verification of site controls and other professional engineering confirmation and certification related to the execution of the work.

Courtesy of the Construction Specifications Institute, Masterformat

Figure 10.17 *List of Sections Typical of Division 1 Topics*

SECTION 01090 - REFERENCE STANDARDS

This section describes and lists the organizations capable of providing published reference standards offered or required by the various specification sections.

SECTION 01100 - SPECIAL PROJECT PROCEDURES

This section describes any specialized or unusual procedures, out of the ordinary, that must be observed by the contractor in the conduct of the work. This section is used rarely in cases of sensitive or unusual owner requirements.

SECTION 01152 - APPLICATIONS FOR PAYMENT

This section describes procedures, specifies forms to be used and information to be contained in contractor's applications for payment.

SECTION 01200 - PROJECT MEETINGS

This section describes procedures in conducting meetings during the process of construction for purposes of coordinating the activities of those related to the work and others.

SECTION 01300 - SUBMITTALS

This section describes the requirements related to submittals of various kinds that require design professional approval.

SECTION 01400 - QUALITY CONTROL

This section describes the procedures to be followed in achieving, determining and verifying specified quality of materials and methods during construction.

SECTION 01410 - TESTING LABORATORY SERVICES

This section describes the standards, procedures and conditions related to testing of materials and applications. Normally specified in Section 01400, this section is commonly used if testing is to be paid for or conducted in some manner other than as required by Paragraph 7.7 of AIA Document A201 - General Conditions of the Contract for Construction.

SECTION 01500 - CONSTRUCTION FACILITIES TEMPORARY CONTROLS

This section describes the requirements and restrictions placed on the use of equipment, site, utilities, temporary facilities, safety measures and other procedures related to the conduct of the work.

Courtesy of the Construction Specifications Institute, Masterformat

Figure 10.17 *List of Sections Typical of Division 1 Topics (continued)*

SECTION 01600 - MATERIAL AND EQUIPMENT

This section describes the requirements of product quality control, transportation to the site, storage and protection, product options, procedures related to substitutions and required certifications.

SECTION 01700 - CONTRACT CLOSE OUT

This section describes the procedures and requirements, final submittals and other information related to the completion and close out of the project leading to final payment and transition of contractor control to owner control.

SECTION 01720 - PROJECT RECORD DOCUMENTS

This section describes the requirements of records and documentation of the construction process for the owner's benefit that is required of the contractor.

Courtesy of the Construction Specifications Institute, Masterformat

Figure 10.17 *List of Sections Typical of Division 1 Topics (continued)*

materials, assemblies, systems or equipment to be used. Each section should incorporate an expected standard of quality in workmanship, installation, and finish. The "Broadscope" categories in each division are further subdivided into "Mediumscope" and "Narrowscope" listings.

Methods of Specifying

It is not unusual for the specifier to incorporate more than one method of specifying when creating the total specification for a single project. There is no clear rule about using one method of specifying over another. It is clear, however, that the specifier should choose one method as the basis of each separate section and should not attempt to mix methods in specifying basic units of work. The CSI *Manual of Practice* recognizes four basic types of specifications, which are outlined below.

Descriptive Specifications

Descriptive Specifications are defined as written descriptions detailing the required properties of a material, manufacturer's product, assembly of materials or products, or a piece of equipment. The subject of the specification is referred to by its generic description. No manufacturer, trade, or proprietary names are used in this type of specification. The materials are named and qualified. If joined into an assembly, the qualities of that assembly are also described.

A typical descriptive specification is shown in Figure 10.18. Here, the components are described, weights are compared, and the mixture is specified by proportionate weight of each ingredient, including water.

The specifier should always bear in mind that the contractor, to whom the specification is addressed, is responsible only for compliance with the exact parameters stated in the specification. While a competent general contractor knows by experience that the concrete ought to perform in certain ways, he fulfills his obligations to the Contract for Construction by following the specifier's directions for proportioning the mix (illustrated in Figure 10.18).

There are distinct disadvantages to the descriptive specification.

Example: Should the structural assembly have required an ultimate compressive strength of 2500 pounds per square inch (psi) in the concrete, and if the mix was not carefully specified to achieve that end, the design professional could be judged to have made an error and be responsible to the owner for the cost of replacement or repair of the faulty concrete.

Addtional examples of the descriptive specification is illustrated in Figures 10.19 and 10.20. A reinforced flexible flashing is to be used in a masonry cavity wall. Because of restrictions placed by the owner, the specifications must not rely upon proprietary name brand products, but describe the product in such a manner as to allow any and all manufacturers who produce such a product to bid competitively. The descriptive specification describes in detail the assembly, its basic materials, and the means of bonding the materials. It also specifies the expected weight of the membrane after assembly. The specification also lists certain expected performance characteristics as to the material's strength and other properties under adverse temperature exposure.

2.01 MATERIALS - STANDARD STRUCTURAL CONCRETE

   A. Portland Cement: Shall be of domestic manufacture, as approved by Architect. Use only one brand of cement unless otherwise authorized by Architect.

   B. Fine Aggregate: Natural bank sand or river sand, as apporved by the Architect from samples, washed and screened so as to produce a minimum percentage of voids.

   C. Coarse Aggregate: Gravel or crushed lime stone suitably processed, washed and screened, and shall consist of hard, durable particles without adherent coatings of foreign materials. Aggregate shall range from 1/4" to 1-1/4", well graded between the size limits.

   D. Water: Clean, potable, free of injurious amounts of minerals.

   E. Admixtures: In accordance with design mix prepared by testing laboratory:

2.02 PROPORTIONING CONCRETE MIX BY VOLUME

   A. Cement: 1/2 part

   B. Fine Aggregate: 1 part

   C. Coarse Aggregate: 2 parts

   D. Water: As required to produce minimum slump of 4 inches.

Figure 10.18 Descriptive Specification for Concrete

It is not likely that a modern day specifier, familiar with the many proven manufactured products available for the purpose of concealed flexible flashing would wish to research the details of each and every ingredient of a proposed product (such as the description of the woven twill and required weight of the cotton fabric written in the descriptive specification in Figure 10.19). A more satisfactory way of naming the product's performance under stress and weather conditions might be to add certain criteria to the specification as illustrated in Figure 10.20.

Industry Standard Specifications allow the specifier to reference the requirements for such materials and applications such as concrete and flexible flashing. Industry Standard Specifications have relieved the need for the specifier to rely on such detailed descriptive specifications. There are a number of advantages in the use of the descriptive specification. Some advantages of descriptive specifications are listed below:

- The contractor has wide discretion in the selection and purchase of materials and individual components.
- Competition among bidders is maximized.
- Approval of material submittals by the design professional offers a substantial basis for judgments to be rendered.

There also are certain disadvantages in descriptive specifying that should be considered:

- Quality and ultimate performance are difficult to predict and control.
- Unskillful specifying can lead to disputes.
- The time required of the specifier to research and write detailed descriptions of components, applications, and necessary restrictions of use and performance requirements may be prohibitive.

Proprietary Specifications

Proprietary Specifications are defined as specifications that name the product by the manufacturer's (proprietary) name or trade name for a product. A proprietary specification for laminated plastic countertops "Laminated Plastic," can serve as an example of a descriptive specification using the accepted trade name for the product. The term "Formica" is a registered trade name for laminated plastic products as manufactured by the American Cynamid Corporation. A proprietary specification for laminated plastic counter tops under Part 2—Products would list "Formica" as a qualified product for the intended use.

The descriptive specification was widely used and greatly preferred in the days when there were few proven published industry standards. Over the years, however, the need for consistent quality and predictable performance has made the proprietary specification more attractive. It is also much easier to write proprietary specifications. Modern manufacturing continues to produce competitive products for building construction, each designed to satisfy a demand for less labor intensive application and greater performance reliability. As these new products have come into the marketplace, the specifier has tended, more and

---

2.01   MATERIALS - FLEXIBLE FABRIC FLASHING

A.   3 oz. copper base sheet.

B.   Sisal fibers: .006 inch diameter, measuring 160 to the inch weighing 5.59 oz. per sq. yd.

C.   Cotton Fabric: Closely woven twill having combined thread count in warp and filling of at least 130, weighing at least 6.66 oz. per yd. before saturation.

D.   Woven wire mesh: Composed of 21 gauge, plain steel wire fabricated with 2 1/2 meshes per inch in each direction.

D.   Asphalt: ASTM 312.

E.   Kraft Paper: Weighing no less than 45 lbs per 100 sq. ft., creped, impregnated thoroughly with bitumen conforming to ASTM 450.

2.02   FABRICATION

A.   Bond sisal fiber to both sides of copper base with two coats asphalt.

B.   Thoroughly embed wire fabric into asphalt on one side of base sheet, cover with one layer kraft paper.

C.   Thoroughly embed cotton fabric into asphalt on opposite side of base sheet. Coat fabric with one coat asphalt, apply and embed one layer of kraft paper.

2.03   PERFORMANCE

A.   Fabricated flexible flashing shall weigh no less than 17 oz. per square yard.

B.   Fabricated membrane shall have bursting strength of no less than 190 lbs. per square inch.

C.   Membrane shall not crack when bent over a 1/2 inch mandrel at 0 degrees F.

Figure 10.19 *Descriptive Specification for Flexible Flashing*

more, to rely upon the use of named brands in specifying the application and quality he seeks. Figure 10.21 illustrates a proprietary specification for flexible membrane flashing in a masonry cavity wall as produced by a well known manufacturer. This product specification accomplishes a similar result as the descriptive specification illustrated in Figure 10.19 with more assurance of quality and performance and less reliance on the technical and communicative skill of the specifier. Proprietary Specifications identify the desired products by brand name, model number, or trade name and name the manufacturers who produce similar and acceptable products. Sometimes referred to as "single source specifying," this method is considered proprietary, even without mention of the name of the manufacturer, provided the product is only available from one, or a limited number of sources. The proprietary specification provides certain distinct advantages as follows:

- Allows control of product selection.
- Provides technical and performance assurance through manufacturer's data based on product research, testing and performance.
- Provides simplification of the bidding process.

2.01   MATERIALS - FLEXIBLE FABRIC FLASHING

A. 3 oz. copper base sheet.

B. Sisal fibers: .006 inch diameter, measuring 160 to the inch weighing 5.59 oz. per sq. yd.

C. Cotton Fabric: Closely woven twill having combined thread count in warp and filling of at least 130, weighing at least 6.66 oz. per yd. before saturation.

D. Woven wire mesh: Composed of 21 gauge, plain steel wire fabricated with 2 1/2 meshes per inch in each direction.

D. Asphalt: ASTM 312.

E. Kraft Paper: Weighing no less than 45 lbs per 100 sq. ft., creped, impregnated thoroughly with bitumen conforming to ASTM 450.

2.02   FABRICATION

A. Bond sisal fiber to both sides of copper base with two coats asphalt.

B. Thoroughly embed wire fabric into asphalt on one side of base sheet, cover with one layer kraft paper.

C. Thoroughly embed cotton fabric into asphalt on opposite side of base sheet. Coat fabric with one coat asphalt, apply and embed one layer of kraft paper.

2.03   PERFORMANCE

A. Fabricated flexible flashing shall weigh no less than 17 oz. per square yard.

B. Fabricated membrane shall have bursting strength of no less than 190 lbs. per square inch.

C. Membrane shall not crack when bent over a 1/2 inch mandrel at 0 degrees F.

Figure 10.20 Combination Descriptive/Performance Specification for Flexible Flashing

PART 2 - PRODUCTS

2.01   MATERIALS - FLEXIBLE FABRIC FLASHING

    A. Acceptable Products:

        1. Cop-R-Guard as manufactured by ABC Products, Amherst MA.

        2. Flex-Flash as manufactured by Flexible lashings Co., Dimebox TX.

        3. Copper-Fab as manufactured by Flashing Specialties, Reagan, CA.

        4. Substitutions: In accordance with Section 01600.

    B. Material shall weigh no less than 17 oz. per square yard.

    C. Fabricated flashing shall have bursting strength of no less than 190 lbs. per square inch.

    D. Fabricated flashing shall not crack when bent over a 1/2 inch mandrel at 0 degrees F.

Figure 10.21 *Proprietary Specification for Flexible Flashing*

- Allows simplification of technical communication in the OPC relationship.
- Reduces the design professional's exposure to contingent liability for product failure.

The proprietary specification is generally applied in one of two distinct ways: The *Closed Proprietary Specification* names a single product and the manufacturer, and offers the contractor little flexibility in the choice. The *Open Proprietary Specification* names two or more products by manufacturer and product name, but also specifies the expected performance of the product.

The Closed Proprietary Specification may not consider the contractor's proposal to use a product of equal or similar attribute, quality or performance. However, Section 01030—Alternates/Alternatives may specify a mechanism whereby the constructor may offer alternative products for the name brand specified. In some cases, the specified product is the only available product that satisfies the designer's intention and application. In order to ensure a reasonable degree of competition among manufacturers of similar products, the specifier will often pre-qualify two or more available products from competing manufacturers and list those products as acceptable for use in the subject project. This approach is known as the Open Proprietary Specification, and to some degree overcomes the disadvantage of reduced or non-existent competition characteristic of the Closed Proprietary Specification.

In recent years, where industry has challenged the public owner's insistence against using Proprietary Specifications and expresses a distinct mandate that Non-Proprietary, Performance Specifications be used have been met with some surprising judgements in courts of law. In one such instance, the Supreme Court of a prominent New England state ruled that the State should rely upon the judgement and experience of the design professional in determining the most appropriate product for each intended use in a publicly owned building, since the design professional is (1) licensed by the state for professional practice which means that his education and experience are a satisfactory basis for decisions in the best interest of the project, and (2) to allow such decisions strictly to the contractor's discretion may not always be in the best interest of the project. In other words, the courts have effectively stated to the public owner "You pay the design professional a fee for his judgement and expertise and you should certainly take full advantage of that expertise." Such courts have found that the Open Proprietary Specification meets the intent of most open bidding laws if the specification is written to include the following:

In Part 1—General, a reference to appropriate Division 1 specifications that provide a mechanism for a bidder to submit a competitive product for consideration, and ...

In Part 2—Products, three or more proprietary products, each of which the design professional is willing to accept as being satisfactory for the intended use, and ...

In Part 3—Execution, a performance specification for a generic product.

Performance Specifications

Performance Specifications are a third type of specification which does not require lengthy descriptions of materials, assemblies, applications or fabrication or mix. The Performance Specification is non-proprietary, yet establishes parameters whereby the contractor can understand the function and required results intended for the specified item as well as the criteria by which compliance can be verified. Figure 10.22 is a performance specification for concrete. Figure 10.18 illustrates a comparative descriptive specification for concrete. The performance specification does not provide the proportions of the materials to be used in the mix, but specifies that the concrete shall, after 28 days attain a minimum compressive strength of 2500 psi.

The Performance Specification makes a statement about the results expected from a material, assembly, or piece of equipment. It also provides criteria whereby compliance with those results can be verified. Figure 10.23 illustrates a performance specification for flexible membrane flashing intended for use in a masonry cavity wall. Figures 10.20 illustrates a descriptive specification for Flexible Flashing, 10.21 illustrates a proprietary specification for Flexible Flashing, and 10.23 illustrates a performance specification for Flexible Flashing offer a comparison of descriptive, proprietary, and performance specifying for similar application of flexible flashing material.

The advantages of performance specifying are listed below:

- Improved products and applications are often elicited from innovative industrial producers.
- Constructors competing for the Contract have greater flexibility in eliciting competitive bids.
- The specifier has more latitude in combining descriptive

specifying techniques with performance criteria (as illustrated in Figure 10.20).

- This method generally satisfies government and public project non-proprietary requirements.

Although the advantages of performance specifying seem to represent an "ideal" approach, there are also certain disadvantages, the most prominent of which are listed below:

- The specifier must be sure that current technology and manufacturers are capable and willing to meet the criteria of the performance specification. Confirmation may be necessary.

2.06 CONCRETE STRENGTH

A. Standard Structural Concrete: Compressive strengths of standard structural concrete shall be capable of minimum allowable compressive strength developed at 28 days as follows:

1. Class AA Concrete: 3750 psi.

2. Class A Concrete: 3000 psi.

3. Class C Concrete: 2500 psi.

4. Class D Concrete: 2000 psi.

B. Non-Structural Concrete: all non-structural concrete used for drives, approaches, walks, curbs, drains, etc. shall have a strength of at least 3000 p.s.i. after 28 days, unless otherwise required by the drawings.

2.07 CONCRETE PROPORTIONING

A. Standard and Lightweight Structural Concrete:

1. The testing laboratory shall establish exact quantities of ingredients required to produce specified concrete.

2. In addition to the above requirements the concrete shall:

a. Have a slump of 4 inches unless otherwise called for on drawings.

b. Work readily into corners and angles of forms and reinforcements without excessive vibration and without permitting materials to segregate or free water to collect on surface.

c. In general, improve workability by adjusting grading rather than by adding water.

Figure 10.22 Example Performance Specification for Concrete

PART 2 - PRODUCTS

2.01 MATERIALS - FLEXIBLE FABRIC FLASHING

A. Fabricate from 3 oz. copper reinforced with sisal fibers; cotton fabric, composed of closely woven twill having combined thread count in warp and filling of at least 130, weighing at least 6.66 oz. per yd. before saturation; woven wire mesh, composed of 21 gauge, plain steel wire fabricated with 2 1/2 meshes per inch in each direction; asphaltic binder conforming to ASTM 312; covered both sides with kraft paper, weighing no less than 45 lbs per 100 sq. ft., creped, impregnated thoroughly with bitumen conforming to ASTM 450.

B. Fabricated flexible flashing shall weigh no less than 17 oz. per square yard.

C. Fabricated membrane shall have bursting strength of no less than 190 lbs. per square inch.

D. Membrane shall not crack when bent over a 1/2 inch mandrel at 0 degrees F.

Figure 10.23 Example Performance Specification for Flexible Flashing

- An incomplete performance specification can result in loss of quality control for the materials, assemblies, equipment, and workmanship that go into a project.
- If performance criteria are the primary means of specifying, many or most of the related Contract Documents must also be specially written and designed in order not to create ambiguities and conflicts.
- The seeming advantage of encouraging "creative innovation" from manufacturers and competing constructors may be more than can be realistically expected within the time limits set for availability of Contract Documents and the bidding process.

Reference Standard Specifications

Reference Standard Specifications are defined as specifications which describe the attributes of a product in terms of an accepted industry standard or testing process by which to measure the performance for the product selected. Industry standards are frequently used as references throughout the Contract Documents. Industry standards are documented criteria, often produced by industry associations, professional societies, and private research organizations. By general usage throughout the construction industry, these standards have become accepted and applied to describe and further specify the attributes, performance, and accepted usage of a particular material, assembly, or piece of equipment required for the project. Such industry standards, also called Reference Standards, can be included as shown in Figure 10.24, a typical specification for cast-in-place concrete by use of Reference Standards. Note that reference standards of the American Society of Testing Materials (ASTM) and the American Concrete Institute (ACI) are used most extensively under Part 2—Products of specification sections.

As can be seen from these illustrations, the frequent use of these and other referenced industry standards from a variety of sources has become an integral part of the common language of the modern day technical construction specification.

As with the other three major methods of specifying recognized by this text, reference standard specifying has certain distinct advantages, some of which are similar to the benefits of other methods, and some of which are unique to reference standard specifying. The more unique advantages of Reference Standard specifying can be summed up as follows:

- By skillfully incorporating well-known standards into the specification, the writer can often avoid tedious and lengthy descriptions of materials and applications.
- This technique allows for the blending of descriptive specifying with performance specifying. In this way, the information included can be used by the contractor in a most economical and efficient manner.
- By incorporating related industry standards, the design professional calls upon the most advanced technology available from recognized specialists in the specified field.
- Properly applied, the referenced standard serves as an additional resource to the design professional's judgment and choice of materials and application.

Unfortunately, not all industry standards are adequate for every purpose. It is vitally important that the specifier study and be intimately acquainted with all of the information contained in the standard to which he refers. He should also be able to produce a copy of that standard if challenged. Even among the most commonly referenced standards there may be certain information that is not in keeping with the design professional's intentions for the subject at hand. For example, although certain provisions within the referenced standard ASTM C 150 may be adequate for the specifier's intention, other provisions published in the same standard may confuse or even conflict with the specifier's intent. Close inspection of ASTM C 150 reveals the fact that the standard for Portland Cement covers not one but five types of Portland Cement. Several of the types have further subcategories, so that there are actually eight distinct types of Portland Cement covered by the document. All are arranged and described in the context of the different applications that may be employed for their use. Clearly, the specifier must be careful to state the type of Portland Cement he intends (see Figure 10.24), rather than to simply specify Portland Cement. As often happens with the "unspecific" use of the reference standard, the contractor may base his contract price on the least expensive of the eight types of material covered by the standard. This least expensive type may not be satisfactory for the designer's intent or the structural adequacy of the building. ASTM C 150 also specifies some 18 other ASTM standards that may be applied to the subject at hand. These other incorporated standards do have a direct bearing on the specification. The specifier must be certain that he is familiar with the provisions of the reference standards because he may otherwise be including specifications contrary to his intent, the owner's budget, and the safety and welfare of those who shall ultimately occupy that building.

Specifying Techniques

Figure 10.25 illustrates Section 01020—Cash Allowances. The Cash Allowance is a commonly used specification technique which allows a particular product to be determined at a later time. A cash allowance provides for certain materials, assemblies or applications to be included in the *contract price* provided by the bidder or contractor. It does not restrict or require an exact specification concurrent with the execution of the Contract for Construction. Cash allowances can be specified to provide certain amounts to be included in the Contract Sum for the purchase of the subject material, assembly, or piece of equipment. In this case, the amount provided for is usually restricted to the purchase, packaging, pick-up, transportation, delivery, protection, storage, and payment of any required sales or use taxes connected with providing the identified subject. The contractor may be responsible (by requirements included in the specification) for calculating the entire quantity needed and providing in the Contract Sum an adequate provision for the tools, labor, and accessories necessary to incorporate the subject into the Work. On the other hand, the cash allowance may be related to the entire cost of a particular unit of work, in which case the intention must be clearly specified (as illustrated by the example in Figure 10.25).

Another similar specifying technique is the use of the *Contingency Allowance* which provides a specific amount of money to be included

SECTION 03300
CAST-IN-PLACE CONCRETE

PART 1 - GENERAL

1.01   REQUIREMENTS INCLUDED

Poured-in place concrete, foundations and other concrete items specified in other Sections.

1.02   RELATED REQUIREMENTS

A.   Section 02800 - Site Improvements.

B.   Section 03100 - Concrete Formwork.

C.   Section 03200 - Concrete Reinforcement.

D.   Section 03320 - Concrete Topping: Concrete topping and curbs over existing construction.

E.   Section 03346 - Finishing Concrete Surfaces.

1.03   QUALITY ASSURANCE

A.   Reference Standards: Comply with all applicable Federal, State and local codes, safety regulations, Portland Cement Assoc. Standards, Ready Mixed Concrete Assoc. Standards, Texas Aggregates Assoc. Standards and others referred to herein.

B.   Tests and Submittals in accordance with Section 01410.

1.   Mix Design and Tests: The mix design for all concrete be established by a testing laboratory under provisions of Section 01410. All tests shall be performed in accordance with standard procedures as follows:

a.   ASTM C 172 Standard Method of Sampling fresh concrete

b.   ASTM C 31 Standard Method of Making and Curing Concrete compressive and Flexural Strength. Test Specimens in the field.

c.   ASTM C 143 Standard Method of test for Slump of Portland Cement Concrete.

d.   ASTM C 39 Standard Method of test for Compressive Strength of Molded Concrete Cylinders.

2.   Access: The Architect shall have access to all places where materials are stored, proportioned or mixed.

3.   Proportions: The testing laboratory shall submit, prior to the start of concrete work, contemplated proportions and the results of preliminary 7 day compression test. Submit a separate set of proportions and test results for pumpcrete if used.

4.   Slump test shall be made by the testing laboratory of concrete delivered to the site for each set of test cylinders.

5.   Standard test cylinders of all concrete placed in the work shall be made by the testing laboratory. One (1) set of four (4) cylinders shall be taken for each 100 cubic yards or fraction there of poured on each day.

6.   Two (2) cylinders of each set shall be tested at 7 days and two (2) cylinders to be tested at 28 days

7.   Reports of above tests and field quality control tests: Provide copies of test reports:

1 copy to Engineer

2 copies to Architect

2 copies to Contractor

8.   Mill reports: The Contractor shall furnish mill reports of test of cement showing compliance with specifications.

9.   All expenses for concrete design and testing shall be paid by the General Contractor

Section 03300 Page 1

Figure 10.24 *A Reference Standard Specification for Concrete ("Cast-in-place-Concrete")*

C. Inspection: Inspection of Reinforcing Steel and Concrete Placement: Before any concrete is poured on any particular portion of project, reinforcing steel will be checked and approved by Architect or Engineer. Correct any errors or discrepancies before concrete is placed. Such checking and approval shall not relieve Contractor from his responsibility to comply with the Contract requirements.

1.04   REFERENCE STANDARDS

A. ASTM C33 - Concrete Aggregates.

B. ASTM C150 - Portland Cement

C. ACI 318 - Building Code Requirements for Reinforced Concrete

D. ASTM C494 - Chemical Admixtures for Concrete.

E. ASTM C94 - Ready-Mixed Concrete.

F. ACI 304 - Recommended Practice for Measuring, Mixing, Transporting and Placing Concrete.

G. ACI 305 - Recommended Practice for Hot Weather Concreting.

H. ACI 306 - Recommended Practice for Cold weather Concreting

I. ACI 301 - Specifications for Structural Concrete for Buildings

J. ACI 311 - Recommended Practice for Concrete Inspection.

1.05   SUBMITTALS

A. Submit product data in accordance with Section 01300.

B. Provide product data for specified products.

C. Submit manufactures' instructions in accordance with Section 01400.

D. Provide shop Drawings showing construction joints.

E. Provide schedule of pouring operations for approval before concreting operations begin.

F. Conform to Mix Design in accordance with 1.03-B.

1.06   PRODUCT DELIVERY, STORAGE AND HANDLING

Store materials delivered to the job and protect from foreign matter and exposure to any element which would reduce the properties of the material.

1.07   COORDINATION

A. Obtain information and instructions from other trades and suppliers in ample time to schedule and coordinate the installation of items furnished by them to be embedded in concrete so provisions for their work can be made without delaying the project.

B. Do any cutting and patching made necessary by failure or delay in complying with these requirements at no cost to Owner.

PART 2 - PRODUCTS

2.01   MATERIALS - STANDARD STRUCTURAL CONCRETE

A. Portland Cement: Type I and III shall conform to "Standard Specifications for Portland Cement" (ASTM C - 150) and shall be of domestic manufacture. Use only one brand of cement unless otherwise authorized by Architect.

B. Fine Aggregate: ASTM C33, natural bank sand or river sand, washed and screened so as to produce a minimum percentage of voids.

C. Normal Weight Coarse Aggregate: ASTM C33, gravel or crushed stone suitably processed, washed and screened, and shall consist of hard, durable particles without adherent coatings. Aggregate shall range from 1/4" to 1-1/4", well graded between the size limits.

Section 03300 Page 2

Figure 10.24 *A Reference Standard Specification for Concrete (continued)*

SECTION 01020
CASH ALLOWANCES

PART 1 - GENERAL

1.01   REQUIREMENTS INCLUDED

    A. Schedule of monetary amounts of allowances in Contract Sum for purchase and delivery of designated products.

    B. Costs in Contract Sum other than in Allowance.

    C. Procedures for administration of Allowances.

    D. The allowances stated herein shall be included in the Base Bid.

1.02   RELATED REQUIREMENTS

    Article 4.8 - General Conditions

1.03   UNIT MATERIAL ALLOWANCES

    A. For Brick Masonry (Section 04300)

        1. For brick masonry type "A" provide a unit price allowance of $ 2000.00_ per one thousand (1000) units as required to complete the installation of masonry according to the drawings.

        2. For brick masonry type "B" provide a unit price allowance of $ 1,500.00_ per one thousand (1000) units as required to complete the installation of masonry according to the drawings.

        3. For brick masonry type "C" provide a unit price allowance of $ 1,500.00 per one thousand (1000) units as required to complete the installation of masonry according to the drawings.

        4. For brick masonry type "D" provide a unit price allowance of $ 2,000.00 per one thousand (1000) units as required to complete the installation of masonry according to the drawings.

        5. Contractor (Bidder) is responsible for determining total quantity of brick of each type required including overage for selection, cutting and wastage.

    B. Carpet - Glue Down Type (Section 09697)

        1. For Carpet (CPT) scheduled type "A", provide a unit price allowance of $ 14.00 per yard for the total volume of type "A" carpet required.

        2. For Carpet Tile (CPT) scheduled type "B", provide a unit price allowance of $ 17.00 per yard for the total volume of type "B" carpet required.

        3. Contractor (Bidder) is responsible for determining total quantity of carpet of each type required including overage for cutting and wastage.

    C. Wall Coverings (Section 09952)

        1. For Vinyl Wall Covering (VWC) scheduled on the drawings, provide a unit price allowance of $ 25.00 per roll to the extent of material required.

        2. Contractor (Bidder) is responsible for determining the total quantity of VWC required for the project, including overage required for cutting and wastage.

    D. Ceramic Tile

        1. For Ceramic Mosaic tile as scheduled for the floors (Section 09311) provide a unit price allowance of $ 2.50 per square foot of tile required.

        2. For Ceramic Tile as scheduled for walls (Section 09312) provide a unit price allowance of $ 2.50 per square foot of tile required.

        3. Contractor (Bidder) is responsible for determining the total quantity of Ceramic Tile required for the project, including overage required for selection, cutting and wastage.

Figure 10.25 *Section 01020 Cash Allowances*

C. Paving Tile

    1. For paving tile as scheduled for certain floors (Section 09314), provide a unit price allowance of $ 7.00 per square foot of tile required.

    2. Contractor (Bidder) is responsible for determining toe total quantity of Paving Tile required for the project, including overage required for selection, cutting and wastage.

1.04   LUMP SUM ALLOWANCES

  A. Interior Sinage (Section 10440): Provide an allowance of $ 500.00 for the purchase of interior signage as required by the Contract Documents.

  B. Exterior Signage (Section 10430): Provide an allowance of $ 2,000.00 for the purchase of exterior signage including building letters as required by the Contract Documents.

  C. Landscaping - Section 02900: Provide and allowance of $ 10,000.00 for landscaping plants, materials, accessories, labor, transportation costs, and all other costs incidental thereto.

  D. Building Plaque: Provide an allowance of $ 1,000.00 for building plaque including accessories and labor to install.

  E. Note: The inclusion of labor and other expenses related to installation is contrary to the General Provisions of Paragraph 1.05.

1.05   COSTS INCLUDED IN ALLOWANCES

  A. Unless otherwise specified in the Allowance description in Paragraph 1.03, costs included in allowances shall include cost of product to Contractor or subcontractor, less applicable trade discounts.

  B. Delivery to site.

1.06   CONTRACTOR COSTS INCLUDED IN CONTRACT SUM (Not in Allowances)

  A. Products handling at site, including unloading, uncrating and storage.

  B. Protection of products from elements and from damage.

  C. Unless otherwise specified in Paragraph 1.03, Contract Sum shall include labor for installation and finishing.

  D. Unless otherwise specified in Paragraph 1.03, Contract Sum shall include other expenses required to complete installation.

  E. Contractor overhead and profit.

1.07   ARCHITECT RESPONSIBILITIES

  A. Consult with Contractor in consideration of products, suppliers and installers.

  B. Select products, obtain Owner's written decision and transmit full information to Contractor:

    1. Manufacturer, product, catalog number and finishes.

    2. Supplier and installer as applicable.

    3. Cost to Contractor, delivered to the site and installed.

  C. Prepare Change Order in accordance with Section 01028.

1.08   CONTRACTOR RESPONSIBILITIES

  A. Assist Architect in determining suppliers and installers; obtain proposals when requested.

  B. Make recommendations for Architect consideration.

  C. Promptly notify Architect of any reasonable objections against supplier or installer.

  D. On notification of selection execute purchase agreement with designated supplier and installer.

Section 01020 Page 2

Figure 10.25 *Section 01020 Cash Allowances (continued)*

in bidding documents, for possible inclusion in the final contract price to be used at the complete discretion of the owner. The very nature of competitive bidding precludes an exact or finite completed cost that can be estimated with 100% accuracy prior to bidding or negotiating procedures or the agreement on a final Contract Sum. Because of this common uncertainty, a contingency is often used to add a percentage of the total estimate, or a certain sum is intended to apply in case the estimate of cost proves to be low when a contract price is bid or negotiated. In many cases, corporate boards and groups of public officials must establish budgets to fund construction projects. Any appropriations from this budget are determined before contracts for construction can be awarded with the full authority of the owner (who may be not a single individual, but many stockholders, or the public at large). The contingency allowance provides a "cushion" that can be applied to improve, correct, or add to the Work without the need to go through a tedious, often futile process of gaining additional appropriations for such expenditures.

The term *Nonrestrictive Specification* refers to a *technique* of specifying rather than a *method* of specifying. It can be seen that the methods of specifying identified as descriptive, performance, and reference standard specifications can all be referred to as *nonrestrictive specifications* in that no clear restriction to a single proprietary or exclusionary product is stated or implied. Provided that a number of alternate but acceptable products are listed, the open proprietary specification can be classified as nonrestrictive. There has been a concerted effort by public sector officials and legislators to enforce standards of specifying so that they do not restrict the acquisition and use of materials and products to certain producers to the unfair and discriminatory exclusion of others. At the same time, this type of specifying also allows for the greatest possible latitude of competition. A typical statute from the volumes of public law is shown in the excerpt from Public Law 92-500, Federal Water Pollution Control Act, Section 204(a)(6) which states:

> ... *no specification for bids in connection with such works shall be written in such a manner as to contain proprietary, exclusionary or discriminatory requirements, other than those based on performance, unless such requirements are necessary to test or demonstrate a specific thing or to provide for necessary interchangeability of parts and equipment, or at least followed by the words "or equal...."*

The "Or Equal" Statement

The statement in the previous example is typical of a sometimes misunderstood and often misused principle that assumes that two materials or items of equipment may be similar in all respects and are therefore somehow "equal" in application, performance and intended use in the project.

The fact is that while some items are similar, it is highly unlikely that any two items, so compared, will be exactly alike in all respects. Traditionally, the term *or equal* has been commonly applied to specifications which name one or more products in an attempt to "loosen" the restriction by implying that if the bidder or contractor can provide a substitute product of "equal" performance, application, use, and quality, the substitute product will be approved.

There are a number of problems that occur with the use of the "or equal" statement:

- Does not make clear how the so-called equality of any substitute product will be determined.
- Does not make clear how the determination of so-called equality between the specified product and the substitute item will be determined.
- Does not make clear a provision for review and approval of the substitute product by the design professional prior to the receipt of bids.

Without a clear provision for an alternate material or product to be disclosed and subsequently approved by the design professional during the bidding process, it is highly likely that the potential for dispute occurs for a number of reasons:

- Substitutions may not be "equal" at all, therefore one bidder gains an unfair advantage over other bidders.
- If no provision is made for the substitution of the so-called "equal" product to be confirmed as acceptable by the design professional before receipt of bids, subsequent discovery of any inferiority in the substitute product may lead to a dispute that can affect the validity of the contract price or the contract itself.

A more satisfactory approach to the specification technique which does not rely upon the "or equal" statement, involves taking the following steps:

- Provide a Division 1 statement in Section 01600—Materials and Equipment, specifying a procedure for achieving approval of substitutions before the receipt of bids.
- Thoroughly investigate and subsequently specify no less than three products produced by manufacturers of substantial means and ability. Determine the reliability of each product by requiring and reviewing qualified testing laboratory data as to attributes that would not be obvious to the casual inspector. List no less than three products (if possible) that prove to be "reasonably" equivalent to the needs of the project as being acceptable for the intended use as illustrated in Figure 10.21.
- Write performance criteria in Part 1 of the specification that can be measured by the testing laboratory.
- Section 01600—Material and Equipment, is the Division 1 Section of the specifications that provides the general parameters for controlling the quality of materials and equipment in the project. Figure 10.26 (paragraph 1.07 from that section) provides a procedure for substitutions to be considered and approved by the design professional. Subparagraph H makes the contractor responsible if the substitute product fails.

Testing of Materials and Systems

To protect the owner's interest and investment, and the reputations of the design and the construction professional, there is no substitute for the safeguard provided in the required testing of various key materials, manufacturer's products, assemblies and equipment that go into the construction of modern buildings. With the major emphasis on economy, the testing of materials to ensure adequacy is one of the few "checks and balances" that are afforded the OPC equation.

Testing has come to be more and more of a necessity as construction in the United States has entered the "high tech" age and as the documented evidence of building failures has affected the lives and fortunes of more and more owners, building professionals, contractors and building occupants. Section 01400—Quality Control is the Division 1 section which establishes the criteria for testing of materials.

The National Institute of Standards and Technology

The National Institute of Standards and Technology (NIST) formally known as the National Bureau of Standards (NBS), an agency of the United States government, Department of Commerce, Environmental Sciences Administration was officially established on March 3, 1903. From its inception, NIST has been responsible for the custody, preparation, and testing of standards, as well as solving standard problems and determining the physical constants and critical properties of materials. NIST is empowered to render services to scientific societies, colleges and universities, and business firms. NIST has, from the beginning, been instrumental in establishing the basis for most of the industry standards previously discussed. NIST is the creator and custodian of the nation's system of measurement in all things physical and scientific. For a fee, NIST is equipped and qualified to set testing standards, calibrate testing equipment, and certify private testing laboratories as being properly equipped to conduct a variety of tests for building materials, systems, and related areas.

The American Society for Testing Materials

The American Society for Testing Materials (ASTM), organized in the early 1900s, is a non-profit, educational organization dedicated to the publication of voluntary consensus standards to benefit more than 30,000 members worldwide. ASTM's membership includes engineers, designers, business persons, industrialists, researchers, administrators and consumers from both the private and public sector. The multiple-volume *Annual Book of ASTM Standards* contains thousands of separate documents dedicated to technical information, specifications and standards dealing with a wide variety of scientific subjects. Originally focused only on materials such as steel and cement, ASTM now develops standards for such diverse subjects as robotics, security systems, textiles, resource recovery, sports equipment, and medical devices. ASTM is organized into more than 140 technical committees which accomplish the actual writing of standards. ASTM committee members contribute their time and talent to create standards that affect their own work and the Work of others.

Cost of Testing

There appear to be at least two distinct "schools of thought" as to how the cost of testing should be administered and financed. Proprietary documents prepared by the American Institute of Architects (AIA) state *unless otherwise provided, the contractor shall make arrangements for such tests.* Other statements may state *the design professional shall give notice of any required testing not included in previous paragraphs."* Such statements do not clearly state who pays for testing. This matter must be determined by the design professional and stipulated in appropriate Division 1 sections.

Many owners and design professionals prefer to require that the contractor cover the costs of all testing, and stipulate that the testing laboratory be approved by the design professional. Section 01400—Quality Control is illustrated in Figure 10.27. This Section of Division 1 normally contains the general provisions for testing. When the contractor is required to pay for testing, related procedures are generally included in Section 01400 as illustrated as Paragraph 1.07 in Figure 10.28. On the other hand, many owners and design professionals prefer that testing be controlled by the owner, in which case the owner selects the laboratory and pays for the testing. When this approach is used, the provisions stated in Section 01400 should appear as shown in Figure 10.28. In addition, the design professional may wish to add a special Section such as Section 01410—Testing Laboratory Services to Division 1 to establish criteria for the testing laboratory (Figure 10.29 illustrates an alternative paragraph 1.07).

Once the responsibility for testing materials has been resolved and established by the appropriate Division 1 sections, more detailed testing information should be stated in Part 1 of the individual specification sections.

Disputes

The matter of resolving disputes in the construction process has been discussed in previous chapters. (See Chapter 6, "Legal Concerns and Insurance".) There is growing interest and concern among the many participants in the construction industry on the subject of Risk Management. Risk management implies that disputes can and will be avoided if the principals in the OPC relationship establish sound, well documented, contractual relationships toward the joint goal of producing sound, well-constructed building projects to the profit and credit of all concerned. To successfully avoid risk, the design professional begins with the creation of well thought out, well coordinated, thorough Contract Documents. Unless the full intention of the contract document requirements is clearly " spelled out" and placed into the Project Manual in a uniform and consistent manner, disputes and misunderstandings are almost inevitable.

The General Conditions of the Contract may name the design professional and establish him as the interpreter of the intent of the Contract Documents. It describes in detail the duties of the design professional. Good, sound, responsible specifications ensure the design professional's ability to fulfill this responsibility to the mutual benefit of all parties to the OPC relationship.

The "Master" Specification

Creating a "master file" of specification sections (generally applicable to the types of projects encountered in professional practice) may be the design professional's best support for producing sound, meaningful specifications. Most design firms, government agencies, and large corporations use master specifications on a mandatory basis. A properly maintained, continually updated master specification file will return dividends more than worth the investment in its creation and maintenance.

SECTION 01600
MATERIAL AND EQUIPMENT

PART 1 - GENERAL

1.01 REQUIREMENTS INCLUDED

A. Products.

B. Workmanship.

C. Manufacturers' Instructions.

D. Transportation and Handling.

E. Storage and Protection.

F. Substitutions and Product Options.

1.02 RELATED REQUIREMENTS

A. Section 01010 - Summary of Work: Owner-furnished Products. Reference Standards.

B. Section 01300 - Submittals: Submittal of manufacturers' certificates.

C. Section 01700 - Contract Closeout: Operation and maintenance data. Warranties and Bonds.

1.03 PRODUCTS

A. Products include material, equipment and systems.

B. Comply with Specifications and referenced standards as minimum requirements.

C. Components required to be supplied in quantity within a Specification section shall be the same, and shall be interchangeable.

1.04 TRANSPORTATION AND HANDLING

A. Transport products by methods to avoid product damage; deliver in undamaged condition in manufacturer's unopened containers or packaging, dry.

B. Provide equipment and personnel to handle products by methods to prevent soiling or damage.

C. Promptly inspect shipments to assure that products comply with requirements, quantities are correct, and products are undamaged.

1.05 STORAGE AND PROTECTION

A. Store products in accordance with manufacturer's instructions, with seals and labels intact and legible. Store sensitive products in weather-tight enclosures; maintain within temperature and humidity ranges required by manufacturer's instructions.

B. For exterior storage of fabricated products, place on sloped supports above ground. Cover products subject to deterioration with impervious sheet covering; provide ventilation to avoid condensation.

C. Store loose granular materials on solid surfaces in a well-drained area; prevent mixing with foreign matter.

D. Arrange storage to provide access for inspection. Periodically inspect to assure products are undamaged, and are maintained under required conditions.

E. After installation, provide coverings to protect products from damage from traffic and construction operations, remove when no longer needed.

Figure 10.26 Section 01600—Material and Equipment

1.06 PRODUCT OPTIONS

    A. Within 10 days after date of Contract, submit complete list of major products proposed, with name of manufacturer, trade name, and model.

    B. Options:

        1. Products Specified by Reference Standards or by Description Only: Any Product meeting those standards.

        2. Products Specified by Naming One or More Manufacturers within a Substitute Paragraph: Submit a request for substitution for any manufacturer not specifically named.

        3. Products Specified by Naming Several Manufacturers: Products of named manufacturers meeting specifications; no options, no substitutions allowed.

        4. Products specified by naming only one manufacturer: substitutions shall be considered in accordance with Paragraph 1.08..

1.07 SUBSTITUTIONS

    A. The listing of product manufacturers in the various sections of the Specifications, or on the drawings, is intended to establish a standard of quality only and is not intended to preclude open, competitive bidding. See Instructions to Bidders for instructions as to proposing substitutions prior to receipt of bids.

    B. Equal products of other manufacturers will be acceptable provided the applicable provisions of the GENERAL CONDITIONS and SUPPLEMENTARY GENERAL CONDITIONS are complied with.

    C. Substitution requests made by the Contractor after the execuition of the Agreement Between Owner and Contractor must be received by the Architect within 10 days of the Order to Proceed with the work.

        1. Document each request with complete data substantiating compliance of proposed substitution with Contract Documents. Substitution requests shall include the name of the material or equipment for which it is to be substituted and a complete description of the proposed substitute including drawings, details, samples, performance and test data and any other information necessary for an evaluation, including modifications required for other parts of the Work.

        2. Substantiate the motivation of the requested substitution and include any proposed savings in cost that would accrue to the Owner if the substitution were approved.

        3. Request constitutes a representation that Contractor:

            a. Has investigated proposed product and determined that it meets or exceeds, in all respects, specified product.

            b. Will provide the same warranty for substitution as for specified product.

            c. Will coordinate installation and make other changes which may be required for Work to be complete in all respects.

            d. Waives claims for additional costs or time which may subsequently become apparent.

    D. After execution of the Contract Agreement, proposed substitutions will be considered only if there is no increase in cost to the Owner, no decrease in quality, and only when submitted by or through and bearing the approval of the General Contractor.

    E. Substitutions will not be considered when they are indicated or implied on shop drawing or product data submittals without separate written request, or when acceptance will require substantial revision of Contract Documents.

    F. The burden of proof of the merit of the proposed substitute is upon the Contractor. The Architect's decision of approval or disapproval of a proposed substitution shall be final.

    G. Requests for time extensions will NOT be approved for delays due to rejected substitutions. NO substitution will be allowed without the Architect's approval in writing.

    H. Should a substitution be approved under the foregoing provisions, and subsequently prove to be defective or otherwise unsatisfactory for the service for which it was intended, the Contractor shall, without cost to Owner, and without obligation on the part of the Architects, replace the same with the material originally specified.

Section 01600 Page 2

Figure 10.26   *Section 01600—Material and Equipment (continued)*

SECTION 01400
QUALITY CONTROL

PART 1 - GENERAL

1.01   REQUIREMENTS INCLUDED

   A.   General Quality Control.

   B.   Workmanship.

   C.   Manufacturer's Instructions.

   D.   Manufacturer's Certificates.

   E.   Manufacturers' Field Services.

   F.   Testing of Materials, assemblies to ascertain quality of work.

1.02   RELATED REQUIREMENTS

   A.   Section 01010 - Summary of the Work

   B.   Section 01020 - Allowances

   C.   Section 01300 - Submittals

1.03   QUALITY CONTROL, GENERAL

        Maintain quality control over suppliers, manufacturers, products, services, site conditions, and
        workmanship, to produce work of specified quality and in any event, work conforming to the best
        standards of the industry or trade.

1.04   WORKMANSHIP

   A.   Comply with industry standards except when more restrictive tolerances or specified requirements
        indicate more rigid standards or more precise workmanship. Conform to Reference Standards specified
        in individual Sections of the Specifications.

   B.   Perform work by persons experienced in the particular unit of Work and who are otherwise qualified to
        produce workmanship of specified quality. Submit evidence of qualification if required to do so by
        the individual Section of the Specifications.

   C.   Secure products in place in accordance with manufacturer's instructions and recommendations, with
        positive anchorage devices designed and sized to withstand stresses, vibration, and racking, using
        such accessories, devices or compounds that are compatible with the material or as recommended by the
        manufacturer.

1.05   MANUFACTURERS' INSTRUCTIONS

        Comply with instructions in full detail, including each step in sequence. Should instructions
        conflict with Contract Documents, request clarification from Architect before proceeding.

1.06   MANUFACTURERS' CERTIFICATES

        When required by individual Specifications Sections, submit manufacturer's certificate, in
        triplicate, that products meet or exceed specified requirements.

1.07   TESTING OF MATERIALS, SYSTEMS, ASSEMBLIES

   A.   Owner will employ, under the provisions of Section 01410 the services of an Independent Testing
        Laboratory approved by the Architect to perform inspections, tests, and other services required by
        individual Specification Sections. Employment of Testing Laboratory by Owner, in
        no way relieves the Contractor of the obligation to perform the Work in strict accordance with the
        Contract Documents.

   B.   Retesting: When the results of the Testing Laboratory's work show that any portion of the Work does
        not meet the requirements of the Contract Documents or other authority, the Contractor shall pay for
        retesting of corrected Work until satisfactory results to approval of Architect have been achieved.

Section 01400 Page 1

Figure 10.27 Section 01400—Quality Control

C. Contractor shall cooperate with Testing Laboratory personnel, furnish tools, samples of materials, equipment, storage and assistance as requested.

D. The Contractor shall notify the Architect and the Testing Laboratory 24 hours prior to expected time for operations requiring testing services.

1.08 MINIMUM TESTING REQUIREMENTS

A. Soils Testing: In accordance with requirements of Section 02220 - Structure Base, Fill and Backfill, and Section 02265 - Landscape Grading.

B. Soil Compaction Tests: In accordance with Section 02220 - Structural Base, Fill and Backfilling.

C. Pavement Material and Base: In accordance with requirements of Section 02513 - Asphaltic Concrete Paving, and Section 02514 - Portland Cement Concrete Paving.

D. Concrete Tests: In accordance with Section 03300 - Cast-In-Place Concrete.

E. Other Specified Tests: In accordance with individual Sections of the Specifications.

F. Additional Tests not specified: In such instances where, in the opinion of the Architect, items may not meet the standards specified, additional tests may be required and so ordered by the Architect. If such tests reveal that specified standards have been met, the Contractor shall pay for the tests under the provisions of the Allowance for Testing specified in Section 01020. In the event that such tests reveal that specified standards have not been met, the Contractor shall pay for the tests from his own funds, at no cost to the Owner plus any retesting of corrected material that may be required additionally by the Architect.

PART 2 - PRODUCTS

Not Used

PART 3 - EXECUTION

Not Used

END OF SECTION

Figure 10.27 Section 01400—Quality Control (continued)

1.07 TESTING OF MATERIALS, SYSTEMS, ASSEMBLIES

A. Contractor will employ the services of an Independent Testing Laboratory approved by the Architect to perform inspections, tests, and other services required by individual Specification Sections.

B. Retesting: When the results of the Testing Laboratory's work show that any portion of the Work does not meet the requirements of the Contract Documents or other authority, the Contractor shall pay for retesting of corrected Work until satisfactory results to approval of Architect have been achieved.

C. Contractor shall cooperate with Testing Laboratory personnel, furnish tools, samples of materials, equipment, storage and assistance as requested.

D. The Contractor shall notify the Architect and the Testing Laboratory 24 hours prior to expected time for operations requiring testing services.

E. Provide copies of Testing Laboratory reports as follows:

1. One copy to Owner

2. Two copies to Architect.

3. Retain 3 copies, 1 at jobsite.

1.08 MINIMUM TESTING REQUIREMENTS

A. Soils Testing: In accordance with requirements of Section 02220 - Structure Base, Fill and Backfill, and Section 02265 - Landscape Grading.

B. Soil Compaction Tests: In accordance with Section 02220 - Structural Base, Fill and Backfilling.

C. Pavement Material and Base: In accordance with requirements of Section 02513 - Asphaltic Concrete Paving, and Section 02514 - Portland Cement Concrete Paving.

D. Concrete Tests: In accordance with Section 03300 - Cast-In-Place Concrete.

E. Other Specified Tests: In accordance with individual Sections of the Specifications.

F. Additional Tests not specified: In such instances where, in the opinion of the Architect, items may not meet the standards specified, additional tests may be required and so ordered by the Architect. If such tests reveal that specified standards have been met, the Contractor shall pay for the tests under the provisions of the Allowance for Testing specified in Section 01020. In the event that such tests reveal that specified standards have not been met, the Contractor shall pay for the tests from his own funds, at no cost to the Owner plus any retesting of corrected material that may be required additionally by the Architect.

Figure 10.28 *Paragraph 1.07 from Section 01400—Quality Control*

1.07 TESTING OF MATERIALS, SYSTEMS, ASSEMBLIES

A. Owner will employ, under the provisions of Section 01410 the services of an Independent Testing Laboratory approved by the Architect to perform inspections, tests, and other services required by individual Specification Sections. Employment of Testing Laboratory by Owner, in no way relieves the Contractor of the obligation to perform the Work in strict accordance with the Contract Documents.

B. Retesting: When the results of the Testing Laboratory's work show that any portion of the Work does not meet the requirements of the Contract Documents or other authority, the Contractor shall pay for retesting of corrected Work until satisfactory results to approval of Architect have been achieved.

C. Contractor shall cooperate with Testing Laboratory personnel, furnish tools, samples of materials, equipment, storage and assistance as requested.

D. The Contractor shall notify the Architect and the Testing Laboratory 24 hours prior to expected time for operations requiring testing services.

1.08 MINIMUM TESTING REQUIREMENTS

A. Soils Testing: In accordance with requirements of Section 02220 - Structure Base, Fill and Backfill, and Section 02265 - Landscape Grading.

B. Soil Compaction Tests: In accordance with Section 02220 - Structural Base, Fill and Backfilling.

C. Pavement Material and Base: In accordance with requirements of Section 02513 - Asphaltic Concrete Paving, and Section 02514 - Portland Cement Concrete Paving.

D. Concrete Tests: In accordance with Section 03300 - Cast-In-Place Concrete.

E. Other Specified Tests: In accordance with individual Sections of the Specifications.

F. Additional Tests not specified: In such instances where, in the opinion of the Architect, items may not meet the standards specified, additional tests may be required and so ordered by the Architect. If such tests reveal that specified standards have been met, the Contractor shall pay for the tests under the provisions of the Allowance for Testing specified in Section 01020. In the event that such tests reveal that specified standards have not been met, the Contractor shall pay for the tests from his own funds, at no cost to the Owner plus any retesting of corrected material that may be required additionally by the Architect.

Figure 10.29 *Alternate Paragraph 1.07 from Section 01400—Quality Control*

A reasonably complete master specifications system will include the following:

- Pre-written master specification sections filed in "hard" copy and, if available, on electronic media.
- An office manual consisting of notes, bulletins, industry publications and other data. This information should be organized and responsive to the drawings and information contained in the *Project Manual.*
- A series of checklists for the contents of the individual specification section and the Project Manual.
- A list or file of frequently specified products, design standards and details, and industry reference standards frequently used for associated projects.
- A digest and listing of information about products, materials, systems, codes and standards, research reports, and other information that has a bearing upon the specifications and their content.
- References on costs and the availability of materials and methods.

The primary advantages of a master specification file are summarized below:

- Studies conducted by knowledgeable institutions indicate that savings in technical labor can be cut 50-70% by the use of such a system. The use of electronic media devices makes this system even more efficient.
- A master specification system documenting a wide range of standards and choices expands the decision-making process considerably. A professional design firm is able to save and document the results of research and decisions involving past work.
- Project development in the office can be made more efficient and timely. Use of the master system allows for development of the specifications parallel to the development of drawings and other Contract Documents.
- Repetitive work can be greatly minimized.
- Errors and omissions can be minimized, thereby reducing the risk of liability.

The "Outline" Specification

Early in the step-by-step development of the modern construction project, an abbreviated specification known as the Outline Specification is often used. Outline specifications cover the essential descriptive provisions of the final specification and serve the purpose of "outlining" or basically describing the information contained in the final document to be produced as part of the Contract Documents. The outline specification may be thought of as relating to the final specification much as "design development" drawings and sketches relate to final construction drawings. Figure 10.30 illustrates an outline specification for steel windows. This outline specification is prepared by the design professional as he seeks the owner's final approval for the design and budget requirements for a particular project. Figure 10.31 illustrates the final open proprietary specification for steel windows.

SECTION 08510
STEEL WINDOWS

PART 1 GENERAL

A. OUTLINE OF REQUIREMENTS

  1. Fixed sash steel windows.

  2. Factory applied enamel finish.

B. SYSTEMS DESCRIPTION

  Windows, prefinished baked on color, with fixed glazing in steel frames.

C. PERFORMANCE

  1. Window components to provide for expansion and contraction caused by a cycling temperature range of 170F
     degrees without causing detrimental effects to components.

  2. Design and size members to withstand dead loads and live loads caused by pressure and suction of wind to a
     design pressure based on 95 mph, exposure C, category 3, importance factor 1.11. Maximum deformation of
     frame or sash member: 1/360 of span length.

  3. Limit mullion deflection to 1/200 of flexure limit of glass with full recovery of glazing materials,
     whichever is less.

  4. Drain water entering joints, condensation occurring in glazing channels, of migrating moisture occurring
     within system, to exterior.

  5. Limit air infiltration through assembly to 0.10 cu.ft. per sq ft. of assembly surface area, measured at a
     reference differential pressure across assembly of 0.3 inches water gauge as measured in accordance with
     ANSI/ASTM E283.

PART 2 PRODUCTS

A. MANUFACTURE

  Acceptable Product: 1000 Series Fixed Heavy Intermediate Steel Windows as manufactured by XYZ Architectural
  Products.

B. MATERIALS

  1. Heavy fixed intermediate steel windows shall be manufactured from solid hot rolled steel shapes.

     a. Sections: New billet steel with integral flanges rolled at the mill.

     b. Perimeter frames shall have unobstructed glazing surface of at least 3/4 inch.

     c. Glazing rebate surfaces shall be perpendicular to the web or stem of the section. Tapered rebate
         surfaces are not acceptable.

     d.   Provide 3 anchors per jamb.

  2. Combined weight of frame shall be no less than 3.5 pounds per lineal foot.

  3. Muntins: Steel Tees:

     a. Hot rolled from new billet steel with integral flanges rolled at the mill.

     b. Glazing rebate surfaces shall be as specified in A above.

     c. 1 3/8 inch tee shall weigh no less than 1.55 pounds per lineal foot.

Figure 10.30 *Section 08510—Steel Windows—Outline Specifications*

FACTORY FINISHING

1. Hot dip galvanize components after fabrication.

2. Steel window frames and muntins shall be zinc-phosphate treated in a continuous five stage
process as a preparation for painting.

   a. Following pre-treatment, one coat of primer is applied and oven cured.

   b. Following prime coat and baking, all exposed surfaces shall be given two coats of acrylic enamel.

3. Finish color as selected by Architect.

4. Apply one coat of bituminous paint or zinc-chromate paint to concealed steel surfaces in contract with
cementitous or dissimilar materials.

5. Apply strippable protective coating to finished surfaces prior to shipping from factory.

END OF OUTLINE SECTION

Figure 10.30 *Section 08510—Steel Windows—Outline Specifications (continued)*

PART 1   GENERAL

1.01 REQUIREMENTS INCLUDED

   A. Fixed sash steel windows.

   B. Factory applied enamel finish.

1.02 REQUIREMENTS INSTALLED BUT SPECIFIED IN OTHER SECTIONS

   A. Section 07900 - Joint Sealants: Sealants for use surrounding window frames.

   B. Section 08800 - Glass and Glazing: Glazing of steel windows.

1.03 RELATED REQUIREMENTS

   A. Section 04300 - Masonry: Masonry openings at windows.

   B. Section 06100 - Rough Carpentry: Wood perimeter shims.

   C. Section 07900 - Sealants: Perimeter sealant and back-up materials.

   D. Section 08800 - Glass and Glazing.

   E. Section 09260 - Gypsum Wallboard Systems: Adjacent finishes.

1.04 SYSTEMS DESCRIPTION

   Windows, prefinished baked on color, with fixed glazing in steel frames.

1.05 PERFORMANCE

   A. Window components to provide for expansion and contraction caused by a cycling temperature range of 170F degrees without causing detrimental effects to components.

   B. Design and size members to withstand dead loads and live loads caused by pressure and suction of wind to a design pressure based on 95 mph, exposure C, category 3, importance factor 1.11. Maximum deformation of frame or sash member: 1/360 of span length.

   C. Limit mullion deflection to 1/200 of flexure limit of glass with full recovery of glazing materials, whichever is less.

   D. Drain water entering joints, condensation occurring in glazing channels, of migrating moisture occurring within system, to exterior.

   E. Limit air infiltration through assembly to 0.10 cu.ft. per sq ft. of assembly surface area, measured at a reference differential pressure across assembly of 0.3 inches water gauge as measured in accordance with ANSI/ASTM E283.

1.04 REFERENCES

   A. ASTM A36 - Structural Steel.

   B. ANSI/ASTM E283 - Rate of Air Leakage through Exterior Windows, Curtain Walls and Doors.

   C. ANSI/ASTM E330 - Structural Performance of Exterior Windows, Curtain Walls, and Doors by Uniform Static Air Pressure Difference.

   D. FS TT-P-645 - Primer, Paint, Zinc Chromate, Alkyd Type.

1.05 SUBMITTALS

   A. Submit shop drawings and product data in accordance with Section 01300.

   B. Include materials, sections, finish, wall opening and component dimensions; wall opening tolerances required; anchorage and fasteners; affected related work and installation requirements.

   C. Submit manufacturer's installation instruction in accordance with Section 01600.

Figure 10.31   *Section 08510—Steel Windows—Final Specification*

1.06 SAMPLES

    A. Submit samples in accordance with Section 01300.

    B. Submit one sample assembly, 18 inches high x 24 inches wide illustrating window frame sections, corner section, mullion section, of fixed glass assembly.

1.07 DELIVERY, STORAGE AND HANDLING

    A. Deliver, handle, store and protect window units in accordance with Section 01600.

    B. Provide wrapping or protective coating to protect prefinished aluminum surfaces.

1.08 WARRANTY

    A. Provide one year manufacturer's warranty in accordance with Section 01700.

    B. Warranty: Cover complete window system for failure to meet specified requirements.

PART 2 PRODUCTS

2.01 MANUFACTURE

    A. Acceptable Product: 1000 Series Fixed Heavy Intermediate Steel Windows as manufactured by XYZ Architectural Products.

    B. Substitutions: In accordance with Section 01600.

2.02 MATERIALS

    A. Heavy fixed intermediate steel windows shall be manufactured from solid hot rolled steel shapes.

        1. Sections: New billet steel with integral flanges rolled at the mill.

        2. Perimeter frames shall have unobstructed glazing surface of at least 3/4 inch.

        3. Glazing rebat surfaces shall be perpendicular to the web or stem of the section. Tapered rebate surfaces are not acceptable.

        4. Provide 3 anchors per jamb.

        5. Combined weight of frame shall be no less than 3.5 pounds per lineal foot.

    B. Muntins: Steel Tees

        1. Hot rolled from new billet steel with integral flanges rolled at the mill.

        2. Glazing rebate surfaces shall be as specified in A above.

        3. 1 3/8 inch tee shall weigh no less than 1.55 pounds per lineal foot.

2.03 FABRICATION

    A. Fabricate steel windows in accordance with approved shop drawings.

    B. Prior to fabrication, all hot rolled steel sections shall be cleaned by shot blasting.

    C. Corners of frames shall be mitered or coped then solidly welded in accordance with AWI standards. Exposed and contact surfaces shall be finished smooth flush with adjacent surfaces.

    D. Steel tee muntins shall be tenioned and welded to the perimeter frame. Muntin intersections shall be slotted and cross notched.

    E. Fabricate windows allowing for minimum clearances and shim spacing around perimeter of assembly, yet enabling installation.

    F. Develop drainage holes with moisture pattern to exterior.

    G. Prepare components to receive anchor devices. Fabricate anchorage items as required by drawings.

Section 08510 Page 2

Figure 10.31 Section 08510—Steel Windows—Final Specification (continued)

2.04 FACTORY FINISHING

    A. Hot dip galvanize components after fabrication.

    B. Steel window frames and muntins shall be zinc-phosphate treated in a continuous five stage process as a preparation for painting.

        1. Following pre-treatment, one coat of primer is applied and oven cured.

        2. Following prime coat and baking, all exposed surfaces shall be given two coats of acrylic enamel.

    C. Finish color as selected by Architect.

    D. Apply one coat of bituminous paint or zinc-chromate paint to concealed steel surfaces in contract with cementitous or dissimilar materials.

    E. Apply strippable protective coating to finished surfaces prior to shipping from factory.

2.05 GLASS AND GLAZING MATERIALS

    A. Glass and Glazing Materials: Specified in Section 08800.

PART 3 EXECUTION

3.01 INSPECTION

    A. Verify wall openings and adjoining air seal materials are ready to receive work of this Section.

    B. Field verify openings prior to fabrication.

    C. Beginning of installation means acceptance of existing conditions.

3.02 INSTALLATION

    A. Install window frames, in accordance with manufacturer's instructions.

    B. Use anchorage devices to securely attach frame to structure.

    C. Align window frame plumb and level, free of warp of twist. Maintain dimensional tolerances, aligning with adjacent work.

    D. Pack fibrous insulation in shim spaces at perimeter to maintain continuity of thermal barrier in accordance with Section 07115.

    E. Install perimeter sealant and backing materials in accordance with Section 07900.

3.03 PROTECTION

    A. Protect against damage by other Trades. Replace any defaced, defective steel work or broken glass caused by improper installation at no cost to Owner.

    B. After setting sills, immediately protect with board or other approved non-staining covering. Maintain protection in place until completion of masonry and plastering.

3.04 CLEANING

    A. Remove protective material from prefinished steel surfaces.

    B. Wash down exposed surfaces using a solution of mild detergent in warm water, applied with soft, clean wiping cloths. Take care to remove dirt from corners. Wipe surfaces clean.

END OF SECTION

Section 08510 Page 3

Figure 10.31 *Section 08510—Steel Windows—Final Specification (continued)*

266

Summary   George Bernard Shaw, the great English playwright once said, "English speaking people are separated by a common language." Mr. Shaw could have been describing the project definition, an imperfect endeavor, at best, and a costly, sometimes confrontational process, at it's worst. At the beginning of the 20th century there was little, if any, uniformity to the language and format of specifications or the organization and graphic symbolism of the drawings. The final drawings of the design professional were produced by hand, drawn on specially treated linen cloth in ink and reproduced by a wet, time consuming chemical process called "blueprinting." The language and organization of specifications was as unique as the design professional who produced them. The design professional spent more time on the job, communicating with the constructor, one-to-one, getting what Frank Lloyd Wright described to this author as "a little mortar under the fingernails."

At the close of the 20th century most drawings are produced by computer and are reproduced electrostatically. The symbols used by one design professional are similar, if not identical, to those used by another. Specifications are uniformally produced in sixteen divisions of information that is more understandable than ever before in the history of building.

The imperfection in project definition is not technical; it is not graphic; it is not in the language. The imperfection has never resided in the "tools" of the profession. The imperfection in project definition is, as George Bernard Shaw observed, by human beings, "separated by a common language." That is why the process is called professional *practice*.

Chapter Eleven

The Project Manual

Construction specifications have traditionally been written and bound apart from the contract drawings, as a matter of convenience. As the various trades became familiar with the "Book of Specifications" this bound document became known as the "specs." Over the years, practitioners included bidding information, conditions of the Contract, and other data necessary to bidding or negotiating for the contract. Contract Documents are more important today than ever before because more and more legal, technical, and qualitative information is demanded by the OPC (Owner-Professional-Contractor) relationship. The Contract Documents (along with the specifications) have commonly been written, reproduced, and bound into a booklet intended to accompany the drawings. This bound volume has come to be called the *Project Manual*.

The American Institute of Architects (AIA) is credited with having coined the term *Project Manual* in the early 1960s. This period represented a time of professional re-evaluation, which saw design professionals streamlining the language of specifications. The AIA improved and expanded the uniform published forms used to supplement the Contract Documents for common building projects. Upon reflection, many design professionals recognized that much of the information contained in the "specs," while related to the Work, was not technical specification data. The Bidding Requirements, for instance, commonly bound into the *specs,* were neither Contract Documents nor Specifications, but were included as a matter of convenience to facilitate the award of the Contract. To this day, many practitioners within the construction industry continue to refer to the bound documents used during bidding and construction as *specs.* The term *Project Manual* more clearly and correctly expresses the use and intention of this collection of information, while at the same time, implies that something other than the technical specifications resides within the manual. This chapter is dedicated to the organization, content, and use of the *Project Manual*.

Today's Project Manual contains, but is not limited to the following documents by category of information:

Bidding Requirements
    Invitation to Bid
    Instructions to Bidders
    Information Available to Bidders
    Property Survey
    Soil Analysis

Related Construction Documents
Bid Forms
Form of Bid Bond

Supplemental Forms
Form of Agreement
Form of Performance Bond
Form of Payment Bond
Certificate of Insurance
Certificate of Compliance

Conditions of the Contract
General Conditions
Supplementary General Conditions
Regulatory Conditions
Wage Rates
Equal Opportunity Requirements
Domestic Materials Requirements
Index of Drawings
A list or schedule of all drawings that are part of the Contract
    Documents

Technical Specifications
Division 1—General Requirements
Division 2—Sitework
Division 3—Concrete
Division 4—Masonry
Division 5—Metals
Division 6—Wood and Plastics
Division 7—Thermal and Moisture Protection
Division 8—Doors and Windows
Division 9—Finishes
Division 10—Specialties
Division 11—Equipment
Division 12—Furnishings
Division 13—Special Construction
Division 14—Conveying Systems
Division 15—Mechanical
Division 16—Electrical

Modifications to the Contract

Invitation to Bid

It is customary that the owner advertise his intention to receive competitive bids. In the case of public work, open competitive bidding is usually mandated by law, and the advertisement for bids must be published in the local media. Some statutes require that the advertisement appear for a specific length of time in one or more local newspapers. Figure 11.1 is an example of a typical public project advertisement to be found in the classified section of a local newspaper. (Chapter 7, "Project Delivery," discusses alternatives available to the owner in procuring his project, and discusses procedures and issues related to competitive bidding and negotiation for the award of the Contract for Construction.)

In the case of private projects, it is more common to offer an Invitation to Bid to selected firms. The private owner may advertise if he so

ADVERTISEMENT FOR BIDS

A. Project Identification: Name, project number, and date of issue. Name and address of architect or engineer.

Bids: November 2, 1992
STATE UNIVERSITY
SCIENCE BUILDING
SMITHVILLE, OH
Project No. 3813

October 1, 1992

Jones and Brown, Architects
5555 Main Street
Smithville, OH 44000
Phone: (999) 888-7777

B. Description of Work

The Board of Governors, State University, Smithville, Ohio, will receive sealed bids on a General Contract, including mechanical and electrical work, for a two-story, thin-shell concrete, circular Science Building, approximately four hundred feet in diameter.

C. Type of Bid

Bids shall be on a stipulated sum basis; segregated bids will not be accepted.

D. Time of Completion: (Not included in this sample.)

E. Bid Opening

The State University Board of Governors will receive bids until 3:00 p.m. Eastern Standard Time on Tuesday, November 2, 1992, at 233 Uptown Street, Room 313, Smithville, Ohio. Bids received after this time will not be accepted. Bids will be opened and publicly read aloud immediately after specified closing time. All interested parties are invited to attend.

F. Examination and Procurement of Documents

Bidding Documents may be examined at the Architect's office and at:

The Plan Center
382 West Third Street
Smithville, OH

Associated Plan Bureau
1177 South Barnes
Smithville, OH

Copies of the Bidding Documents may be obtained at the Architect's office in accordance with the Instructions to Bidders upon depositing the sum of $100.00 for each set of documents.

G. Bid Security

Bid Security in the amount of five percent of the bid must accompany each bid in accordance with the Instructions to Bidders.

H. Bidder's Qualifications (Not Included in this sample.)

Any bidder upon returning the documents in good condition immediately following the public opening of the bids, shall be returned the deposit in full. Any non-bidder returning the documents in good condition will be returned the sum of $75.00.

I. Owner's Right to Reject Bids

Contracts for work under this bid will obligate the Contractor and subcontractors not to discriminate in employment practices. Bidders shall submit a compliance report in conformity with Executive Order No. 11246.

J. Laws and Regulations: usually required for legal advertisements

This contract is Federally assisted. The Contractor must comply with the Davis-Bacon Act, The Anti-Kickback Act, and the Contract Work Hours Standard.

The Board of Governors reserves the right to waive irregularities and to reject bids.

By order of the Board of Governors

STATE UNIVERSITY
SMITHVILLE, OHIO

Note: This sample is reasonably complete. It touches on all major points included in most Advertisements for Bids. The user should recognize that each project may have specific requirements that may not be emphasized in this sample document.

Courtesy of the Construction Specifications Institute

Figure 11.1 Sample Advertisement to Bid

desires. However, he may also privately invite whoever he pleases to enter the bidding competition, or he may pre-select the constructor and negotiate the Contract for Construction. Figure 11.2 is a common form of an Invitation to Bid. The Invitation to Bid and the Advertisement for Bids accomplish the same basic function, that is to attract bids from constructors in order to award the Contract.

Both the Advertisement for Bids and the Invitation to Bid should incorporate certain information. As a minimum requirement these documents should include the following:

- Project Identification.
- Name of Project.
- Address of Project.
- Name of Owner.
- Contract Authority (if required).
- Name of Design Professional.
- Address of Design Professional.
- Telephone Number of Design Professional.
- Name of Design Professional's Project Manager.

The body of these documents should include: a brief description of the project; the owner's requirements for time of completion; the types of bids required; the date of the bid opening; the availability and procurement of bidding documents; any pre-qualification required of bidders; bid security requirements; and a statement regarding the owner's right to reject any or all bids. In the case of public work, statements applicable to governing laws should be included.

Instructions to Bidders

The key document to the bidding process is the *Instructions to Bidders*. This document should include the following information:

A list of *all* documents that comprise the *Bid Documents* including the following:

- Advertisement or Invitation to Bid.
- Instructions to Bidders.
- Bid Form.
- Form of Contract (Agreement Between Owner and Contractor).
- Conditions of the Contract.
- Supplemental Contract Conditions.
- Schedule of Drawings.
- Specifications.
- Addenda (Issued prior to execution of the Contract).

Definitions of all terms that are related to the Bid and the implications that are consistent with the submission of a Bid including the following:

- *Addenda*—written or graphic instruments issued by owner (or design professional) prior to the execution of the Contract for Construction. They modify or interpret the Bid Documents by additions, deletions, clarifications, or corrections.
- *A Bid*—a written, signed, and complete proposal to do the Work for the sum(s) stipulated therein in accordance with the Bid Documents.
- *Bidder*—a company (or individual) submitting a written proposal in response to the Invitation to Bid or The Advertisement to Bid

A. Project Identification: Name, project number, and date of issue. Name and address of architect or engineer.	Jones and Brown, Architects 5555 Main Street Smithville, OH 44000 Phone (999) 888-7777

INVITATION TO BID
STATE UNIVERSITY SCIENCE BUILDING
Project No. 3813
October 1, 1992

B. Description of Work

C. Type of Bid

You are invited to bid on a General Contract, including mechanical and electrical work, for a two-story, thin-shell concrete, circular Science Building, approximately four hundred feet in diameter. Bids shall be on a stipulated sum basis; segregated bids will not be accepted.

D. Time of Completion

Project is to be completed within 480 calendar days from the date of award of contract.

E. Bid Opening

The State University Board of Governors will receive bids until 3:00 p.m. Eastern Standard Time on Tuesday, November 2, 1992, at 233 Uptown Street, Room 313, Smithville, Ohio. Bids received after this time will not be accepted. Bids will be opened publicly and read aloud immediately after specified closing time. All interested parties are invited to attend.

Bidding Documents may be examined at the Architect's office and at:

F. Examination and Procurement of Documents

The Plan Center 382 West Third Street Smithville, OH	Associated Plan Bureau 1177 South Barnes Smithville, OH

Copies of the Bidding Documents may be obtained at the Architect's office in accordance with the Instructions to Bidders upon depositing the sum of $100.00 for each set of documents.

Any bidder upon returning the documents in good condition immediately following the public opening of the bids, shall be returned deposit in full. Any non-bidder returning the documents in good condition will be returned the sum of $75.00.

H. Bidder's Qualifications

Bidders are required to be prequalified for this project and may obtain appropriate qualification forms from the Architect's office.

G. Bid Security

Bid Security in the amount of five percent of the bid must accompany each bid in accordance with the Instructions to Bidders.

I. Owner's Right to Reject Bids

The Board of Governors reserves the right to waive irregularities and to reject bids.

By order of the Board of Governors

State University
Smithville, Ohio

Hirmats J. Downe, Secretary

J. Laws and Regulations: (Not included in this sample.)

Note: This sample is reasonably complete. It touches on all major points included in most Invitations to Bid. The user should recognize that each project may have specific requirements that may not be emphasized in this sample document.

Courtesy of the Construction Specifications Institute

Figure 11.2 *Sample Invitation to Bid*

and offers to accomplish the Work in accordance with the Bid Documents.

- *Sub-Bidder*—a company (or individual) submitting a proposal for a defined portion or sub-division of the Work to the Bidder.
- *The Base Bid Sum*—the sum stated in the *Form of Proposal* for which the *Bidder* offers to perform the Work described in the Bid Documents. It is the basic Contract Sum to which may be added or substracted sums stipulated in any Alternate Bids as described in the Instructions to Bidders.
- *Alternate Bid*—is an amount stated in the Form of Proposal for which the Bidder offers to add or subtract from the Base Bid Sum if the Alternate Work described in the Bid Documents is accepted at the discretion of the owner.
- *Unit Price*—an amount stated in the Form of Proposal as a price per unit of measurement for materials, equipment, or services for a portion of Work as described in the Bid Documents.

Bidder's Representations

These state that by submitting a Bid, the Bidder represents that:

- The Bidder has read and understands the full intent of all the *Bid Documents* and that the *Bid* is made in accordance with the Bid Documents.
- The Bidder has visited the site, is familiar with and understands local conditions under which the Work is to be performed, and has correlated the Bidder's personal observations with the requirements of the Bid Documents.
- The Bid is based upon the labor required, the materials to be incorporated, and the equipment and systems required without exception.

Bid Documents

The purpose of this article is to describe the access to, use of, and legal attributes of the bid documents. Suggested statements should include:

- Address for access to the Bid Documents and conditions under which a prospective Bidder may obtain copies of the Bid Documents. Note: It is quite appropriate for the Bidder to be required to pay a fee that adequately covers the reproduction and other incidental costs of providing the documents. The Bid Document fee may or may not be refunded at the owner's discretion, however, the Instructions to Bidders must make both the amount and the final disposition of the fee clear.
- The Bid Documents are the property of the owner. Any use of Bid Documents for purposes other than complying with the Instruction to Bidders or the Advertisement for Bids is strictly prohibited. Furthermore, use or duplication of the Bid Documents should not extend beyond the scope of the project described in the Invitation to Bid or Advertisement for Bids.
- The Bid shall be based upon a complete set of Bid Documents. Neither the owner nor the design professional shall be responsible for any errors, or mis-interpretations of the Bid Documents or any portions of the Bid Documents.
- Bid Documents will not be issued to Sub Bidders unless specifically offered in either the Invitation to Bid or the Advertisement for Bids.

Pre-Bid Conference

It is suggested that the bidding procedures include a time and place for a pre-bid conference. The conference offers the design professional an opportunity to make a statement describing the project and the bidding procedures, and allows prospective bidders to ask questions. It serves as an opportunity for the owner or the owner's representative to state the owner's objectives in the project.

Interpretation or Correction of Bidding Documents

The Bidder is responsible for studying the Bid Documents, for comparing the documents, and for being aware of any other Work that may affect the Bid. The Bidder is expected to familiarize himself with local conditions, codes and code enforcement, as well as with state and federal codes and regulations.

- Bidder shall report any inconsistancies, errors, or apparent omissions in the Bid Documents to the design professional of record.

Bidders and Sub-Bidders requiring clarification or intrepetation of Bid Documents may submit a written Request for Information (RFI) addressed to the design professional at least five calendar days before the pre-bid conference. If there is no pre-bid conference, then RFIs should be tendered seven days before the date for receipt of bids.

- Interpretations, clarifications, changes, and responses to RFIs will be made by Addendum. NOTE: Bidders should be cautioned that interpretations, clarifications, changes, and responses to RFIs received in any manner other than by Addendum issued by the design professional should be ignored, as they can be unreliable.

Substitutions

It is the intent of the Bid Documents that the materials, products, and equipment described in the Bid Documents establish a standard of required function, dimension, appearance and quality to be met by any substitution. The Instructions can and should state rules for acceptance of Bidder initiated substitutions:

- No substitution will be considered prior to receipt of bids unless written approval of the design professional has been published by Addendum.

Form of Proposal

The content of a proposal submitted as a result of the bidding process will come with many practical and legal implications. It is important that these implications be detailed in the Instructions to Bidders. The acceptance of a bid implies that the proposal is based on the site as it exists, the bidding documents as they are written, and the materials and systems as specified. The validity of the entire competitive bidding process is based on the principle that each competitor is working with identical criteria.

Establishing proper bidding procedures is crucial when instructing bidders. The bid forms used should be carefully designed and the forms submitted by each bidder should be identical. A legal problem can occur if there is any variation in the form or the wording of the proposal provisions, or any deviation in its content. General practice dictates that the design professional furnish the bidders with forms that require only the filling in of blanks for responses. Figure 11.3 illustrates a typical three-page Form of Proposal for a public works project. This form asks bidders to respond with a proposed Contract Sum (base bid), a proposed number of days for project completion, and the bidder's proposal for any alternate items that may be identified in the Bid Documents. The inclusion of alternates in the Bid Document suggests that certain portions of the Work may be desirable to the owner, but not essential to his needs. These alternates allow the owner the options of either accepting the proposed price for the alternate item, or rejecting it altogether. If the item is accepted, the proposed amount is added to the base bid price. If rejected, the proposed amount in the base bid is unaffected.

By designing the bidding documents to allow for additive rather than subtractive alternates, the contractor is able to include a non-disclosed, but sufficient amount for overhead and profit as part of his base bid. It is a natural expectation that the lump sum price offered for an additive alternative would include a non-disclosed amount for additional overhead and profit. The lump sum price offered as a subtractive alternate, however, may leave doubt from the owner's view as to whether a proportional amount of overhead and profit has also been included in the amount to be deducted from the base bid. The subtractive alternate, therefore has a potential for disagreement or dispute and should be avoided.

The protocol for receiving, accepting, opening and considering bids, and the amount of time that the owner requires for considering the bids should be covered in the Instructions to Bidders.

In the case of public work, the owner may be mandated to accept the lowest responsible bid. "Contractor responsibility" is key to the owner. Whether a project is public or private project, a serious situation arises if the chosen bidder proves unable to complete the Work. Experience reveals that although a contractor may be bonded, this alone is no guarantee that he will be able to fulfill the requirements of the Contract for Construction by submitting a bid in accordance with the Instruction to Bidders. It is good policy to require a "screening" process whereby bidders are required to file their credentials. These credentials should reveal their current financial condition, the extent of their current work load, and examples of completed work, with names of owners and design professionals who can furnish references. The AIA, for example, publishes a document called the *Contractor's Qualification Statement.* It is frequent practice that the Contractor's Qualification Statement is filed with the owner prior to the opening of bids. This practice tends to discourage overextended or under-qualified constructors from submitting a bid, and gives the owner (usually acting through the design professional) valuable time to conduct the screening process. When the contractor's qualification statement is a pre-bid requirement, the owner, particularly a public owner, has the opportunity to evaluate the apparent competency and capability of those who respond to the "open" invitation to bid. For instance, if the required Contractor's Qualification Statement were not prepared and filed as instructed, the owner would be justified in returning the sealed bid to the bidder unopened and unconsidered.

PROPOSAL FORM - GENERAL CONSTRUCTION

PROPOSAL OF: _____
                              (Name of Bidder)

TO: City of (Name of City, State)
     (Name of party to receive bids)
     (Street address where bids are to be delivered)
     (Name of City, State, Zip Code)

FOR: Prime Contract for General Construction
     (Address of project site)
     (Name of city, State, Zip Code)

Gentlemen:

The Undersigned has received the Bidding Documents (Project Manual and Drawings) for the referenced project including Addenda numbered _____. The provisions of these Addenda have been included in this Proposal. The undersigned has examined both the site and the documents, and is fully informed on the scope and conditions of the work.

The Undersigned hereby proposes to furnish all labor and materials and perform all work related to the Prime Contract for General Construction for the new (Name of Project as it appears on all contract documents) located at (Address of site), in strict accordance with the Contract Documents included or listed in the Project Manual, for the consideration of the following:

BASE BID: For all labor and materials and all work related to the General Construction of the proposed project, including the Plumbing, Mechanical and Electrical work, in full consideration of all that is required by the Contract Documents for the sum of:

_____DOLLARS

            ($_____)

            City Hall Building Proposal Page 1

Figure 11.3 Sample Proposal Form

Furthermore:

1. If awarded the Prime Contract for General Construction, the undersigned agrees to complete the Work on or before the expiration of _____ calendar days from date of written Notice to Proceed.

2. In accordance with Additive Alternate Item No. 1, understood to be (name of item to be bid as an additive alternate) as described in Section (Provide appropriate specification section number) of the specifications, and as shown on the drawings, the undersigned offers to include, at the owner's option, this additive alternate for a total consideration, to be added to the amount shown above as the "Base Bid", the sum of:

    _____ Dollars.

    ($ _____.__)

    Furthermore, if the Owner elects to accept our offer for Additive Alternate Item No. 1 to be added to the Base Bid, the undersigned would require _____ days to be added to the number of calendar days required for completion of the work first stated in Paragraph 2 above.

The undersigned hereby certifies to have complied with all conditions stated in the Instructions to Bidders.

Bid Security in the form of a certified check or bid bond in the sum of five percent (5%) of the greatest possible amount of the Contract Sum as bid is attached hereto, as a guarantee of the execution of a satisfactory contract and furnishing of bonds as required by the Contract Documents.

It is understood and agreed that the Owner has the right to reject any and all bids and to waive any technicalities. Furthermore, it is understood that the Owner, at his option, may accept or reject any offer stated in Paragraphs 2 through 5 above for possible inclusion in the Prime Contract for General Construction.

City Hall Building Proposal Page 2

Figure 11.3 Sample Proposal Form (continued)

If written notice of the acceptance of Bid is mailed, faxed or delivered to the undersigned within (90) days after the date of opening bids, or at any time thereafter before this bid is withdrawn by writing, the undersigned agrees that he will execute and deliver a contract, in accordance with the bid as accepted, all within ten (10) days (unless a longer period of time is allowed) after the prescribed forms are presented to him for signature.

Notice of acceptance should be mailed, faxed or delivered to the undersigned at the following address:

Signed _____

For _____
                  Legal Name of Bidder

Address _____

_____

SEAL
(If Bid is by a Corporation)

NOTE: Amounts shall be shown in both written form and figures. In case of discrepancy between the written amount and the figures, the written amount will govern.

If Bidder is a Corporation, write State of Incorporation under signature and if a Partnership, give full names of all parties.

Caution: This Bid may be rejected if not accompanied by a Guarantee in the amount specified. Any Certified Checks may be held uncollected at the risk of the Bidder submitting them.

END OF PROPOSAL FORM

City Hall Building Proposal Page 3

Figure 11.3 *Sample Proposal Form (continued)*

If for any reason a bidder becomes unwilling to commit to a Contract for Construction based upon the proposal he has submitted, the owner may have the right to collect the amount of the bid security included in the bid package as liquidated damages for such refusal. It should be stressed that compliance with the requirements of the Instructions to Bidders should be followed in all respects and with no exceptions. Receipt of bids ends at the exact hour on the date stated in the Advertisement or Invitation. Any bid received after the stipulated time can be returned to the bidder unopened. Any bid that is found incomplete in any way can be set aside, not read aloud, and returned to the bidder with an explanation of the rejection. Telephone calls or other communication not in accordance with the Instructions should not be accepted. Bidders are not allowed to add any kind of unique statements of qualification to the Form of Proposal. Finally, no commitment should be made as to award of the Contract until both owner and design professional have had sufficient time to study each proposal, reflect upon the bidders' qualifications, review the proposed list of subcontractors, and verify the availability of the specified performance and payment bonds.

Information Available to Bidders

The General Conditions of the Contract should list the information normally furnished to bidders. Other information which would further the bidder's understanding of the project may include:

- Soils investigation and recommendations.
- Local weather information.
- Owner's financial qualifications, financial statement or authority to commit construction funds.
- Property survey and existing conditions, including:
  —Existing improvements
  —"As built" drawings
  —Existing utilities

Conditions of the Contract

Conditions of the Contract are related documents which complement the Contract for Construction. Conditions of the Contract define the basic rights, responsibilities, and relationships of the parties involved in the construction process, namely the owner, the design professional, the contractor, the subcontractor and the sub-subcontractor. Conditions of the Contract normally appear in the two related documents described below.

The General Conditions of the Contract normally contain general statements defining the responsibilities of the parties during the construction process. In most instances, the forms prepared by national professional organizations such as the AIA are used. These kinds of forms published by a reliable professional society or institution, usually represent a consensus among various groups within the building industry.

The Supplemental Conditions document is used to modify and expand the General Conditions as needed, and address any requirements unique to the individual project.

The General Conditions of the Contract along with its companion document, the Supplemental General Conditions, are discussed, in Chapter 9, "Conditions of the Contract."

Specifications

Techniques of specification writing and organization are discussed in Chapter 10, "Project Definition." The word "specify" is defined as the action required to name or to state in detail. Construction specifications have been defined as the qualitative requirements for products, materials, and workmanship upon which the Contract for Construction is based.

During the period following World War II, many design professionals became concerned with specification writing practices. The Construction Specifications Institute soon came into being for the express purpose of improving the quality, uniformity, and usefulness of construction specifications. Many design professionals began to publicly discuss the many concerns the industry shared regarding the creation and use of Contract Documents. An article that appeared in the March 1949 edition of the *National Architect,* (an AIA publication and a forerunner of today's *Architecture* magazine) discussed the discovery of a set of specifications written for a residential project in New England at about 1835. The *Carpenter's Specification* section is reported to have included the following description:

> ... *Base 12 inches including moldings not inferior to Dan'l Smith's house on fifth street ...*

While this statement was probably specific enough for 1835, today, a more appropriate specification would probably include the following language:

> *Hardwood base: plain sliced, clear red oak (Quercus Rubra), meeting the requirements of PS 20 and ASTM D 2555, shaped to traditional base No. WM 6186, prepared for transparent finish as specified in Section 09900.*

In modern specifications, stating the Latin name for red oak is intended to establish the certainty of the species desired, instead of relying on a common name that could be misunderstood if the nomenclature for certain wood species varied from one locale to another. *Standard PS-20* refers to a voluntary standard for wood products, developed and published by the National Institute of Standards and Technology (NIST), formerly known as the National Bureau of Standards. These designations establish dimensional requirements for standard sizes of wood, and technical requirements for uniform manufacture and grading of wood products. ASTM D 2555, commonly called *the clear wood standard*, is a standard specification published by the American Society for Testing Materials (ASTM). *Traditional Base WM 6185* refers to a certain shape and size of molding, established as a standard by the Wood Molding and Millwork Producers Association.

The techniques of specification writing have clearly changed since 1835. In today's highly competitive, technological world, construction specifiers must keep pace with the times in language and technical proficiency.

Project Manual Functions

In order to understand the organization and content of the Project Manual, the following should be clearly understood and observed:

Bidding Requirements
- Are not specifications.
- Are procedures that apply to the competition for award of the Contract for Construction.

- Remain in effect only until the signing of the Contract for Construction or during the construction process.

Conditions of the Contract
- Include both the General and Supplemental Conditions.
- Are not specifications.
- Are an integral part of the Contract.
- With the Contract, govern the content of the entire contract.
- Contain contractual principles applicable to most projects with supplemental provisions for individual projects.

General Conditions
- Are broad contractual conditions.
- Contain requirements, establish relationships, and define obligations.

Supplemental General Conditions
- Modify the General Conditions.
- Modify the constraints for a specific region or project.
- Take precedence over General Conditions.
- Must be written separately for each project.

General Requirements
- Are specifications.
- Establish procedural and administrative requirements.
- Are enforceable under the Contract for Construction.
- Must be written separately for each project.

Finally, in conceiving the organization and application of the Project Manual, the design professional should consider the overall relationship of the various components of the Bidding and Contract Documents to the Project Manual as these documents are prepared and issued to prospective bidders.

Figure 11.4 illustrates the relationship of the various documents that make up the "Bidding Package," which becomes the basis for the Contract for Construction.

Creating the Project Manual

Clear, concise, and thorough communications throughout the Contract Documents are the key to effective economy and success in building construction. Effective communication of design intent depends largely on the content of the Project Manual.

Information must be presented in such a manner as to be readily accessible, logically and obviously placed, clearly written, simply stated, and systematically coordinated. Everyone involved in the process of building construction benefits from a well-conceived, properly written Project Manual.

The preparation of the Project Manual falls under the domain of the prime design professional. It is generally the Specification Writer who ultimately coordinates the team that prepares the Project Manual. This is true regardless of whether the design professional is a single practitioner acting as the specification writer, or exists as part of a team within a multi-disciplined office. Figure 11.5 illustrates the process by which the Project Manual is developed.

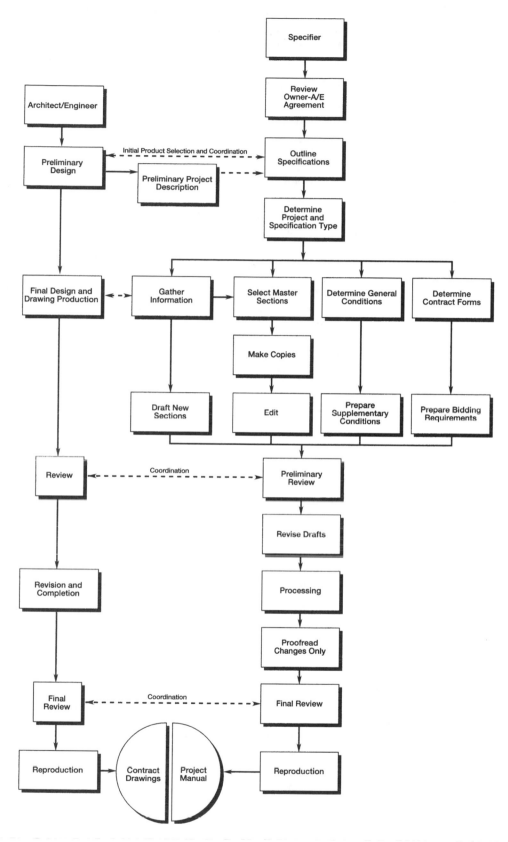

Figure 11.4 Document Relationships

The Specification Writer

The specification writer may be an independent practitioner who works as a consultant to the design professional. Just as the language and content of the Contract Documents have become more important to the success of the finished project, so have the qualities and attributes of the specification writer become more critical to his role in the construction process. Because his responsibility involves a specific use of language, the specification writer must be knowledgeable of grammar, punctuation, and word definition. Statements must be precisely written and presented in a manner that is clear to a great number and diversity of people. Many readers of the Project Manual will not be trained in technical reading or writing.

The specification writer must also be able to deal skillfully with a profusion of details and technical elements. A great deal of reading and in-depth research are necessary. The specification writer must also oversee the voluminous quantities of technical data that must be handled, stored, retrieved, and appropriately applied to a wide variety of project types with differing requirements.

There is no single educational program specifically designed to train the construction specifier. An academic background must be supplemented with experience that can be gained only in professional practice before one can become a qualified specifier. The academic credentials for an aspiring construction specifier would include, in order of preferen ce:

- A bachelor's degree in architecture and engineering.
- A vocational associate degree in architecture or engineering.
- A high school diploma supplemented with on-the-job training in architecture or engineering.

The following are among the personality traits that are desirable in a construction specifier:

- Keen observation and attention to detail.
- Ability to visualize three-dimensional objects.
- Ability to organize thoughts into orderly statements.
- Ability to isolate essential elements of a problem.
- Ability to listen and accurately understand other people.
- Ability to reach equitable agreements without compromising important principles.
- Ability to accurately express ideas and concepts.

The accomplished specifier should be able to use the above listed personality traits to develop specific skills that should include:

- A thorough understanding of construction materials and construction methods.
- Well developed written communications skills.
- Ability to understand graphic information presented in drawings, tables, and charts.
- Ability to negotiate successfully.
- Ability to coordinate the activities of others.
- Ability to manage time in order to meet critical production schedules.
- Ability to know resources in order to effectively perform in-depth research.
- A thorough knowledge of construction law.

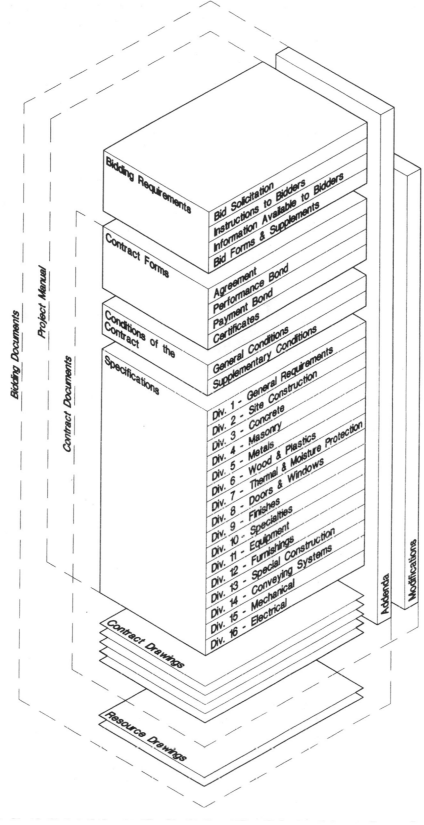

Bidding Requirements
- Bid Solicitation
- Instructions to Bidders
- Information Available to Bidders
- Bid Forms & Supplements

Contract Forms
- Agreement
- Performance Bond
- Payment Bond
- Certificates

Conditions of the Contract
- General Conditions
- Supplementary Conditions

Specifications
- Div. 1 - General Requirements
- Div. 2 - Site Construction
- Div. 3 - Concrete
- Div. 4 - Masonry
- Div. 5 - Metals
- Div. 6 - Wood & Plastics
- Div. 7 - Thermal & Moisture Protection
- Div. 8 - Doors & Windows
- Div. 9 - Finishes
- Div. 10 - Specialties
- Div. 11 - Equipment
- Div. 12 - Furnishings
- Div. 13 - Special Construction
- Div. 14 - Conveying Systems
- Div. 15 - Mechanical
- Div. 16 - Electrical

Bidding Documents
Project Manual
Contract Documents
Addenda
Modifications
Contract Drawings
Resource Drawings

Courtesy of the Construction Specifications Institute

Figure 11.5 *Project Manual Development*

- A thorough knowledge of building codes and ordinances.
- A thorough knowledge of insurance and bonds as they apply to the construction industry.
- A thorough knowledge of construction trade jurisdictions and customary divisions of work.

In the mid-1970s, the board of directors of the Construction Specifications Institute (CSI) authorized the Institute to create and maintain a system for examining qualified professionals engaged in the writing or developing of construction specifications. The goal has been to recognize and certify the qualified specifier as a Certified Construction Specifier (CCS).

Documents Associated with the Project Manual

The Bidding Package

Various documents included in the Bidding Package are interrelated with the documents in the Project Manual. The project documentation is not complete without all its parts. The following describes the documents in the Bidding Documents "package."

The Drawings

A layman is likely to associate an architect with tee squares, drawing boards, and rolls of drawings. When thinking of the engineer, he adds to that picture a transit and a slide rule. For many generations, the drawings produced by architects and engineers were thought to be, and probably were, the most important of the documents produced by the design professional. Because of the need to diagram building assemblies to scale with dimensions, material symbols, cross sections, details and schedules in order to clearly create a "picture" of the project, the drawings continue to perform a critical function in complementing the other Contract Documents. Nevertheless, the drawings, even with sophisticated photography, computer aided design (CAD) and other visual aids, are still not of a convenient size to be "read," or bound into the Project Manual. An index of the drawings is usually included as a separate document in the Project Manual. The drawings, thus, are "tied-in" as an integral part of the Project Manual, and by reference, are a part of the Contract Documents "package."

Modification Documents

The bidding process often produces requests for information that may require the design professional to create modifications to the Bid Documents "package."

Addendum/Addenda

The Project Manual is designed to assist in the bidding or negotiating activities that lead to the Contract for Construction, but it also continues to serve the project during construction. At the time that project is being bid, modifications to the Contract Documents are often made by a published Addendum. The Addendum serves to link the bidding process and the Contract Documents. It informs the bidders of modifications that may affect project requirements and therefore the Contract Sum during the bidding process. It then becomes one of the Contract Documents after the Contract is signed. It should be attached to or become part of the Project Manual. Figure 11.6 is a typical addendum published during the bidding period. Each addendum should contain the following information:

- Addendum number and date of issue.
- Reference to the project by title and project number if applicable.
- Name and address of party issuing the addendum, usually the design professional.
- Identification of parties to whom the addenda is directed or addressed.
- A brief explanation of the purpose of the addendum, the documents that it intends to modify and a reminder to bidders that acknowledgment of receipt of addendum is required on the bid form.

An Addendum can be designed to modify any of the following:

- Changes to prior addenda.
- Changes to bidding requirements.
- Changes to information available to bidders.
- Changes to conditions to the Contract.
- Changes to the specifications.
- Changes to the drawings.

Field Orders

Once the Contract for Construction has been executed and construction has begun, the design professional may need to issue, from time to time, supplemental instructions that do the following:

- Clarify a specific intent of the Contract Documents.
- Approve a minor change in the Work.
- Instruct the contractor on a matter pertaining to the execution of the Work.

The *Field Order,* sometimes called *Supplemental Instructions,* is useful for making minor modifications to the Contract for Construction as long as these changes do not increase or decrease the Contract Sum, or change the scheduled date of completion. Modifications that would in any way alter the Contract Sum or require additional time for completion must be prepared in the form of a *Change Order.*

Change Order

The Change Order is an instrument through which significant changes in the Contract for Construction can be made. Changes to the contract can affect the Contract Sum or the number of days required for completion of the Contract. A Change Order requires the agreement of the parties to the Contract for Construction (owner and contractor) as well as the design professional. Figure 11.7 illustrates a Means Contract Change Order.

Construction Change Directive

In the most recent edition of its *General Conditions of the Contract for Construction,* the AIA introduced a method of directing certain owner-initiated changes in the Work called the *Construction Change Directive* (CCD). The CCD is designed for use in cases of disagreement between the Owner and Contractor on the terms and conditions that would otherwise be used in a Change Order. It is designed to document a change in the work that may or may not be followed by a Change Order that will identify any change in Contract Price or Schedule for Construction. The intent of the CCD is to facilitate the continuation of construction while any changes that may affect the Contract Price or the Schedule for Construction are being negotiated

A. Number and Date	**ADDENDUM NO. 2, May 1, 1992**
B. Project Identification	RE: First National Bank of Brownsville Project No. 11863
C. Name & address of A/E	FROM: JONES and SMITH, Architects and Engineers John Doe Building Washington, D.C. (202) 555-8888
D. To Whom Addendum is Issued	TO: Prospective Bidders
E. Opening Remarks and Notice to Bidders	This Addendum forms a part of the Contract Documents and modifies the original Bidding Documents dated April 15, 1992, and Addendum No. 1, dated April 20, 1992, as noted below. Acknowledge receipt of this Addendum in the space provided on the Bid Form. Failure to do so may subject Bidder to disqualification. This Addendum consists of one page and the attached drawing, Sheet S-9-A, with the revised date of April 20, 1992.
F. Changes to Prior Addenda	CHANGES TO PRIOR ADDENDA: 1. Addendum No.1, Item No. 13, Page AD-1-1, change the number of the referenced drawing from "G-1" to "G-7."
G. Changes to Bidding Requirements	CHANGES TO BIDDING REQUIREMENTS: 2. Instructions to Bidders, Page 00200-2, Item 15, replace first sentence with "Proposed substitutions must be submitted in writing at least 15 days before the date for opening of bids."
H. Changes to Agreement: (Not included in this sample.)	
I. Changes to Conditions of the Contract	CHANGES TO CONDITIONS OF THE CONTRACT: 3. Supplementary Conditions Item No. 12, Page 00800-3, change limit of public liability from "$100,000/$500,000" to "$300,000/$500,000."

J. Changes to Specifications	CHANGES TO SPECIFICATIONS:
	
	4. Section 09250 – Gypsum Board, subparagraph 2.01 C.3, add the following:
	"3. Smooth shank nail:
	     a. ASTM C 514
	     b. Length: 1-3/8 inches (35mm)."
	
	5. Section 15600 – Refrigeration Equipment, subparagraph 2.03 B.2, change total square feet (square meters) of surface from "298 (27.68)" to "316 (29.36)."

K. Changes to Drawings	CHANGES TO DRAWINGS: 6. Delete Sheet S-9 – Beam Schedule, and replace with attached Sheet S-9-A. 7. Sheet M-1 – Mechanical Plan, at Room 602, change "12 x 6" exhaust duct, to "12 x 18."

END OF ADDENDUM

Note: This sample is reasonably complete. It touches on all major points included in most Addenda. The user should recognize that each project may have specific requirements that may not be emphasized in this sample document.

Courtesy of the Construction Specifications Institute

Figure 11.6 *Typical Addendum*

Means
CONTRACT
CHANGE ORDER

FROM:

_____

_____

_____

_____

TO:

_____

_____

_____

_____

CHANGE ORDER NO.							
DATE							
PROJECT							
LOCATION							
JOB NO.							
ORIGINAL CONTRACT AMOUNT	$						
TOTAL PREVIOUS CONTRACT CHANGES							
TOTAL BEFORE THIS CHANGE ORDER							
AMOUNT OF THIS CHANGE ORDER							
REVISED CONTRACT TO DATE							

Gentlemen:

This CHANGE ORDER includes all Material, Labor and Equipment necessary to complete the following work and to adjust the total contract as indicated;

☐ the work below to be paid for at actual cost of Labor, Materials and Equipment plus_____percent (_____%)

☐ the work below to be completed for the sum of_____

_____ dollars ($_____)

_____

_____

_____

_____

_____

_____

_____

_____

_____

_____

_____

_____

_____

_____

_____

_____

_____

_____

_____

_____

_____

_____

CHANGES APPROVED

The work covered by this order shall be performed under the same Terms and Conditions as that included in the original contract unless stated otherwise above.

_____

By_____

_____

By_____

Signed_____

By _____

Figure 11.7 *Form of Change Order*

resulting in a formal Change Order. The CCD is discussed in more detail in Chapter 9, "Conditions of the Contract." The CCD has been proven to be fair to both owner and contractor; however, because it allows the scope of work to be agreed upon without an adjustment to contract price, there is potential for claims at a later time. It should therefore be used only when the advice of a knowledgable attorney has been obtained.

Industry Resources

The construction industry-at-large offers and provides a number of resources to assist the design professional in the preparation of the Project Manual.

Masterformat

Previous chapters have noted the unique and invaluable role of the Construction Specifications Institute in the development of uniform language, format, content and approach to the Contract Documents—particularly specifications for modern construction. CSI developed the 16 Division Format for the primary purpose of organizing the technical specifications. The "16 Division Format" approach to classifying technical construction data has been applied to accounting, cost estimating, filing, and other functions related to information handling and classification in construction. In 1978, CSI and its Canadian counterpart, Construction Specifications Canada (CSC) developed an organizational system called the *Masterformat*. The Masterformat, provides a numeric identity, or "address," and numerical order for each of the major components of the Contract Documents. Figure 11.8 illustrates the basic organization and numbering system recommended by Masterformat for the contents of the Project Manual.

Uniformat

Uniformat is an alternate method of information organization that is defined by building systems rather than divisions or "families"of materials and equipment (as is the Sixteen Division Masterformat). The Uniformat system is often the choice of public owners for cost estimating purposes. Uniformat has been endorsed by the American Society for Testing Materials (ASTM) and the National Institute of Standards and Technology (NIST).

Uniformat is subdivided into twelve major categories of information as illustrated in Figure 11.9 that generally follow the sequence of construction of a typical project.

Reference Standards and Technical Information

Reference Standards are requirements set by authority, custom, or general consensus. Composition, quality, and workmanship can be measured based on these standards of the industry. Typical reference standards are authored by those who represent manufacturers, producers, and installers, and others who are extremely knowledgeable on the subject. Various standards, currently accepted in the industry, are published by trade associations, government and institutional, and professional organizations. As technology and experience expand, standards are frequently re-written and new standards emerge, creating a vital, self-improving, ever-expanding support for new methods and new ideas in the construction industry.

Bidding Requirements
Contract Forms
Contract Conditions

00100 Bid Solicitation
00200 Instruction To Bidders
00210 Supplementary Instructions to Bidders
00220 Bid Scopes
00250 Pre-Bid Meeting
00300 Information Available To Bidders
00310 Preliminary Schedules
00320 Geotechnical Data
00330 Existing Conditions
00340 Environmental Assessment Information
00350 Project Financial Information
00360 Permit Application
00400 Bid Forms And Supplements
00410 Bid Form
00430 Bid Form Supplements
00450 Representations and Certifications
00490 Bidding Addenda
Contracting Requirements
00500 Agreement
00510 Notice of Award
00520 Agreement From
00540 Attachments to Agreement Form00550 Notice to Proceed
00570 Definitions
00600 Bonds And Certificates
00610 Bonds
00620 Certificates
00640 Release of Liens
00650 Statutory Declaration Forms
00700 General Conditions
00800 Supplementary Conditions
00890 Permits
00900 Addenda and Modifications
00910 Addenda
00920 Claims
00930 Clarifications and Proposals
00940 Modifications

Note: The sections listed above are not specifications. CSI *Masterformat* does not recognize Division O. The list above are part of the Bidding Documents

Division 1—General Requirements

01100 Summary
01110 Summary or Work
01120 Multiple Contract Summary
01140 Work Restrictions
01180 Project Utility Sources

01200 Price And Payment Procedures
01210 Allowances
01230 Alternates
01240 Value Analysis
01250 Contract Modification Procedures
01270 Unit Prices
01290 Payment Procedures
01300 Administrative Requirements
01310 Project Management and Coordination
01320 Construction Progress Documentation
01330 Submittal Procedures
01350 Special Procedures
01400 Quality Requirements
01410 Regulatory Requirements
01420 References
01430 Quality Assurance
01450 Quality Control
01500 Temporary Facilities And Controls
01510 Temporary Utilities
01520 Construction Facilities
01530 Temporary Construction
01540 Construction Aids
01550 Vehicular Access and Parking
01560 Temporary Barriers and Enclosures
01570 Temporary Controls
01580 Project Identification
01600 Product Requirements
01610 Basic Product Requirements
01620 Product Options
01630 Product Substitution Procedures
01640 Owner-Furnished Products
01650 Product Delivery Requirements
01660 Product Storage and Handling
01700 Execution Requirements
01710 Examination
01720 Preparation
01730 Execution
01740 Cleaning
01750 Starting and Adjusting
01760 Protecting Installed Construction
01770 Closeout Procedures
01780 Closeout Submittals
01800 Facility Operation
01810 Commissioning
01820 Demonstration and Training
01830 Operation and Maintenance
01890 Reconstruction
01900 Facility Decommissioning

Division 2—Site Work

02050 Basic Site Materials And Methods
02055 Soils
02060 Aggregate
02065 Cement and Concrete
02070 Geo-Synthetics
02080 Utility Materials
02090 Joint Materials
02100 Site Remediation
02105 Chemical Sampling and Analysis
02110 Excavation, Removal, & Handling of Hazardous Materials
02115 Underground Storage Tank Removal
02120 Off-SiteTransportation and Disposal
02125 Drum Handling
02130 Site Decontamination
02140 Landfill Construction and Storage
02145 Groundwater Treatment Systems
02150 Hazardous Waste Recovery Processes
02160 Physical Treatment
02170 Chemical Treatment
02180 Thermal Processes
02190 Biological Processes
02195 Remediation Soil Stabilization
02200 Site Preparation
02210 Subsurface Investigation
02220 Site Demolition
02230 Site Cleaning
02240 De-Watering
02250 Shoring and Underpinning
02260 Excavation Support and Protection
02285 Rebuilt Miscellaneous Structures
02290 Site Monitoring
02300 Earthwork
02310 Grading
02315 Excavation and Fill
02325 Dredging
02330 Embankment
02335 Sub-Grade and Roadbed
02340 Soil Stabilization
02360 Soil Treatment
02370 Erosion and Sedimentation Control
02380 Scour Protection
02390 Shoreline Protection and Mooring Structures
02400 Tunneling, Boring And Jacking
02410 Tunnel Excavation
02420 Initial Tunnel Support Systems
02425 Tunnel Linings

Figure 11.8 Masterformat

02430 Tunnel Grouting
02440 Immersed and Sunken Tube Tunnels
02441 Micro-Tunneling
02442 Cut and Cover Tunnels
02443 Tunnel Leak Repairs
02444 Shaft Construction
02445 Boring and Jacking Conduits
02450 Foundation and Load-Bearing Elements
02455 Driven Piles
02465 Bored Piles
02475 Caissons
02480 Foundation Walls
02490 Anchors
02500 Utility Services
02510 Water Distribution
02520 Wells
02530 Sanitary Sewerage
02540 Septic Tank Systems
02550 Piped Energy Distribution
02570 Process Materials Distribution Structures
02580 Electrical and Communication Structures
02590 Site Grounding
02610 Pipe Culverts
02620 Sub-Drainage
02630 Storm Drainage
02640 Culverts and Manufactured Construction
02660 Ponds and Reservoirs
02670 Constructed Wetlands
02700 Bases, Ballasts, Pavements, And Appurtenances
02710 Bound Base Courses
02720 Unbound Base Courses and Ballasts
02730 Aggregate Surfacing
02740 Flexible Pavement
02750 Rigid Pavement
02760 Paving Specialties
02770 Curbs and Gutters
02775 Sidewalks
02780 Unit Pavers
02785 Flexible Pavement Coating and Micro-Surfacing
02790 Athletic and Recreational Surfaces
02795 Porous Pavement
02800 Site Improvements and Amenities
02810 Irrigation System
02815 Fountains
02820 Fences and Gates
02830 Retaining Walls
02840 Walk, Road, and Parking Appurtenances
02850 Prefabricated Bridges
02860 Screening Devices
02870 Site Furnishings
02875 Site and Street Shelters

02880 Play Field Equipment and Structures
02890 Traffic Signs and Signals
02895 Markers and Monuments
02900 Planting
02905 Transplanting
02910 Plant Preparation
02920 Lawns and Grasses
02930 Exterior Plants
02935 Plant Maintenance
02945 Planting Accessories
02965 Flexible and Bituminous Pavement Recycling
02975 Flexible and Bituminous Pavement Reinforcement and Crack and Joint Sealants
02980 Rigid Pavement Rehabilitation
02990 Structure Moving

Division 3—Concrete

03050 Basic Concrete Materials and Methods
03100 Concrete Forms And Accessories
03110 Structural Cast-in-Place Concrete Forms
03120 Architectural Cast-in-Place Concrete Forms
03130 Permanent Forms
03150 Concrete Accessories
03200 Concrete Reinforcement
03210 Reinforcing Steel
03220 Welded Wire Fabric
03230 Stressing Tendons
03240 Fibrous Reinforcing
03250 Post-Tensioning
03310 Structural Concrete
03330 Architectural Concrete
03340 Low Density Concrete
03350 Concrete Finishing
03360 Concrete Finishes
03370 Specially Placed Concrete
03380 Post-Tensioned Concrete
03390 Concrete Curing
03400 Pre-Cast Concrete
03410 Plant-Pre-Cast Structural Concrete
03420 Plant-Pre-Cast Structural Post-Tensioned Concrete
03430 Site-Pre-Cast Structural Concrete
03450 Plant-Pre-Cast Architectural Concrete
03460 Site-Pre-Cast Architectural Concrete
03470 Tilt-Up Pre-Cast Concrete
03480 Pre-Cast Concrete Specialties
03490 Glass-Fiber-Reinforced Pre-Cast Concrete

03500 Cementitious Decks and Under-Layment
03510 Cementitious Roof Deck
03520 Lightweight Concrete Roof Insulation
03530 Concrete Topping
03540 Cementitious Under-Layment
03600 Grouts
03700 Mass Concrete
03900 Concrete Restoration And Cleaning
03910 Concrete Cleaning
03920 Concrete Resurfacing
03930 Concrete Rehabilitation

Division 4—Masonry

04050 Basic Masonry Materials And Methods
04060 Masonry Mortar
04070 Masonry Grout
04080 Masonry Anchorage and Reinforcement
04090 Masonry Accessories
04200 Masonry Units
04210 Clay Masonry Units
04220 Concrete Masonry Units
04230 Calcium Silicate Masonry Units
04270 Glass Masonry Units
04290 Adobe Masonry Units
04400 Stone
04410 Stone Materials
04420 Collected Stone
04430 Quarried Stone
04500 Refractories
04550 Flue Liners
04560 Combustion Chambers
04570 Castable Refractories
04580 Refractory Brick
04600 Corrosion-Resistant Masonry
04610 Chemical-Resistant Brick
04620 Vitrified Clay Liner Plates
04700 Simulated Masonry
04710 Simulated Brick
04720 Cast Stone
04730 Simulated Stone
04800 Masonry Assemblies
04810 Unit Masonry Assemblies
04820 Reinforced Unit Masonry Assemblies
04830 Non-Reinforced Unit Masonry Assemblies
04850 Stone Assemblies
04880 Masonry Fireplaces
04900 Masonry Restoration And Cleaning
04910 Unit Masonry Restoration
04920 Stone Restoration
04930 Unit Masonry Cleaning
04940 Stone Cleaning

Figure 11.8 *Masterformat (continued)*

Division 5—Metals

05050 Basic Metal Materials And Methods
05060 Metal Materials
05080 Factory-Applied Metal Coatings
05090 Metal Fastenings
05100 Structural Metal Framing
05120 Structural Steel
05140 Structural Aluminum
05150 Wire Rope Assemblies
05160 Metal Framing Systems
05200 Metal Joists
05210 Steel Joists
05250 Aluminum Joists
05260 Composite Joist Assemblies
05300 Metal Deck
05310 Steel Deck
05320 Raceway Deck Systems
05330 Aluminum Deck
05340 Acoustical Metal Deck
05400 Cold-Formed Metal Framing
05410 Load-Bearing Metal Studs
05420 Cold-Formed Metal Joists
05430 Slotted Channel Framing
05450 Metal Support
05550 Metal Fabrications
05510 Metal Stairs and Ladders
05520 Handrails and Railings
05530 Gratings
05540 Floor Plates
05550 Stair Treads and Nosings
05560 Metal Castings
05580 Formed Metal Fabrications
05600 Hydraulic Fabrications
05650 Railroad Track And Accessories
05700 Ornamental Metal
05710 Ornamental Stairs
05715 Fabricated Spiral Stairs
05720 Ornamental Handrails and Railings
05725 Ornamental Metal Castings
05730 Ornamental Formed Metal
05740 Ornamental Forged Metal
05800 Expansion Control
05810 Expansion Joint Cover Assemblies
05820 Slide Bearings
05830 Bridge Expansion Joint Assemblies
05900 Metal Restoration And Cleaning

Division 6—Wood and Plastics

06050 Basic Wood And Plastic Materials And Methods
06060 Wood Materials
06065 Plastic Materials
06070 Wood Treatment
06080 Factory-Applied Wood Coatings
06090 Wood and Plastic Fastenings
06100 Rough Carpentry
06110 Wood Framing
06120 Structural Panels
06130 Heavy Timber Construction
06140 Treated Wood Foundations
06150 Wood Decking
06160 Sheathing
06170 Prefabricated Structural Wood
06180 Glued-Laminated Construction
06200 Finish Carpentry
06220 Millwork
06250 Pre-Finished Paneling
06260 Board Paneling
06270 Closet and Utility Wood Shelving
06400 Architectural Woodwork
06410 Custom Cabinets
06415 Countertops
06420 Paneling
06430 Wood Stairs and Railings
06440 Wood Ornaments
06445 Simulated Wood Ornaments
06450 Standing and Running Trim
06455 Simulated Wood Trim
06460 Wood Frames
06470 Screens, Blinds, and Shutters
06500 Structural Plastics
06510 Structural Plastic Shapes and Plates
06520 Plastic Structural Assemblies
06600 Plastic Fabrications
06900 Wood and Plastics Restoration and Cleaning
06910 Wood Restoration and Cleaning
06920 Plastic Restoration and Cleaning

Division 7—Thermal and Moisture Proofing

07050 Basic Thermal And Moisture Protection Materials And Methods
07100 Dampproofing And Waterproofing
07110 Dampproofing
07120 Built-Up Bituminous Waterproofing
07130 Sheet Waterproofing
07140 Fluid-Applied Waterproofing
07150 Sheet Metal Waterproofing
07160 Cementitious and Reactive Waterproofing
07170 Bentonite Waterproofing
07180 Traffic Coatings
07190 Water Repellents
07200 Thermal Protection
07210 Building Insulation
07220 Roof and Deck Insulation
07240 Exterior Insulation and Finish Systems (EIFS)
07260 Vapor Retarders
07270 Air Barriers
07300 Shingles, Roof Tiles, and Roof Coverings
07310 Shingles
07320 Roof Tiles
07330 Roof Coverings
07400 Roofing And Siding Panels
07410 Metal Roof and Wall Panels
07420 Plastic Roof and Wall Panels
07430 Composite Panels
07440 Faced Panels
07450 Fiber-Reinforced Cementitious Panels
07460 Siding
07470 Wood Roof and Wall Panels
07480 Exterior Wall Assemblies
07500 Membrane Roofing
07510 Built-Up Bituminous Roofing
07520 Cold-Applied Bituminous Roofing
07530 Elastomeric Membrane Roofing
07540 Thermoplastic Membrane Roofing
07550 Modified Bituminous Membrane Roofing
07560 Fluid-Applied Roofing
07570 Coated Foamed Roofing
07580 Roll Roofing
07590 Roof Maintenance and Repairs
07600 Flashing And Sheet Metal
07610 Sheet Metal Roofing
07620 Sheet Metal Flashing and Trim
07630 Sheet Metal Roofing Specialties
07650 Flexible Flashing
07700 Roof Specialties and Accessories
07710 Manufactured Roof Specialties
07720 Roof Accessories
07760 Roof Pavers
07800 Fire And Smoke Protection
07810 Applied Fireproofing
07820 Board Fireproofing
07840 Firestopping
07860 Smoke Seals
07870 Smoke Containment Barriers
07900 Joint Sealers
07910 Preformed Joint Seals
07920 Joint Sealants

Figure 11.8 Masterformat (continued)

Division 8—Doors and Windows

08050 Basic Door And Window Materials And Methods
08100 Metal Doors And Frames
08110 Steel Doors and Frames
08120 Aluminum Doors and Frames
08130 Stainless Steel Doors and Frames
08140 Bronze Doors and Frames
08150 Pre-assembled Metal Door and Frame Units
08160 Sliding Metal Doors and Grilles
08180 Metal Screen and Storm Doors
08190 Metal Door Restoration
08200 Wood And Plastic Doors
08210 Wood Doors
08220 Plastic Doors
08250 Pre-assembled Wood and Plastic Door and Frame Units
08260 Sliding Wood and Plastic Doors
08280 Wood and Plastic Storm and Screen Doors
08290 Wood and Plastic Door Restoration
08300 Specialty Doors
08310 Access Doors and Panels
08320 Detention Doors and Frames
08330 Coiling Doors and Grilles
83340 Special Function Doors
08350 Folding Doors and Grilles
08360 Overhead Doors
08370 Vertical Lift Doors
08380 Traffic Doors
08390 Pressure-Resistant Doors
08400 Entrances and Storefronts
08410 Metal-Framed Storefronts
08450 All-Glass Entrances and Storefronts
08460 Automatic Entrance Doors
08470 Revolving Entrance Doors
08480 Balanced Entrance Doors
08490 Sliding Storefronts
08500 Windows
08510 Steel Windows
08520 Aluminum Windows
08530 Stainless Steel Windows
08540 Bronze Windows
08550 Wood Windows
08560 Plastic Windows
08570 Composite Windows
08580 Special Function Windows
08590 Window Restoration and Replacement
08600 Skylights
08610 Roof Windows
08620 Unit Skylights
08630 Metal-Framed Skylights
08700 Hardware
08710 Door Hardware
08720 Weather-stripping and Seals
08740 Electro-Mechanical Hardware
08750 Window Hardware
08770 Door and Window Accessories
08780 Special Function Hardware
08790 Hardware Restoration
08800 Glazing
08810 Glass
08830 Mirrors
08840 Plastic Glazing
08850 Glazing Accessories
08890 Glazing Restoration
08900 Glazed Curtain Wall
08910 Metal Framed Curtain Wall
08950 Translucent Wall and Roof Assemblies
08960 Sloped Glazing Assemblies
08970 Structural Glass Curtain Walls
08990 Glazed Curtain Wall Restoration

Division 9—Finishes

09050 Basic Finish Materials And Methods
09100 Metal Support Assemblies
09110 Non-Load Bearing Wall Framing
09120 Ceiling Suspension
09130 Acoustical Suspension
09190 Metal Frame Restoration
09200 Plaster And Gypsum Board
09205 Furring and Lathing
09210 Gypsum Plaster
09220 Portland Cement Plaster
09230 Plaster Fabrications
09250 Gypsum Board
09260 Gypsum Board Assemblies
09270 Gypsum Board Accessories
09280 Plaster Restoration
09300 Tile
09305 Tile Setting Materials and Accessories
09310 Ceramic Tile
09330 Quarry Tile
09340 Paver Tile
09350 Glass Mosaics
09360 Plastic Tile
09370 Metal Tile
09380 Cut Natural Stone Tile
09390 Tile Restoration
09400 Terrazzo
09410 Portland Cement Terrazzo
09420 Precast Terrazzo
09430 Conductive Terrazzo
09440 Plastic Matrix Terrazzo
09490 Terrazzo Restoration
09500 Ceilings
09510 Acoustical Ceilings
09545 Specialty Ceilings
09550 Mirror Panel Ceilings
09560 Textured Ceilings
09570 Linear Wood Ceiling
09580 Suspended Decorative Grids
09590 Ceiling Assembly Restoration
09600 Flooring
09610 Floor Treatment
09620 Specialty Flooring
09630 Masonry Flooring
09640 Wood Flooring
09650 Resilient Flooring
09660 Static Control Flooring
09670 Fluid-Applied Flooring
09680 Carpet
09690 Flooring Restoration
09700 Wall Finishes
09710 Acoustical Wall Finishes
09720 Wall Covering
09730 Wall Carpet
09740 Flexible Wood Sheets
09750 Stone Facing
09760 Plastic Blocks
09770 Special Wall Surfaces
09790 Wall Finish Restoration
09800 Acoustical Treatment
09810 Acoustical Space Units
09820 Acoustical Insulation and Sealants
09830 Acoustical Barriers
09840 Acoustical Wall Treatment
09900 Paints And Coatings
09910 Paints
09930 Stains and Transparent Finishes
09940 Decorative Finishes
09960 High-Performance Coatings
09970 Coatings for Steel
09980 Coatings for Concrete and Masonry
09990 Paint Restoration

Division 10—Specialties

10100 Visual Display Boards
10110 Chalkboards
10115 Markerboards
10120 Tackboard and Visual Aid Boards
10130 Operable Board Units
10140 Display Track Assemblies
10145 Visual Aid Board Units
10150 Compartments And Cubicles
10160 Metal Toilet Compartments
10165 Plastic Laminate Toilet Compartments
10170 Plastic Toilet Compartments
10175 Particleboard Toilet Compartments

Figure 11.8 *Masterformat (continued)*

10180 Stone Toilet Compartments
10185 Shower and Dressing
Compartments
10190 Cubicles
10200 Louvers And Vents
10210 Wall Louvers
10220 Louvered Equipment
Enclosures
10225 Door Louvers
10230 Vents
10240 Grilles And Screens
10250 Service Walls
10260 Wall And Corner Guards
10270 Access Flooring
10290 Pest Control
10300 Fireplaces And Stoves
10305 Manufactured Fireplaces
10310 Fireplace Specialties and
Accessories
10320 Stoves
10330 Fireplace and Stove
Restoration
10340 Manufactured Exterior
Specialties
10345 Exterior Specialties
Restoration
10350 Flagpoles
10400 Identification Devices
10410 Directories
10420 Plaques
10430 Exterior Signage
10440 Interior Signage
10450 Pedestrian Control Devices
10500 Lockers
10520 Fire Protection Specialties
10530 Protective Covers
10550 Postal Specialties
10600 Partitions
10605 Wire Mesh Partitions
10610 Folding Gates
10615 Demountable Partitions
10630 Portable Partitions, Screens,
and Panels
10650 Operable Partitions
10670 Storage Shelving
10700 Exterior Protection
10705 Exterior Sun Control Devices
10710 Exterior Shutters
10715 Storm Panels
10720 Exterior Louvers
10750 Telephone Specialties
10800 Toilet, Bath, And Laundry
Accessories
10810 Toilet Accessories
10820 Bath Accessories
10830 Laundry Accessories
10880 Scales
10900 Wardrobe And Closet
Specialties

Division 11—Equipment

11010 Maintenance Equipment

11020 Security And Vault
Equipment
11030 Teller And Service
Equipment
11040 Ecclesiastical Equipment
11050 Library Equipment
11060 Theater And Stage
Equipment
11070 Instrumental Equipment
11080 Registration Equipment
11090 Checkroom Equipment
11100 Mercantile Equipment
11110 Commercial Laundry And
Dry Cleaning Equipment
11120 Vending Equipment
11130 Audio-Visual Equipment
11140 Vehicle Service Equipment
11150 Parking Control Equipment
11160 Loading Dock Equipment
11170 Solid Waste Handling
Equipment
11190 Detention Equipment
11200 Water Supply And
Treatment Equipment
11210 Supply and Treatment
Pumps
11220 Mixers and Flocculators
11225 Clarifiers
11230 Water Aeration Equipment
11240 Chemical Feed Equipment
11250 Water Softening Equipment
11260 Disinfectant Feed Equipment
11270 Fluoridation Equipment
11280 Hydraulic Gates And Valves
11285 Hydraulic Gates
11295 Hydraulic Valves
11300 Fluid Waste Treatment and
Disposal Equipment
11310 Sewage and Sludge Pumps
11320 Grit Collecting Equipment
11330 Screening and Grinding
Equipment
11335 Sedimentation Tank
Equipment
11340 Scum Removal Equipment
11345 Chemical Equipment
11350 Sludge Handling and
Treatment Equipment
11360 Filter Press Equipment
11365 Trickling Filter Equipment
11370 Compressors
11375 Aeration Equipment
11380 Sludge Digestion Equipment
11385 Digester Mixing Equipment
11390 Package Sewage Treatment
Plants
11400 Food Service Equipment
11405 Food Storage Equipment
11410 Food Preparation Equipment
11415 Food Delivery Carts and
Conveyors
11420 Food Cooking Equipment

11425 Hood and Ventilation
Equipment
11430 Food Dispensing Equipment
11435 Ice Machines
11440 Cleaning and Disposal
Equipment
11450 Residential Equipment
11460 Unit Kitchens
11470 Darkroom Equipment
11480 Athletic, Recreational, and
Therapeutic Equipment
11500 Industrial and Process
Equipment
11600 Laboratory Equipment
11650 Planetarium Equipment
11660 Observatory Equipment
11680 Office Equipment
11700 Medical Equipment
11710 Medical Sterilizing
Equipment
11720 Examination and Treatment
Equipment
11730 Patient Care Equipment
11740 Dental Equipment
11750 Optical Equipment
11760 Operating Room Equipment
11770 Radiology Equipment
11780 Mortuary Equipment
11850 Navigation Equipment
11870 Agricultural Equipment
11900 Exhibit Equipment

Division 12—Furnishings

12050 Fabrics
12100 Art
12110 Murals
12120 Wall Decorations
12140 Sculptures
12170 Art Glass
12190 Ecclesiastical Art
12300 Manufactured Casework
12310 Manufactured Metal
Casework
12320 Manufactured Wood
Casework
12350 Specialty Casework
12400 Furnishing and Accessories
12410 Office Accessories
12420 Table Accessories
12430 Portable Lamps
12440 Bath Furnishings
12450 Bedroom Furnishings
12460 Furnishing Accessories
12480 Rugs and Mats
12490 Window Treatments
12500 Furniture
12510 Office Furniture
12520 Seating
12540 Hospitality Furniture
12560 Institutional Furniture
12580 Residential Furniture
12600 Multiple Seating

Figure 11.8 Masterformat (*continued*)

12610 Fixed Audience Seating
12620 Portable Audience Seating
12630 Stadium and Arena Seating
12640 Booths and Tables
12650 Multiple-Use Fixed Seating
12660 Telescoping Stands
12670 Pews and Benches
12680 Seat and Table Assemblies
12700 Systems Furniture
12710 Panel-Hung Component
      System Furniture
12720 Free-Standing Component
      System Furniture
12730 Beam System Furniture
12740 Desk System Furniture
12800 Interior Plants and Planters
12810 Interior Live Plants
12820 Interior Artificial Plants
12830 Interior Planters
12840 Interior Landscape
      Accessories
12850 Interior Plant Maintenance
12900 Furnishings Restoration and
      Repair

Division 13—Special Construction

13010 Air-Supported Structures
13020 Building Modules
13030 Special Purpose Rooms
13080 Sound, Vibration, and
      Seismic Control
13090 Radiation Protection
13100 Lightning Protection
13110 Cathodic Protection
13120 Pre-Engineered Structures
13150 Swimming Pools
13160 Aquariums
13165 Aquatic Park Facilities
13170 Tubs and Pools
13175 Ice Rinks
13185 Kennels and Animal Shelters
13190 Site-Constructed
      Incinerators
13200 Storage Tanks
13220 Filter Underdrains and
      Media
13230 Digester Covers and
      Appurtenances
13240 Oxygenation Systems
13260 Sludge Conditioning
      Systems
13280 Hazardous Material
      Remediation
13400 Measurement and Control
      Instrumentation
13410 Basic Measurement and
      Control Instrumentation
      Materials and Methods
13420 Instruments
13430 Boxes, Panels, and Control
      Centers

13440 Indicators, Recorders, and
      Controllers
13450 Central Control
13480 Instrument Lists and Reports
13490 Measurement and Control
      Commissioning
13500 Recording Instrumentation
13510 Stress Instrumentation
13520 Seismic Instrumentation
13530 Meteorological
      Instrumentation
13550 Transportation Control
      Instrumentation
13560 Airport Control
      Instrumentation
13570 Railroad Control
      Instrumentation
13580 Subway Control
      Instrumentation
13590 Transit Vehicle Control
      Instrumentation
13600 Solar and Wind Energy
      Equipment
13610 Solar Flat Plate Collectors
13620 Solar Concentrating
      Collectors
13625 Solar Vacuum Tube
      Collectors
13630 Solar Collector Components
13640 Packaged Solar Equipment
13650 Photovoltaic Collectors
13660 Wind Energy Equipment
13700 Security Access and
      Surveillance
13800 Building Automation and
      Control
13850 Detection and Alarm
13900 Fire Suppression
13910 Basic Fire Suppression
      Materials and Methods
13920 Fire Pumps
13930 Wet-Pipe Fire Suppression
      Sprinklers
13935 Dry-Pipe Fire Suppression
      Sprinklers
13940 Pre-Action Fire Suppression
      Sprinklers
13945 Combination Dry-Pipe and
      Pre-Action Fire Suppression
      Sprinklers
13950 Deluge Fire Suppression
      Sprinklers
13955 Foam Fire Extinguishing
13960 Carbon Dioxide Fire
      Extinguishing
13965 Alternative Fire
      Extinguishing Systems
13970 Dry Chemical Fire
      Extinguishing
13975 Standpipes and Hoses

Division 14—Conveying Systems

14100 Dumbwaiters
14110 Manual Dumbwaiters
14120 Electric Dumbwaiters
14140 Hydraulic Dumbwaiters
14200 Elevators
14210 Electric Traction Elevators
14240 Hydraulic Elevators
14270 Custom Elevator Cabs
14280 Elevator Equipment and
      Controls
14290 Elevator Renovation
14300 Escalators and Moving
      Walks
14400 Lifts
14410 People Lifts
14420 Wheelchair Lifts
14430 Platform Lifts
14440 Sidewalk Lifts
14450 Vehicle Lifts
14500 Material Handling
14510 Material Transport
14530 Postal Conveying
14540 Baggage Conveying and
      Dispensing
14550 Conveyors
14560 Chutes
14570 Feeder Equipment
14580 Pneumatic Tube Systems
14600 Hoists and Cranes
14605 Crane Rails
14610 Fixed Hoists
14620 Trolley Hoists
14630 Bridge Cranes
14640 Gantry Cranes
14650 Jib Cranes
14670 Tower Cranes
14680 Mobile Cranes
14690 Derricks
14700 Turntables
14800 Scaffolding
14810 Suspended Scaffolding
14820 Rope Climbers
14830 Telescoping Platforms
14840 Powered Scaffolding
14900 Transportation
14910 People Movers
14920 Monorails
14930 Funiculars
14940 Aerial Tramways
14950 Aircraft Passenger Loading

Division 15—Mechanical

15050 Basic Mechanical Materials
      and Methods
15060 Hangers and Supports
15070 Mechanical Sound,
      Vibration, and Seismic
      Control
15075 Mechanical Identification

Figure 11.8 *Masterformat (continued)*

15080 Mechanical Insulation
15090 Mechanical Restoration and
Retrofit
15100 Building Services Piping
15105 Pipes and Tubes
15110 Valves
15120 Piping Specialties
15130 Pumps
15140 Domestic Water Piping
15150 Sanitary Waste and Vent
Piping
15160 Storm Drainage Piping
15170 Swimming Pool and
Fountain Piping
15180 Heating and Cooling Piping
15190 Fuel Piping
15200 Process Piping
15210 Process Air and Gas Piping
15220 Process Water and Waste
Piping
15230 Industrial Process Piping
15300 Fire Protection Piping
15400 Plumbing Fixtures and
Equipment
15410 Plumbing Fixtures
15440 Plumbing Pumps
15450 Potable Water Storage
Tanks
15460 Domestic Water
Conditioning Equipment
15470 Domestic Water Filtrating
Equipment
15480 Domestic Water Heaters
15490 Pool and Fountain
Equipment
15500 Heat-Generation Equipment
15510 Heating Boilers and
Accessories
15520 Feedwater Equipment
15530 Furnaces
15540 Fuel-Fired Heaters
15550 Breechings, Chimneys, and
Stacks
15600 Refrigeration Equipment
15610 Refrigeration Compressors
15620 Packaged Water Chillers
15630 Refrigerant Monitoring
Systems
15640 Packaged Cooling Towers
15650 Field-Erected Cooling
Towers
15660 Liquid Coolers and
Evaporative Condensers
15670 Refrigerant Condensing
Units
15700 Heating, Ventilating, and Air
Conditioning Equipment
15710 Heat Exchangers
15720 Air Handling Units
15730 Unitary Air Conditioning
Equipment
15740 Heat Pumps

15750 Humidity Control Equipment
15760 Terminal Heating and
Cooling Units
15770 Floor-Heating and Snow-
Melting Equipment
15780 Energy Recovery Equipment
15800 Air Distribution
15810 Ducts
15820 Duct Accessories
15830 Fans
15840 Air Terminal Units
15850 Air Outlets and Inlets
15860 Air Cleaning Devices
15900 HVAC Instrumentation and
Controls
15905 HVAC Instrumentation
15910 Direct Digital Controls
15915 Electric and Electronic
Control
15920 Pneumatic Controls
15925 Pneumatic and Electric
Controls
15930 Self-Powered Controls
15935 Building Systems Controls
15940 Sequence of Operation
15950 Testing, Adjusting, and
Balancing

Division 16—Electrical

16050 Basic Electrical Materials
and Methods
16060 Grounding and Bonding
16070 Hangers and Supports
16075 Electrical Identification
16080 Electrical Testing
16090 Restoration and Repair
16100 Wiring Methods
16120 Conductors and Cables
16130 Raceway and Boxes
16140 Wiring Devices
16150 Wiring Connections
16200 Electrical Power
16210 Electrical Utility Services
16220 Motors and Generators
16230 Generator Assemblies
16240 Battery Equipment
16260 Static Power Converters
16270 Transformers
16280 Power Filters and
Conditioners
16290 Power Measurement and
Control
16300 Transmission and
Distribution
16310 Transmission and
Distribution Accessories
16320 High-Voltage Switching and
Protection
16330 Medium-Voltage Switching
and Protection
16340 Medium-Voltage Switching
and Protection Assemblies

16360 Unit Substations
16400 Low-Voltage Distribution
16410 Enclosed Switches and
Circuit Breakers
16420 Enclosed Controllers
16430 Low-Voltage Switchgear
16440 Switchboards, Panelboards,
and Control Centers
16450 Enclosed Bus Assemblies
16460 Low-Voltage Transformers
16470 Power Distribution Units
16490 Low-Voltage Distribution
Components and
Accessories
16500 Lighting
16510 Interior Luminaires
16520 Exterior Luminaires
16530 Emergency Lighting
16540 Classified Location Lighting
16550 Special Purpose Lighting
16560 Signal Lighting
16570 Dimming Control
16580 Lighting Accessories
16590 Lighting Restoration and
Repair
16700 Communications
16710 Communications Circuits
16720 Telephone and
Intercommunication
Equipment
16740 Communication and Data
Processing Equipment
16770 Cable Transmission and
Reception Equipment
16780 Broadcast Transmission and
Reception Equipment
16790 Microwave Transmission
and Reception Equipment
16800 Sound and Video
16810 Sound and Video Circuits
16820 Sound Reinforcement
16830 Broadcast Studio Audio
Equipment
16840 Broadcast Studio Video
Equipment
16850 Television Equipment
16880 Multimedia Equipment

Figure 11.8 Masterformat (continued)

The Uniformat System

01	Foundations	011	Standard Foundation Systems
		012	Special Foundation Conditions
02	Substructure	021	Slab on Grade
		022	Basement Excavation
		023	Basement Walls
03	Superstructure	031	Floor Construction
		032	Roof Construction
		033	Stair Construction
04	Exterior Closure	041	Exterior Walls
		042	Exterior Doors and Windows
05	Roofing	051	Roofing Systems and Sheet Metal
06	Interior Construction	061	Partitions
		062	Interior Finishes
		063	Specialties
07	Conveying Systems	071	Elevators
08	Mechanical Systems	081	Plumbing
		082	Heating, Ventilating and Air Conditioning
		083	Fire Protection
		084	Special Mechanical Systems
		085	Mechanical Service and Distribution
09	Electrical	091	Electrical Service and Distribution
		092	Lighting and Power
		093	Special Electrical Systems
10	General Conditions	101	Contractor's OH&P
11	Equipment	111	Fixed and Movable Equipment
		112	Furnishings
		113	Special Construction
12	Sitework	121	Site Preparation
		122	Site Improvements
		123	Site Utilities
		123	Off Site Construction

Figure 11.9 Uniformat

In order to save time, specifiers frequently reference certain standards in specification sections. The following is a concrete specification with a reference to certain industry standards:

Cement: Shall be standard brand Portland Cement, conforming to ASTM Specification C-150, the latest edition.

At first reading, it may seem as if the specifier has covered the subject sufficiently. However, a review of the referenced document shows that ASTM C150-83a specifies eight types of cement, and refers to several other published reference standards. Thus, the type of Portland Cement to be used has not been clearly stated. While reference standard specifying is a valid method for writing specifications, it requires a thorough and careful approach to avoid the kinds of errors shown above. Reference standard specifying is discussed in more detail in Chapter 9, "Conditions of the Contract."

A number of trade unions, industry organizations, and government agencies produce published standards that are recognized and used throughout the construction industry. So that the source of a reference standard can be identified, the various organizations are recognized by initials, and the standard by number and date. In the above example, "ASTM" refers to the *American Society for Testing Materials,* and "C150" is the number identifying the particular specification established by ASTM. The figure "83a" represents the year and sequence of order during the year in which the standard was written. A listing of industry organizations is included in the Appendix.

Manufacturers' Literature

The most reliable information resource for both the design professional and the specification writer is the literature produced by manufacturers of building materials, products, and assemblies. Many construction industry services provide annual catalogues as a service to design professionals. In fact, most licensed practitioners receive a profusion of manufacturers' literature by mail. This literature can serve as a library of general product data.

Most manufacturers of major building products provide the services of a manufacturer's representative. The manufacturer's representative usually keeps the company's literature up to date, makes himself available to answer questions about his company's products, and makes suggestions as to proper use, cost considerations, availability, restrictions and similar data.

To promote uniformity in commercial product literature, the Construction Specifications Institute provides a suggested format. This system is used by manufacturers for the presentation of data to design professionals. It uses the Spec-Data Sheet. The standard Spec-Data Sheet, as designed by the Construction Specifications Institute, organizes product data into ten groups (headings) of related information. This is an excellent format for the specifier to classify any product. These Spec-Data headings are listed below:

- Product name.
- Manufacturer.
- Product description.
- Technical data.
- Installation.

- Availability and cost.
- Warranty.
- Maintenance.
- Technical services.
- Filing systems.

Professional and Industry Publications and Web Sites

Most professional institutes and societies publish print journals and offer web sites featuring articles, research studies, and editorials on subjects of interest to their members. Membership in such organizations provides many benefits to the construction specifier, including the journals which can become a part of a professional library.

A number of construction-related industries produce their own trade magazines and publications in print and on-line. These publications feature articles on projects, legal matters, new product development and evaluations, and the work and practice of outstanding practitioners. To catalogue and store great numbers of magazines may not be practical, but several indexes are available that cross reference industry publications by year and month with listings by author, subject, and general content. Most publications are available at libraries or through vendors. A good construction index of products and methods is essential to the library of today's construction professional.

The Professional Library

A complete and well implemented library and a command of Internet search techniques are essential to the needs of today's design professional and the specifier. Such a library should contain the following items:

- Current catalogues of building products, equipment, and furnishings.
- Current volumes of applicable published building codes.
- Industry reference standards and specifications.
- Professional journals.
- Current texts on construction industry subjects and innovations.
- Graphic and construction standards.
- Dictionary of construction terms and usage.
- Current guides to estimated construction costs.
- Project manuals for previous projects.

Continuing Education

Finally, regardless of education, experience, and success, today's construction professional must pursue a course of continuing education throughout the course of professional life. Just as ignorance of the law is no defense in legal matters, ignorance of construction's ever-changing technology is no excuse for the modern construction professional.

Chapter Twelve
Contract Administration

Modern building construction requires a great deal of skill and expertise on the part of those who organize, schedule, supervise, coordinate, administer, and keep records of the various projects. The interrelationships between the owner, design professional, constructor, and subcontractor can be sensitive because of the exposure to liability and financial risk associated with any errors and omissions in design and construction, injury on the job, and possible failure of materials and assemblies (and workers) to perform as expected.

Building construction has become an extremely complex endeavor involving the careful orchestration of large capital expenditures, the employment of specialized design and engineering resources, as well as construction management expertise. In addition, a variety of crafts, trades, and labor must be coordinated. All of these elements must come together in the assembly of different materials and systems. The finished product must be delivered within a specified period of time for a prearranged cost if a project is to be successful. At no time in history has the building process been more complicated by a combination of economic factors and government regulations. In its zeal to protect, government has created law that regulates location, size, shape, structure, envelope, ingress and egress, and even the ultimate use of the modern building. At the same time, government has come to regulate wages, work, safety conditions, record keeping, and the accountability of those who employ and manage. Because of its size and influence on the general economy, building construction is extremely sensitive to changes in the general health of business and commerce. Figure 12.1 illustrates the interrelationships of function and the flow of money, effort, resource, and records that must occur between owner, design professional, constructor, and community (government) during the construction of a modern building. These relationships, although they may vary greatly from project to project, may be thought of as a wheel kept constantly turning by the transfer of energy from one spoke to another in a single coordinated direction. As with any machine, a major expenditure of collective energy is required to start the construction "wheel" in rotation, and a continuous transfer of energy is needed to maintain the rotation. The failure of any sector to transfer energy to the next sector, or any reversal of the flow, will slow or perhaps even stop the progress of construction. In order to start up again, considerable extra energy and cost must be expended to overcome the inertia, reach its former momentum, and continue that motion through the process of completion.

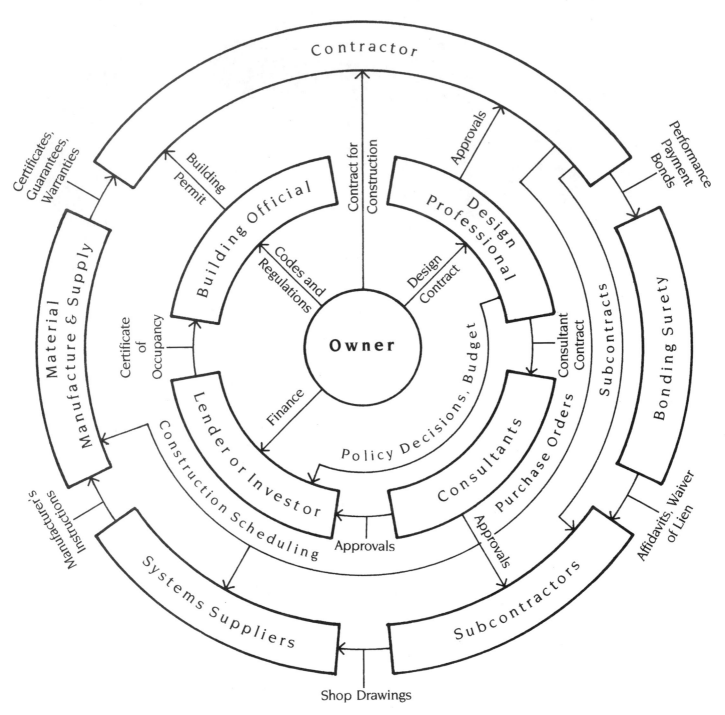

Contractor

Certificates, Guarantees, Warranties

Building Permit

Building Official

Contract for Construction

Approvals

Design Professional

Performance Payment Bonds

Material Manufacture & Supply

Codes and Regulations

Design Contract

Consultant Contract

Subcontracts

Bonding Surety

Certificate of Occupancy

Owner

Policy Decisions, Budget

Lender or Investor

Finance

Consultants

Purchase Orders

Construction Scheduling

Approvals

Manufacturer's Instructions

Systems Suppliers

Approvals

Affidavits, Waiver of Lien

Subcontractors

Shop Drawings

Courtesy of the Construction Specifications Institute

Figure 12.1 *Wheel of Construction Progress*

The Function of Government

The fundamental purpose of government in the United States is to represent and safeguard the public interest, health and economy, to provide basic services, and to establish and maintain order. Chapter 2, "The Owner," discusses government as owner. Chapter 5, "Labor and Government" discusses the history of government and the influence of various government bodies on the construction industry.

The function of local government in the process of building construction is established by legislation which gives local government the ability to:

- Adopt zoning regulations, which are usually administered by an appointed commission of knowledgeable and responsible citizens. Such a commission controls land use in terms of function and potential nuisance, e.g., limiting the height of buildings and building density. The secondary objectives of a zoning commission may be to preserve a percentage and quality of free or open space for the benefit of the community and to establish guidelines for community, planning for future growth, communication, transportation, and basic utility and sanitary services.
- Establish ordinances, building codes, and other authority under the administration of an appointed building official, as well as regulations regarding the type, occupancy, and appropriate construction of buildings in accordance with zoning requirements, and safe practices concerning the safety and welfare of building occupants and the public at large.

Taxation and Fees

The functions of government are funded by various taxes, and by fees collected for the services it renders. In regard to building construction, most municipalities require that a Building Permit be issued prior to commencement of construction. This process involves collection of a fee based on the size and value of the construction. The fee covers the cost of review and approval of the construction documents as well as periodic inspection of the Work by the Building Official. Certain portions of the construction, such as plumbing, mechanical, and electrical work may require issuance of additional permits and licensing of certain associated subcontractors. Some jurisdictions require that the general contractor and other major subcontractors be licensed. The building permit establishes the relative value of the improved property. The relative value is later entered in the tax record for future tax collection purposes. Meters are installed to collect fees for utilities such as water, gas, and electricity. Other forms of taxation may include sales tax on certain materials, as well as tax on income. Generally, it is the private owner who generates the majority of tax revenues to the community. Publicly owned buildings are usually exempt from payment of property, sales and other taxes.

After the building permit has been reviewed, and in order for the proposed building to be approved, the municipal building department may require reviews by the departments which administer public utility services, engineering, traffic and transportation, zoning, and/or city planning, fire protection, police, and health and sanitation. These reviews confirm compliance with building codes and other applicable ordinances. Once the appropriate permits are issued, various members of the building inspection department may make required periodic visits and inspections of the Work. These officials can issue citations for the violation of codes and ordinances as well as refuse to issue the Certificate of Occupancy—which is usually required before permanent utilities can be turned on and occupancy of the building can take place. The building official has the power to demand that materials and assemblies be tested to ensure that they comply with codes and other regulations. The cost of such tests must therefore be included as part of the project cost. Contract Documents usually provide contractor responsibility for the cost of building permits and testing required by government authorities. The Supplemental General Conditions may expand upon these responsibilities for the individual project. See Chapter 10, "Project Definition." Preparation of Specifications, for a discussion of testing requirements that are included in a technical specification.

The OPC Relationship—Duties and Objectives

The OPC (Owner-Professional-Constructor) relationship is discussed in Chapter 1, "The Construction Industry" and the duties of each party in the OPC have been discussed at length in earlier chapters of this book. It is appropriate at this point to recognize and profile the representatives of each of these parties who may be employed to carry out the duties and responsibilities of their employers on the job site, either by continuous or part-time on-site representation. Following is a review of the roles and responsibilities of each of the major participants, along with the roles of the members of their support staffs.

The Owner's Duties and Objectives

The first party in the OPC relationship, the owner, is discussed in Chapter 2, "The Owner." The owner is the source of the project's capital and direction. The owner initiates the project by identifying a need, and then arranging the financial resources to meet that need. The owner retains the design professional who confirms the owner's need and draws up a program of design and improvement within the scope of the owner's financial capacity. Contract Documents are drawn up by the design professional, competitive bids or negotiations for construction are arranged, the Contract for Construction is agreed upon, and construction begins.

Most owners in building construction today are corporate entities. The owners who make, by far, the largest contribution to total building construction, consist of boards of directors of major corporations, municipal councils, county commissions, school boards, boards of governors, state legislatures, and the government of the United States. This is not to ignore the individual owner who is, for the most part, the homeowner, small businessperson and, in many instances, the individual private investor.

The owner, whether a corporation or an individual, has at least three primary and three secondary goals in commissioning the design and construction of a modern building. The primary goals of an owner are typically:

- Construction of a building that will house some function vital to certain needs and objectives.
- Creation of maximum space and utility for minimum expenditure of capital.

- A resulting building of beauty and functional efficiency, which reflects the owner's objectives, character, and personality.

The secondary objectives of the owner may be:

- A cost savings over the existing operation or facility, or an alternative suitable to his needs and objectives.
- Structured shelter from taxation.
- Recognition in the community.

Figure 12.2 shows the typical organization and immediate resources needed by the owner. It includes employment of the design professional and selection of the constructor.

Among the owner's duties and responsibilities are:

- Provision of adequate funds, a site, and information necessary to define his need.
- Employment of competent professionals to design and engineer the project.
- Selection and employment of construction professionals to build the project.
- Administration of the budget and payment of monies earned and due.
- Rendering of approvals and instructions when appropriate.
- Coordination of separate items of work.
- Inspection and acceptance of the completed project.

The Design Professional's Duties and Objectives

The second member of the OPC relationship, the design professional is discussed in Chapter 3, "The Design Professional." The design professional, like the owner, is seldom a single individual, but a carefully coordinated team of professionals, each of whom is a specialist in certain disciplines. Together this group establishes the building's design under the direction, responsibility, and coordination of the architect or engineer identified as the prime design professional. Figure 12.3 is a diagram of the design professional's organization, resources, and disciplines.

The primary objectives of the design professional are as follows:

- To serve the owner's needs and objectives competently and completely at an adequate profit to himself and his associates.
- To create a design that can be delivered within the owner's budget requirements, that will serve adequately for many years, and that will satisfy the concerns and regulations of the community in which it is constructed.
- To be recognized as a participant in a successful project that will bring credit to himself and all who participated in the endeavor.

The design professional, by training and experience, is the appropriate administrator of decisions and the author of documentation that delineate the final design of the project. As such, he or she is the logical party to make judgments and recommendations to the owner regarding appropriate materials, size, shape, function, arrangement of the envelope, and the immediate environment of the building and site. In principle, he is an extension of the owner, utilizing the owner's resources to accomplish the owner's objectives. Once the design is

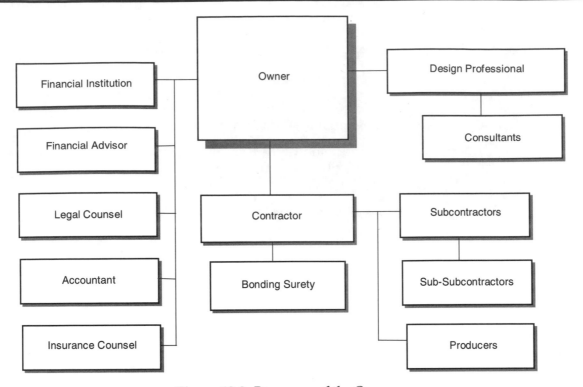

Figure 12.2 *Resources of the Owner*

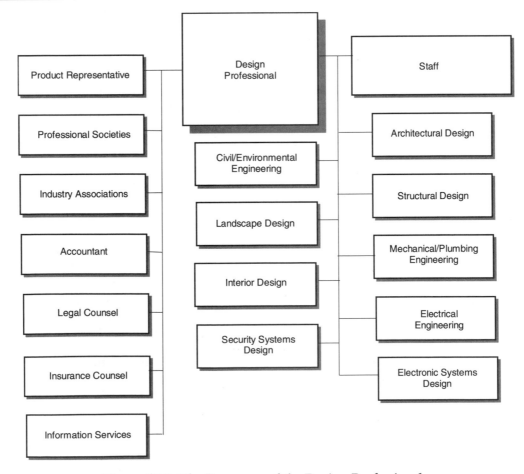

Figure 12.3 *The Resources of the Design Professional*

complete and documented, and the constructor has been chosen and the construction begun, the design professional is the owner's representative, participating in the process by observing and administering the Contract for Construction.

The Constructor's Duties and Objectives

The third party of the OPC relationship, the constructor is discussed in Chapter 4, "The Constructor." The constructor, identified by the Contract for Construction as the (general) contractor, is the implementor of the construction process. Figure 12.4 shows the resources and organization of the typical constructor including personnel, subcontract resources, and source of supply. Such organizations vary greatly depending upon the size of the company and its capacity to accomplish work with "in-house" employees and equipment. The illustration is based on the typical medium-sized constructor and assumes that the constructor is capable of performing approximately 20% of the Work with his own forces, with 80% accomplished by subcontractors.

It is the constructor's duty to organize and provide the labor, skills, supervision, materials, systems, equipment, tools and other resources necessary for the proper construction and completion of the project. The constructor's primary responsibilities are typically:

- To adequately estimate the cost and time required to construct the proposed building, keeping in mind that the final result must be acceptable to both the owner and the design professional. At the same time, the constructor must be competitive, and maintain an adequate margin of profit and increased business potential.
- To administer the construction process, management, and procurement of the material, systems, means, resources and personnel required to construct the building while maintaining or exceeding the profit objectives established when the Contract Sum was offered.
- To complete the Work in a competent, efficient, and timely manner that will bring credit to himself, his organization and the construction industry.

In the typical Contract for Construction, the constructor, and the constructor alone, is responsible for the means and methods of construction. He is responsible for observing and adhering to the full intent and content of the Contract Documents, authored by the design professional. The Contract Documents establish the duties and responsibilities of the owner, design professional, constructor, subcontractor, and sub-subcontractor. They also illustrate the building and its components and establish the quality of materials, components, assemblies, equipment, workmanship and delivery requirements of the project. The constructor has full discretion (with certain controls for the owner's approval and protection) to pursue and execute the Work in the most appropriate and expeditious manner available under the guidance of the Contract Documents. The constructor is responsible for safety at the job site, for adhering to federal and state law, employment principals, and adhering to local building codes and ordinances.

The Construction Manager

Because of the complexity of modern building construction, some owners—both private and public—may wish to hire an independent

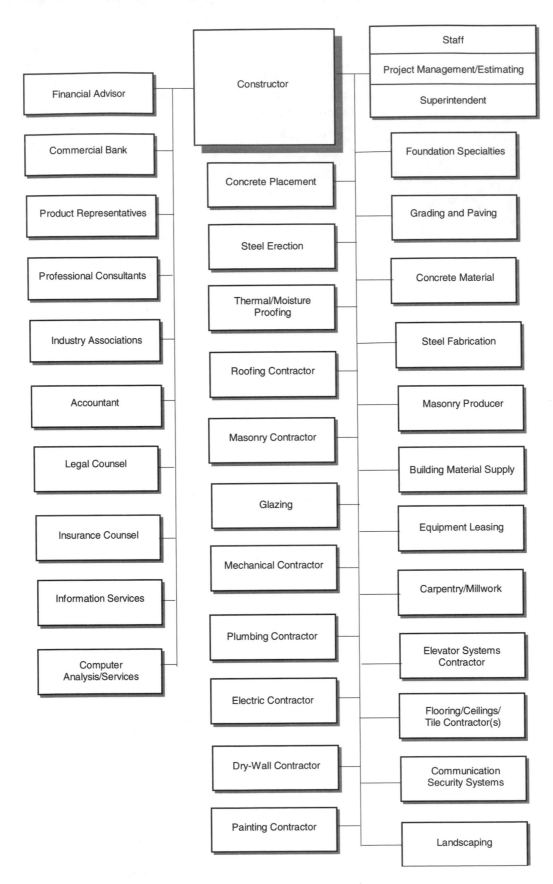

Figure 12.4 *The Constructor's Resources*

Construction Manager to represent their interests during the critical construction phase of the project. (See Chapter 7, "Project Delivery"). In this role, the construction manager serves as liaison between owner, design professional, constructor and building official. In some respects, the construction manager's duties may overlap, and even conflict with the design professional's. Appropriate measures must be taken while modifying the Contract Documents to avoid any conflict or confusion. The agreement between owner and design professional should make clear the fact that unless otherwise provided, the design professional " ... *shall not be required to make exhaustive or continuous on-site inspections to check the quality or quantity of the Work ...* " The duties of the construction manager, employed by the owner, should properly include "*continuous and regular on-site inspections to check the quality and quantity of the Work, ... and detailed reports to the owner of these inspections.*" Depending on the type of contract, the construction manager may be an independent construction professional, with the design professional acting under an extension to the basic services agreement, or in certain contracting methods, a construction manager may be employed instead of a general contractor. In the latter case, the construction manager is responsible for coordinating the Work under a series of subcontracts (or multiple prime contracts) and purchase orders for materials and manufactured items.

The Owner's Representative

The owner, particularly the corporate owner, may wish to employ an Owner's Representative in lieu of a Construction Manager. The role of an owner's representative is to be available on a full-time basis to represent the owner's interests in the Work. In addition, this representative would see that the owner's duties and responsibilities, special work and separate contracts, and other related duties and privileges are carried out, properly coordinated and completed according to the provisions of the various contracts and agreements. The owner's representative may be one of the following:

- An Architect or Engineer.
- An additional service of the prime design professional.
- If not a licensed professional, someone with training and experience in building construction and administration.
- An individual with an eye for detail and keen powers of observation.
- Someone with a distinct and proven ability to draw up and maintain records, conduct and chair meetings, and the capacity of understanding the content, meaning, and application of the various Contract Documents.

Representatives of the Design Professional

A design professional's representative, or Construction Administrator, may be employed to assist in the many responsibilities of the design professional during the construction process. Such an individual, sufficiently experienced and qualified, can be a valuable source of information and criticism regarding the continuing quality standards of the design professional's practice. This representative can also act as an observer and reporter on the construction process of particular projects. A qualified project representative should:

- Have experience in building construction as contractor or contractor's superintendent.

- Be familiar with all aspects, materials, and methods of the particular types of construction he is asked to observe.
- Be intimately familiar with the Contract Documents of the project, particularly the drawings and specifications.
- Have a keen eye for detail and know the proper sequence of construction, as well as the provisions of and schedule for inspections of various portions of the Work before they are covered.
- Finally, his integrity, background and general character should be above reproach.

The Construction Superintendent

The Construction Superintendent plays a key role in the ultimate success and quality of the construction project. This is true regardless of the capability, integrity, and experience of other representatives of the owner and design professional. The construction superintendent is the coordinator of the constructor's responsibilities. He implements the construction schedule, marshals the power and effort of workers on the job, receives materials, and arranges for the storage, inventory and protection of the construction materials. He coordinates the work of subcontractors and sub-subcontractors and communicates with the design professional and his staff, as well as the construction manager and owner's representatives. A construction superintendent should:

- Be thoroughly experienced in building construction and possess strong leadership ability in the field.
- Have a good rapport with the various elements of the construction industry.
- Be able to direct, and communicate effectively with worker and professional alike, and display a strong sense of responsibility and trust.
- Be able to maintain positive control during times of crisis, criticism, dispute, and emergency.
- Be familiar with all aspects of applicable building codes, government regulations, industry standards, safety requirements, and procedures.
- Be thoroughly knowledgeable of required and applicable labor rates and requirements, equal opportunity requirements and procedures, rules and regulations concerning hiring practices, and other labor-related legislation and procedures.
- Have a thorough understanding of the requirements and intent of the Contract Documents.
- Be able to plan ahead and anticipate the needs of the project several weeks or months beyond the work in progress. Planning ahead is necessary to coordinate the activities of many different workers, tradesmen, subcontractors, suppliers and others involved in executing the Work.

Constructor's Project Manager

Many constructors responsible for a number of concurrent projects may employ executive assistants with the title of Project Manager. The project manager performs a variety of middle management functions in the construction process, serving as a liaison between field and office. The project manager may supervise the ordering of material and equipment as well as the subcontracting record keeping, correspondence, and handling of submittals and other communications.

Subcontractors

In today's highly specialized world, a great percentage of buildings may be constructed by subcontractors selected, contracted, and supervised by the constructor. Although this practice is convenient for the constructor, reducing his continuing overhead cost of personnel and inventory, subcontracting can also pose some difficulties. Among the challenges are: getting some subcontractors to return to the job site for completion of minor items or repair of damage, and the problems of coordinating many trade activities in a complicated sequence of work.

The general contractor is responsible for the entire project. Portions of the Contract Sum may be retained by the owner until the project is completed, including "punch list" items discovered by the owner's representative and/or the design professional.

For example, with a building project valued at $1,000,000, a retainage of 5% would amount to $50,000. In a project of this size, the painting subcontract could amount to $50,000. If the constructor followed suit with his subcontractors and retained 5% of the Contract Sum against final completion, the amount retained from the painting subcontract would be only $2,500.00. A busy painter, working in an active job market may find it costly to return to a project for touch-up work at the constructor's convenience when such a small sum is outstanding. He may instead choose to return at his own convenience, making it difficult for the constructor to finish the building on time. If substantial portions (approaching 100%) of the Work are accomplished by subcontractors, and the retainage is 5% or less, it may be difficult, if not impossible, to complete the Work on a timely basis. For this reason, many owners and design professionals choose to qualify bidders on the basis that 20% or more of the Work be accomplished using the constructors' own forces.

It is difficult for the constructor, subject to the competitive bidding process, to readily identify the subcontractors he intends to employ at the time the bids are due. Competition is keen for subcontractor awards, and confidentiality is not always strictly observed among competing subcontractors. A practice known as "shopping" often takes place. In this practice, a constructor may reveal the sub-bid proposal of one subcontractor to another in an effort to force the price of that work down, and thus increasing his own potential profit. This practice has become so widespread that many astute subcontractors will wait until the last minutes before the candidate constructor seals the bid to the owner to reveal his price for the subcontract work. Most general requirements (Division 1 of the specifications) require the constructor to provide a list of proposed subcontractors within 10 days or so of the bid opening for the owner's and/or design professional's approval before executing the Contract for Construction. This practice is in the owner's best interest and tends to help prevent subcontractors with a questionable reputation or inferior credit rating from becoming involved in the project.

Producers, Manufacturers, and Materials

The specifications are frequently written in such a way as to give the constructor the widest possible latitude in achieving competition in the price of materials, assemblies, equipment, and other components of the building. In the case of public contracts, nonproprietary specifying is often a requirement. It is common practice to require the apparent lowbidder, prior to award of contract, to draw up a listing by the Construction Specifications Institute (CSI) number of the materials and manufacturers he intends to use for the building construction. This listing is submitted to the design professional for approval.

Project Meetings

Project meetings can be time-consuming, expensive, and inconvenient, but they are also necessary to the enormous task of coordinating the project. Such meetings are essential to the collective interests of the OPC relationship, and are to be preserved and enforced. Properly prepared Division 1 sections will require certain meetings to be attended by all concerned parties from time to time during the project development.

Pre-Bid Conference:
The pre-bid conference allows questions, bidding instructions, and other pertinent information to be discussed among the competitors, their major subcontractors, the owner's representative, and the design professional who has prepared the Contract and bidding documents. Much time can be saved if all attend, as confusion and potential misunderstandings can be cleared up at such meetings.

Pre-Construction Conference:
A pre-construction conference may be held prior to the order to proceed with construction. Such a meeting is often helpful in clearing up any unfulfilled submittal or qualification items as well as to establish construction scheduling, coordination of the Work, and any remaining uncertainty as to the role to be played by the various members of the construction "team."

Progress and Coordination Meetings:
The general contractor should call frequent meetings between his superintendent, project manager, and major subcontractors in order to better schedule start dates and coordination between the work of different trades, much of which will take place at the same time in the same space. The owner and the design professional may find it useful to hold monthly, or even weekly, progress meetings with the constructor and his superintendent. Such a meeting provides an opportunity to discuss monthly pay requests, the current percentage of completion, concerns of the owner and the design professional's representatives, and the overall progress of the Work. This practice can do much to prevent future disputes and legal problems.

Transmittals

The need to transmit information, instructions, drawings, samples, and correspondence between the various elements in the construction process is both significant and frequent. Time is the essence of the Contract and documentation must be kept of the transactions. Figure 12.5 illustrates a Means Letter of Transmittal. This (or a similar) form allows the sender to communicate considerable information about the particular transmittal including: the date, the name of the individual and company to whom it is addressed, the nature and purpose of the transmittal, and the action required as a result. Also included is a description of what is being transmitted and a provision for any remarks or explanations.

Means
LETTER
OF TRANSMITTAL

FROM:
_____
_____
_____
_____

TO:
_____
_____
_____
_____

DATE _____
PROJECT _____
LOCATION _____
ATTENTION _____
RE: _____
_____
_____
_____
_____

Gentlemen:

WE ARE SENDING YOU ☐ HEREWITH ☐ DELIVERED BY HAND ☐ UNDER SEPARATE COVER

VIA _____ THE FOLLOWING ITEMS:

☐ PLANS ☐ PRINTS ☐ SHOP DRAWINGS ☐ SAMPLES ☐ SPECIFICATIONS

☐ ESTIMATES ☐ COPY OF LETTER ☐ _____

COPIES	DATE OR NO.	DESCRIPTION

THESE ARE TRANSMITTED AS INDICATED BELOW

☐ FOR YOUR USE   ☐ APPROVED AS NOTED   ☐ RETURN _____ CORRECTED PRINTS
☐ FOR APPROVAL   ☐ APPROVED FOR CONSTRUCTION   ☐ SUBMIT _____ COPIES FOR_____
☐ AS REQUESTED   ☐ RETURNED FOR CORRECTIONS   ☐ RESUBMIT_____ COPIES FOR_____
☐ FOR REVIEW AND COMMENT ☐ RETURNED AFTER LOAN TO US   ☐ FOR BIDS DUE_____
☐ _____

REMARKS: _____
_____
_____
_____
_____
_____
_____

IF ENCLOSURES ARE NOT AS INDICATED,   SIGNED:_____
PLEASE NOTIFY US AT ONCE.

Figure 12.5 Letter of Transmittal

The transmittal form or letter serves several functions explained as follows:

- It establishes the date and fact of transmittal. Such a record is useful should data be lost, misplaced, or misdirected.
- It establishes when, why, and how a significant piece of information is transmitted.
- It provides a permanent record of the sender's compliance with his responsibilities under the Contract for Construction.

Submittals

Other chapters have addressed the subject of submittals in various contexts. The following is a review of some of the submittals that may be required of the constructor during the construction process:

- Samples of materials and finishes.
- Samples of manufactured assemblies.
- Manufacturer's literature, installation or application instructions, maintenance data and similar information.
- Certification that a material, assembly, or piece of equipment complies with the requirements of the Contract Documents.
- Test results that may be required by the building inspector or by a specification provision.
- Shop drawings indicating the fabrication, assembly, installation, and other physical aspects of a construction component.
- Progress schedules, construction sequence, compliance with time requirements, and other data concerning the completion of the Work.
- Requests for clarification, information, action, approval or any other interaction between the participants in the construction process.

The process of requesting, receiving, and processing submittals during construction serves a number of major purposes. In general, submittals document compliance with the intent and requirements of the Contract Documents. When submittals are required, the constructor must prevail upon his subcontractors, vendors, selected manufacturers, and others to document the materials, assemblies, equipment, and/or systems as needed. The design professional generally writes specifications and creates drawings that are generic in order to allow a wide margin for competition in price and labor. The various submittals, when transmitted according to the requirements of the Contract Documents, allow the design professional the opportunity to confirm or reject the proposed product. If the proposal is rejected, the design professional can communicate his objection, and indicate why the submittal is unsatisfactory. Figure 12.6 shows the form and content of a stamp typically used by design professionals to indicate their actions regarding a particular submittal. The statement made by the approval stamp is, in effect, a disclaimer. The design professional's approval acknowledges general compliance with the intent of the Contract Documents. The design professional does not assume any responsibility for the correctness of dimension, correlation of job site conditions, or construction means and methods. This statement is generally in accord with typical published forms of the General Conditions which set forth the design professional's responsibilities regarding administration of the Contract for Construction.

```
  □  NO EXCEPTION TAKEN        □  EXCEPTIONS NOTED

  □  SUBMIT SPECIFIED ITEM     □  REVISE & RESUBMIT

  Checking is only for general conformance with design concept of
  project and general compliance with Contract Documents.
  Contractor is responsible for confirming and correlating
  dimensions at job site: for information which pertains to
  fabrication processes of construction techniques and for
  coordination of work of all trades. Checking of shop drawings
  shall not relieve Contractor of responsibility for deviation from
  requirements of Contract Documents nor for errors or omissions in
  shop drawings.

  BY: _____         DATE: _____


              WALLER S. POAGE, ARCHITECT
```

Figure 12.6 Submittal Approval Stamp

Samples

Submittals of materials and product samples illustrating color, texture, composition, and other attributes allow the design professional to approve and confirm the material to be used in the construction. If the approved samples are kept at the job site, they can also provide a basis of comparison to confirm that the requirements and intent of the Contract Documents have been met. Many products made by different manufacturers are similar in nature, but competitive in price and availability. The constructor will choose the product he intends to use, but if required, must seek the design professional's approval before the material is ordered or otherwise committed to the project. In most instances the design professional specifies the material or product in such a way that any one of several products can satisfy the design requirement. Approved samples confirm agreement between design professional and constructor on a particular product.

Manufacturers' Literature

Many products used in building construction have been carefully formulated, designed, and manufactured for specific applications and uses. In many instances, the design professional will require that manufacturer's literature regarding specific products be submitted prior to approval. In this way, the manufacturer's responsibility for the use and reliability of the product is reasonably assured. The huge quantity of capital expended by a manufacturer to develop and produce the product, and make it available to the market, means that he has, in all likelihood, tested and explored the limits and capabilities of the product. Chances are the product has been classified among commonly accepted industry standards and comes with general warranties and limited guarantees as to its performance and use in accordance with the manufacturers' instructions and recommendations. The manufacturer is generally the best source of information as to the methods, advantages, disadvantages and limitations of the product's use and what accessory items, tools, fasteners, adhesives and other processes should be employed in its application or installation. By requiring the constructor to use, apply, or install the product in strict accordance with the manufacturer's instructions and recommendations, the design professional provides himself and the owner with an additional layer of protection against the failure of building components. As a result, the manufacturer is added to the list of those responsible for the performance and compatibility of a specified product used in the building's construction. The implications of manufacturers' guarantees and warranties are discussed in some detail in subsequent paragraphs.

Certifications

A *Certificate* is a document that serves as evidence or testimony as to the status, qualification, privilege, or truth of a matter that must be substantiated. Certificates play an important role in establishing evidence that a certain requirement of the Contract is, has, or can be met in a particular way. It is often necessary to require a manufacturer to certify in writing that his material has been used in a project in accordance with his best intent for that product and that the installation or application has been accomplished in accordance with the proper methods and intent of that product. In many instances, certification by a constructor, subcontractor, manufacturer, or vendor is the most satisfactory method whereby the owner can be assured that certain building components meet or exceed his performance expectations.

Test Results

Testing is the most satisfactory method of ensuring the adequacy and performance capability of a preparation, a material, a mixture of materials, an assembly, or fabrication of components. It is also a way to judge the operation of a system or piece of equipment, or the stability of a structural component used in building construction. The types and capabilities of testing and the responsibility for this aspect of the project are discussed in Chapter 9, "Conditions of the Contract" and Chapter 10, "Project Definition."

In the absence of certification, testing is often required by the building official to prove that a certain component meets or exceeds the requirements of the building code. In other cases, the design professional requires testing of certain items to confirm compliance with the Contract Documents as construction proceeds. Such tests, common to most building projects may include the following:

- Testing of the quality, bearing capacity, nature, and composition of soils and subsoils.

- Testing of mixtures such as asphalt, concrete, and mortar for structural and other performance properties once they are mixed, placed, and cured.
- Testing of structural and other components for performance under conditions of stress, strain, compression, and tension.
- Testing of joining methods such as welding, gluing, fastening, and other means of connecting materials and components.
- Testing of various materials for thermal expansion and contraction, hardness, flame spread and support, smoke contribution when subjected to fire, and similar properties.
- Testing of various materials and assemblies for thermal and acoustical properties.
- Testing of various materials, assemblies, and enclosures for resistance to fire and smoke.
- Testing of various materials for compatibility when used in conjunction with other materials.
- Testing of piping assemblies for resistance to pressure and leaks.
- Testing of mechanical and electrical systems.

Shop Drawings

Shop drawings prepared under the direction of the constructor confirm the design and detailing of fabricated components, equipment, assemblies, and systems by illustrating the exact properties, dimensions, materials, finishes, installation methods, and / or other attributes of the construction elements to be provided. As with other types of submittals, shop drawings give the design professional and the constructor the opportunity to communicate and agree upon construction details. The design professional's approval of shop drawings indicates agreement, but (as the design professional's approval stamp in Figure 12.6 indicates) does not waive the constructor's responsibility to meet the requirements of the Contract Documents.

Schedules

The art and technique of scheduling the modern construction project is a science worthy of a separate volume unto itself. For the purposes of this discussion, it is sufficient to touch briefly upon the requirements for construction schedule preparation and submittal in terms of the Contract Documents.

As discussed in the General Conditions of the Contract, time is the "essence" of the Contract. When the Contract for Construction is executed, the constructor has usually agreed to complete the Work in a specific number of calendar days. The construction schedule required by the design professional serves a number of purposes, as follows:

- It confirms the constructor's commitment as to when construction shall be complete.
- It provides a "road map" of how and in what sequence the Work will be achieved.
- It provides a ready reference as to the timeliness of the construction progress at the time of each monthly pay request.
- It shows the impact of changes to the Contract on the time of completion.
- It serves as a planning guide to all participants in the construction process.

Figure 12.7 is a simple bar-graph type construction schedule that plots various kinds of work on a straight line basis over time plotted in terms of months. Figure 12.8 is an example of a more sophisticated construction schedule prepared by use of network scheduling. It identifies the "critical path" of the construction process. This critical path method (CPM) considers the earliest and latest starting dates that various sequences of the Work can be accomplished while keeping in proper sequence with other trades.

In the early 1900s the growth of industry led to the creation of organizations like the National Bureau of Standards, now known as the National Institure of Standards and Technology (NIST) and the American Society for Testing Materials (ASTM). At this time, scientific management pioneers Henry L. Gantt and Fredrick W. Taylor began to work with graphic representations of work versus time. Their technique soon became known as Gantt Charts and are the forerunners of today's bar charts of activity vs. time (as illustrated in Figure 12.7).

The basic problem with construction scheduling by the bar chart method is that the simple bar graph is limited in terms of the information it can present. A major drawback is its inability to present opportunities for saving time and money. Preparation of a bar chart is often influenced by an assumed completion date rather than a predicted and more realistic date based on a network of events. The network, or CPM method (illustrated in Figure 12.8), considers each event from the standpoint of earliest start and completion date. It then relates subsequent events that can take place concurrently, along with the earliest and the latest dates that they can begin. By placing all the events in a graphic network, the best possible completion date for the entire project can be predicted.

The Critical Path Method (CPM) of planning and scheduling began in the mid-1950s when the E.I. Du Pont Company first used a computer to schedule and correlate management of the company's engineering functions for an expanded building program. The resulting computerized scheduling technique became known as the Kelley-Walker Method. This procedure was the forerunner of what we know today as CPM. In the late 1950s, the Special Projects Office of the U. S. Navy Bureau of Ordinance developed a similar program called Program Evaluation Research Task or (PERT) to assist with the development of a missile program. Today variations and combinations of CPM and PERT are used to generate sophisticated construction schedules. Compared to traditional methods, such schedules can help reduce construction time by as much as 40%.

Mock-Ups

Often, the design of a particular building requires the assembly of certain materials and systems whose workmanship, detailing, finish or other physical characteristics are critical to the quality and objectives of the designer's art and intention. This critical attention to detail usually applies to systems and components that require either a mix of basic ingredients, such as concrete or pre-cast concrete, or the assembly of many pieces such as occurs with various kinds of masonry. A mock-up, or sample panel or section of certain critical design components, can be helpful to both designer and constructor and may be constructed for approval by the design professional. This sample may serve as a

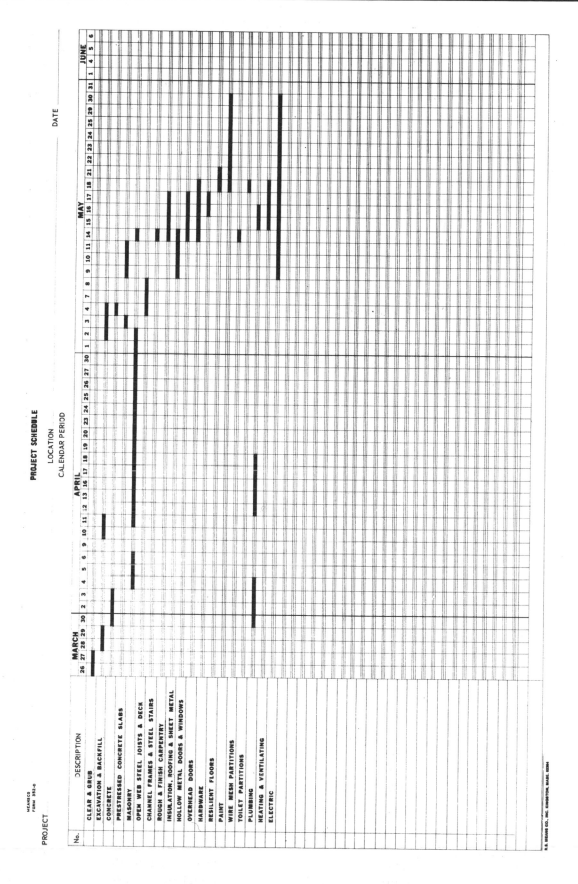

Figure 12.7 *Bar Graph Schedule*

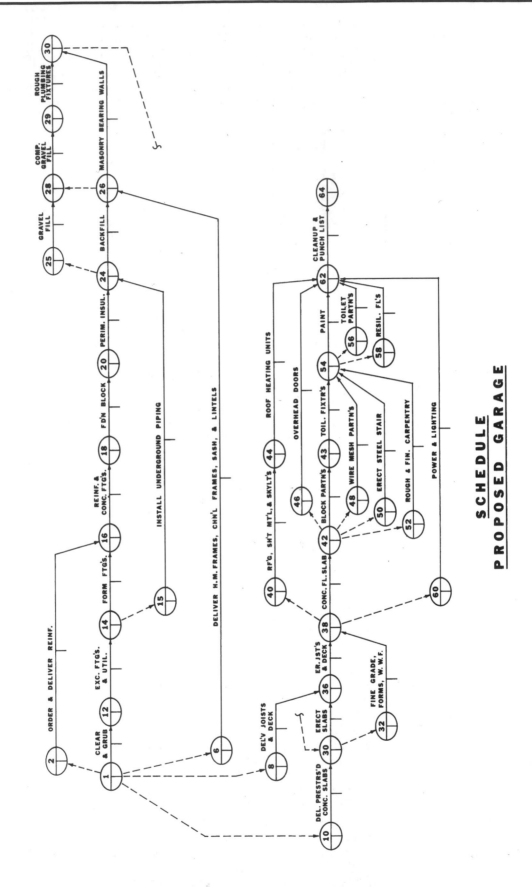

Figure 12.8 *Critical Path Schedule*

standard of quality and consistency for the actual work. Sometimes the mock-up is constructed in such a way that it can later be incorporated into the Work. In other cases, the mock-up is placed at some conspicuous location on the site where it remains for study and comparison until it no longer serves a useful purpose. It is then discarded. Mock-ups may be required of any number of different systems including those listed below:

- Architectural Pre-cast Concrete Panels.
- Masonry.
- Window Wall.
- Plaster Work.
- Ornamental Metal.
- Special Architectural Features.
- Special Finishes.
- Millwork.
- Woodwork.
- Windows.
- Doors.

Requests and Certificates for Payment

The Contract Documents normally make provision for the constructor to be paid on a specific periodic basis. Most contracts provide the owner the right to retain a certain percentage of the amount due. This withheld amount, or "retainage," gives the owner a slight leverage in the matter of final completion and closeout of the contract. Depending upon the nature of the project, whether it is public or private work, and any local law regulating the owner's rights to retain such a percentage, most contracts recognize an adequate retainage to be between 5% and 10%. The contract language concerning retainage may appear as follows:

> On or about the tenth day of each month, the constructor shall be paid an amount equal to 90 percent of the value, based on the Contract prices of labor and materials incorporated in the Work and 50 percent of materials suitably stored at the site up to the first day of that month, as estimated by the Design Professional, less the aggregate of previous payments; and upon substantial completion of the entire work, a sum sufficient to increase the total payments to 95 percent of the Contract price.

Payment for materials delivered and suitably stored at the site (prior to installation) varies depending upon the locality and other factors. In 1980, the high losses from theft prompted many insurance carriers to exclude any material from theft coverage that has not been incorporated into the Work. For this reason, many owners will not pay the constructor for material not yet "in-place." The design professional should determine the owner's policy on this matter and specify (or exclude) provisions for such payments in the Contract Documents. In this way, bidders know what to expect when submitting proposals.

A document sometimes referred to as the Application and Certificate for Payment is used to facilitate the process by which the constructor is compensated. The Application and Certificate for Payment is usually designed so that each application builds upon the information provided in the previous application. The application form is initiated by the constructor, who first prepares a form similar to the Schedule of Values as illustrated in Figure 12.9. The form should list each item established in the Schedule of Values. The first column provides space

Schedule of Values

Contract Component	Original Contract Amount	Contract Changes to Date of Report	Total Contract Amount to Date	Percent Complete	Amount Complete to Date
Division 1—General Requirements					
Contingency Fund					
Insurance					
Bonds					
Division 2—Site Work					
Sub Grading					
U/G Utilities					
Division 3—Concrete					
Foundations					
Concrete Work					
Division 4—Masonry					
Masonry					
Division 5—Metals					
Structural Steel					
Division 6—Wood & Plastics					
Carpentry					
Division 7—Thermal and Moisture Protection					
Insulation					
Waterproofing					
Division 15—Mechanical					
HVAC Systems					
Plumbing					
Division 16—Electrical					
Electrical Rough-In					
Fixtures and Trim					

Totals

Work Complete to Date: _____

Stored Material (See Attached) _____

Sub Total _____

Less Retainage at 10% _____(_____)

Sub Total _____

TOTAL AMOUNT EARNED TO DATE

Date of Report: _____

Figure 12.9 *Schedule of Values*

for a break-down of the total value of each item of work in the original contract. The second column provides space for the total of any changes to the value of any item on the schedule. The third column provides space for the total of the original amount plus any change for a total at the date the schedule is published. The fourth column provides space for the constructor to estimate the percentage of completion for each item in the schedule. The last column provides space for the value of each item that has been completed.

The Application may include a value for material and equipment that has been stored but not yet installed if the Contract for Construction allows payment for those assets. The total retainage through the current application should be calculated. "Total Earned Less Retainage" is determined and recorded as instructed by the Conditions of the Contract. The total of payments made to date is recorded and the amount of the current payment due is then calculated. The balance to finish is also calculated as instructed, and recorded. The "Application for Payment" portion of the Application is completed by the constructor, and the "Certificate For Payment" portion is completed by the design professional. The constructor should sign the application in the presence of a Notary Public. The application is then transmitted to the design professional, who verifies the constructor's numbers based on his own records and observations. The amount verified and approved by the design professional as due and payable to the constructor is recorded and communicated to the owner. The application is then transmitted to the owner and payment is made to the constructor.

The design professional has the responsibility of certifying the constructor's applications for payment. The design professional should be aware that in the event that the constructor is certified for amounts that, in effect, overpay him for the value of the Work, the Design Professional could be liable for losses sustained by surety in case the constructor defaults and surety is called upon to complete the Work.

Substantial Completion

Substantial Completion is usually defined in the Conditions of the Contract for Construction (see Chapter 9, "Conditions of the Contract"). When this stage of the construction is reached, all work should be finished with only minor items, if any, left to be completed.

The "Punch List"

At the point of presumed substantial completion, notice is given by the constructor, together with a list of items that remain to be completed. The design professional will then inspect the Work, make notes of his observations, and prepare an independent list of items to be completed, repaired, or replaced. This list of items is often called the "punch list." The constructor must then correct these deficiencies before receiving final payment. The term "punch list" comes from a 19th-century custom whereby the superintendent used a special paper punch as his "seal," and punched a hole beside each item as it was completed, repaired, or replaced.

Certificate of Substantial Completion

Once the constructor and the design professional agree that Substantial Completion has been reached, a *Certificate of Substantial Completion* is signed by the design professional, the constructor, and the owner. Provisions are made for the owner and constructor to agree on the disposition of security, maintenance, heat, utilities, any damage to the work that may occur after the date of Substantial Completion, and insurance coverage required beyond that date. Normally, the owner takes possession of the property and makes arrangement for the items named above. However, depending upon the nature and extent of the Work that remains to be completed, alternate arrangements may need to be made through the time of final completion. A number of functions must take place at the time of Substantial Completion.

One of these functions is the notification of the surety who has provided the Performance Bond and the Payment Bond for materials and labor. Another function that must be performed at this time is making arrangements that are in keeping with the surety's responsibility to the owner. Communications required by the surety may include the following:

- Contractor's Affidavit of Release of Liens.
- Contractor's Affidavit of Payment of Debts and Claims.

An affidavit is, in the legal sense, an oath sworn before a public official. Using such an affidavit, the constructor testifies that he has paid in full all obligations for materials, equipment, labor, and services performed. The affidavit may also include statements that the constructor has resolved all known indebtedness and claims against him (for which the owner or surety may be held responsible) that are in any way connected with the performance of the Contract for Construction. If the constructor cannot so warrant, arrangements may be made to continue to withhold funds from the retainage; or, the constructor may provide additional bonding in an amount sufficient to cover any outstanding obligations, claims, or both. Supporting documents should include the following:

- Consent of surety to a reduction in and partial release of retainage or final payment.
- Separate releases or waivers of liens from subconstructors and material and equipment suppliers to the satisfaction of the owner.

One of the owner's greatest areas of vulnerability during the construction process is a claim from a third party who has not been paid for the work, materials, or equipment that he has provided for the project. The Construction Contract is an agreement between the owner and the constructor; thus it is the constructor alone who is paid for the work of all those he employs to accomplish the project. While it is the constructor's duty to pay others, there is nothing in the contract to guarantee that such payment will in fact take place. The owner's vulnerability comes from the lien rights provided by law for each mechanic and materialman who does any work on the project. Although the surety has provided a bond as additional protection for the owner, the most satisfactory method of ensuring that no liens shall be filed is to require that waivers of such lien rights be obtained from all concerned prior to release of any retainage or final payment.

Project Closeout

There is an expression, *"Building construction is much like reading a very dull book; it is easy to start but difficult to finish...."* However the process of closing out a project is as critical to the owner's interest as any stage of the project. Procedures that are necessary to ensure compliance with the Contract Documents include the following:

Documentation

As project construction nears completion, the constructor is generally remanded to collect all documentation required by the Contract Documents. The following items may be included:

- Guarantees.
- Warranties.
- Affidavits attesting that all payrolls and bills have been paid (waivers of lien).
- Consent of surety to final payment.
- Certificates of inspection.
- Operating manuals for: mechanical equipment and controls; electrical equipment and controls; other service equipment including parts list, operating instructions, maintenance instructions, and equipment warranties.
- Keys and keying schedule.
- Project record drawings (if required).
- Miscellaneous items required by the Contract Documents.
- Such documentation should be in accordance with the number of copies specified, and should be delivered to the owner upon completion of the Project.

Certifications

When the constructor considers that the Work has reached final completion, he is usually required to submit written certification that the Contract Documents have been reviewed, that the Work has been inspected by local authorities, and that the Work is complete in accordance with the Contract Documents and ready for the design professional's inspection.

Code Compliance

In addition to the submittals that may be required by the Conditions of the Contract, the constructor should provide any information and certifications that may be required by governing authorities.

Final Accounting

The constructor should submit a final statement of accounting stating the total adjusted Contract Sum, total amount of previous payments, and a statement of the sum including retainage that may be remaining due.

Final Change Order

Upon receipt of the required data, the design professional should issue a final change order reflecting any approved adjustments to the Contract Sum not previously made by change order.

Final Cleaning

These operations are generally required prior to Substantial Completion and again prior to Final Inspection. Specifically, final cleaning entails:

- Cleaning of interior and exterior surfaces that are exposed to view.
- Removal of stains, foreign substances, and temporary labels.

- Polishing of transparent and glossy surfaces, and vacuuming of carpeted and soft surfaces.
- Cleaning of equipment and fixtures.
- Cleaning or replacement of filters on mechanical equipment.
- Cleaning of roofs, and verification that drainage systems are clean and free of all debris.
- Cleaning of site: sweeping of paved areas, raking and cleaning of other surfaces.
- Removal of waste and surplus materials, rubbish, and construction equipment from the buildings and from the site.

Project Record Documents

The constructor is generally required to store and maintain project record documents separately from those used for construction. Such records should be maintained on a daily basis with the caution that no work be permanently concealed until the required information (such as size of components, dimensions as to location and other "as built" information) has been recorded.

Systems Demonstration and Product Certification

Prior to final inspection, the constructor should demonstrate the operation of each system to the design professional and owner and (as required) instruct the owner and his personnel in the adjustment and maintenance of each piece of equipment and other systems. The operation and maintenance data are used as the basis of instruction. The constructor may be required to provide these additional certifications:

- That an authorized representative of each manufacturer of certain materials and/or equipment installed in the Work has personally inspected the installation and operation of his material systems and/or equipment and determined that they are correctly installed and operating properly.
- That inspections and testing have been accomplished for work which is not concealed and for work which is concealed during the course of construction. Inspections should be made both prior to concealment and after completion of the installation.

Warranties and Bonds

The constructor is usually required to provide duplicate, notarized copies of all warranties and bonds including those furnished by subcontractors, suppliers, and manufacturers.

Spare Parts and Maintenance Materials

It is not unusual for the constructor to be required to provide spare parts and maintenance materials for specific items which are usually specified in an individual section of the specifications.

Certificate of Occupancy

The *Certificate of Occupancy* is issued by the building official. It is not only a means of certifying that the finished project meets or exceeds all code requirements, but it is usually a mandatory requirement before the utilities of water, natural gas, and electricity can be delivered on a permanent basis to the owner. The Certificate of Occupancy ensures code compliance from the constructor and major subcontractors.

Chapter Thirteen

Project Record-Keeping and Close-Out

This final chapter is devoted to the importance of record keeping throughout the construction process. It has been shown that there are easily thousands of decisions that must be made and documented in the collective effort required to erect a modern building. The contract conditions and the general requirements, particularly those published by AIA and EJCDC, describe and require appropriate methods for recording the developments and transactions during the construction process. A number of problems that sometimes occur in and between the parties to the OPC relationship can be avoided by proper and consistent documentation leading to final *Project Close-out*.

The Record-Keeping Process

Timely, informative, communicative, and accurate record keeping is not only desirable, but essential to the success of today's construction project. Proper record keeping is also a key ingredient in the fortunes and success of all concerned participants, including the owner, the design professional, the contractor, and the many others who become indirectly involved in the construction process. The advantages of record keeping are many. Among the most obvious benefits are the following:

- Record keeping is the most convenient method of substantiating the fulfillment of an obligation and process of payment for that item or service. Record keeping also documents compliance with the requirements of the Contract Documents. Each party to the construction process is linked to the combined effort by a contract or similar instrument which stipulates a promise and requires some form of consideration. Thus, there is a legal obligation on the part of both parties. Precise and complete records made and kept by all parties to the construction effort will, by no means, eliminate the possibility of dispute and litigation. However, it is safe to say that without such records, frustrating and expensive disputes are far more likely.
- Documenting all modifications, submittals, approvals, agreements, and other transactions expedites the coordination and collective work of all parties to the construction process.
- Written communication between parties to the Contract for Construction is the most effective method of efficiently managing the construction process. Compliance with contract document requirements is recorded in these types of records.

- Records of the exact location of items concealed by construction is extremely important. Such records are used by the owner during the life of the project for maintenance and safety purposes. This kind of documentation often proves invaluable should additions and alterations be made to the project in the future.

The American Institute of Architects, the Engineers Joint Contract Documents Committee, the Associated General Contractors, the Construction Specifications Institute, and many private vendors, including the R. S. Means Company and others publish many forms of prepared documents which can be used throughout design and construction. These forms and related documents can prove valuable as time-saving instruments to all building professionals. Several such forms are described and mentioned in this book.

Pre-Construction Submittals

The Contract Documents often, and should, require the contractor to submit a significant amount of written information prior to the commencement of the construction process. Pre-construction submittals generally consist of documents describing how and by whom the construction process is to be conducted. Chapter 9, "Conditions of the Contract," and Chapter 10, "Project Definition," discuss project documentation in more detail.

Bonds

The bonding or surety company (for projects where bonding is required) has a responsibility to the owner that may transcend the period of construction. Under most construction contracts, the contractor's general warranty applies to a minimum one-year period. Individual warranties for some specific building components may cover longer periods. If a guarantee or warranty needs to be enforced, or if the contractor is unable or unwilling to fulfill such obligations, the bonding company could be called upon to enforce it.

Performance Bond

The Performance Bond provides a guarantee from a surety that the Contract for Construction will be fulfilled in the event of failure or default by the contractor. The performance responsibility includes any guarantees and warranties that may be required of the contractor by the Contract Documents. Should the building or any portion of it experience a failure resulting from faulty workmanship by the contractor, the bonding company's responsibility may extend through the term of the statutes of limitations (transcending the period of construction as well as the general warranty period) subject to any time limitations contained in the bond itself. For this reason, the bond becomes a valuable permanent record to be retained by the owner, the design professional, and the contractor.

Labor and Materials Payment Bond

Previous chapters have noted how important it is that the owner obtain releases of lien from the contractor, various subcontractors, material suppliers, and others who may have a claim for payment before the project is closed out and the final payment made. Despite diligent effort made to obtain waivers of lien from all potential claimants, it is always possible that liens may be filed after the contract close-out.

Many jurisdictions have established statutes of limitation that allow an alleged creditor to make a claim after total payment has been made and the contract closed out. Some unforeseen claims may come from tax authorities not satisfied by the amounts paid by the contractor or those he employs. For example, under federal law, the Internal Revenue Service requires any employer to be responsible for withholding and paying certain payroll taxes. If the contractor or any subcontractor fails to pay such taxes, a federal tax lien can be filed against the owner's property. As is often the case, unsatisfied tax liability may not appear until some time after the Work has been completed. If the responsible party does not satisfy the claim by the taxing authority, the bonding company has an obligation to protect the owner. A *Labor and Material Payment Bond* is used for this purpose.

Certificate of Insurance

The AIA and others publish forms for the purpose of establishing the basis and obligation for Labor and Material bond which is usually provided by the company who has provided the Bid and Performance Bonds for the constructor. (See Chapter 4, "The Constructor" Bonding and Insurance).

Under the insurance requirements stated in most forms of General Conditions of the Contract (and in any supplemental conditions, See Chapter 9, "Conditions of the Contract," the contractor's insurance carrier must submit certification that adequate insurance has been provided and is in force at the time construction begins. Some insurance coverage, such as the "completed operations" coverage under the contractor's commercial general liability policy may transcend the period of construction for several potential loss categories. For example, if a worker develops an illness or incapacity that can be proven to be related to work on a project, such a claim can be made after completion of the project (within the limits of any jurisdictional statute of limitation that may apply). In other cases, damage to persons or property proven to result from a failure during construction may be covered by the contractor's liability insurance (in force during the construction process).

List of Subcontractors

An owner or design professional may reasonably require that a contractor provide a list of proposed subcontractors for a project. This approach gives the owner or design professional the chance to make any reasonable objection to any subcontractor named. As a permanent record, the list of subcontractors in an owner's database is a valuable directory for the owner's use in maintaining, repairing, replacing, or altering building components throughout the life of the project.

The owner's concern with approving subcontractors is not without foundation. Major subcontracts for mechanical and electrical work alone may involve as much as 30% to 40% of the total Contract Sum. Any failure of one of these subcontractors could jeopardize the contractor's ability to complete the project. It is becoming a common practice to stipulate in the Contract Documents that major subcontractors be bonded. Major subcontractors may also be required to carry specified limits on liability insurance.

Schedule of Values

The schedule of values is a breakdown of the Contract Sum by category of work. Figure 13.1.a illustrates a sample schedule of values with work categories listed according to the CSI Masterformat. Figure 13.1.b illustrates a sample schedule of values with work categories listed according to Uniformat. Chapter 11, "The Project Manual" discusses Masterformat and Uniformat.

The Schedule of Values is discussed more thoroughly in Chapter 12, "Contract Administration."

The schedule of values becomes the basis by which periodic payments are made to the contractor. As work in the various categories is completed, the contractor and design professional may certify the percentage of completion and the amount of material received by the contractor. At the time of each periodic payment, an accounting is made of the amount of work accomplished since the last application for payment was made. The current level of completion is computed monthly and an assessment is made of previous payments and retainage in order to compute the amount due the contractor. The Continuation and up-date of this schedule can be used to record the schedule of values and a summary of work completed at the time of each periodic payment. An *Application and Certification for Payment* is used to compile the data from the schedule of values, and to determine the current payment due, which is certified by the design professional or construction manager.

Construction Schedule

The construction schedule sets forth the contractor's estimate of completion for the project. One of the functions of this document should be to indicate the approximate degree of completion that the owner can expect at each period of application and certification of payment. Chapter 12, "Contract Administration" discusses scheduling the process of construction.

Construction Submittals

Most submittal documents are meant to provide verification or certification of requirements of the construction specifications. Submittals often required of the contractor include material samples, manufacturers' literature and certification, test results, shop drawings, and schedules of progress. Chapter 12, "Contract Administration" discusses these types of requirements in more detail. Such documentation serves a two-fold purpose. First, submittals provide data which assists the design professional in approving materials, payments, and other components of the project. Second, as permanent project records, submittals may provide valuable information project (on maintenance, replacement, future additions, and alterations) for the owner's use during the life of the project.

While project data is a high priority among project records, the job file maintained by the design professional is no less important. The job file is the repository of all written communication between the parties to the Contract for Construction. The job file should organize and contain all correspondence between the parties including transmittal records, legal notices, memos, written instructions, and the minutes of project meetings. While it may not be considered part of the Contract Documents, the job file, when properly administered and organized,

Contract Component	Original Contract Amount	Contract Changes to Date of Report	Total Contract Amount to Date	Percent Complete	Amount Complete to Date
Division 1—General Requirements					
Contingency Fund					
Insurance					
Bonds					
Division 2—Site Work					
Sub Grading					
U/G Utilities					
Division 3—Concrete					
Foundations					
Concrete Work					
Division 4—Masonry					
Masonry					
Division 5—Metals					
Structural Steel					
Division 6—Wood & Plastics					
Carpentry					
Division 7—Thermal and Moisture Protection					
Insulation					
Waterproofing					
Division 15—Mechanical					
HVAC Systems					
Plumbing					
Division 16—Electrical					
Electrical Rough-In					
Fixtures and Trim					

Totals

Work Complete to Date: _____

Stored Material (See Attached) _____

Sub Total _____

Less Retainage at 10% _____(_____)

Sub Total _____

TOTAL AMOUNT EARNED TO DATE

Date of Report: _____

Figure 13.1.a Schedule of Values (Based on Masterformat)

Contract Component	Original Contract Amount	Contract Changes to Date of Report	Total Contract Amount to Date	Percent Complete	Amount Complete to Date
01—Foundations					
011 Foundation Systems					
02—Substructure					
021 Slab on Grade					
022 Basement Excavation					
023 Basement Walls					
03—Superstructure					
031 Floor Construction					
032 Roof Construction					
033 Stair Construction					
04—Exterior Closure					
041 Exterior Walls					
042 Exterior Doors and Windows					
05—Roofing					
051 Roofing and Sheet Metal					
06—Interior Construction					
061 Partitions					
062 Interior Finishes					
063 Specialties					
07—Conveying Systems					
071 Elevators					
08—Mechanical Systems					
081 Plumbing					
082 HVAC					
083 Fire Protection					
084 Special Mechanical Systems					
085 Mech Service and Distribution					
09—Electrical					
091 Elect Service and Distribution					
092 Lighting and Power					
093 Special Electrical Systems					
10—General Conditions					
101 Contractor's OH&P					
11—Equipment					
111 Fixed and Movable Equipment					
112 Furnishings					
113 Special Construction					
12—Sitework					
121 Site Preparation					
122 Site Improvements					
123 Site Utilities					
123 Off Site Construction					

Totals

Work Complete to Date: _____

Stored Material (See Attached) _____

Sub Total _____

Less Retainage at 10%   _____(_____)

Sub Total _____

TOTAL AMOUNT EARNED TO DATE

Date of Report: _____

Figure 13.1.b Schedule of Values (Based on Uniformat)

may serve as a "diary" of the construction process. The data in the job file provides a wealth of information, such as recall of agreements, instructions, and transactions that take place during the course of the project.

Correspondence

Correspondence is any form of written communication that occurs between any two or more of the parties to the Contract for Construction. Correspondence usually comes in the form of letters, memos, email transmissions, or any other written communication, and should be kept in the job file.

Transmittal Records

Transmittals are used to direct a piece of information to its intended party or parties in the approval or notification process. The job construction file is the proper repository for transmittal forms once they have served their purpose. The Contract Documents often specify time requirements for submittals (i.e., shop drawings and manufacturers' literature). The organized handling and filing of transmittals by both the contractor and the design professional can settle arguments and disputes that result from delays that may or may not have been caused by the approval process. A well documented job file containing complete records with dates indicating when information was transmitted, how, or by what means it was transmitted, and the date it was received and processed, can serve as evidence in such disputes.

Notices

The Contract Documents often require formal written correspondence (in the form of legal notices) from the parties to the Contract for Construction. Legal notices establish evidence of communication related to several critical provisions of the Contract for Construction. For example, the Notice to Proceed, usually issued by the design professional, establishes the official date when construction begins. The Notice to Proceed can therefore be fundamental in establishing the date of Substantial Completion. Other legal notices may be required if either party to the Contract needs to inform the other of any requirement not fulfilled according to the agreement. Such notices should become part of the job file and, if necessary, serve as evidence of the procedures necessary to establish compliance with the legal duties of the parties to the Contract for Construction.

Supplemental Instructions

From time to time, the design professional or the construction manager must issue supplemental instructions to the contractor regarding some aspect of the construction process. These supplemental instructions often have implications that may affect or become part of the Contract Documents. These instructions must, therefore, be carefully handled within the procedures set forth in the family of Contract Documents. It is not good policy to rely upon verbal agreements in the construction process. All related communication should rather be put in writing. A complete and written record establishes and documents the facts as they occur. Such records become invaluable in the case of any costly disputes that may occur much later when the memory of those concerned has dimmed. Among the communications that should be documented during construction are the following:

Instructions of the Design Professional

The American Institute of Architects (AIA) publishes a form titled *Architect's Supplemental Instructions* that is designed to record and transmit supplemental instructions given during the construction process. The design professional should either select or design an appropriate form of this kind to facilitate frequent instructions related to the intent of the Contract Documents in response to Requests for Information (RFI) from the Contractor during the construction process.

Field Reports

The design professional should endeavor to document compliance with the duty of periodic job site observation. The AIA publishes a form for this purpose called *Architect's Field Report* that is designed to document the design professional's compliance with contractural duties during construction.

Change Orders

The *Construction Change Order* or "Authorization," is intended to document any agreement made during the construction process that facilitates a change and causes a change in the Contract Sum. As a matter of procedure, this document is normally used in order to avoid delay in the project while an official Change Order is being processed. Figure 13.2 illustrates a Means Contract Change Order, a document for creating modifications to the Contract for Construction.

Minutes of Meetings

Written notes taken during meetings between the parties to the Contract for Construction serve a number of useful, even essential purposes—and are important project records. Copies of these notes, or minutes, should be kept in the job files of the owner, design professional, and contractor. Like other documentation, such records minimize the potential for misunderstandings, disputes, delays, and litigation that may occur after construction. When any participant, during the course of a project meeting, is asked to complete an assignment, the meeting minutes may reflect an *action list*. An action list or schedule acts as a memorandum on how duties and responsibilities of participants will be divided. The action list also assists in documenting who will be held accountable for which tasks.

Accounting Records

The Contract for Construction most often requires that accounting records be maintained and available for review if necessary, for legal or tax purposes. In public projects, the law may demand that the contractor (and subcontractors) pay workers according to established minimum wage requirements. Chapter 5, "Labor and Government," discusses the influence of both government and organized labor on wages in the construction industry. Payroll and other accounting records may have to be reviewed by authorities to establish compliance with the law. The contractor's insurance carrier may require an audit of payroll records to establish premiums for Workers' Compensation Insurance. The contractor's financial records of overhead, labor, and material costs may also become part of the Contract for Construction where the contractor's compensation is based on cost plus a fee.

Means
CONTRACT
CHANGE ORDER

FROM: _____

_____

_____

_____

TO: _____

_____

_____

_____

CHANGE ORDER NO. _____		
DATE _____		
PROJECT _____		
LOCATION _____		
JOB NO. _____		
ORIGINAL CONTRACT AMOUNT	$	
TOTAL PREVIOUS CONTRACT CHANGES		
TOTAL BEFORE THIS CHANGE ORDER		
AMOUNT OF THIS CHANGE ORDER		
REVISED CONTRACT TO DATE		

Gentlemen:

This CHANGE ORDER includes all Material, Labor and Equipment necessary to complete the following work and to adjust the total contract as indicated;

☐ the work below to be paid for at actual cost of Labor, Materials and Equipment plus_____percent (_____%)

☐ the work below to be completed for the sum of_____

_____ dollars ($_____)

_____

_____

_____

_____

_____

_____

_____

_____

_____

_____

_____

_____

_____

_____

_____

_____

_____

_____

_____

_____

_____

_____

_____

CHANGES APPROVED

The work covered by this order shall be performed under the same Terms and Conditions as that included in the original contract unless stated otherwise above.

By_____

By_____

Signed_____

Dy_____

Figure 13.2 Form of Change Order

Subcontracts

The subcontractor's financial records are as much a part of the project requirement as the contractor's. The subcontractor must conform to any minimum wage scale or Workers' Compensation Insurance requirements. Records of payment to subcontractors (by the contractor) become part of the procedure of waiver of lien, compliance with the law, and good business policy.

Construction Records

The contractor, in order to fulfill his contract obligation to the owner, is responsible (either directly or indirectly) for the employment of all labor and the purchase of all materials and products to be incorporated into the project. He has an obligation to see that all participants are paid according to the various contracts and laws regarding the construction process. At the time of periodic payment, and particularly the time of final payment, the contractor may be required to show documented proof of compliance with the compensation requirements regarding labor, purchase of materials, and payment of federal, state, and local taxes. Furthermore, the contractor may be required to prove that he has met all other contract document requirements including building codes, zoning restrictions, and other statutory requirements having jurisdiction over the project. Proper record keeping during the construction process is key to the contractor's ability to substantiate such compliance.

Time Sheets

Figure 13.3 illustrates a Means Daily Time Sheet form. The contractor and the subcontractor can use this type of form to establish a record of labor performed during construction. The cost of labor in a typical construction project can be 50% or more of the total cost; thus, management of labor on a daily basis is fundamental to preserving the contractor's profit margin. Carefully maintained labor records enter the process of cost accounting and are fundamental to the contractor's ability to manage the project, while complying with the law, union, and insurance requirements.

Material Cost Records

Records of the purchase of materials, assemblies, and equipment are also important to cost accounting. Prices of items purchased for construction vary considerably. A Purchase Order Page is a form that can be used by a purchaser (such as a contractor) of project materials. This form, when accepted by both purchaser and vendor (seller), is a type of contract that records who ordered the items and from what source. It also records when the transaction was made, the price that was agreed upon, and the terms by which payment shall be made. Additional information might include any discounts offered for early payment and the anticipated date and method of delivery.

Once the transaction is complete, the vendor presents an invoice to the contractor for payment. This invoice can be compared to the purchase order to confirm that the transaction has been completed within the agreed upon terms.

Daily Construction Report

Figure 13.4 is an example of a Means Daily Construction Report form, designed to provide daily records of all activities at the job site. These

Means Forms
DAILY
TIME SHEET

PROJECT _____

FOREMAN _____

WEATHER CONDITIONS _____

TEMPERATURE _____

DATE _____

SHEET NO. _____

NO.	NAME	DESCRIPTION OF WORK								TOTAL HOURS REG-ULAR	TOTAL HOURS OVER-TIME	RATES REG-ULAR	RATES OVER-TIME	OUTPUT	
		HOURS													
		UNITS													
		HOURS													
		UNITS													
		HOURS													
		UNITS													
		HOURS													
		UNITS													
		HOURS													
		UNITS													
		HOURS													
		UNITS													
		HOURS													
		UNITS													
		HOURS													
		UNITS													
		HOURS													
		UNITS													
		HOURS													
		UNITS													
		HOURS													
		UNITS													
		HOURS													
		UNITS													
		HOURS													
		UNITS													
		HOURS													
		UNITS													
	TOTALS	HOURS													
	EQUIPMENT	UNITS													

Figure 13.3 *Daily Time Sheet (Means Form)*

daily records, when accurate and up-to-date, can provide a valuable foundation to support the other documents and records that the contractor must keep.

The Daily Construction Report can have an important influence on the contractor's financial records, the construction schedule, and applications for payment. This form is also reviewed during any audit that may be requested to determine compliance with contract obligations and other legal requirements.

Job Progress Report

Figure 13.5 is a Means Job Progress Report form, designed to provide a periodic computation of work completed by certain key dates during the construction process. As a continuing record, developed and updated periodically, the Job Progress Report can be the basis of periodic application for payment as well as the contractor's accounting system.

Project Inspection Reports

While making periodic job site inspections, the design professional may make and record observations. There are a number of published Project Inspection Report forms that are useful for this purpose. Such forms are used for recording of information by the design professional during his or her duty of construction progress observation. The Project Inspection form prepared by the design professional roughly corresponds to the job progress reports that are used to record the contractor's observations. Well documented observations of the construction progress by the design professional are valuable as a basis in approving the contractor's monthly pay requests. Project Inspection Reports are also valuable in mediating any claims or disputes that may arise before project close out. The importance of thorough and consistent written documentation of the design professional's observations during construction cannot be emphasized too strongly.

Progress Photographs

Progress photographs are supplemental to other, written records of the progress of construction. While photographs may not always be required by the construction documents, they perform a valuable function in the documentation of a project. A photograph can rectify a dispute about what may have occurred after the fact. Progress photos taken on a regular basis may prove to be a minor overhead cost when compared to the major cost of delay or litigation that may result from a dispute that cannot be settled without photographic evidence.

Project Record Documents

A modern building project is a complicated organism composed of many interrelated systems that may be usefully compared to the functions and components of the human body. The supporting structure or "skeleton" may be thought of as the "bones" of the building, the enclosing envelope as the "skin," the plumbing, mechanical and electrical components as the "veins and arteries." The drawings prepared by the design professional illustrate the work to be done. Many of the components are often represented schematically for convenience. As the construction proceeds, the final design and location of many vital building components is decided and executed. The Contract Documents, prepared by the design professional are reliable illustrations of the completed project. They do not, however, provide

338

Means Forms

DAILY
CONSTRUCTION REPORT

JOB NO.

DATE

PROJECT

SUBMITTED BY

ARCHITECT

WEATHER

TEMPERATURE   AM   PM

CODE NO.	WORK CLASSIFICATION	FOREMEN	MECHANICS	LABORERS	SUB-CONTR'S	TOTAL HOURS	DESCRIPTION OF WORK
	General Conditions						
	Site Work: Demolition						
	Excavation & Dewatering						
	Caissons & Piling						
	Drainage & Utilities						
	Roads, Walks & Landscaping						
	Concrete: Formwork						
	Reinforcing						
	Placing						
	Precast						
	Masonry: Brickwork & Stonework						
	Block & Tile						
	Metals: Structural						
	Decks						
	Miscellaneous & Ornamental						
	Carpentry: Rough						
	Finish						
	Moisture Protection: Waterproofing						
	Insulation						
	Roofing & Siding						
	Doors & Windows						
	Glass & Glazing						
	Finishes: Lath, Plaster & Stucco						
	Drywall						
	Tile & Terrazzo						
	Acoustical Ceilings						
	Floor Covering						
	Painting & Wallcovering						
	Specialities						
	Equipment						
	Furnishings						
	Special Construction						
	Conveying Systems						
	Mechanical: Plumbing						
	HVAC						
	Electrical						

Figure 13.4 *Daily Construction Report*

EQUIPMENT ON PROJECT	NUMBER	DESCRIPTION OF OPERATION	TOTAL HOURS

EQUIPMENT RENTAL - ITEM	TIME IN	TIME OUT	SUPPLIER	REMARKS

MATERIAL RECEIVED	QUANTITY	DELIVERY SLIP NO.	SUPPLIER	USE

CHANGE ORDERS, BACKCHARGES AND/OR EXTRA WORK

ORAL DISCUSSIONS AND/OR INSTRUCTIONS

VISITORS TO SITE

JOB REQUIREMENTS

Figure 13.4 Daily Construction Report (continued)

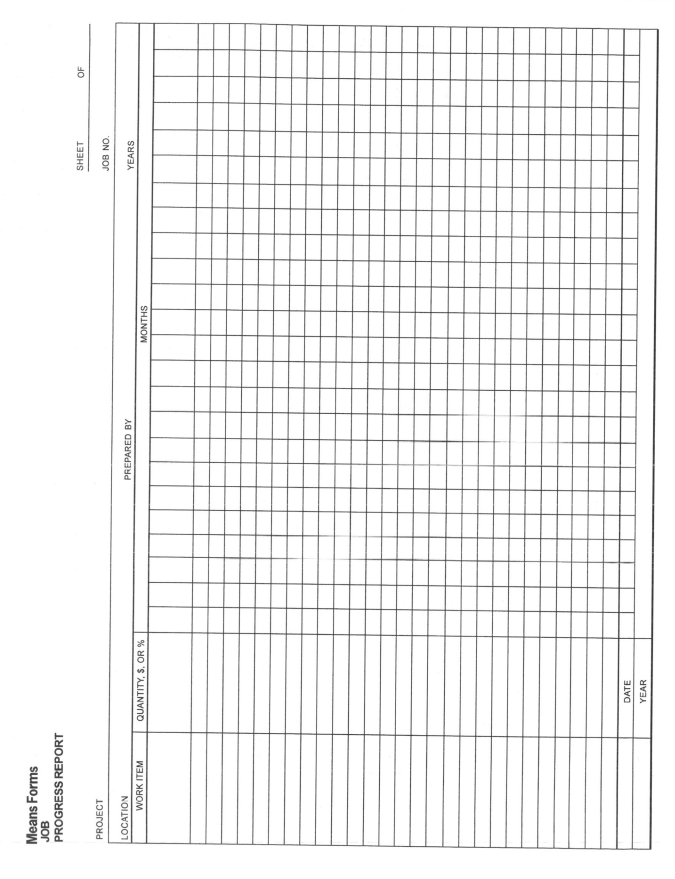

Figure 13.5 Job Progress Report

341

a complete or reliable record of the actual components installed in the project. The Contract Documents which are diagrammic in nature do not offer a reliable "map" to locations of vital elements that are concealed once the project is completed.

Project Record Documents sometimes referred to as "as built drawings" respond to the need for a reliable record of how the project was actually built. The intention of the requirement for the creation of project record documents is to record the size, configuration, and location of materials and methods used. They serve as a permanent record for the owner as he maintains, uses, and perhaps alters the building during its useful "life." Creating and maintaining data during construction in the form of project record documents is often a requirement of the Contract Documents. It need not be a difficult or expensive function, provided the contractor keeps accurate and useful documents and records throughout the building process. Most final design data relating to material, configuration, size, and location of various components will be shown on shop drawings or manufacturers' literature. Other information can be recorded with photographs and sketches made during placement, before subsequent operations conceal such items as mechanical and electrical components. The constant influx of data is recorded on special copies of the contract drawings and specifications that may be provided by the design professional. This process allows for a final compilation and permanent record of "as built" data at the time of completion. The finalized version should be recorded by competent drafters on reproductions of the design professional's documents, and preserved for future reference.

The term *project record documents* is preferred over the more commonly used term "as built documents" for a number of reasons. The term "as built" may be misleading in that it loosely connotes or may infer a degree of accuracy or perfection in the product that may be unreasonable if not impossible for the constructor to attain. For example, the project record site plan is seldom reliable in "pinpointing" the exact location of underground utilities, it should indicate the size and "general" location of such elements. The value of the record document is that it is a reliable record of the final design and is of great value if the owner makes signifiant additions and alterations to the original project. At the time that a change is anticipated, the exact location of underground utilities, for example, will be able to be located by a specialist using equipment designed for that purpose.

Modifications to the Contract

The Contract for Construction makes provision for changes or modifications in the Work. Such modifications can involve additions to the project, changes in material or equipment, or the deletion of some portion of the Work. The design professional may recommend a change that would improve the design or function of the project or correct a condition that becomes apparent once construction has begun. The contractor may also recommend a change to expedite the Work, substitute an item for one that becomes unavailable, improve the Work, or produce a cost savings. The Conditions of the Contract for Construction may describe procedures that can be used to make changes in the Work. To alter the Contract for Construction, the owner, the design professional, and the contractor must draw up a written agreement.

The Request for Proposal

In most cases, an anticipated modification in the Contract for Construction will require a change in the Contract Sum, the number of calendar days required for construction, or both. A Request for Proposal is usually prepared by the owner or by the design professional on behalf of the owner, and allows the contractor to respond formally with a disclosure of the information necessary to accomplish a change. Such information is transmitted to the owner via the design professional, and the anticipated work is either accepted, modified, or rejected.

Construction Change Authorization

The documentation of contract modifications may require considerable time for study, negotiation, agreement, and finally, three-way approval. When delays are inevitable and the owner is willing to accept a change with certain conditions, the design professional may issue a *Construction Change Authorization*. This form allows the contractor to proceed with the change on the basis that the finally negotiated cost and time extension shall not exceed certain limits established in the authorization document.

Change Orders

Figure 13.2 illustrates a Means Contract Change Order which has been previously discussed in this text. The Change Order is used to document the modification to the Contract for Construction. Change orders should be carefully documented, placed in consecutive order, and coordinated with each current application for payment.

Close-Out Documents

All documents and procedures described below are included for demonstration purposes. Actual documents and procedures may vary from project to project depending on contractual obligations, municipal, legal, and/or other requirements.

Figures 13.6 illustrates an example of Specification Section 01700—Project Close-out, typically included in Division 1—General Requirements of the Specifications. This section specifies the normal procedures for closing out the Contract for Construction for typical projects. Figure 13.7 illustrates Section 01720, Project Record Documents. This is a companion section to 01700, also included in Division One (1). This section specifies the procedures and data generally required of the contractor.

Substantial Completion

The General Conditions of the Contract define Substantial Completion as that point in the construction at which the project is complete enough for the owner to take possession of the building. When the contractor believes that Substantial Completion has been achieved, he notifies the design professional, who then makes an inspection for confirmation. If the design professional agrees, the owner and the surety who has issued the performance and payment bonds may be notified by a *Certificate of Substantial Completion*. Subject to any items requiring completion (that may be listed in the design professional's "punch list"), the owner may receive a semifinal Application and Certification for Payment. The owner may then pay the contractor an amount including retainage to bring the sum of all payments to 95% or more of

SECTION 01700
CONTRACT CLOSEOUT

PART 1 - GENERAL

1.01   REQUIREMENTS INCLUDED

   A.   Closeout Procedures.

   B.   Final Cleaning.

   C.   Operation and Maintenance Data.

   D.   Systems Demonstration.

   E.   Guarantees, Warranties and Bonds.

1.03   RELATED REQUIREMENTS

   A.   Conditions of the Contract: Fiscal provisions, legal submittals and other administrative requirements.

   B.   As the construction of the Project nears completion, collect all guarantees, warranties, affidavits that all payrolls and bills have been paid, Consent of Surety to final payment, certificates of inspection, operating manuals, keys and keying schedule, Project Record Drawings and other items required, in the number of copies specified, to be delivered to the Owner upon completion of the Project.

   C.   When Contractor considers Work has reached final completion, submit written certification that Contract Documents have been reviewed, Work has been inspected, and that Work is complete in accordance with Contract Documents and ready for Architect's and Engineer's inspection.

   D.   In addition to submittals required by the conditions of the Contract, provide submittals required by governing authorities, and submit a final statement of accounting giving total adjusted Contract Sum, previous payments, and sum remaining due.

   E.   Architect will issue a final Change Order reflecting approved adjustments to Contract Sum not previously made by Change Order.

1.04   FINAL CLEANING

   A.   Execute prior to Substantial Completion and again prior to Final Inspection.

   B.   Clean interior and exterior surfaces exposed to view; remove temporary labels, stains and foreign substances, polish transparent and glossy surfaces, vacuum carpeted and soft surfaces. Clean equipment and fixtures to a sanitary condition, clean or replace filters of mechanical equipment. Clean roofs, and verify that drainage systems are clean and free of all debris of any kind.

   C.   Clean site; sweep paved areas, rake clean other surfaces.

   D.   Remove waste and surplus materials, rubbish, and construction facilities from the Project and from the site.

1.05   PROJECT RECORD DOCUMENTS

   A.   Store Project Record Documents separate from those used for construction and in accordance with Section 01720.

   B.   Keep documents current; do not permanently conceal any work until required information has been recorded.

   C.   At Contract closeout, submit documents with transmittal letter containing date, Project title, Contractor's name and address, list of documents, and signature of Contractor.

Figure 13.6 Project Close-out Requirements

1.06 OPERATION AND MAINTENANCE DATA

   A. General Contractor shall provide data for:

      1. Specialties - Division 10.

      2. Equipment - Division 11.

      3. Furnishings - Division 12.

      4. Mechanical equipment and controls - Division 15.

      5. Electrical equipment and controls - Division 16.

   B. Submit minimum of 3 sets of required information prior to final inspection, bound in 8-1/2 x 11 inch three-ring side binders with durable plastic covers. If a system is accepted prior to final acceptance of Contract, submit 1 set at time of system acceptance and the other 2 sets prior to final acceptance.

   C. Provide a separate volume for each system, with a table of contents and index tabs for each volume.

   D. Part 1: Directory, listing names, addresses, and telephone numbers of: Architect, Architect's Consultants, Contractor, Subcontractors, Manufacturers, Material Suppliers and any other entity related to the work.

   F. Part 2: Operation and maintenance instructions, arranged by system. For each system, list:

      1. Identify parties listed in Part 1 who are associated with the subject system.

      2. Appropriate design criteria.

      3. List of equipment.

      4. Parts list.

      5. Operating instructions.

      6. Maintenance instructions, equipment.

      7. Maintenance Instructions, finishes.

      8. Shop Drawings and product data.

      9. Warranties and Guarantees.

1.07 SYSTEMS DEMONSTRATION AND PRODUCT CERTIFICATION

   A. Prior to final inspection, demonstrate operation of each system to Architect and Owner.

   B. Instruct Owner's personnel in operation, adjustment, and maintenance of equipment and systems, using the operation and maintenance data as the basis of instruction.

   C. Prior to Final Acceptance of the Work, for items so designated in individual specification Sections, an authorized representative of each manufacturer of materials and/or equipment installed in the Work shall personally inspect the installation and operation of his materials systems, and/or equipment to determine that they are correctly installed and operating properly.

      1. Inspection and testing shall be accomplished:

         a. For work which will be concealed: during the course of the Work, after completion of installation and prior to concealment.

         b. For work which will not be concealed: at completion of the Work.

      2. Each representative shall submit a signed statement to the Architect, through the General Contractor, certifying to his personal inspection and to the correct installation and proper operation of materials, systems and/or equipment. Their certification shall list the items included.

      3. The General Contractor shall transmit all such certifications to the Architect at or prior to the Final Acceptance Inspection. The transmittal shall include a list of all certifications included.

Figure 13.6 Project Close-out Requirements (continued)

1.08   WARRANTIES, GUARRANTIES AND BONDS

   A.   Provide duplicate, notarized copies. Execute Contractor's submittals and assemble documents executed
        by subcontractors, suppliers, and manufacturers. Provide table of contents and assemble in binder
        with durable plastic cover.

   B.   Submit material prior to final application for payment.   For equipment put into use with Owner's
        permission during construction, submit within 10 days after first operation. For items of Work
        delayed materially beyond Date of Substantial Completion, provide updated submittal within ten days
        after acceptance, listing date of acceptance as start of warranty period.

1.09   SPARE PARTS AND MAINTENANCE MATERIALS

   Provide products, spare parts, and maintenance materials in quantities specified in each section, in addition
   to that required for completion of Work. Coordinate with Owner, deliver to Project site and obtain receipt
   prior to final payment.

1.10   DELIVERY SCHEDULE

   A.   Keys and Keying Schedule, and one copy of equipment operating manuals shall be delivered at the time
        of the Substantial Completion Inspection for each separately accepted portion of the Work.

        1.   Deliver Keys and Keying Schedule to the Owner, with copy of signed receipt to the Architect.

        2.   Deliver other items to the Architect for his transmittal to the Owner.

   B.   Deliver all other items at the Final Inspection.

PART 2 - PRODUCTS

Not required.

PART 3 - EXECUTION

Not Required

END OF SECTION

Figure 13.6 *Project Close-out Requirements (continued)*

SECTION 01720
PROJECT RECORD DOCUMENTS

PART 1 - GENERAL

1.01   REQUIREMENTS INCLUDED

    A. Maintenance of Record Documents and Samples.

    B. Submittal of Record Documents and Samples.

1.02   RELATED REQUIREMENTS

    A. Section 01300 - Submittals: Shop drawings, product data, and samples.

    B. Section 01700 - Contract Closeout: Closeout procedures.

    C. Individual Specifications Sections: Manufacturer's certificates and certificates of inspection.

1.03   MAINTENANCE OF DOCUMENTS AND SAMPLES

    A. Contractor shall maintain at the site for Owner, one record copy of:

        1. Contract Drawings.

        2. Specifications.

        3. Addenda.

        4. Change Orders and other modifications to the Contract.

        5. Reviewed shop drawings, product data, and samples.

        6. Inspection certificates.

        7. Manufacturer's certificates.

    B. Store Record Documents and samples in Field Office apart from documents used for construction. Provide files, racks, and secure storage for Record Documents and samples.

    C. Label and file Record Documents and samples in accordance with Section number listings in Table of Contents of this Project Manual. Label each document "PROJECT RECORD" in neat, large, printed letters.

    D. Maintain Record Documents in a clean, dry and legible condition. Do not use Record Documents for construction purposes.

    E. Keep Record Documents and samples available for inspection by Architect.

1.04   RECORDING

    A. Record information on a set of blue line prints of drawings and bound Project Manual provided by Owner.

    B. Provide felt tip marking pens, maintaining separate colors for each major system, for recording information.

    C. Record information concurrently with construction progress. Do not conceal any work until required information is recorded.

    D. Contract Drawings and Shop Drawings: Legibly mark each item to record actual construction, including:

        1. Measured locations of internal utilities and appurtenances concealed in construction, referenced, by dimension and otherwise, to visible and accessible features of construction.

        2. Field changes of dimension and detail.

        3. Changes made by modifications.

        4. Details not on original Contract Drawings.

        5. References to related shop drawings and Modifications.

Example Project

Figure 13.7 Project Record Documents

E. Specifications: Legibly mark each item to record actual construction, including:

   1. Manufacturer, trade name, and catalog number of each product actually installed, particularly optional items and substitute items.

   2. Changes made by Addenda and Modifications.

F. Other Documents: Maintain manufacturer's certifications, inspection certifications, field tests and start up, records, and other information required by individual Specifications sections.

1.05 "AS BUILT" DRAWINGS

A. General Contractor shall have drafted, a set of "as-built" drawings of the project, on reproducible media, for Owner's final record.

B. Using data accumulated on blue line prints as specified in paragraph 1.04, place all information on a set of sepia reproducible drawings furnished by the Owner,

C. Use only experienced draftspersons for this work.

D. Use industry standards for drafting, keep lines and lettering uniform, legible.

1.06 SUBMITTALS

A. At Contract closeout, deliver Record Documents and samples under provisions of Section 01700.

B. Transmit with cover letter in duplicate, listing:

   1. Date.

   2. Project title and number.

   3. Contractor's name, address, and telephone number.

   4. Number and title of each Record Document.

   5. Signature of Contractor or authorized representative.

PART 2 - PRODUCTS

   Not Used.

PART 3 - EXECUTION

   Not Used.

END OF SECTION

Figure 13.7 *Project Record Documents (continued)*

the Contract Sum (or as negotiated and specified in the Contract). This payment may be dependent on the contractor's certification that all debts and claims have been paid, together with an affidavit of release or waiver of liens. Under the provisions of the bonds provided by the surety, the owner may be required to withhold the retainage until the surety has issued a consent for its release. Other documents may include *Contractor's Affidavit of Payment of Debts and Claims* and *Contractor's Affidavit of Release of Liens*, may provide some legal protection for both owner and surety (as well as for the contractor) when the contractor is paid a substantial amount of the retainage. A form called *Consent of Surety to Reduction in Retainage* may be issued to the owner before any retainage is paid to the contractor.

Once the contractor has complied with all required provisions of the Project Close-out, and all items shown on the semifinal punch list have been completed, the design professional may issue a final Certificate for Payment. This document notifies the owner that he can, subject to the consent of the surety, release an amount to the contractor that will bring the total payments to 100% of the Contract Sum.

Beneficial Occupancy

The General Conditions of the Contract for Construction may require the contractor to be responsible for the acquisition of building permit(s), and for compliance with all codes, ordinances and other matters of regulation and authority of the building official. Many jurisdictions require a Certificate of Occupancy to be issued by the building official before the owner will be allowed to occupy the completed project. The term *beneficial occupancy* as it is often used in Contract Documents means occupancy of the building by owner after a certificate of occupancy by the building official, but before a certificate of final completion is issued. The Certificate of Occupancy is the building official's certification that the building meets the requirements of the building code and/or other applicable ordinances and therefore, when required, must be considered as an important and integral part of the finalization of the project. It should be noted that the building official is the interpreter of the building code, not the contract documents. The design professional will not issue the Final Certificate for Payment until owner, design professional, and constructor have agreed that all work is complete and the "punch-list" has been satisfied.

Summary

It has been the purpose of this text to review the process of building construction from the standpoint of the interrelated functions of owner, design professional, and constructor expressed in terms of what we have called the OPC Relationship. This basic relationship has been seen in terms of the duties of the primary parties to the Contract for Construction (i.e., the owner and constructor). The owner may choose to be represented in the construction process solely by the design professional, or may choose to employ a construction administrator, or construction manager, to oversee the fulfillment of the Contract, in addition to the services provided by the design professional.

The constructor (identified as the contractor by the Contract Documents), in order to fulfill his obligation under the Contract for Construction, becomes entirely responsible for the construction process and its completion. The contractor is responsible by separate agreement for subcontractors, material and equipment suppliers, and others who supply and process the work of construction.

The design professional acts as the interpreter of the content and intent of the Contract Documents, and in concert with other professionals, advises the owner. One of the primary duties of the design professional is to periodically observe the construction process and report to the owner on the contractor's apparent conformity with the requirements of the Contract Documents. The design professional either employs professional specialists or separately contracts with professional consultants to implement specialized technical design. The instruments by which the building process is organized and implemented, commonly called Contract Documents are usually created by the design professional. These instruments are formally named the Contract Documents. Basic to the Contract Documents are the defined responsibilities of each member of the OPC relationship, a complete description of the Work to be done, and provision for such ancillary requirements as bonding, insurance, administrative requirements, evidence of conformity to design and specifications, and instructions for record keeping.

Under the code of common conduct and responsibility is an unwritten element of mutual faith that relies on all of the parties to adhere to the principals of common law, generally accepted good practices of the construction industry, and the integrity that is characteristic of that which we call professionalism. The construction industry is far from being an instrument of perfect science. The legal profession will always be needed to oversee contracts and to litigate claims. However, the genius of the justice system in the United States is that common law is based not upon what is perfect, but upon what is reasonable.

Appendix

Professional Associations

ARI **Air-Conditioning and Refrigeration Institute**
4301 N. Fairfax Drive, Suite 425
Arlington, VA 22203
Tel: (703) 524-8800
URL: www.ari.org

ADC **Air Diffusion Council**
104 S. Michigan Avenue, Suite 1500
Chicago, IL 60603
Tel: (312) 201-0101
URL: www.flexibleduct.org

AMCA **Air Movement and Control Association**
30 West University Drive
Arlington Heights, IL 60004
Tel: (847) 394-0150
URL: www.amca.org

AA **Aluminum Association**
900 19th Street, N.W.
Washington, DC 20006
Tel: (202) 862-5100
URL: www.aluminum.org

ACI **American Concrete Institute**
P.O. Box 9094
Farmington Hills, MI 48333
Tel: (248) 848-3700
URL: www.aci-int.org

ACEC **American Consulting Engineers Council**
1015 15th Street, N.W.
Washington, DC 20005
Tel: (202) 347-7474
URL: www.acec.org

AIA **American Institute of Architects**
1735 New York Avenue, N.W.
Washington, DC 20006
Tel: (202) 626-7300
URL: www.aiaonline.com

AISC **American Institute of Steel Construction**
One E. Wacker Drive, Suite 3100
Chicago, IL 60601
Tel: (312) 670-2400
URL: www.arcat.com/arcatcos/cos36/arc36780.cfm

AISI	American Iron and Steel Institute
	1101 17th St., N.W., Suite 1300
	Washington, DC 20036
	Tel: (202) 452-7100
	URL: www.steel.org

ANSI	American National Standards Institute
	1819 L Street N.W.
	Washington, DC 20036
	Tel: (212) 642-4900
	URL: www.ansi.org

APA	The Engineered Wood Association
	(formerly the American Plywood Association)
	Box 11700
	Tocoma, WA 98411
	Tel: (253) 565-6600
	URL: www.apawood.org

ASCE	American Society of Civil Engineers
	1801 Alexander Bell Drive
	Reston, VA 20191-4400
	Tel: (800) 548-2723
	URL: www.asce.org

ASHRAE	American Society of Heating, Refrigeration and Air Conditioning Engineers
	1791 Tullie Circle N.E.
	Atlanta, GA 30329
	Tel: (404) 636-8400
	URL: www.ashrae.org

ASME	American Society of Mechanical Engineers
	Three Park Avenue
	New York, NY 10016
	Tel: (800) 843-2763
	URL: www.asme.org

ASTM	American Society for Testing and Materials
	100 Barr Harbor Drive
	West Conshohocken, PA 19428-2959
	Tel: (610) 832-9585
	URL: www.astm.org

AWWA	American Water Works Association
	6666 West Quincy Avenue
	Denver, CO 80235
	Tel: (303) 794-7711
	URL: www.awwa.org

AWS	American Welding Society
	550 N.W. LeJeune Road
	Miami, FL 33126
	Tel: (800) 443-9353
	URL: www.amweld.org

AWC	**American Wood Council** 1111 19th Street N.W., Suite 800 Washington, DC 20036 Tel: (202) 463-2766 URL: www.awc.org
AWPA	**American Wood-Preserver's Association** P.O. Box 5690 Granbury, TX 76049 Tel: (817) 326-6300 URL: www.awpa.com
AWI	**Architectural Woodwork Institute** 1952 Isaac Newton Square West Reston, VA 20190 Tel: (703) 733-0600 URL: www.awinet.org
AI	**Asphalt Institute** Research Park Drive P.O. Box 14052 Lexington, KY 40512 Tel: (859) 288-4960 URL: www.asphaltinstitute.org
ABC	**Associated Builders and Contractors** 1300 N. Seventeenth Street, Suite 800 Rosslyn, VA 22209 Tel: (703) 812-2000 URL: www.abc.org
AGC	**Associated General Contractors of America** 333 John Carlyle Street, Suite 200 Alexandria, VA 22314 Tel: (703) 548-3118 URL: www.agc.org
CLFMI	**Chain Link Fence Manufacturers Institute** 9891 Broken Land Parkway, Suite 300 Columbia, MD 21046 Tel: (301) 596-2583 URL: www.chainlinkinfo.org/members.html
CSI	**Construction Specifications Institute** 99 Canal Center Plaza, Suite 300 Alexandria, VA 22314 Tel: (800) 689-2900 URL: www.csinet.org
CRSI	**Concrete Reinforcing Steel Institute** 933 N. Plum Grove Road Schaumburg, IL 60195 Tel: (312) 517-1200 URL: www.crsi.org

DBIA   **Design-Build Institute of America**
1010 Massachusetts Avenue, NW, Suite 350
Washington, D.C. 20001
Tel: (202) 682-0110
URL: www.dbia.org

CDA   **Copper Development Association**
260 Madison Avenue, 16th floor
New York, NY 10016
Tel: (212) 251-7200
URL: www.copper.org

EJCDC   **Engineer's Joint Contract Documents Committee**
American Consulting Engineers Council
1015 15th Street N.W.
Washington, DC 20005
Tel: (202) 347-7474
URL: www.acec.org

FM   **Factory Mutual**
1151 Boston-Providence Turnpike
Norwood, MA 02062
Tel: (781) 762-4300
URL: www.fmglobal.com

Federal Specifications are available through:
GSA   **General Services Administration**
Federal Supply Service, Bureau Specifications Section
(3FBP-W)
470 L'Enfant Plaza S.W., Suite 8100
Washington, DC 20407
Tel: (202) 755-0325
URL: www.gsa.gov

FGMA   **Flat Glass Marketing Association**
3310 Harrison
White Lakes Professional Building
Topeka, KS 66611
Tel: (913) 266-7013
URL: www.recycle.net/recycle/assn/glass_28.html

GA   **Gypsum Association**
810 First St., NE, #510
Washington DC, 20002
Tel: (202)-289-5440
URL: www.gypsum.org

EEEI   **Electrical and Electronics Engineers, Inc.**
1828 L Street, N.W., Suite 1202
Washington, D.C. 20036
Tel: (202) 785-0017
URL: www.ieee.org

IMI	**International Masonry Institute** The James Brice House 42 East Street Annapolis, MD 21401 Tel: (410) 280-1305 URL: www.imiweb.org
SSMA	**Steel Stud Manufacturers Association** 8 S. Michigan Avenue, Suite 1000 Chicago, IL 60603 Tel: (312) 456-5590 URL: www.steel.org
DAPS	*For Military Specifications* **Defense Automated Printing Service— Customer Service** 700 Robbins Avenue Building 4-D Philadelphia, PA 19111 Tel: (215) 697-2179 URL: pcim.com/glos/refl.htm
NAAMM	**National Association of Architectural Metal Manufacturers** 8 South Michigan Avenue, Suite 100 Chicago, IL 60603 Tel: (312) 332-0405 URL: www.naamm.org
NEMA	**National Electrical Manufacturers' Association** 1300 North 17th Street, Suite 1847 Roslyn, Virginia 22209 Tel: (703) 841-3200 URL: www.nema.org
NEBB	**National Environmental Balancing Bureau** 8575 Grovemont Circle Gaithersburg, MD 20877 Tel: (301) 977-3698 URL: www.nebb.org
NFPA	**National Fire Protection Association** 1 Batterymarch Park P.O. Box 9101 Quincy, MA 02269-9101 Tel: (617) 770-3000 URL: www.nfpa.org
NSPE	**National Society of Professional Engineers** 1420 King Street Alexandria, VA 22314 Tel: (703) 684-2800 URL: www.nspe.org
NSWMA	**National Solid Wastes Management Association** 4301 Connecticut Avenue, NW, Suite 300 Washington, DC 20008 Tel: (202) 244-4700 URL: www.envasns.org

NRCA	**National Roofing Contractors Association** 10255 W, Higgins Road, Suite 600 Rosemont, IL 60018 Tel: (847) 299-9070 URL: www.nrca.net
PCA	**Portland Cement Association** 5420 Old Orchard Road Skokie, IL 60077 Tel: (847) 966-6200 URL: www.portcement.org
NIST	**National Institute of Standards and Technology** 100 Bureau Drive, Stop 3460 Gaithersburg, MD 20899 Tel: (301) 975-6478 URL: www.nist.gov
SAVE	**SAVE International** "The Value Society" 60 Revere Drive, Suite 500 Northbrook, IL 60062 Tel: (847) 480-1730 URL:www.value-eng.com
SIGMA	**Sealed Insulating Glass Manufacturers Association** 401 N. Michigan Ave. Chicago, IL 60611 Tel: (312) 644-6610 URL: www.recycle.net/recycle/assn/glass_34.html
SMACNA	**Sheet Metal and Air Conditioning Contractors' National Association** (National Office) 4201 Lafayette Center Drive Chantilly, VA 20151 Tel: (703) 803-2980 URL: www.smacna.org
SDI	**Steel Door Institute** 30200 Detroit Road Cleveland, OH 44145 Tel: (440) 899-0010 URL: www.wherryassoc.com/steeldoor.org
SSPC	**Steel Structures Painting Council** 40 24th Street, Suite 600 Pittsburgh, PA 15213 Tel: (412) 281-2331 URL: www.kellymoore-nw.com/architect/SSPC.html
TAS	**Technical Aid Series** Construction Specifications Institute 99 Canal Center Plaza, Suite 300 Alexandria, VA 22314 Tel: (800) 689-2900 URL: www.csinet.org

TCA	**Tile Council of America** 100 Clemson Research Blvd. Anderson, SC 29625 Tel: (864) 646-8453 URL: www.tileusa.com/index.html
ULI	**Underwriters' Laboratories, Inc.** 333 Pfingsten Road Northbrook, IL 60062 Tel: (847) 272-8800 URL: www.ul.com
WCLIB	**West Coast Lumber Inspection Bureau** Box 23145 Portland, OR 97281 Tel: (503) 639-0651 URL: www.wclib.org

Glossary of Terms

Addenda
Plural form of Addendum.

Addendum
Document describing an addition, change, correction or modification to the Contract Documents. An addendum is issued by the design professional during the bidding phase or prior to the award of the contract for construction, and is the primary method of informing bidders of modifications to the work, published during the bidding process. Addenda become part of the Contract Documents "package."

Advertisement for Bids
A published notice of an owner's intention to award a contract for construction to a qualified constructor who submits a proposal according to Instructions to Bidders. In its usual form, the advertisement published in a convenient form of news media in order to attract constructors who are willing to prepare and submit proposals for the performance of the work.

Action Item
Description of an element of work, research, design or other task that is assigned to a participant or other individual. The item establishes the expectation that the named participant or participants will complete the described task for delivery according to a specific requirement at a time that may be agreed or assigned during a process such as a meeting or work plan.

AFL-CIO
A major union, formed by the merger of AFL (American Federation of Labor) and CIO (Committee for Industrial Organizations) under the leadership of John L. Lewis in 1955. The AFL-CIO represents the interests of various types of member-workers in industry and other endeavors (construction) for the purpose of negotiating with management for wages, benefits, and other material interests of worker-employees.

Agreement
A consensus of two or more parties concerning a particular subject. Regarding matters of construction or services of a design professional, the term "agreement" is synonymous with contract. Examples include the Agreement Between Owner and Design Professional and the Agreement Between Owner and Contractor.

All-Risk Insurance
An insurance policy that can be written separately to add coverage against certain specific risks of damage or loss from any number of potential events. These risks represent potential losses in excess of coverage by other forms of insurance purchased for the purpose of protecting the owner, design professional and contractor during and after the construction process.

Allowance

A stated requirement of the Contract Documents whereby a specified sum of money is incorporated, or allowed, into the Contract Price in order to sustain the cost of a stipulated material, assembly, piece of equipment or other part of a construction contract. This device is convenient in cases where the particular item cannot be fully described in the contract documents. The allowance can be stated as a Lump Sum or as a Unit Sum and includes specific instructions as to whether or not the cost of the material and labor to install the material is to be included in the amount of the allowance. In the case of the Unit Cost Allowance, the constructor (bidder) or a third party Quantity Surveyor in the employ of the owner is to be responsible for determining the quantity to be applied. In this way, a sum can be calculated that will adequately cover the work required by the Contract Documents.

Alternate

A specified item of construction that is set apart by separate sum. An alternate may or may not be incorporated into the Contract Price at the discretion and approval of the owner at the time of contract award.

American Federation of Labor

A labor organization or union formed in the United States under the leadership of Samuel Gompers in 1866. The American Federation of Labor (AFL) provided an "umbrella" organization the purpose of which was to represent to management the collective interests of workers in the various trades, crafts and other skilled disciplines related to manufacture and construction.

Application for Payment

A statement prepared by the Contractor stating the amount of work completed, and materials purchased and properly stored and otherwise protected to date. The statement includes the sum of previous payments, the sum of any retain age amounts that may be agreed and the current amount requested in accordance with payment provisions of the Contract Documents.

Arbitration

A procedure whereby disputes regarding matters of contract responsibility can be mediated without litigation in a court of law. Under arbitration, a panel of knowledgeable arbitrators is impaneled to review the evidence and testimony of the parties to the dispute. The parties to the contract would have agreed in advance to accept the decision rendered by the panel of arbitrators.

Architect

A design professional who, by education, experience, and examination is licensed by state government to practice the art of building design and technology. Derived from the root words "arch" and "technology," this term is roughly translated as "technician of the arch."

As-Built-Drawings

A "loosely associated" term usually intended to mean "record drawings and associated documents" made from information collected during construction to record the locations, sizes and nature of concealed items such as structural components, accessories, equipment, devices, plumbing lines, valves, mechanical equipment, and the like. The preferred term is *Project Record Documents* which more closely describes the intent of providing a reasonable record of the size and placement of concealed building components for the owner's use and reference.

Assemblies Estimate (See Building Systems Estimate)

Bar Graph

Graphic representations of simultaneous events charted with reference to time. A technique developed by Henry Gantt and Frederick W. Taylor around 1900. Early forms were called Gantt Charts. A bar graph is a simplified method of charting events that occur in sequence, such as the processes of building construction. The horizontal axis of the chart is scaled to increments of time, the various events are charted vertically. The duration of the event is charted by a horizontal line or bar beginning at the time the event begins and ending at the time the event is scheduled to be complete. At any point in time, the reader can observe the number of events that are occurring simultaneously.

Basic Services

A group of services provided for the owner by the design professional, under a contract or agreement for design, that are considered to be the minimum services necessary to lead to a contract for construction with an acceptable constructor.

Bid

A term commonly used for a complete and properly executed proposal to perform work that has been described in the Contract Documents and submitted in accordance with Instructions to Bidders.

Bid Bond

A form of Bid Security purchased by the bidder from a Surety. A bid bond is provided, subject to forfeit, to guarantee that a bidder will enter into a contract for construction within a specified time and furnish any required bonds such as Performance Bond and Payment Bond.

Bid Opening

A formal meeting held at a specified place, date and hour at which sealed bids are opened, tabulated and read aloud.

Bid Security

A Bid Bond or other form of security such as a Cashier's Check or other thing of value that is acceptable to the owner. Bid Security is provided as a guarantee that the bidder will enter into a contract for construction within a specified time and furnish any bonds or other requirements of the Bid Documents.

Bidding Documents

Documents usually including Advertisement or Invitation to Bidders, Instructions to Bidders, Bid Form, Form of Contract, forms of Bonds, Conditions of the Contract, Specifications, Drawings and any other information necessary to completely describe the work by which candidate constructors can adequately prepare proposals or Bids for the owner's consideration.

Bidding Phase

The period of time required for competing constructors to study and respond to the owner's invitation or advertisement for competitive bids to construct a project.

Bidding Process

A process, managed by the owner, assisted by the design professional, by which competing constructors are invited to study and respond to the owner's invitation or advertisement for competitive bids to construct a project.

Blue Print
A paper sensitized with a mixture of ferric ammonium citrate and potassium ferricynide used for reproductions of drawings. When subjected to a strong light source and washed in a solution of potassium dichromate, the exposed portion will turn a dark blue color. By placing the drawing over the sensitized medium, and performing the light exposure, the dark image on the drawing blocks a corresponding area on the print. When developed, the original is reproduced in reverse image.

Bonds
Written documents, provided by a Surety in the name of a Principal to obligee to guarantee a specific obligation. In construction, the principal types of bonds are the Bid Bond, the Performance Bond and the Payment Bond.

Bonus Provisions
Provisions in the Contract for Construction by which the owner may offer monetary rewards to the contractor for achieving some savings that benefit the owner. For example, a stipulated bonus may be offered for early completion of the work, or the achievement of some accountable savings in construction cost.

Breach
A term applied to the failure of one or more parties to a contract to perform according to the exact terms of the contract.

Broadscope
A term describing the content of a section of the specifications, as established by the Construction Specifications Institute. A broadscope section covers a wide variety of related materials and workmanship requirements. (Narrowscope sections denote a section a single material. Mediumscope sections denote a section describing dealing with a "family" of materials.)

Budget
The total amount of money that an owner is prepared to spend in the procurement of a project.

Building Codes
The minimum legal requirements established or adopted by a government such as a municipality. Building codes are established by ordinance and govern the design and construction of buildings with focus on assuring the safety and welfare of the general community at large.

Building Official
An appointed officer of a body of government, responsible for enforcing the Building Code. Sometimes called the Building Inspector, the building official may approve the issuance of a Building Permit, review the Contract Documents, inspect the construction and approve the issuance of a Certificate of Occupancy.

Building Permit
A written authorization required by ordinance for a specific project. A building permit allows construction to proceed in accordance with construction documents approved by the building official.

Building Systems Estimate
An estimate of probable Contract Price prepared during the design process by defining, measuring and pricing unit assemblies of materials and other components intended for inclusion in the construction of a project. The building systems estimate is most

appropriately used during the traditional Design Development phase of the design professional's work.

Business
An entity or individual enterprise that produces goods and services.

Cash Allowance
A specified sum of money to be included into the Contract Price for an element, group of elements, assembly, system, piece of equipment or other described item to be included in the work under specified conditions.

Certificate
A written document appropriately signed by responsible parties testifying to a matter of fact in accordance with a requirement of the contract documents.

Certificate of Insurance
A written document signed by a duly authorized representative of an insurance company which states the exact coverage and period of time for which the coverage is applicable in accordance with the contract documents.

Certificate of Occupancy
A written document issued by the governing authority in accordance with the Building Permit. The Certificate of Occupancy indicates that the project, in the opinion of the Building Official, has been completed in accordance with the Building Code. The document authorizes the owner to occupy and use the premises for the intended purpose.

Certified Construction Specifier
A building professional who by experience and examination by the Construction Specifications Institute has been certified as being proficient in the art of preparing technical specifications, part of the contract documents, for any project.

Certified Value Specialist
A building professional who by experience and examination by the Society of American Value Engineers as being proficient in Value Engineering or Value Management and is capable of leading a team of professionals in the conduct of a Value Engineering study of the design of building projects.

Change Order
A written document signed by the owner, design professional and contractor detailing a change or modification to the contract for construction.

Civil Rights Act
Legislation enacted by the Congress and President of the United States in 1964 and amended in subsequent years. The Civil Rights Act prohibits any act that would discriminate against an individual for any reason, but particularly because of sex, race, ethnic origin or religion. In 1990, the Congress and the President signed into law the Americans with Disabilities Act (ADA) which recognizes the rights of individuals with disabilities to accommodated access to the "built" environment of the United States. ADA also prohibits discrimination against individuals with disabilities in the work place.

Clayton Act
Legislation enacted by the Congress and President of the United States in 1914. The Clayton Act was intended to lessen the negative effects of the Sherman Anti-Trust Act by allowing labor to organize for the purposes of negotiating with a single employer.

Closed Bidding
A common term meaning Closed Competitive Selection.

Closed Competitive Selection
The preferred term for Closed Bidding, a process of competitive bidding where the owner limits the list of bidders to companies he or she has selected and invited to bid.

Closed Shop
A term applied to a trade or skill that requires membership in a particular union to the exclusion of non-union members.

Committee for Industrial Organizations (CIO)
A labor union organized in 1935 for the purpose of representing industrial workers. The CIO was created as the result of a dispute with the AFL. John L. Lewis, president of the United Mine Workers, a member of the CIO, was instrumental in merging the AFL-CIO in 1955.

Competition
A term used in the study of economics describing a situation that exists when many suppliers try to sell the same kinds of things to the same buyers.

Concept
(1) Something conceived in the mind such as a thought or a notion. An abstract or generalized idea drawn from particular data, such as a design concept. (2) A vision of something to be achieved or created that satisfies a defined goal.

Concept Documents
A series of drawings, and other definitive documents that illustrate a design professionals concept for a project.

Conditions of the Contract
A document detailing the rights, responsibilities, and relationships of the parties to the Contract for Construction.

Consideration
A term used to describe the compensation that shall be paid to one party to a contract by another party in return for services and/or products rendered.

Construction Administrator
One who oversees the fulfillment of the responsibilities of all parties to the Contract for Construction, for the primary benefit of the owner. In the typical project involving an owner, a design professional and a (single) contractor, construction administration is usually provided by the contractor, while administration of the contract for construction may be provided by the design professional acting on behalf of the owner. A separate Construction Administrator may be required by an owner who contracts independently with multiple constructors.

Construction Drawings
A component of the Contract Documents, documents that provide graphic representations of the work to be done in the construction of a project.

Construction Manager

One with authority, from the owner to direct the process of construction. The Construction Manager-as-Agent of the owner provides management of multiple contracts held by the owner for a stipulated fee. The Construction Manager-At Risk is responsible for providing multiple contracts held by the construction manager with the promise of project delivery for a stipulated Contract Price.

Constructor

One who is in the business of providing construction services. A contractor is a constructor who is acting under the specific terms of a contract for construction between the constructor and the owner.

Consulting Engineer

An engineer, licensed for a particular discipline or disciplines of engineering practice by a state or district, who performs specific portions of a project design under a subcontract and in coordination with the services of a (prime) design professional.

Contingency

A term describing an allotment or an assigned amount included in an estimate of probable Contract Price which represents a portion of a project which is unknown, or more specifically is unknown or undefined at the time the estimate is prepared. In the case of an estimate of probable cost, depending upon the resource, the most convenient method of applying a contingency to a prediction of contract price is to add a percentage of the derived cost to the total of the estimate.

Contingency Allowance

A specific amount of money included in the contract price, with approval and understanding of the owner, that is intended to adjust the result of an estimate of probable contract price in order to cover the cost of portions of the project that may remain undetermined or to allow for unforeseen economic conditions that may cause fluctuations in predictable contract price at the time the bidding or negotiations are scheduled to take place.

Continuing Education

A term applied to a regimen of attendance and application of special study toward specific subject matter. Many states require a specific number of Continuing Education Units (CEUs) annually for design professionals seeking renewal of their state licenses for professional practice.

Contract

An agreement between two or more individuals where mutual consent occurs, giving rise to a specified promise or series of promises to be performed, for which consideration is given.

Contract Documents

A term applied to any combination of related documents that collectively define the extent of an agreement between two or more parties. As regards the Contract for Construction, the contract documents generally consist of the Agreement (Contract), the Bonds, the Certificates, the Conditions of the Contract, the Specifications, the Drawings and the Modifications.

Contract for Construction
An agreement between owner and contractor whereby the contractor agrees to construct the owner's building or other described project in accordance with the Contract Documents within a specified amount of time for consideration to be paid as mutually agreed.

Contract Documents Phase
The phase of the design professional's services reserved for the preparation of final Contract Documents. The Contract Documents Phase is usually dependent upon completion of a prior a sequence of services including, but not entirely dependent upon, the Pre-Design Phase, the Schematic Design Phase and the Design Development Phase, the sum of which provide an orderly and systematic sequence of events by which to thoroughly confirm the owner's requirements and budget rest rants with opportunity for owner to have approved the design professional's documented solution for the intended project.

Contract Price
A single, lump sum of money named as the price which a candidate for the contract for construction offers according to bidding instructions or as a final price during negotiations as total compensation for the delivery of the project described in the Contract Documents.

Contractor
A constructor who is a party to the Contract for Construction, pledged to the owner to perform the work of construction in accordance with the Contract Documents.

Contractor's Qualification Statement
A statement of the contractor's qualifications, experience, financial condition, business history, and staff composition. This statement together with listed business and professional references provides evidence of the contractor's competence to perform the Work and assume the responsibilities required by the Contract Documents.

Contributory Negligence
A term used to describe legal responsibility for an error or fault by one or more parties who have allegedly contributed in whole or in part to a loss or damage suffered by another party as a result of a specific occurrence.

Corporation
An association of individuals for the purpose of conducting business established under certain legal requirements. A corporation exists independently of its members and has powers and liabilities distinct and apart from its members.

Corporation Law
A body of law that governs the formation and operation of business corporations. It deals mainly with the powers and obligations of management and the rights of stockholders. *Corporation law* is often classed together with contract and commercial law and may be described as *Business Law*.

Covenant
A term used to describe one or more specific points of agreement that may be set forth in a Contract.

Critical Path

A term used to describe the order of events, each of a defined duration, that results in the least amount of time to complete a series of tasks, or to complete a project.

Davis-Bacon Act

An act by the Congress and President of the United States, enacted into law in 1931. The Davis-Bacon Act provides that wages and fringe benefits paid to workers employed by contractors under contract with the federal government be no less than the prevailing rates for each trade in that location.

Deductible

A term used to describe a specified amount that will be deducted from the total of compensation paid in event of loss covered under an insurance policy.

Demand

In terms of economics, the amount of goods or services that users desire to purchase at alternative prices.

Descriptive Specification

A type of specification described as a written description detailing the required properties of a material, manufacturer's product, assembly of materials or products, or a piece of equipment.

Design Concept

A representation, either graphic or written, often a combination of both which describes the design professional's early or preliminary ideas for a building's design.

Design Development Phase

The phase of the design professional's services reserved for the preparation of final documents that define and otherwise explain the total intent of the design of the project. The Design Development Phase is usually dependent upon completion of a prior sequence of services including, but not entirely dependent upon, the Pre-Design Phase and the Schematic Design Phase, the sum of which provides an orderly and systematic sequence of information by which to thoroughly confirm the owner's requirements and budget restraints with opportunity for owner to understand and approve the design professional's detailed design approach for the intended project.

Design Professional

A generic term that identifies the party responsible for creating the contract documents. As used in this text, the term design professional refers to one licensed by appropriate government to deliver design services to an owner. Design professional can mean architect, engineer, architect/engineer, interior designer or landscape architect.

Design to Budget

A requirement in the contract between owner and design professional which requires the design professional to re-design the project if the contract price exceeds the owner's budget.

Diazo

A group of chemical compounds, such as benzenediazo hydroxide or diazomethane, generally used as a light sensitive emulsion on a support such as paper or plastic. When this material is exposed, as in a photographic process by the passage of light through an original drawing and developed by the reaction of a coupler, either an acid compound or an alkaline agent, a positive image called a "whiteprint," is produced. (Also see *Whiteprint*.)

Direct Selection

A process whereby the owner selects a constructor for the purpose of constructing the project. The selection is made at the owner's discretion based upon the constructor's experience, availability and capability. The terms of the Contract for Construction are reached by negotiation rather than through the process of competitive bidding.

Economy

A system for managing the production, distribution and consumption of goods in a particular society.

Engineering Drawing

A term used to describe drawings, prepared with precision, to scale, for purpose of illustrating details and design characteristics of an object to be fabricated, assembled or constructed.

Equal Employment Opportunity Commission (EEOC)

An agency of the United States Government under the Department of Labor. This agency is dedicated to enforcing the provisions of Title IV of the Civil Rights Act of 1964, which forbids discrimination by an employer on the basis of race, color, religion, sex or national origin of a potential employee.

Escrow

A legal device used in conjunction with a contract, whereby something of value is placed with a third party acting as trustee. The escrow serves as a guarantee of performance to the conditions of the contract.

Estimator

One who is capable of predicting the probable *contract price* of a project prior to, or during the bidding or negotiating phase of a project's development.

Estimating

The process of predicting the probable *contract price* of a project prior to, or during the bidding or negotiating phase of a project's development.

Exclusionary Provision

A provision in an insurance policy covering potential loss whereby specific types or origins of loss are specifically excluded (by description) from the coverage provided.

Fair Labor Standards Act

An act of the Congress of the United States enacted in 1936, and the subject of numerous amendments to the present day. This act is commonly referred to as the Minimum Wage Law; the act establishes a minimum wage for all workers with the exception of agriculture workers. It provides a maximum of a 40-hour work week for straight time pay for employees earning hourly wages.

Fast Track

A term used to describe a time driven process whereby a project is both designed and constructed in subsequent phases, called "bid packages." The method allows portions of the construction to begin before the entire package of contract documents for the project has been completed. The contract documents are delivered in sequenced "bid-packages" such as foundations, followed by superstructure, followed by exterior envelope, etc. The construction is likewise conducted in phases, each starting following to the issuance of each sequential "bid package." Each "bid package" can be competitively bid as separate contract, or a Construction Manager-At-Risk can negotiate each phase under a master agreement to complete the project.

Federal Mediation and Conciliation Service
An agency of the United States Department of Labor which acts as a mediator in the settlement of disputes as provided by the Labor Relations Act of 1935 and the Labor Relations Act of 1947.

Field Order
A written modification to the Contract for Construction, made by the design professional or the Construction Administrator.

General Conditions
Formally known as the *General Conditions of the Contract for Construction*, the part of the contract documents that defines rights, responsibilities and relationships between the parties to the Contract for Construction.

General Contractor
A constructor whose primary business activity is the primary responsibility for construction under contract with various owners.

General Obligation Bonds
An instrument of obligation, which by permission of the public through *referendum*, is in turn issued to investors by a subdivision of government. These bonds promise incremental payment of principal and interest from revenues collected annually by the government. In return, funds are supplied by investors to pay for the construction of publicly owned buildings or other public works projects.

General Requirements
Division 1 of 16 divisions of the specifications organized under Masterformat created by the Construction Specifications Institute (CSI). The General Requirements, in sequential sections, detail the general administration requirements of the project in careful coordination with the various conditions of the Contract for Construction.

Generic
A term used to describe a material, product, assembly or piece of equipment, as in the *Descriptive Specification*, rather than specifying a manufacturer's trade name or specific source of manufacture or named distributor.

Guarantee
A warrant, pledge or formal assurance for the fulfillment of a condition such as an assurance of the quality to be expected from a product often with a promise of reimbursement if the product fails during a certain period of time.

Guaranteed Maximum Price Contract
A contract for construction wherein the contractor's compensation is stated as accountable accumulated cost plus a fee, with a promise, by the contractor, that the total accumulated cost plus fee to be paid by the owner will not exceed a specific amount agreed in advance. This type of contract often has provision of financial reward to the contractor as an incentive to deliver the project a cost below the guaranteed maximum price.

Geo-Technical Engineer
A term often used to describe an engineering specialty in the field of civil or structural engineering by application of the science of geology

and mechanics of soils including the sampling and testing of bearing capacity of soils at the project site leading to recommendations for design of foundation structures.

Gross Building Area
Often referred to as GBA, the total area of the building based on measurement from outside of exterior wall to outside of exterior wall including sum of all floors, wings and appendages and other portions of the building.

Interest
A certain fee derived from the lending of a sum of money or other thing of value for a period of time collected by a lender from a borrower.

Interest Rate
Usually a percentage of the amount borrowed applied as interest to be earned by the lender annually during the period of the loan.

Inclusive Coverage
A provision in an insurance policy covering potential loss where specific types or origins of loss are included by description under the coverage provided.

Industry Standard
Readily available information in the form of published specifications, technical reports, and disclosures, test procedures and results, codes and other technical information and data. Such data should be verifiable, professionally endorsed, with general acceptance and proven use by the construction industry.

Industry Standard Specification
A published specification meeting the general definition of an industry standard.

Instructions to Bidders
A document, part of the bidding requirements, usually prepared by the design professional, providing detailed instructions to candidate bidders on procedures, expectations of the owner, disclaimers by the owner, and other necessary information for the preparation of proposals for consideration of the owner for a competitive bid.

Insurance
Coverage by contract in which one party agrees to indemnify or reimburse another party for any loss that may occur within the terms of the *insurance policy*.

Insurance Policy
A contract which provides *insurance* against specific loss.

Invitation to Bid
A written notice of an owner's intention to receive competitive bids for a construction project wherein a select group of candidate constructors are invited to submit proposals of *contract price*.

Joint Venture
A joining of two or more individuals, partnerships or corporations for the single purpose of jointly sharing the responsibility for and compensation from a single endeavor such as the design or construction of a building project.

Journeyman
A term applied to the second or intermediate level of development of proficiency in a particular trade or skill. As related to building

construction, a journeyman's license, earned by a combination of education, supervised experience and examination, is required in many jurisdictions for those employed as intermediate level mechanics in certain trades (e.g. plumbing, mechanical and electrical work).

Judgment

A judicial decision rendered as a result of a cause of action in a court of law.

Labor Union

An organization or confederation of workers with the same or similar skills who are joined in a common cause (such as collective bargaining) with management or other employers for workplace conditions, wage rates and/or employee benefits.

Landrum-Griffin Act

Enacted by Congress in 1959, this act requires labor union management to be subject to audit for the funds of union members for which they are responsible.

Legal Notice

A covenant, often incorporated into the language of an agreement between two or more parties to an agreement that requires communication in writing, serving notice from one party to another in accordance with the terms of the agreement.

Lender

A common term for a commercial financial institution that loans money to individuals or businesses for capital leverage.

Liability

Exposure to potential claim by which a first party may be subject to pay compensation to a second party in the case of loss or damage occurring to the second party for acts attributable to the responsibility of the first party.

Lien

A legal means of establishing or giving notice of a claim or an unsatisfied charge in the form of a debt, obligation or duty. A lien is filed with government authorities against title to real property. Liens must be adjudicated or satisfied before title can be transferred.

Life Cycle

A term often used to describe the period of time that a building can be expected to actively and adequately serve its intended function.

Litigation

Legal action or process in a court of law.

Loss of Use Insurance

A type of insurance coverage that compensates the owner for the loss of use of his property in the case of a mishap such as fire or other damage.

Lump Sum

An amount of money stated in a contract or a bid representation the total cost of an item of work, or as proposed the contract price.

Market

A place or situation in which people buy and sell goods or services.

Mark-Up

A percentage of the sum or of other sums that is added to the total of *direct costs* to determine a sales price or *contract price*.

In construction practice, the mark-up usually represents two factors important to the contractor. The first factor is the estimated cost of *indirect expense* often referred to as overhead. The second factor is an amount representing profit for the contractor.

Master
A term applied to the third and highest level of achievement for a tradesman or mechanic who by supervision, experience and examination has earned a master's license attesting that he is a master of the trade and no longer requires supervision of his work as is the case with the journeyman or apprentice levels.

Master Builder
A term applied to one who performs the functions of both design and construction. The master builder approach to building construction has been a practice commonplace in much of the world for many centuries. In the United States, design and construction are traditionally seen as two separate and distinct functions.

MASTERFORMAT
The name created and copyrighted by the Construction Specifications Institute (CSI) of the United States and Construction Specifications Canada (CSC) denoting a numerical system of organization for construction related information and data based on a 16 division format.

Materialman
A term applied to one through whom the contractor may obtain the materials of construction. The materialman may be a representative of a manufacturer or he may be a distributor or salesman of the tools, products, materials, assemblies and equipment vital to the process of construction.

Mechanics Lien
A type of lien filed by one who has performed work related to the real property for which compensation is either in dispute or remains unsatisfied.

Mediumscope
A term established by the Construction Specifications Institute to denote a section of the specifications that describes a family of related or integrated materials and workmanship requirements. (*Narrowscope* specifications denote a single product. *Broadscope* specifications denote a section describing differing materials used in a related manner.)

Minimum Wage Law
A common term used to describe the Fair Labor Standards Act enacted by Congress in 1938. The act establishes a minimum wage for workers and the forty hour work week.

Mock-Up
Materials and products assembled as a sample or demonstration faithful to the finished product in terms of color, texture, manufacture and/or workmanship, as it will be installed into the building. Mock-ups are useful for review and approval of the owner, design professionals and others.

Model Codes
Professionally prepared building regulations and codes, regularly attended and revised, designed to be adopted by municipalities and appropriate political subdivisions by ordinance for use in regulating building construction for the welfare and safety of the general public.

Modifications

A term applied to changes that may be made from time to time to the Contract Documents and/or the Contract for Construction. Modifications made prior to the award of contract are called *Addenda,* modifications made after the contract is in force are called *Change Orders* or *Field Orders.*

Monopoly

A term used in economics meaning singular control of the supply of a product or service for which no substitute is available

Multiple Prime Contract

This type of contract is used in a situation where one or more constructors are employed under separate contracts to perform work on the same project, either in a sequence or coincidentally.

Mutual Companies

Insurance companies by many individuals who are also the insured. The "pooling" of this combined capital is a form of mutual assurance.

Mylar

A term used to describe a thin, tough, smooth surfaced polyester film used for drawings. The term is also used to describe plastics used for preserving foods, for recording tapes and as an insulator for electrical wiring.

Narrowscope

A term established by the Construction Specifications Institute (CSI) to denote a section of the specifications that describes a single product. (See also *Mediumscope* and *Broadscope*).

National Labor Relations Act

An act of Congress sometimes known as the Wagner Act, enacted in 1935. This act mandated a framework of procedure and regulation by which management and labor relations are to be conducted.

Negotiation

A process used to determine a mutually satisfactory *contract price* and terms to be included in the Contract for Construction. In negotiations, the owner directly selects the constructor and the two, often with assistance of the design professional, derive by compromise and meeting of the minds the scope of the project and its cost.

Network Schedule

A method of scheduling the construction process where various and related events are programmed into a sequential network on the basis of starting and finishing dates.

Net Building Area

Often referred to as (NBA), the sum of the net-functional area of a building that results from measuring the useful spaces in a building design before consideration of the area occupied by walls, horizontal common circulation (corridors and hallways), vertical circulation (stairs, escalators and elevators), service and utility areas (lobbies, public toilets, and janitor's closets), mechanical and electrical equipment functions (boiler and chiller rooms, electrical closets and switch gear rooms, telephone equipment rooms and electronic equipment rooms).

Non-Restrictive Specification

A technique of specifying in which no clear restriction to a single proprietary or exclusionary product is either stated or implied.

Norris-LaGuardia Act
Enacted by Congress in 1932, this act was the first piece of major legislation designed to diminish the power of management over labor.

Obligation
A result of custom, law or agreement by which an individual is duty bound to fulfill an act or other responsibility.

Occupational Safety and Health Act (OSHA)
Enacted by Congress in 1970, this act is sometimes referred to as the Williams-Steiger Act, it was designed to improve job safety under administration of the United States Department of Labor, with provision of fines and penalties for non-compliance.

OPC Relationship
A term, unique to this text, which defines the basic contract relationship between owner, (design) professional and constructor as the fundamental contract relationship or mechanism by which the majority of building construction in the United States of America is accomplished.

Open Bidding
A common, colloquial term meaning the process of constructor selection known as Open Competitive Selection.

Open Competitive Selection
The proper term for *Open Bidding* defined as a process of constructor selection whereby an Advertisement to Bidders is published in the news media notifying qualified constructors of owner's intention to receive and consider sealed competitive bids leading to award of a Contract for Construction (usually to the qualified bidder submitting the lowest responsive bid with other considerations being given in accordance with published Instructions to Bidders.)

Order of Magnitude Estimate
An estimate of probable cost of construction that is based on generalities such as historical costs associated with building type and function, applied to approximate gross building area, number of floors, date of probable construction and general locality of the project.

Ordinance
An authoritative rule of law, public decree or regulation enacted by a municipality or other political subdivision fully enforceable through the court system of the municipality or other political subdivision.

Orthographic Drawing
A term used to describe a geometrical procedure of projecting the image of an object on the plane of the drawing by perpendicular projection.

Outline Specification
An abbreviated or preliminary form of specification, intended for preliminary evaluation, stating basic, but not necessarily complete descriptions of the products, materials and workmanship upon which the Contract for Construction will eventually be based.

Overhead
Term used to describe business expenses (as rent, insurance, or heating) not chargeable to a particular part of the work or product.

Overtime
A term applied to the numbers of hours worked in excess of eight (8) hours in any one day or in excess of forty (40) in any one week.

Parchment
A term originally used to describe a writing medium made from the skins of sheep or goats used for hand written manuscripts also called *vellum*. Today the term parchment usually refers to a thin glossy paper that resembles parchment, usually made by soaking an unsized paper in dilute sulfuric acid, then washed and dried under pressure.

Part 1–General
The first of three parts of a specification which contains the administrative and procedural requirements unique to the item or items of work which the specification is designed to address.

Part 2–Products
The second of three parts of a specification which deals exclusively with the material or product, or related products, including (if applicable) the manufacturer or manufacturing process.

Part 3–Execution
The third of three parts of a specification which addresses issues involving the incorporation of the products addressed in Part 2 of the specification into the Work.

Partnership
The joining of two or more individuals for a business purpose whereby profits and liabilities are shared.

Payment Bond
A form of security purchased by the contractor from a surety, which is to provide a third party guarantee that the contractor will pay all costs of labor, materials and other services related to the project for which the contractor is responsible under the Contract for Construction.

Payments Withheld
A provision of the General Conditions of the Contract for Construction which provides that the owner may withhold payments to the contractor, if, in the opinion of the design professional or the owner, the work falls behind the schedule of construction, or in the event that the work deviates from the provisions of the Contract Documents.

Performance
(1) A term meaning fulfillment of a promise made by one party to a contract or agreement in return for compensation. (2) The manner in which or efficiency by which something acts or reacts in the manner to which it is intended to perform.

Performance Bond
A form of security purchased by the contractor from a surety, which is provided to guarantee that the contractor will satisfactorily perform all work and other services related to a project for which he is responsible under the contract for construction.

Performance Specification
A description of the desired results or performance of a product, material or assembly, or piece of equipment with criteria for verifying compliance.

Plan Rooms

A service provided by construction industry organizations or service companies, sometimes available to interested contractors, producers, vendors and manufacturers. Plan rooms provide access to contract documents for projects currently in the process of receiving competitive or negotiated bids.

Pre-Design Phase

A group of services conducted by the design professional for the benefit of the owner which may include selection of adequate site, development of a program of design and the establishment of the owner's budget for building construction including site and building(s).

Primary Subcontractors

Subcontractors who may perform major portions of the work in a construction project such as installation of plumbing, mechanical or electrical systems.

Prime Professional Service

The chief among multiple entities (each under separate contracts with the prime professional) responsible for providing services to an owner.

Principal

(1) The principal authority or person responsible for a business such as architecture, engineering or construction. (2) The capital amount of a loan or other obligation as distinguished from the interest.

Private Owner

An individual or other collective entity from the private sector of the economy who by ownership interest initiates the OPC relationship to produce the design and construction of a project.

Probable Contract Price

The design professional's estimate of the most probable price that may be offered by a qualified constructor in response to request for the base bid for the work of constructing a project.

Product Data

Information furnished and certified by the manufacturer of a product which offers technical data as to the composition of the product or material, recommended use or application, test data, advantages and disadvantages of use, physical properties and characteristics, guarantees and warrantees normally provided by the manufacturer and other specific information that may be requested by the design professional.

Professional Corporation

A corporation created expressly for the purpose of providing professional practice and related services which may have special requirements under the law as opposed to requirements for corporations in general.

Profit Sharing

Provisions in special agreements or contracts for construction where the contractor, as an incentive to save money for the owner, is paid in addition to the final Contract Price, some percentage of any net savings he may achieve if he is able to deliver the finished project to the owner's satisfaction at a total cost which is below a specified limiting amount, which may or may not have been guaranteed by the contractor.

Program

An orderly statement and explanation of the requirements of space and function that are major considerations to be applied or incorporated into the design of a project.

Progress Schedule

A schedule showing time relationships of various elements of the construction progress of a project. A progress schedule serves to verify whether or not a project, under construction, is progressing as intended.

Program of Design

A written description of the owner's project that defines the project in sufficient terms to guide the design process. The program may include descriptions of rooms or functional space characteristics including net floor area, room or space name, adjacency requirements and general description of the functions that will take place in that space.

Programmed Building Area

Often referred to as (PBA), the sum of the space and functional area of a building that has been determined as the result of the conduct of a program of design.

Project

(1) A broad term used by this text synonymous with a building or other undertaking requiring design and construction services. (2) A term used to describe something that is contemplated, planned, devised or intended to be produced. In construction terms, the total intention of the work of construction to be accomplished such as a building, real estate improvement, or structure.

Project Closeout Phase

A term used to describe the period in which completion of the work is verified and accepted and all documentation related to project completion (Project Record Documents) required by the Contract Documents are submitted for approval and acceptance by the owner (and design professional).

Project Manual

A bound booklet which (with the possible exception of drawings of large size which may be bound separately) contains the Contract Documents and, if appropriate, the Bidding Requirements related to the Contract for Construction.

Project Record Documents

The documents, certificates and other information relating to the work, materials, products, assemblies that the contractor is required to accumulate during construction and convey to the owner for his use prior to final payment and project closeout.

Project Team

A collection of professional entities directed or otherwise coordinated to perform work or services for a project.

Property Law

A body of laws that govern the ownership and use of property. Property may be categorized as real property (such as land and buildings) or personal property (such as an automobile and clothing).

Promissory Note

A legal instrument, agreement or contract made between a lender and a borrower by which the lender conveys to the borrower a sum of money or other consideration known as principal for which the borrower promises repayment of the principal amount plus interest under conditions set forth in the agreement.

Proprietary Specification
A technique of specifying by which the specifier names the product by the manufacturer's (proprietary) name or trade name for a product. Sometimes referred to as "single source" specifying.

Protocol
A procedure or practice established by long or traditional usage and currently accepted by a majority of practitioners in similar professions or trades. Protocol represents the generally accepted method of action or reaction that may be expected to be followed in a transaction.

Punch List
A list of items within a project, prepared by the contractor, confirmed by the owner or his representative, which may remain to be replaced or completed in accordance with the requirements of the Contract for Construction at the time of Substantial Completion.

Purchase Order
A written contract or similar agreement made between a buyer and seller that details the items to be purchased, the price of such items and the method and responsibility for delivery and acceptance of the items. A purchase order also formalizes the intentions of both parties to the transaction.

Purchasing Plan
The constructor's business plan by which to purchase or otherwise provide the management, labor, materials, tools, equipment, services, taxes, fees and incidentals required to construct the project for the contract price offered.

Real Estate Broker
A qualified professional, licensed by the state or other jurisdiction, who agrees to facilitate the sale or purchase of real estate on behalf of either a buyer or seller.

Realtor
A term generally used to describe a qualified professional who offers the service of facilitating the sale or purchase of real estate.

Receipt of Bids
The official action of an owner in receiving sealed bids that have been invited or advertised in accordance with the owner's intention to award a contract for construction.

Reference Standard
Professionally prepared generic specifications and technical data compiled and published by competent organizations generally recognized and accepted by the construction industry. These standards are sometimes used as criteria by which the acceptability and/or performance of a product, material, assembly or piece of equipment can be judged.

Reference Standard Specification
A type of non-proprietary specification that relies on accepted industry standards as referenced in Part 1 of the specification to describe a product, material, assembly or piece of equipment to be incorporated into a project.

Referendum

(1) A special election in a jurisdictional subdivision which establishes public approval (e.g., for elected officials to sell General Obligation Bonds as a means of financing a public project). (2) The principle or practice of submitting to popular vote a measure passed on or proposed by a legislative body. (3) Approval by election of a legislative or other measure submitted by a legislative body of government.

Risk Management

An approach by management and procedure which is designed to prevent occurrence of culpability, potential liability, contravention of law or other potential risk that could bring about loss in the process of building construction.

Samples

Physical examples of materials, products, equipment or workmanship that establish standards by which the acceptability of work will be judged.

Schedule

The constructor's plan for the orderly sequence of work in a period of time.

Schedule of Values

A listing of the elements systems, items, or other subdivisions of the Work, establishing a value for each, the total of which equals the Contract Price. The schedule of values is used for (1) establishing a basis for approval of progress payments to the contractor during construction, (2) establishing the cash flow of a project.

Schematic Design

Typically a phase of the Design Professional's services wherein the design professional provides basic definition to the project and illustrates the scale and relationship of project components.

Seal

A legal term used to describe the signature or other representation of an individual agreeing to the terms and conditions of an agreement or contract.

Secondary Subcontractor

A subcontractor employed by the contractor to complete minor portions of the Work, or a subcontractor other than those identified as Primary or Prime Subcontractors.

Selective Bidding

A process of competitive bidding for award of the Contract for Construction whereby the owner selects certain constructors who are, in turn, invited to bid to the exclusion of others as occurs in the process of Open Bidding.

Separate Contracts

A procedure whereby an owner may issue individual contracts to separate trades or specialty constructors, each intended for completion of a specific portion of the Work.

Sherman Anti-Trust Act

An Act of the U. S. Congress in 1890, designed to prevent the unchecked growth of "big" business by preventing companies or individuals from holding or creating a business monopoly or controlling prices in certain areas of commerce.

Shop Drawings
Drawings or other illustrations created by a contractor, subcontractor or producer, manufacturer, vendor, or other entity that illustrate construction details, methods, materials, dimensions, installation, and other pertinent information for the incorporation of an element or item into the construction.

Single Prime Contractor
A term describing a constructor acting alone to fulfill the contractor's responsibility under the Contract for Construction.

Spec Data
A copyrighted name, owned by the Construction Specifications Institute (CSI), for a document, written or approved and published by CSI, presenting all pertinent properties and technical data related to a particular product. The Spec Data publication is useful to design professionals, particularly to specifiers in the preparation of uniform Contract Documents and to constructors in conforming with Contract Documents during the construction process.

Specifications
Documents that describe the attributes of a product in terms of an accepted industry standard or testing process by which to measure the performance for the product selected.

Specifier
One who writes, edits or otherwise prepares specifications.

Statutes of Limitation
Provision by law establishing a certain time limit from an occurrence during which a judgment may be sought from a court of law.

Statutory Requirements
Requirements that are embodied in the law.

Stock Companies
Insurance companies owned by a group of stockholders for the purpose of selling insurance.

Subcontract
An agreement between a constructor, specializing in a particular trade or other construction specialty, and a prime contractor for the completion of a portion of the Work for which the prime contractor is responsible.

Subcontractor
A constructor, specializing in a particular trade or other construction specialty, under contract to a prime contractor for the completion of a portion of the Work for which the prime contractor is responsible.

Submittal
A sample, manufacturer's data, shop drawing or other such item submitted to the owner or the design professional by the contractor, in accordance with the Contract Documents, for the purpose of establishing the contractor's intent in completing some portion of the work for which the contractor seeks approval or other action.

Substantial Completion
The condition when the Work of a project is substantially complete, ready for owner acceptance and occupancy. Any items remaining to be completed should, at this point, be duly noted or stipulated in writing.

Sub-Subcontractor
One under contract to a subcontractor for completion of a portion of the Work for which the subcontractor is responsible.

Superintendent
The title usually applied to one who is the senior supervisor of the work at a construction site, acting on behalf of the contractor.

Supplemental General Conditions
Written modifications to the General Conditions that become part of the Contract Documents.

Supplemental Instructions to Bidders
Written modifications to the Instructions to Bidders that become part of the Contract Documents.

Supply
A term commonly used in the study of economics meaning the amount of goods or services that are offered for sale.

Surety
An individual or company that provides a bond or pledge to guarantee that another individual or company will perform in accordance with the terms of an agreement or contract.

Taft-Hartley Act
An act of the U. S. Congress in 1947, otherwise known as the Labor Management Relations Act, which modified and lessened the power of management over labor and provides that labor participate in some management decisions.

Test Case
A term used by legal practitioners to denote a trial whose pleadings and merits have the potential to form a precedence for future judgments in similar cases.

Testing
Action whereby a portion or sample of a material is subjected to procedures designed to prove performance charcteristics.

Title
A legal term meaning the right of ownership to real property or real estate.

Tort Law
A legal remedy to a wrong or injury a person suffers because of the action or negligence of the person or persons responsible.

Transmittal
A form or letter conveying the action to be taken on an item being transmitted from one party to another.

Tracing
A term commonly used to describe a drawing prepared on translucent material which can be reproduced on light sensitive material by direct contact in a process requiring an exposure of strong light and development by photographic means. Such material allows a final drawing to be created by tracing a copy over an original which is visible below the drawing surface.

Trial
A term commonly applied to an action in a court of law.

Turn-Key
A contract that provides all of the services required to produce a building or other construction project.

Unit of Measure Estimate
An estimate of cost of construction based upon line items of material and/or labor multiplied by a measured quantity of defined units, multiplied by a reliable cost per unit.

Value Engineering
A science related to the study of the function, primary and secondary, and attributes that determine the value of various materials and manufacturing and/or construction techniques. Value engineering considers the initial cost of construction or manufacture coupled with the estimated cost of maintenance, energy consumption, useful life expectancy and cycle of replacement.

Value Engineering Study
A special procedure, not usually part of the basic services of the design professional, where an independent team of design professionals evaluates the intended design under the coordination of a Certified Value Specialist (CVS), a practitioner duly certified by the Society of American Cost Engineers (SAVE) with the purpose of offering a series of proposals that may improve the intended function, or save cost or otherwise improve the value of the project and thus provide added benefit the owner's objectives.

Value of the Project
The worth of defined attributes of a project that the owner confirms as being satisfactory to his or her needs.

Vellum
A thin but tough paper material used as a drawing medium by design professionals for design drawings. The term is synonymous with *parchment*, both drawing mediums having originated from preserved animal skins.

Wage Rate
The amount in currency paid a worker per hour of work by an employer.

Warranty
Manufacturer's certification of quality and performance that may include a limited guarantee of satisfaction.

White Print
(1) A reproduction of a drawing or other document that is a positive image of the original. (2) A term sometimes used to describe a reproduction by the diazo method of reproduction. (Also see *Diazo*).

Workman's Compensation Insurance
Insurance carried by employers, mandated by law, that provides compensation for bodily injury and loss of wages for a work-related accident.

Work Plan
The constructor's plan for the orderly and timely accomplishment of the work of construction, the assignment of responsibility and accountability in conjunction with the purchasing plan and the schedule.

Working Drawings
A colloquial term commonly used to describe contract or construction drawings used to illustrate the construction of a building.

Index